Yugoslavia in the British Imagination

Yugoslavia in the British Imagination

Peace, War and Peasants before Tito

Samuel Foster

BLOOMSBURY ACADEMIC
LONDON • NEW YORK • OXFORD • NEW DELHI • SYDNEY

BLOOMSBURY ACADEMIC
Bloomsbury Publishing Plc
50 Bedford Square, London, WC1B 3DP, UK
1385 Broadway, New York, NY 10018, USA
29 Earlsfort Terrace, Dublin 2, Ireland

BLOOMSBURY, BLOOMSBURY ACADEMIC and the Diana logo are trademarks of Bloomsbury Publishing Plc

First published in Great Britain 2021
Paperback edition published in 2023

Copyright © Samuel Foster, 2021

Samuel Foster has asserted his right under the Copyright, Designs and Patents Act, 1988, to be identified as Author of this work.

Cover image: Peasants dancing, Bosnia, Austro-Hungary, between ca. 1890 and ca. 1900 (Library of Congress Prints and Photographs Division Washington, D.C. 20540 USA)

All rights reserved. No part of this publication may be reproduced or transmitted in any form or by any means, electronic or mechanical, including photocopying, recording, or any information storage or retrieval system, without prior permission in writing from the publishers.

Bloomsbury Publishing Plc does not have any control over, or responsibility for, any third-party websites referred to or in this book. All internet addresses given in this book were correct at the time of going to press. The author and publisher regret any inconvenience caused if addresses have changed or sites have ceased to exist, but can accept no responsibility for any such changes.

Every effort has been made to trace copyright holders and to obtain their permissions for the use of copyright material. The publisher apologizes for any errors or omissions and would be grateful if notified of any corrections that should be incorporated in future reprints or editions of this book.

A catalogue record for this book is available from the British Library.

A catalog record for this book is available from the Library of Congress.

Library of Congress Cataloging-in-Publication Data
Names: Foster, Samuel, 1987- author.
Title: Yugoslavia in the British imagination: peace, war and peasants before Tito / Samuel Foster.
Other titles: Peace, war and peasants before Tito
Description: London; New York: Bloomsbury Academic, 2021. | Includes bibliographical references and index. |
Identifiers: LCCN 2021000355 (print) | LCCN 2021000356 (ebook) | ISBN 9781350114609 (hb) | ISBN 9781350114616 (ePDF) | ISBN 9781350114623 (eBook)
Subjects: LCSH: Yugoslavia–Foreign public opinion, British. | Great Britain–Relations–Yugoslavia. | Yugoslavia–Relations–Great Britain. | Peasants–Yugoslavia–Public opinion. | Public opinion–Great Britain. | Yugoslavia–History–1918-1945. | Balkan Peninsula–History–War of 1912-1913–Foreign public opinion, British. | World War, 1914-1918–Moral and ethical aspects–Great Britain. | National characteristics, British.
Classification: LCC DR1258.G7 F67 2021 (print) | LCC DR1258.G7 (ebook) | DDC 949.702/1–dc23
LC record available at https://lccn.loc.gov/2021000355
LC ebook record available at https://lccn.loc.gov/2021000356

ISBN: HB: 978-1-3501-1460-9
PB: 978-1-3502-4807-6
ePDF: 978-1-3501-1461-6
eBook: 978-1-3501-1462-3

Typeset by Deanta Global Publishing Services, Chennai, India

To find out more about our authors and books visit www.bloomsbury.com and sign up for our newsletters.

To my parents

Contents

List of Illustrations	ix
Acknowledgements	x
A note on names and transliteration	xi
Abbreviations	xii
Maps	xiii
Introduction	1

Part I The era of the *fin de siècle*

1	Before the twentieth century	13
	Early representations	14
	1878 and the rise of cultural pessimism	19
	Conclusion	24
2	A new age of anxieties	25
	The 'national efficiency' paradigm	26
	Echoes of the Long Depression	32
	Peasants and the city	36
	Romancing remoteness	39
	Conclusion	45
3	The victimhood archetype?	46
	Organized opinion	47
	The 'civilizing mission'	51
	Women as metaphor	56
	Reimagining violence	59
	Conclusion	63

Part II The era of the Great War

4	The years of crisis	67
	The Balkan Wars through British eyes	67
	The new humanism	71
	From Sarajevo to Cer	73
	Conclusion	76

5 The British and the Balkan front	77
'English sestre' and peasant soldiers	78
Forgotten alliances at war	84
Peasant society in war and exile	88
The British panacea?	95
Conclusion	100
6 Yugoslavia as British propaganda	102
Draining 'Serbia's cup of sorrow'	103
Visions of a Yugoslav nation	106
The limits of propaganda	113
Conclusion	115

Part III The era of the 'New Europe'

7 Yugoslavia in the 'Anglo-British' mind	119
An Anglo-British paradigm?	120
Commodifying the 'New Europe'	125
Uncovering the 'Yugoslav type'	130
Conclusion	135
8 The shape of things to come?	137
Allegories for a 'Morbid Age'	138
The 'east end of Europe'	141
Witnesses to 'the passing of Arcadia'	147
Conclusion	150
Conclusion	152
Notes	157
Bibliography	202
Index	221

Illustrations

Figures

1	'A Nice Time of It; or, The New Constable and the Naughty Boys', *Punch; or, The London Charivari*, 1878	22
2	Peasants in the Market at Spalato (Split), c. 1907	34
3	Miss Alice Tebbutt and members of the Serbian Army at large troughs or basins, Serbia, c. 1914–1915	82
4	Serbian infantry marching to their camp at Mikra near Salonika (Thessaloniki) following the voyage from Corfu, 1916	85
5	British officer and Dr Katherine Stewart MacPhail of the Scottish Women's Hospital dancing the *Kolo* at a Serbian Slava or regimental festival at Salonika, 1916	92
6	Unit of the Scottish Women's Hospital during the Serbian military retreat, 1915	94
7	A dead Serbian soldier lying on the side of the road during the retreat to the Adriatic Sea coast, November to December 1915	95
8	Victoria and Albert Museum's West Hall during Ivan Meštrović's *Kosovo* exhibition, June to July 1915	110
9	'Heroic Serbia', poster promoting 'Kossovo Day', June 1916	111
10	'Serbo-Turkish Villages', by Cora Gordon, 1921	132
11	'The Kolo', by Cora Gordon, 1921	139
12	Vox Populi (*Evening Standard*, 29 January 1929)	143

Maps

1	South Slavic Balkans, 1878	xiii
2	South Slavic Balkans, 1914	xiv
3	Kingdom of Yugoslavia, 1929–39	xv

Acknowledgements

Considering this book's focus on cultural (mis)perceptions, it feels ironic that the process of researching and writing is often viewed as a mostly solo effort. For me, this endeavour would have been impossible without the help and support of many, many friends and colleagues. For all their constructive feedback, help with style and structuring, or simply offering encouragement in times of ebbing morale, I would like to thank Chris Jones, Mark Vincent, Olena Palko, Richard Mills, Francis King, Alex Drace-Francis, Mark Thompson and Graham Harris. Above all, I am forever indebted to my PhD supervisor and mentor Cathie Carmichael, who planted the idea for this project in my impulsive undergraduate mind all the way back in 2011, and whose advice has been nothing short of indispensable ever since.

On the subject of broadening horizons, I have been fortunate for the immense support in navigating the linguistic barrier. For this, my thanks to Biljana Babić at the University of Novi Sad's Centre for Serbian as a Foreign Language and Lazar Stričević of the Norfolk and Norwich Novi Sad Association.

Throughout my research I was fortunate to have explored several archives across the UK, Serbia and Slovenia and wish to thank those who helped me access their collections, especially the staff of the Royal Anthropological Institute, UCL School of Slavonic and East European Studies, Matica srpska in Novi Sad, Narodna biblioteka Srbije in Belgrade and the Imperial War Museum. My sincerest thanks also go to Jon Gregory for designing and editing the maps, and Ken Bryant at *The Jan and Cora Gordon pages* for allowing me to reproduce the titular artists' impressions of 1920s Bosnia-Herzegovina. I am no less grateful to Tom Stottar, who originally picked this project up, and Rhodri Mogford and Laura Reeves at Bloomsbury who helped guide it to publication.

Finally, thank you to all my family and closest friends, in particular Karen, John, Carol, Keith, Alexandra, Elizabeth, Victoria, Andrew, Ruth, my sister Lucy and my mother Gill, for supporting and humouring my innumerable idiosyncrasies from beginning to end. And to my father Tony, who found the term 'Serbo-Croat' hilarious. I somehow doubt reading this book would have changed his mind!

A note on names and transliteration

Before the 1890s, British writing on the Slavic Balkans typically adopted non-Slavic (usually German, Greek, Italian, Latin or Turkish) exonyms for various place names. The most obvious examples were those of countries such as *Servia* (Serbia) or major towns and cities including *Agram* (Zagreb), *Laibach* (Ljubljana), *Sara* (Sarajevo) and *Uskub* (Skopje). Conversely, authors who used the Slavic equivalents would often attempt to anglicize them by substituting the native diacritics for phonetic approximations (e.g. Čedomilj Mijatović as 'Chedomille Mijatovich'). By 1914, improvements in comprehension saw the adoption of Slavic nomenclature. More casual observers, however, often continued to use non-Slavic exonyms for historically important locations such as *Cattaro* (Kotor), *Monastir* (Bitola) and *Ragusa* (Dubrovnik). In the interests of brevity, this study uses the contemporary variations in all cases unless quoting directly or an established English equivalent, like Belgrade (*Beograd*), Croatia (*Hrvatska*), Montenegro (*Crna Gora*) or Yugoslavia (*Jugoslavija*), is available; the term 'Macedonia' refers only to the territory of the modern Republic of North Macedonia. The study also applies this rule to all other non-Slavic and non-Balkan place names, notably *Constantinople* (Istanbul) and *Salonica* (Thessaloniki).

Abbreviations

BC	Balkan Committee
BL	British Library
BSF	British Salonica Forces
FO	(British) Foreign Office
IWM	Imperial War Museum (Archive and Sound Archives)
JO	*Jugoslovenski odbor* (Yugoslav Committee)
KPJ	*Komunistička partija Jugoslavije* (Communist Party of Yugoslavia)
M-O	Mass-Observation
MRF	Macedonian Relief Fund
RAI	Royal Anthropological Institute (of Great Britain and Ireland)
RAMC	Royal Army Medical Corps
SRF	Serbian Relief Fund
SSEES	School of Slavonic and East European Studies
SWH	Scottish Women's Hospitals (for Foreign Service)
VMRO	*Vnatrešna makedonska revolucionerna organizacija* (Internal Macedonian Revolutionary Organisation)

Maps

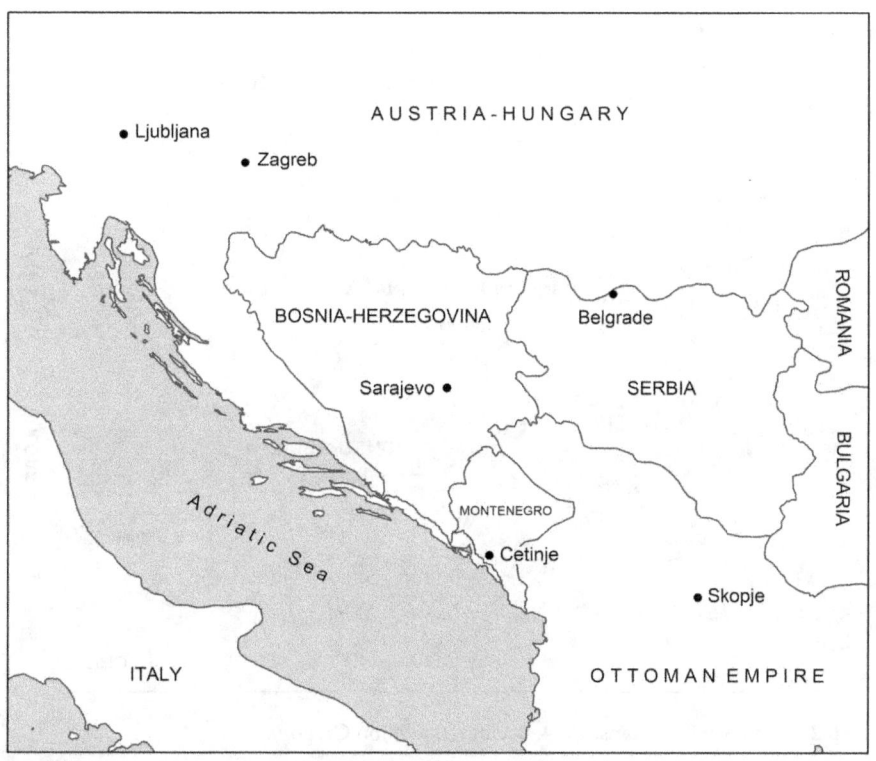

Map 1 South Slavic Balkans, 1878. © Courtesy of Jon Gregory.

Map 2 South Slavic Balkans, 1914. © Courtesy of Jon Gregory.

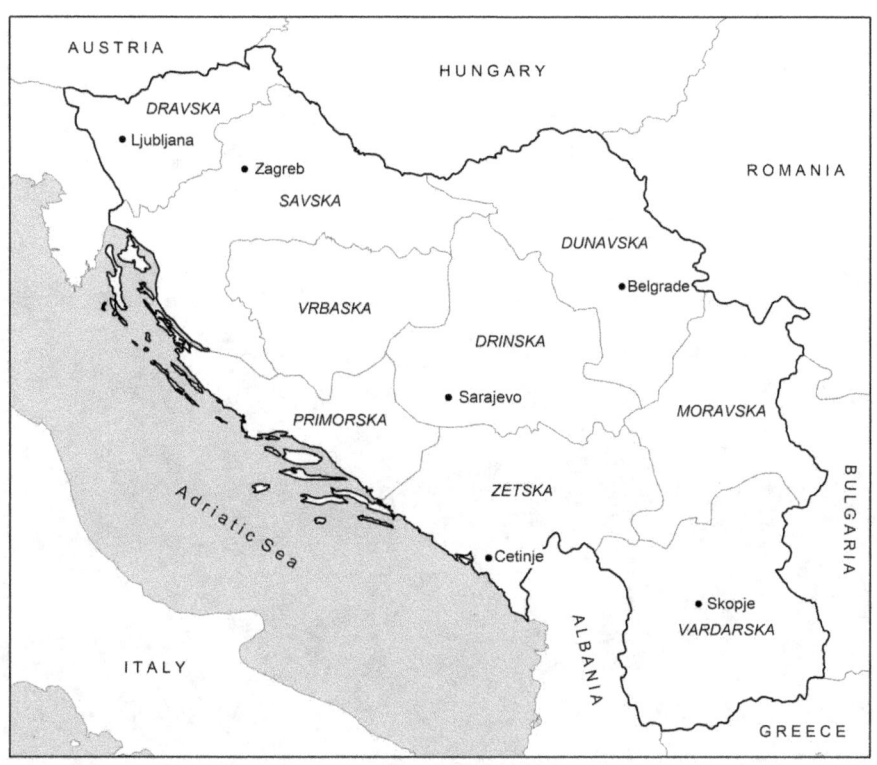

Map 3 Kingdom of Yugoslavia, 1929–39. © Courtesy of Jon Gregory.

Introduction

When the British journalist Rebecca West visited the Kingdom of Yugoslavia[1] in the spring of 1937, accompanied by her husband, she did so in the knowledge that accounts of such journeys had played a pivotal role in shaping understanding of other cultures. An early chapter in her own 1,239-page travelogue, *Black Lamb and Grey Falcon*, appears almost as a distillation of the stratified cultural perceptions of southeastern Europe's Balkan Peninsula prevalent in early-twentieth-century Britain. While touring what is today north Croatia, the couple's car became briefly stuck in a snowdrift only to be saved by a group of jovial peasants 'shouting with laughter because machinery had made a fool of itself'. Remarking on how quickly it had happened, West mused that their rescuers must have been 'anxious to get back and tell a horse about it'.[2] As late as 1937, one could, so it seemed, still gaze out from that hilltop onto a previous age. Her depictions of the local peasantry in particular appear emblematic of Edward Said's 'imagined geography': a spatial ordering of the world in which foreign lands are presented through exaggerated cultural embellishments, rather than objective falsehoods.[3] Yet, these romanticized idylls did not simply reflect some entrenched misconception of the Balkans as a vast ethnographic museum. West was following an established literary pattern in which foreign peoples became framing devices for articulating the many latent anxieties surrounding the nature of British identity.

From the late 1890s, British writers, guided by these anxieties, started to cast those living in less industrialized corners of the world like the, mostly agrarian, South Slavic peoples of the future Yugoslavia: Croats, Serbs, Slovenes, Montenegrins, Bosnian Muslims and Macedonian Slavs, as embodying a pre-industrial ideal. Episodes of violent upheaval, such as the Balkan Wars of 1912 and 1913, served to spread and cement this view, while also bringing the plight of the region's peasant population to wider public attention. A recurrent archetype in British depictions of the Balkans since the 1870s, the once inconspicuous figure of the South Slavic peasant increasingly appeared through a prism of pathos and victimization, perpetuated by insidious, corrupt and, above all, modernistic trends – an allegory for uncertain times.[4]

This study explores how this confluence of motifs evolved in tandem with twentieth-century Britain's changing domestic context before the rise of the Communist Party of Yugoslavia (KPJ), under Josip Broz Tito, as the main resistance to the Axis Powers' occupation of the western Balkans during the Second World War. By considering these questions, it seeks to fill a lacuna in the current historiography of Anglo-Yugoslavian relations through two interconnected analytical aims. First, it examines how representations of South Slavic peasant communities developed transnational links with domestic issues prevalent in the British public sphere. These connections presented a positive vision of the South Slavs as a moralistic allegory for Britain's shifting social climate, finding wider resonance among the general public than more direct depictions. This would emerge in tandem with a nascent sense of British identity – given form by the public's collective experience of the First World War.

Second, it aims to assess how these social transitions determined British attitudes towards the Yugoslavian state project before and after the country's founding on 1 December 1918. Despite Yugoslavia's prominence in modern Balkan history, no comprehensive analysis has been undertaken as to how its formation interrelated with the West's changing perceptions of southeastern Europe, beyond elite political and intellectual circles. By situating the first Yugoslavia's creation in British imaginative geography as part of a broader social, rather than narrowly political, phenomenon, it looks to advance historical understanding of the interplay between Britain's evolving sense of statehood and efforts to validate its place in the wider world. Historical contingencies are therefore central to both objectives.

From the 1880s to 1920s, British scholarship on the Balkans, and other such areas, existed not only to inform audiences, but convey or reinforce ideological perspectives. Works of 'popular' anthropology in particular, usually carried sub-commentaries on domestic questions, reflecting Britain's 'loss of self-confidence [that] it had once enjoyed as the first industrialized nation and economic leader of the world'.[5] Concurrently, anthropologists from the region, such as the Serb geographer Jovan Cvijić, often tied their research into the nation-building process. Rural customs and social organization, like the peasant village or familial *zadruga*,[6] appeared in 'national myth-making discourses' as evidence of shared historical identities and scientific justification for territorial claims.[7]

Although Western 'ignorance' of the Balkans had been rebuked long before 1945, research into these external perspectives only began to appear from the mid-1950s.[8] A 1955 article by the diplomatic historian Barbara Jelavich, discussing Victorian-era travel writing on the Slavic Balkans under the rule of the Ottoman Empire as informal social commentary, can be read as the earliest known critical analysis of the region's history from a British literary perspective.[9] Until the 1980s, however, further research was mostly limited to anthropological and ethnographic field studies; Vera Stein Ehrlich's interwar survey of some 300 Yugoslavian villages, *Family in Transition* (1966), provided an early precedent.[10]

Following the 'cultural turn'[11] of the 1970s, scholarly interest in the West's relationship with the wider world started to place greater emphasis on the evolution of stereotypes. Post-colonialist critiques, such as Said's *Orientalism* (1978), link these portrayals or 'images' to the imperialist societies that produced them. In Said's case, the Islamic 'Orient' – North Africa and the Middle East – was the most prominent example, existing as an inferior and stagnant inversion of the culturally dynamic 'West'.[12] This approach can more accurately be termed 'imagology': a form of comparative literature concerned with the study of cross-national cultural, political, racial and social perceptions, images and stereotypes.[13]

By the 1980s, a growing academic backlash to the perceived Western tendency for defining the world as a series of indigenous 'peripherals' surrounding a 'European core' was increasingly reflected within historical scholarship. Benedict Anderson's *Imagined*

Communities (1983) was particularly influential in reinterpreting the idea of 'the nation' as a social construct and product of transnational processes, rather than being historically predetermined as often claimed by nationalists. In the European context especially, Anderson identified the rise of the modern 'nation-state' as imitative of 'the large cluster of new political entities that sprang up' in the former colonial territories of North and South America between 1776 and 1838.[14]

This growing interest in nationalism and national identity prompted a gradual revival of the imagological approach to Anglo-Balkan relations. Writing at the end of the Cold War, Wendy Bracewell expounded on Jelavich's original idea by identifying late-Victorian travel accounts as vicarious opinion pieces on British foreign policy.[15] John Allcock further suggested that the British travel writer had been instrumental in cultivating the region's international image as a cultural extension of Said's 'Orient'. The fact that the more high-profile authors had tended to be women only further popularized this impression among Western audiences.[16]

Socialist Yugoslavia's collapse in the early 1990s triggered the first major wave of imagological research exploring this essentialist imagery's contemporary political relevance. A perceived cultural cynicism among Western observers focused attention on how negative 'patterns of perception' shaped the Balkans wider image following its intellectual 'discovery' in the late eighteenth and nineteenth centuries.[17] Yugoslavia features prominently in this paradigm as 'the heart of what constitutes the cultural sign of the Balkans': nationalist violence, innate ethnic hatreds, political mendacity, social dysfunction and a sense of insalubrious ambiguity, linked to a perceived cultural remoteness.[18] Even identification with 'Europe' was deemed to exist in a contested geographical imaginary. Milica Bakić-Hayden characterizes this as a gradation of 'nesting orientalism' where cultures to the south and east always appear 'more conservative and primitive', highlighting Croat and Slovene efforts to divorce their countries from any historical association with the Balkans.[19] For Larry Wolff, the concept of 'Western' and 'Eastern Europe' is itself an imposition of the French-led Age of Enlightenment that sought to define 'the developmental division of the continent'.[20]

The revisionist impulse driving this initial phase gained momentum following the end of the Bosnian War in 1995. Maria Todorova's seminal *Imagining the Balkans* (1997) codified the imagological approach to Balkan history through her discursive theory of 'Balkanism'. Since the Enlightenment, the idea of south-east Europe crystalized in the West's geographical imagination as a liminal cultural space, representing an amalgamation of the Eastern and Western hemispheres' least edifying qualities. Rather than simply being some vestige of the medieval Orient, the Balkans stands as 'a repository of negative characteristics against which a positive and self-congratulatory image of the "European" and the "West" has been constructed'.[21] Scholars working in a similar vein, notably Ludmilla Kostova and Vesna Goldsworthy, identify British travel literature – the international 'standard' for the genre by 1900 – as having perpetuated many of the negative stereotypes around which these impressions formed.[22] Of particular note was the frequent citing of authors such as West as validation for the 'breezy reductionisms' employed among Western pundits and diplomats throughout the 1990s to explain why the region had ostensibly diverged from 'an assumed European norm'.[23]

This first wave of imagological historiography, alongside more conventional historians such as Robert Donia, John V. A. Fine, Mark Mazower and Misha Glenny, has since formed a robust counter-discourse, exposing many Balkanist pejoratives as inherently European and attributing the region's ascribed instability to decades of external interference.[24] Conversely, opinion remains divided over how Balkanism should be understood. Todorova's 'legalistic-geographical' stance distinguishes the Balkans as unique – having never experienced the same prolonged forms of colonialism as Africa or Southern Asia. By contrast, 'cultural-colonialists' assert that the pejorative meaning of the Balkans is only fully comprehensible when observed through an imperial mind-set. For Western powers, David Norris argues, independent 'small nations' still existed under a veil of 'cultural colonialism' and were also looked upon as 'children with no right to exercise their own voice'.[25] Kostova and Goldsworthy contend that ignorance of the region led to it falling under a 'textual colonization' during the nineteenth century. Viewing its inhabitants as backward and saturated in primitive folklore and superstition, Victorian authors populated the Balkan Peninsula with fantastical 'British creations', most infamously Bram Stoker's *Dracula* (1897).[26] Regardless of form, however, these interpretations adhere to a specific school of imagological thought that this study terms the 'Balkanist thesis': an underlying consensus that southeastern Europe has come to be defined by an integral Otherness, permitting its dismissal in the Western mind 'as a developmental, geographical, historical, religious, cultural and economic borderland'.[27]

It is therefore unsurprising that, following its codification by Todorova, the Balkanist thesis has fallen under increasing critical scrutiny. Much of this stems from the indelible legacy of the Yugoslav Wars which, unsurprisingly, overshadowed these earlier dialogues, with the history of Western involvement often set as a series of teleological narratives. A key criticism of the body of work published in the 1990s and early 2000s has been a tendency to echo some of the epistemological flaws associated with Said. This notably includes an overgeneralized image of continual and monolithic misrepresentation, perpetuated mostly by Western 'outsiders' and entangled in numerous threads of innate historical prejudice and ignorance.[28] As Patrick Finney and Mika Suonpää observe in Britain's case, this fixation on 'outlining the lineaments of the discourse' has too often been to the detriment of non-imagological factors: tangible political realities and the 'concrete connections' that existed between Britain and south-east Europe as a whole. It also carries the risk of minimizing the historical agency of Balkan actors.[29] Moreover, while scholars in other fields have explored Balkanist imagery as transnational 'metaphors' for more contemporary identity issues in the West, this has been limited to the post–Cold War era.[30]

Since the late 2000s, a second wave of imagological scholarship has challenged the Balkanist thesis's core assertions of the region's representative status as habitually peripheral. Diana Mishkova's *Beyond Balkanism* (2018) stands, to date, as the most direct expression of this turn. Pursuing an imagological approach from the perspective of the Balkan countries, Mishkova challenges the Balkanist thesis's claims of a perennial, Eurocentric discourse, positing that Europe was itself merely one of multiple cultural referents in the development of the region's various national identities.[31]

An ancillary feature to this trend has been a cumulative reappraisal of Anglo-Balkan relations. Historical context and Britain's domestic climate have also been granted greater consideration in evaluating how Britons were supposedly conditioned to perceive the region. Andrew Hammond extrapolates that Anglophone literary motifs represent articulations of self-identity, concluding that during the nineteenth and twentieth centuries the Balkans emerged as 'a spectacle from the social margins against which people at the centre gain definition and become individualized'.[32] However, like the Balkanist thesis, Hammond's methodological approach inhibits further scholarly enquiry through its use of periodization and an overreliance on travel accounts: publications with a 'poetic function' that undercuts factual content and amplifies 'analogy, exaggeration and contrast'.[33] As Suonpää contests, this oversimplifies a far more nuanced understanding that was as much informed by religious, military, commercial and satirical narratives rooted in a British domestic context.[34]

The importance attributed to Britain in this second wave has brought new perspectives to the fore, with an increasing focus on the more pragmatic aspects of Anglo-Balkan engagement. Florian Keisinger's exploration of the Balkans in Anglo-German press reportage and Neval Berber's reassessment of Bosnia-Herzegovina's image in British literature, for example, both emphasize domestic matters, rather than cultural prejudice, as the guiding point of reference by 1912.[35] Eugene Michail and James Perkins take this further by focusing on the debates, channels and inter-ideological relations through which Balkan imagery was formed. British liberals, especially, are noted for having come to perceive the Balkans through a multiplicity of concerns, often in opposition to the purported injustices of the nineteenth century.[36]

However, this transition towards more domestic influences has remained limited to studies discussing general cultural impressions of the Balkans as a whole. Besides more engaged individuals or groups, analysis of how British domestic questions served as a transnational bridge to specific countries, excluding Greece, is markedly absent. James Evans and Vesna Drapac follow the Balkanist thesis in asserting that cultural prejudice saw British policymakers consign the majority of South Slavs to a Serb-dominated repression through London's support for the new Yugoslav state. Like Hammond, Drapac pays lip service to transnational issues such as gender, yet offers little clarification as to how these factors influenced opinion.[37] Evans, more wisely, limits his focus to those with an active interest or personal investment in Balkan affairs.[38] This illustrates Michail's observation that despite being appealed to frequently, public opinion has always remained elusive in Western discussions on the Balkans.[39]

This study further explores the transnational social angle through which the South Slavic Balkans evolved in the British geographical imagination by challenging historiographical assumptions of 'Britishness' and the 'West' as fixed concepts. Central to this are two narratives, both resulting from a convergence of several historical contingencies. The first concerns Yugoslavia's emergence and early history as an independent state. Parallel to this was the incipient coalescing of various domestic – as opposed to imperial – cultural strands, fashioned by 'the clarifying effects of the Great War' as a shared national effort, and the resolution of the Irish Home Rule Crisis of 1912 to 1922, into a semi-coherent, and readily pliable, pan-British identity.[40] What bridged these two, ostensibly unrelated, developments was the shifting depiction of the South Slavic peasant as an allegory for more widely discussed domestic issues.

What distinguished Great Britain from Anderson's modern nation-state was the absence of a unitary national idea.[41] In 1900, any concept of 'nationhood' or a sense of 'identity' rooted in a common heritage was firmly associated with the so-called 'Celtic fringe', the great urban centres and those regions of England divorced from the fixtures and conduits of state and imperial power, centred, unsurprisingly, in London and the South East. As Colin Kidd asserts 'in its political manifestations, "Britishness" is *Anglo-British* dependent on a historical allegiance to England's evolving constitution of crown and parliament [emphasis added]' as opposed to a recognized national culture.[42]

Anderson's paradigm has also produced differing interpretations of British identity, notably Linda Colley's contested claim that a unitary national consciousness came into existence between the Act of Union in 1707 and the start of Queen Victoria's reign in 1837. Rather than domestic consensus, this was based on comparisons with other countries, notably France.[43] However, this study builds on Jay Winter's premise that the First World War represented the foundational experience for an Anglo-British identity. Before the 1910s, those formulations viewed as 'British' existed more as a 'blurred' assortment of cultural iconography, prescribed values and competing sociopolitical interests.[44] The Great War merged these elements into a form of transitional commonality that lacked any 'national' element, was limited to the British isles and still used interchangeably with the no-less ambiguous notion of 'Englishness'. With this in mind, the study also follows Brad Beaven, Krishan Kumar and Peter Madler's concept of English identity as unfixed and easily appropriated to reflect specific contexts.[45] By 1914, for instance, Victorian associations with scientific progress appeared less pronounced compared to what Glenda Sluga terms the 'moral hierarchy of civilization': a ranking of cultures based on perceived social stability.[46]

However, as Mandler and Geoffrey Searle argue, any common articulation of Anglo-Britishness at the public level usually amounted to little more than an affinity for the city, or increasingly the suburb, and patterns of materialistic consumption.[47] Beaven further notes that even civic enthusiasm for the Empire was ultimately tied to local identities with the imperial project 'recast to capture the concerns of a locality'.[48] At its core, Anglo-Britishness was reactionary and rooted in contrast, yet also domestically oriented – mostly originating as a response to nationalist mobilization in Ireland from 1873, and the momentum gathering behind Scottish and Welsh autonomy. Depictions of the South Slavic Balkans were thus more often predicated on a heightened sense of intellectual dissatisfaction towards the status quo among a (predominantly) bookish, middle-class audience rather than any romantic sense of rural nostalgia or some innate yearning for a mythologized past.

The transitory nature of public understanding, or even awareness, of southeastern Europe left the political narrative open to manipulation by Balkan actors who increasingly tailored their messages to resonate with the British domestic climate, especially after 1914. In a similar vein, it is important to stress that the study's focus on the South Slavs is indicative of the fact that the popular image of what become Yugoslavia was one largely devoid of racial diversity or nuance. By 1912, non-Slavic minorities such as Albanians or Hungarians were invisible or merely coincidental due to the adjacency of their internationally designated 'homelands'. Indeed, one of the few imagological aspects that acquired a deeper meaning was the peasant archetype.

Although travel literature still represents an important resource, this study looks beyond the medium to incorporate a more diverse selection of material. These include pamphlets, newspapers, social surveys and journals primarily concerned with domestic matters. Private diaries, unpublished memoirs and correspondence from officials and regional experts who attempted to influence 'informed' public understanding, what William Wallace judiciously terms 'organized opinion', are also utilized in order to more accurately trace how domestic influences were projected onto the Balkans as a reflection of Britain's changing self-image.[49] In relation to Yugoslavia, those of the anthropologist Edith Durham and the historian R. W. Seton-Watson are of particular note. Of greater significance, however, are the Imperial War Museum's (IWM) extensive, but overlooked, archival collections detailing the experiences of British nationals deployed to the Balkans during the Great War. The study may therefore also be considered a preliminary investigation of this neglected body of material and its place in Britain's changing geographical imaginary.

Moving analysis away from direct representations towards the more ambiguous question of public attitudes and national identity presents several challenges. Before the introduction of opinion polling and the emergence of social research initiatives, such as Mass-Observation (M-O), in the 1930s, gauging broader public attitudes, beyond economic metrics, was almost impossible. While concepts such as 'popular opinion', 'the public sphere', or the proverbial 'man in the street' were frequently invoked by politicians and pundits, it was usually without substantiation or only in reference to the views of a narrow strata of middle and upper-class 'informed opinion'.[50] The present study's emphasis on domestic concerns partially circumvents this through Gerald Hauser's model of 'rhetorical' public spheres arising from 'the ongoing dialogue on public issues'. Within such forums, audiences play a proactive role without being restricted by socio-economic class. Multiple opinions and overlapping interests are usually present, with notions of universal reason discarded in favour of how well an issue resonates with personal experience and political, economic, or cultural values.[51] This approach finds further articulation in John Dewey's theory of 'many publics' called into being over a shared interest such as war or national emergencies.[52] It was within this framework that the South Slavic peasant acquired an allegorical status.

The study comprises eight chapters spanning the three key phases of Yugoslavia's evolution in British imaginative geography, and the emergence of Anglo-British identity, before 1945. Chapter 1 provides a summary of the historical context and the origins of the concepts and processes under examination. Key to this was growing diversity among literary representations, new channels of engagement and the spread of cultural pessimism amid a rising public fixation on British national efficiency during the 'Long Depression' of 1873 to 1896 and the era of the *fin de siècle*. This coincided with the various strands of cultural iconography that later come to be associated with Anglo-Britishness, notably William Gladstone's appeal to 'British morality' during the Eastern Crisis of 1875 to 1878, and its antithesis in the spectre of Irish nationalism.

Chapter 2 assesses the impact of social change and domestic anxieties in Edwardian Britain following the Second Boer War. In some quarters of the public sphere, even the debate on national efficiency was framed as a veritable 'crisis of civilization', often articulated through calls for a return to the 'normalcy' of an earlier, supposedly more stable, era.[53] Representations of the South Slavs also grew less pejorative as contemporary social issues, particularly urban poverty, were reflected in depictions of local peasant life with earlier motifs of 'organic' village traditions, and an absence of industrialization, becoming imbued with allegorical meaning.

Balkan developments are explored more closely in Chapter 3. Escalating violence from 1903 to 1912, paralleling Britain's own ratcheting domestic tensions, resulted in the peasantry's imaginative status transitioning from backward Other to a sympathetic victim of an industrialized Europe in the throes of its own moral decay. Those 'experts' associated with British organized opinion attempted to influence this shift, with varying degrees of success, by seeking to construe the still crystallizing sense of Anglo-Britishness as a moralistic force within an evolving narrative of peasant victimhood. At the outbreak of the First Balkan War, this new paradigm gave credence to the belief that confronting the evils of modernity was now a moral necessity.

Chapter 4 traces these trajectories through what it terms the 'years of crisis' from 1912 to the opening months of the First World War. Besides intersecting with the various elements which came to form Anglo-British identity, this period marked the critical moment in both of the study's narratives with the outbreak of the First Balkan War having coincided with the beginnings of the Irish Home Rule Crisis and Britain's simmering labour unrest. These convoluted antagonisms, rooted as they were in genuine social concerns, were reflected onto the conflicts in south-east Europe which were increasingly framed in humanitarian terms, decoupled from nationalist politics. This remained the case in 1914, as shown in the British public's reaction to Serbia's alleged role in precipitating the July Crisis.

Chapter 5 focuses on the experiences of British humanitarian and military personnel, comprising mostly women and working-class men, deployed in Serbia and Macedonia from the end of 1914, and the myriad beliefs which framed their engagement with peasant communities and Serb soldiers. These collective experiences engendered a further shift in the peasant's image from victim to cultural arbiter of national identity; Britain, as an emerging force of civilizational morality, was now viewed as honour-bound to provide aid, granting British personnel in the Balkans a foothold within the wartime narratives beginning to underpin the idea of Anglo-Britishness. Nevertheless, this continued to be articulated through earlier motifs, including the 'civilizing mission'.

Returning to the Home Front, Chapter 6 considers how these re-evaluations reached an apotheosis through their integration into Britain's wider propaganda narrative. In contrast to the pre-war years, peasant victimhood now appeared analogous for the struggle between democratic 'freedom' and a malignant form of modernity embodied in the German Empire: a cathartic expression of the new Anglo-Britishness as a moral force. It also surveys the role of pro-Yugoslav activists in attempting to direct narratives of 'peasant martyrdom' into a campaign for the post-war creation of a 'peasant' Yugoslav state and the limits of such propaganda in terms of more practical outcomes.

Chapter 7 assesses how Europe's geopolitical reconstitution from 1918, coupled with war fatigue, saw Yugoslavia disappear from the British public sphere almost entirely.

Despite the public's far greater access to information – and the further consolidation of Anglo-British identity following the establishment of the Irish Free State in 1922 – this fell in conjunction with a loss of earlier communication channels and the stratification of expertise into ever more obscure niches. Furthermore, the rise of a mass consumer-based society and cultural commodification in general, displaced Edwardian domestic tensions as Anglo-Britishness identity's dominant paradigm, resulting in Yugoslavia's reconfiguration as a tourist destination from 1930.

The final chapter traces the modest revival of cultural interest in the 1930s. However, it was through the new Anglo-British commercial milieu that the new country was more acutely defined as an 'alternative' middle-class tourist destination, its 'timeless' agrarian nature offering reprieve from the perceived dreariness of an interwar Britain dominated by consumerism, suburbanization and seemingly implacable economic inequalities. With the outbreak of the Second World War, even this appeared fleeting as observers started to predict the South Slav peasantry's coming disappearance in the face of socio-economic change, exacerbated by the more immediate threat of fascism.

This study does not seek to deconstruct Britain's political involvement in the western Balkans or argue that Yugoslavia was historically inevitable.[54] Neither does it claim to present an accurate picture of British or South Slavic society before 1945, depictions of which were far from impervious to exaggeration and hyperbole. Rather, in framing the first Yugoslavia's creation against Britain's evolving self-image it hopes to provide a window onto the transnational nature of social change in early-twentieth-century Europe.

Part I

The era of *fin de siècle*

1

Before the twentieth century

Despite a presumed 'timelessness' surrounding the various cultural stereotypes and political leitmotifs popularly associated with the Balkans, it was only in the latter half of the nineteenth century that the British geographical imaginary gained coherency.[1] Nevertheless its genealogy could be traced to the Ottoman conquests of the fourteenth century that delineated much of the region as part of the Islamic world immediately adjacent to 'Christendom'. Only 'in the middle of the sixteenth century when the first book in English on the Ottoman Empire appeared' did Westerners begin to perceive the Balkans as a distinctive cultural space.[2]

The emergence of Serbia and other former Ottoman territories as independent countries, for example, has been emphasized as the point at which British writers 'fashioned Europe as an abiding geographical dichotomy', bestowing the Balkan peoples with distinct cultural identities.[3] Yet, this was also reflective of a populist reaction towards Britain's stance on the so-called 'Eastern Question' following the Crimean War.[4] Rising newspaper circulation generated a public appetite for information that was both accessible and unambiguous; Victorian travellers even attempted to present their accounts as a form of reportage, focusing on 'news' that could be easily traced to ongoing foreign policy issues. In the Balkans, this soon became synonymous with sensationalist vignettes on 'the wild beauty and grandeur of the landscape and the recurrent atrocities in the relations of the people dwelling therein'.[5] This was generally predicated on nineteenth-century ideals of progress and a Western morality considered absent from the region.[6]

While early-nineteenth-century philhellenism[7] – notably Lord Byron's involvement in the Greek War of Independence – solicited some interest in the so-called 'little lands' north of Greece, before the 1840s, logistical practicalities limited the possibilities for travel.[8] Correspondingly, the inconsistent flow of information prevented the formation of a contextualized knowledge base before the advent of 'popular anthropology', and accounts oriented towards the domestic and social lives of the region's general populace, often authored by wealthy female travellers, became more widely available to Britain's middle-class 'reading public'.[9] Thus, for much of this longue durée, the figure of the South Slavic peasant appeared as little more than cultural embellishment. Centuries of external dominance, a 'base conservatism' and convoluted linguistic and cultural traditions fixed their place in imaginative geography as a semi-homogenous rural *Lumpenproletariat* or, as Friedrich Engels remarked in 1849, a 'residual fragment of peoples [*Völkerabfälle*]' devoid of any coherent sense of modern nationhood.[10]

At the end of the nineteenth century, the *London Evening Standard*'s former Near East correspondent, Ardern Hulme-Beaman, could still defend such a view. For foreign visitors to Serbia, or other Balkan states, the only effective means of gauging the national character was through interaction with the urban political and commercial elites: 'the specimens given to the critic for dissection'. Local peasants, 'only known vaguely from statistics and by sight', were simple indiscernible:

> As regards to the peasants, there is very little difference between them and their like all over the East. The agriculturalist is generally (not always in Servia) sober, honest, hard-working, and hospitable, whether he was born a Turk, an Arab, a Roumanian, a Bulgarian, or a Serb.[11]

While the peasant and other popular Balkanist archetypes are recognized as having originated in these earlier periods, disagreement persists as to when they acquired cultural substance. However, these pre-twentieth-century readings largely subscribe to various forms of periodization. Todorova and Norris, for example, classify the era before 1900 as one dominated by 'patterns' of imagological 'discovery', resulting in the 'invention' or 'construction' of a Balkan cultural space by external observers.[12] Hammond designates 1850 to 1914 as an opening phase in literary depictions where (predominately) British attitudes remained consistent in their disdain, reflecting the 'pseudo-scientific conceit of a staunchly racialist age'.[13]

Both approaches characterize British engagement as an evolving process yet remain largely silent on the scale of domestic and social change during the Victorian age. The fact Hulme-Beaman felt obliged to even justify his opinions was itself indicative of an awareness in the shifting interests of British audiences by the turn of the century. This chapter will trace the origins of this development in conjunction with the crystallization of the South Slavic peasant archetype, the genesis of Anglo-Britishness and the rising sense of cultural pessimism and ennui that characterized Britain's *fin de siècle* during the 1880s and 1890s.

Early representations

Despite Britain's comparatively minor diplomatic and economic presence, the solidifying of the Balkans as a distinctive cultural and political space in Western imaginative geography was directly linked to an explosion of interest among the Victorian elites. A Serbian bibliography of English-language literature on the Eastern Question published in 1909 illustrates this transition, with 150 of the indexed titles listed as having appeared before 1800. In contrast, almost 1,120 were published between 1840 and 1906 alone.[14] As well as travel, by 1900, British writers were concerning themselves with the region's archaeology, architecture, agriculture, economics, history, geography and natural sciences with specific topics tending to dominate discussions on different territories. Macedonia, for example, was usually associated with Alexander the Great and the Classical Hellenic past, while titles covering the east Adriatic coastal province of Dalmatia tended to focus on its Venetian architectural heritage.[15] This increasing fascination coincided with the arrival of émigré intellectuals from south-east Europe, such as the Romanian-Jewish linguist Moses Gaster in 1885, in whose work British folklore enthusiasts discovered 'a rich field of observations'.[16]

Nevertheless, historiographical fixation on this later period downplays earlier points of engagement. Even before the 1800s information 'about the eastern limits of Christendom' had 'coalesced in England from earlier times' with a steady procession of missionaries, merchants, soldiers, pilgrims and travellers having passed through the western Balkans from at least the eleventh century.[17] Sporadic references to the ancestors of the South Slavs also featured in significant medieval records including the ninth-century Saxon translation of Paulus Orosius (attributed to Alfred the Great), the Icelandic sagas and *The Travels of Sir John Mandeville* (c. 1356), one of the earliest works of European travel literature.[18]

As obscure as such information would have been, it nevertheless revealed an awareness of the region's peoples based on what Kiril Petkov describes as a composite of legal, political, emotive and culturally comparative standards that 'speak of pictures which, over long periods of time, converged and conveyed ideas from one genre to another'.[19] Cathie Carmichael further notes that despite a dearth of published works, subsequent commentaries and debates in the correspondence of medieval and early modern travellers were paradigmatic of 'an intermediate stage between the private mind and the published word'.[20]

Following Elizabeth I's excommunication from Rome in 1570, medieval animosity towards Islam was replaced by a sense of latent approbation as England entered into a series of anti-Catholic alliances with the ascendant Ottoman Empire.[21] This aroused some interest in the sultanate's northwestern territories, including the appearance of several significant English-language texts between the 1580s and 1630s. Of these, the most notable was Henry Blount's *Voyage into the Levant* (1636), which discussed the author's experience of travel, and attempted to offer objective impressions of society, in Ottoman-ruled Bosnia and Serbia.[22] As Berber observes, however, such accounts only provide 'nebulous testimonies' and were likely to be 'imprecise and full of inaccuracies'. Furthermore, this brief flowering in interest had already faded by the mid-seventeenth century as travellers elected to bypass Dalmatia and Bosnia-Herzegovina's mountain trails in favour of a 'gentler northern route' to Istanbul via the Pannonian Basin.[23]

Even at the height of its popularity, Eastern Europe and 'the Orient' rarely featured in the itineraries of the 'Grand Tour': a custom associated with Northern European nobility from the 1660s until the advent of railway travel in the 1840s that focused on visiting historical sites relating to Roman antiquity and the French and Italian Renaissance.[24] Nevertheless, the spread of the Enlightenment as an intellectual phenomenon in the mid-eighteenth century saw a tentative kindling of British interest as Dalmatia's Antiquarian and Venetian architectural heritage drew the attentions of the Royal Society and other scientific institutions. The Scottish architect Robert Adam's study of the ruins of Emperor Diocletian's palace in the Dalmatian port of Split, published in 1764, exemplified this trend as well as a new Western propensity for interpreting European culture around an axiom 'gazing from west to east, instead of from south to north'.[25] The lack of information evident in these texts, however, was demonstrative of 'the *mentalité* and the tastes of the literate upper classes than about what they were trying to describe' with the culture and society of non-elites usually receiving only cursory mention.[26] Adam's survey, for instance, presented Split as an 'outpost of antiquity' in a province that had all but lost its historical identity; the Slavic peasantry had usurped the land and its Roman heritage while being incapable of understanding or appreciating either.[27]

Although this cultural superficiality was gradually expunged in the early nineteenth century, British literary parlance was slow to adopt the newer scientific concepts and terminology circulating on the continent.[28] Even the name 'Balkan Peninsula', coined by the German geographer Johann August Zeune in 1808, only gained currency among English-language writers in the late 1870s when a suitable shorthand was needed to replace the, by then, anachronistic 'Turkey-in-Europe'.[29] Despite these limited and inconstant patterns of engagement, however, English and Scottish polymaths could still explore a more consistent body of knowledge in the internationalized context of the Enlightenment, particularly the theories of identity and human agency fostered by French and German 'cultural nationalists'. Johann Gottfried Herder was arguably the most significant in proposing that the presence of a shared language, rather than the classical dichotomy of 'cultured' and 'uncultured' peoples, represented the pivotal determinant for nationhood. This conflation of language and national identity was subsequently applied to Europe's various 'minor peoples'.[30]

In his 1774 anthropological treatise *Viaggio in Dalmazia* ('Travels into Dalmatia') the Venetian naturalist Alberto Fortis, with generous financial assistance from several wealthy British patrons, applied Herder's theories to the Republic of Venice's territorial possessions in Dalmatia. Central to this were the pastoralist, Slavic-speaking *Morlaci* people inhabiting the coastal hinterland, claimed by Fortis to represent the only distinctive nation in the east Adriatic through what he assumed to be linguistic fidelity.[31] Although based on selective anecdotal observations, Fortis's work proved influential in drawing British interest to the region as an early example of an anthropological field study. Like Herder, his humanistic emphasis on contemporary society and culture proved essential to the underlying philosophies which were to frame British popular understating in the early twentieth century, particularly the conflation of language and a designated national homeland.[32]

Following the French Revolution, British depictions underwent a major tonal shift as cultural romanticism slowly displaced Enlightenment rationalism and direct engagement increased. However, this mostly continued in piecemeal fashion, being reliant on developments directly linked to British interests around which tangible associations could form. Despite considerable naval activity in the Adriatic during the Napoleonic Wars, including the occupation of numerous Dalmatian islands and ports by the Royal Navy, the region commanded little interest in either the public sphere or diplomatic circles. Istanbul's recognition of Montenegro as an independent state in 1789, the Serbian revolutions and acquisition of political autonomy from 1804 to 1817, or other incidences of unrest in the Ottoman Balkans were easily dismissed as 'essentially a local movement with little effect on the rest of the empire', the integrity of which was considered crucial to British interests in a post-Napoleonic Europe.[33] By contrast, the Greek War of Independence from 1821 to 1833 generated a groundswell of popular anti-Turkish sentiment in opposition to London's official pro-Ottoman stance.[34] It also represented the first incidence in which public opinion was directly invoked as grounds for intervention, as reports of atrocities against Hellenic Christians proliferated. Greece's revival as a sovereign state was subsequently achieved in 1830, orchestrated, in part, by British, French and Russian naval intervention.[35]

This invocation of a popular victimhood narrative served to stimulate curiosity in contemporary regional affairs among middle-class British travellers. As with eighteenth-century antiquarianism, information pertaining to local peoples was minimal, yet it did not prevent inquisitive personalities from expressing interest, and even cultural admiration. Andrew Archibald Paton, Britain's consul to Serbia in the 1840s and the Dalmatian city of Dubrovnik in the 1860s, recalled his delight in exploring the peasant communities of Serbia's 'back-woods', who lived without 'a trace of poverty, vice or misery'. Through 'the patriarchal simplicity of their manners, and the poetic originality of their language', this 'large assembly of peasants' formed a near-ideal society that was 'neither poor nor barbarous'.[36] Paton could thus characterize Serbia, and the wider Ottoman Balkans, as part of 'the European family', albeit at its extreme periphery, rather than a cultural extension of 'Arabia'.[37] Conversely, Alexander Kinglake's erudite travelogue *Eōthen* (1844) was unusual in its candid focus on the author's personal experience, seeking to capture a deeper sense of 'intimacy' incidental to 'the realities of Eastern Travel'. Accordingly, Kinglake's narrative remained ambivalent towards anything outside of regional elites, town life, or his travelling companions.[38]

Despite their contrasting presentation styles, Paton's idealized rustic, peasant concord and Kinglake's apparent disregard for anything beyond his personal musings were indicative of the 'middle-class cultural revolution' permeating early Victorian society. As a response to the French Revolution, the more socially diverse 'bourgeoisie' gradually supplanted the aristocracy in determining Britain's 'cultural narrative'. Central to this was the growing prevalence of female authors and a 'feminization' of certain literary genres. This was especially notable in travel writing, traditionally the principal medium through which information on foreign cultures was disseminated. In the case of southeastern Europe, earlier male-dominated preoccupations with classical heritage, governing elites and philhellenism receded as accounts by middle-class women pivoted authorial interest towards more qualitative subjects such as the languages, customs, habits and tribulations of common people.[39]

However, it was the Great Eastern Crisis – a series of revolts against proposed tax increases in Ottoman-ruled Bosnia-Herzegovina and Bulgaria from 1875 to 1878 – that brought the figure of the peasant to the representational fore underpinned, again, by a narrative of victimhood. Significant among these was *Travels in the Slavonic Provinces of Turkey-in-Europe* (1866) by the suffrage campaigners Adeline Paulina Irby and Georgina Muir Mackenzie and the archaeologist Arthur Evans's *Through Bosnia and the Herzegovina* (1876) and *Illyrian Letters* (1878).[40] Having, according to Todorova, 'discovered the South Slavs for the English Public', Irby and Mackenzie's account in particular represented an early intervention in Britain's official stance on the Eastern Question, highlighting abuse, neglect and rumoured atrocities against the Slavic Christian *rayahs*.[41]

The late 1870s also witnessed a refashioning of the debate surrounding the Eastern Question and the continuation of Ottoman rule in south-east Europe. While liberal commentators denigrated it as denying a perceivably Christian majority the right to join 'European' civilization, their counterparts in the more conservative-leaning, pro-Turkish camp argued that international peace was only sustained because Istanbul's hegemony prevented it's 'barbarian' subjects from descending into complete anarchy. Montenegro and Serbia (that had achieved de facto independence in 1867) were presented as a case-in-point, being described as farcical caricatures where peasants-tuned-politicians availed themselves of the trappings of state 'borrowed from civilized countries'. When taken with their 'ignorant' fellows in Bosnia-Herzegovina, calls for an end to Ottoman rule made the prospect of a British withdrawal from Ireland seem 'harmonious and edifying' by comparison.[42] By contrast, Evans lauded the mountaineer warriors of Montenegro (proclaimed a secular principality in 1852) as embodying the 'Homeric' qualities of Classical antiquity.[43]

Following Istanbul's suppression of the 1876 'April Uprising'[44] in Bulgaria, the revived victimhood narrative was elevated to a matter of humanitarian morality by the widespread publicity afforded to violent acts committed against Christian Bulgarians in Gladstone's polemical *Bulgarian Horrors and the Question of the East* (1876). Particular opprobrium was reserved for the Empire's use of *bashi-bazouks*: irregular soldiers with a reputation for violent indiscipline, looting and preying on civilians.[45] Gladstone's inflammatory depictions of a Christian populace languishing under a despotic Islamic Empire turned Britain's official position on the Eastern Crisis into the moralistic fulcrum of his Midlothian Campaign, leading to his re-election to parliament and second term as prime minister in 1880. It also served in directing the attentions of an outraged voting public towards pro-Slav titles such as Irby's and Mackenzie's *Travels*, republished in 1877 with an introduction by Gladstone, and establishing the image of the victimized Slavic Christian peasant as a potent tool for framing Britain's political relations with the region.[46] Particular significance lay in the fact that such appeals were predicated on an alleged need to extend British state protections to foreign strangers rather than just British nationals overseas. This represented a clear divergence from previous acts of direct intervention supposedly underscored by 'moral considerations', such as the military expedition to Ethiopia in 1868.[47]

Midlothian, often cited as British democracy's first modern political campaign, was undoubtedly a political and cultural milestone in Anglo-Balkan relations. Yet, Gladstone's triumphant return to 10 Downing Street was equally distinct in articulating a liberal vision of Britishness, often through direct appeals to working-class audiences, as the manifestation of Christian values that justified radical domestic reform and intervention overseas.[48] By construing regional involvement as a matter of ethical and spiritual urgency, the mid- to late 1870s marked the end of a protracted era that had not only culminated in the South Slavic Balkans' perceived elevation to the European cultural sphere but recast it as an object of reference in mainstream domestic debates. The growing assortment of imagery which developed from public reactions to the Eastern Crisis coalesced into a more coherent vision of the region onto which observers could project their own interests and beliefs. Simultaneously, the vitriolic rhetoric provided the antecedent for early-twentieth-century propaganda; as well as enhancing public knowledge the elucidation of peasant society was now tentatively associated with a type of British moral idealism.[49]

1878 and the rise of cultural pessimism

While the Eastern Crisis cultivated a more distinctive image of the Balkans in the popular imagination, it also represented its apogee as a topic of interest in the Victorian public sphere. Despite the sympathy Gladstonian Liberal moralizing attracted to the cause of Christian Slav liberation, its impassioned dialogue remained mostly divorced from the diplomatic realities. The 1878 Treaty of Berlin brought the Crisis to an end simply by rescaling the local power balance in favour of the Dual Monarchy of Austria-Hungary, granting it administrative control over Bosnia-Herzegovina and the Sandžak of Novi Pazar (although both remained under nominal Ottoman rule). Concurrently, Montenegro and Serbia finally received full international recognition as independent states.[50] Yet, while Istanbul's retaining of Macedonia and other Slav-inhabited territories elicited vehement protest from Evans and other radical voices, the energy of public outrage Gladstone had sought to harness in 1876 and 1877 swiftly dissipated after 1878.[51] Anti-Ottoman rhetoric belied the fact that, as with London's decision to establish direct diplomatic relations with Serbia in 1837, maintaining a bulwark against Russian designs on the eastern Mediterranean remained the British raison d'être in the Balkans.[52] Moreover, rather than an appeal to some idealized British nation, Gladstone's electoral evangelizing reflected the fact that 'Britishness' still existed as a rhetorical device for vehiculating the ideological tenants of the country's ruling factions. The absence of military conscription and the Victorian British state's relatively minor presence in much of public life inhibited any deeper sense of affinity. This continued aversion to unitary nationhood was reinforced by the perennial, and increasingly racialized, question of Irish nationalism, conceived of as a violent aberration 'outside British norms and practices'.[53]

Beyond narrow strategic objectives, efforts to promote closer economic and cultural links with the independent Balkan states proved mostly fruitless due, in part, to a British propensity for denigrating the moral characters of their erstwhile partners.[54] Serbs, and by extension Orthodox Christian communities in Bosnia-Herzegovina, Croatia, Dalmatia, and Montenegro, became intrinsic to discussions of the relationship between Western modernity and the 'lost' territories of Eastern Christendom.[55] Such dialogues oscillated between two strains of thought. Admiration for what Evans termed the 'Homeric' virtues and 'democratic' traditions of the Slav village, the prevalence of peasant land ownership and Serbia and Montenegro's history of resistance to Ottoman rule were counterbalanced by the diplomatic consensus that the violent instability of the 1870s necessitated the continuing need for an (anti-Russian) imperial hegemon. By the end of the 1890s, Austria-Hungary had assumed this role. According to the historian, and self-identified authority on modern Balkan affairs, William Miller, 'centuries of Turkish misrule' had finally been rectified under the aegis of a European authority.[56] Evidence for this could be found in juxtaposing 'the model Balkan state' of Habsburg-administered Bosnia-Herzegovina, against the dismal socio-economic condition and systemic inefficiency of neighbouring Serbia.[57] Some commentators even suggested that regional tensions might be resolved if Montenegro and Serbia were compelled to surrender their national sovereignty to a 'higher' power.[58] Indeed, such sentiment was not without precedent. Following Athens's declaration of bankruptcy in 1893, and Greece's humiliating defeat in the Greco-Turkish War of 1897, an 'International Finance Committee', established by the European Great Powers, exercised full fiscal control over the country's public spending in order to service its extensive foreign debts.[59]

Balkan nationalism also elicited suspicion of 'agitators' and 'conspirators'. Even before Berlin, local grievances, if at all considered, were more likely to be looked upon as guises for extrinsic forces which, if indulged, would 'disorganise and impede' regional stability.[60] This was most acutely felt in Ottoman Macedonia with the appearance of rival Bulgarian, Greek and Serb nationalist institutions and, subsequently, paramilitary bands between the 1880s and 1903. *Vnatrešna makedonska revolucionerna organizacija* (VMRO), founded by pro-Bulgarian Macedonian revolutionaries in 1893, became the largest and most actively militant of these groups, having effectively evolved into a vehicle for Greater Bulgarian irredentism by 1900. In the eyes of late-Victorian pundits, the VMRO's covert activities became synonymous with insurrectionary violence, transforming the Balkans into a space 'where plans are hatched and schemes devized', often correlating with concerns over Ireland.[61]

Goldsworthy asserts that the emergence of a more conceptually cohesive form of imaginative geography in the 1890s was indelibly tied to literary motifs. Popular fiction such as Stoker's *Dracula* or, despite it actually being set in central Europe, *The Prisoner of Zenda* (1894) by Antony Hope cast the Balkans as a geographical 'blank canvas' onto which authors could project fantastical narratives, unencumbered by more obvious political subtext.[62] Beyond this purely imaginative literary sphere, middle-class British audiences found little of the 'seduction' that imbued Italy and the Mediterranean. The South Slavic Balkans instead existed seemingly to serve as an austere diplomatic arena for resolving obscure political disputes; 'an overgrown wilderness' strewn with 'the ruins of forgotten medieval battles' and risible local attempts at mimicking Western urbanity.[63]

Nonetheless, the appearance of Montenegro and Serbia as independent states granted the region a fixed sense of geopolitical distinctiveness. Literary depictions also grew increasingly diffuse, representing a diversifying range of gendered, professional and even ethnic perspectives among authors.[64] By the late 1890s, previously limited channels of engagement had also been significantly widened by a continual growth in communications and shifting social attitudes.[65] Factual information was no longer perceived as a purely rhetorical device for political and intellectual elites but a 'public cultural commodity' through which Britain's aspiring middle classes could pursue a range of topics that augmented 'the scope, audience and content' of publications.[66] This early process of commodification not only heralded a more consistent knowledge base, but represented the most important development in relation to how foreign cultures were presented and received in the wider public sphere.

Britain's gradually changing social context also became apparent in regard to historical and geographical awareness. Serbia's entry in the ninth edition of *Encyclopaedia Britannica*, published in 1886, for example, detailed some 500 years of history, religion and culture, alongside further coverage of neighbouring territories. An earlier entry, appearing in a supplementary volume to the seventh edition in 1842, had simply referred to the country's internal administrative structure and proximity to Istanbul.⁶⁷ This accumulation of knowledge was facilitated by more direct channels of contact – and the advent of organized opinion that had been presaged by Evans. In 1888, the Irish journalist James Bourchier arrived in the Balkans as a special correspondent for *The Times*, a position that was made 'permanent' in 1892. A talent for languages – and his unique status as Britain's only dedicated journalistic presence – gained Bourchier the favour of both the crowned heads of Bulgaria and Greece and access to contacts beyond the reach of most diplomats. Excluding Macedonia, however, Bourchier's remit was principally focused on Bulgaria, Greece and Romania, the South Slavic lands being officially the preserve of his opposite number in Vienna, William Lavino. Bourchier's occasional forays into Serbia (elevated to the status of a kingdom in 1882) usually resulted in brief, second-hand reports on royal scandals and the parlous state of the country's national finances.⁶⁸

Nevertheless, Bourchier's ingrained political affinity for neighbouring Bulgaria marked a critical point of departure from previous forms of British engagement. Michael Foley speculates that as a former teacher, 'haunted by growing deafness and probably homosexual', such empathy was likely to have stemmed from personal impulse and social frustration.⁶⁹ Being perceived outsiders, whose ascribed cultural identity was viewed with ever-growing political suspicion, Irish journalists and writers were obliged to adopt a far more objective and distanced approach in their reporting as a means of winning the favour of an English-dominated media establishment. The decision to identify with a foreign culture, particularly one deemed to exist at the periphery of modern civilization, represented a clandestine act of personal emancipation.⁷⁰

Questions of individual or collective identity would become a significant factor in forging links between the region and Britain's own increasingly visible social fault lines. Bourchier's unconscious associations between his outsider-status and role as correspondent thus illustrated the growing presence of domestic-inspired allegory in imaginative geography. This was particularly overt in earlier parallels between Austria-Hungary's occupation of Bosnia-Herzegovina and British rule in Ireland. Depictions in *Punch* and other publications deemed reflective of middle-class opinion, coupled with pseudo-scientific theorizing of the Irish as an inherently inferior race, partially eliminated geographical proximity as a means of cultural othering; both rural Ireland and Bosnia-Herzegovina now occupied similar places in the hierarchy of civilization as colonial 'peripheries' to a metropolitan Western European 'centre'.⁷¹

Suonpää interprets this through the lens of rising concerns over urban deprivation. *Punch's* caricature of the Habsburg Emperor Franz Joseph as a hapless police constable struggling to impose his authority over, 'Bozzy' and 'Herzy', two delinquent Turkish street children, provided intertextual commentary for its middle-class readership's own anxieties regarding crime and poverty in Britain's larger cities.⁷² Berber concludes that such allegorical connections were indicative of 'discursive strategies' through which these territories came to be understood as an inferior part of the 'European cultural space', as opposed to an 'Oriental other'.⁷³

At a more politically visceral level, popular allegories born of domestic anxiety were prevalent in the fractious public debates over Irish Home Rule which dominated Gladstone's second and third terms of office from 1880 to 1886. The spectre of conflict and wider international unrest emanating from the Balkans appeared paradigmatic of

Figure 1 'A Nice Time of It; or, The New Constable and the Naughty Boys', *Punch; or, The London Charivari*, 31 August, 1878, 86. © Courtesy of Punch Cartoon Library.

the ambiguities in Irish politics, set against rising bellicosity among rival nationalist and unionist factions. This was granted additional substance by the 'Land War' – a prolonged period of civil unrest in rural Ireland, including widespread violence, lasting into the 1890s.[74] Besides an overt racial undertone, the fixation on the Irish Question, much of which was cultivated deliberately by the British press, existed to rationalize the union with Ireland and arguably Britain's existence as a whole. At the heart of this lay a prescribed vision of British destiny to shoulder the burden of having to 'assist, instruct, and when necessary, punish' the Irish for their own long-term benefit.[75] Irish nationalism as a proactive political force signified a historical aberration that jeopardized both the union and the sense of a shared future.

Ireland not only manifested as a political concern but heralded a crucial realignment in how affiliation to the British state was defined in the public sphere. Following Gladstone's conversion to the cause of Home Rule, the ensuing split between Liberals and Liberal Unionists, resulting in the defeat of the First Home Rule Bill and a Conservative landslide in the 1886 general election, saw Britishness appropriated in service to the unionist cause. This further entrenched its association with elitist perceptions of the country's Anglo-Saxon heritage, emphasizing loyalty to historically English institutions such as the monarchy and Royal Navy.[76]

Suonpää further notes the presence of domestic anxieties as also coming to hold a more 'concrete' influence over British regional engagement after 1878. Discussions on strengthening the Anglican Communions' ties with the Eastern Orthodox Church –

specifically those Balkan autocephalies firmly outside of the Russian sphere – during the third and fourth Lambeth Conferences in 1888 and 1897 for instance, were dismissed by most religious pundits. The idea that the rational and orderly Church of England would even entertain a prospective 'reunion' with its 'stagnant', 'mysterious and illogical' East European counterparts was simply inconceivable.[77] Anglo-Catholic traditionalists, however, repudiated this conclusion, citing the Eastern rites' 'unvarying characteristics', impervious to Western scientific rationalism, as evidence of its greater theological purity, placing it closer to the 'undivided' Early Christian Church. Such admiration found precedence during the Eastern Crisis. In rallying behind Gladstone's anti-Ottoman campaign, nonconformists, liberal Anglican clerics and the more Radical segments of his support base secularized the Balkan Orthodox Churches' political image as guardians of their congregations' cultural and national identities.[78]

A more pertinent expression of this emerging cultural pessimism, however, lay in the growing fixation on 'national efficiency' from 1899. The crash of the Vienna stock exchange in 1873 and British industry's failure to fully capitalize on newer technological innovations after 1870 characterized the late nineteenth century as a period of entrenched stagnation. This was compounded by heightened commercial competition from Imperial Germany and the United States and the precipitating 'Long Depression', the economic impact of which was especially pronounced in Britain's agricultural sector. The social consequences of this were soon made visible through rising coverage of rural depopulation and entrenched pockets of unemployment and poverty in the larger cities. Philanthropic studies exploring the social consequences of urban impoverishment and reports of nationalist agitation in India and Ireland merely exacerbated existing anxieties. At the height of the Depression in the early 1890s, commentators were even attributing Britain's perceived state of decline to physiological regression and a loss of national vigour brought about by the 'degenerative' influence of urbanization.[79]

As the nineteenth century drew to a close concerns over Britain's apparently waning cultural and economic assertiveness partly served to generate fresh interest in the Balkans as a potential market for commercial expansion, even informing textual representations.[80] Herbert Vivian's *Servia: The Poor Man's Paradise* (1898) reciprocated many established motifs and clichés, yet offered an uncharacteristically non-pejorative, albeit overly romanticized, portrayal. For Vivian, Serbia's peasant society amounted to the purest expression of nationhood, based on romantic ideals extrapolated from his fixation on medieval chivalry. Serbia's limited industrial development – and the absence of a large organized working class – were viewed as indicative of a 'heroic' agrarian idyll that had long since vanished from British society, echoing earlier sentiments expressed by Paton.[81] To this end, British business was urged to rethink its cultural disinclinations towards Serbia, with Vivian, seemingly unaware of those still operating in the region, proposing that England's struggling entrepreneurs be encouraged to settle in a land 'where they shall be happy and wealthy and wise'.[82] While still demonstrating many of the earlier biases expressed by the likes of Hulme-Beaman, Vivian's text also anticipated many of the positive revaluations that came to shape imaginative geography in early-twentieth-century Britain.

Conclusion

Following his dramatic defeat in 1886, Gladstone authored another pamphlet, *The Irish Question*. While certainly not lacking in moralistic rhetoric, its discussion of the less electorally popular issue of Britain's duty to rectify its own legacy of misrule in Ireland illustrated a shift in socio-political debate. Despite a historiographical preoccupation with the Eastern Crisis, *The Irish Question* was far more revealing than *Bulgarian Horrors* of the cultural anxieties that underpinned representations of the South Slavic Balkans after 1900.[83]

Although improvements in long-distance communications had done much to reduce geographical barriers, by the turn of the century, cultural pessimism and latent anxieties had already corroded the Victorian-era belief in modernity's promise of indefinite scientific and social progress. Throughout the 1880s and 1890s the cultural movements surrounding 'the *fin de siècle* spirit' precipitated a sense of pessimism, cynicism and ennui. Friedrich Nietzsche and other scions of this development found a receptive following for their ideas among Britain's middle class through the 'widespread belief that civilization leads to decadence'.[84] When combined with domestic concerns, this pessimistic intellectual current began to manifest as a sense of wider civilizational decline where the 'thousand faces of degeneration' existed both at home and abroad.[85]

At the dawn of the new century, anxieties over the changing nature of a now mostly urbanized society asserted greater influence over how the South Slavic lands were represented. Although developments in the proceeding decades had been sporadic and inconsistent, they ultimately established the transnational parameters in which the region underwent a cultural reappraisal after 1899.

2

A new age of anxieties

Few would contest Todorova's claim that 'an image of the Balkans had already been shaped in European literature' before 1900.[1] Nevertheless, other imagological historians such as Norris, Hammond, Evans, Berber and Drapac continue to base their analyses on some variation of Eric Hobsbawn's 'long nineteenth century' with 1912 or 1914 as their point of departure. This periodizing of earlier patterns in Anglo-Balkan engagement has not only isolated discursive channels from their formative environment but overlooks a changing historical context not immediately evident within the political and cultural confines of diplomatic dispatches or middle-class travelogues. Consequently, discussion of the Edwardian era often carries a number of misleading presumptions, such as the idea that Britons still perceived themselves as unassailable global hegemons right up to the First World War. According to Hammond and Evans, it was only 'specific engagement with Serbia' from 1914 onwards that signalled the 'rupture' between the Victorian and 'post-Edwardian' paradigms.[2]

Following a prolonged lull in the 1880s and 1890s, the years spanning the end of Queen Victoria's reign to the outbreak of the Great War saw the Balkans play host to a decade of political upheaval from 1903 to 1913, engendering a revival in sporadic British public interest. The turn of the century was also defined by the ongoing reshaping of information as a widely accessible commodity, facilitated by ever-growing newspaper circulation and the appearance of cinema newsreels as a readily consumable form of mass media from 1910.[3] This also permitted the cynicism of the *fin de siècle* to permeate into the public sphere, intermixing with rising social anxieties and the British press's growing editorial propensity for sensationalism.[4]

The Second Boer War, that saw an overconfident and chronically ill-prepared British Empire struggle to subdue the independent Afrikaner republics of Transvaal and Orange Free State, provided the trigger for this cultural pivot, predicated as it was on the socio-economic legacies of the Long Depression and a raft of lingering domestic concerns. The humiliating setbacks of the campaign not only aroused public outrage, but also provoked wider discussion of Britain's comparative global isolation while precipitating calls for greater domestic 'efficiency'. These discourses soon came to revolve around improvements to public health and welfare provision as the basis for overcoming perceived military deficiencies and economic stagnation.

However, the highly sensationalized and febrile manner through which such objectives were framed in the national and metropolitan press tended to imbue such debates with a degree of reactionary alarmism, sublimated into appeals to nostalgia and pseudo-philosophizing. The Victorian tendency for conflating cultural development with science and technological progress was incrementally abandoned in favour of the 'moral hierarchy' of values deemed inherent to 'civic' as opposed to 'ethnic' nations. While tending to shy away from being overtly racialized, these values were viewed as inherent to Western Europeans – specifically the British and French – whose cultures were deemed more stable in adapting to socio-political and economic change. Early industrialization, for instance, had demonstrated a natural talent for ingenuity and innovation while an affinity for democratic plurality made them more successful in politically integrating new ideologies, such as Socialism. At a societal level, firmer grounding in Judeo-Christian heritage created more harmonious interpersonal relationships and a far lower risk of resorting to violent or deviant forms of behaviour in the pursuit of one's interests. It was through this developing intellectual millux that the professed ideals of Anglo-Britishness were initially articulated.[5]

While this new hierarchy invariably set Britain against 'the East', it did not necessarily preclude the latter's inhabitants from occupying a place within it. In the context of rising geopolitical tensions, it also permitted the British to implicitly distance themselves from the rapidly industrializing German Empire.[6] This redefining of civilization's temporal parameters thus instilled further doubt over the current trajectory of modernity: a new 'age of anxieties' where the advent of modernization could erode British power abroad by first weakening it at home. This rhetoric was certainly not unfelt among those writing on the Balkans. By the early 1900s, a tendency to valorize the countryside as the perceived origin of Anglo-British moral values saw South Slavic village culture elevated as a 'palliative for contemporary decadence'.[7]

This chapter will consider how Edwardian Britain's domestic anxieties were expressed through a curious intersection between nineteenth-century literary archetypes and a growing unwillingness, born of 'concrete British-Balkan connections', to simply dismiss the region as an esoteric travel destination 'or raw material for horror stories'.[8] With these developments, representations of the South Slav peasantry also acquired their allegorical meaning, when framed against what was colloquially termed the 'condition of England'.[9]

The 'national efficiency' paradigm

While historians are now inclined to view George Dangerfield's assertion that Britain faced a 'general crisis' by 1914 with some circumspection, few would contest J. B. Priestley's claim that the so-called 'long Edwardian summer' was an invention of 1920s cultural nostalgia.[10] Since the 1880s, entrenched middle- and upper-class domestic concerns over urban poverty were compounded by several sensationalized exposés which had made it even more visible in the public sphere. This occurred in conjunction with a series of highly publicized events, such as the London unemployment riots of 1886 and 1887, set against rising trade union membership and the ever-expanding labour movement. By the 1906 general election, these anxieties overlapped with other domestic issues including the Irish Question and the growing momentum of the women's suffrage campaign. Following the Boer War, such demands for radical change were amalgamated within the discourse of 'national efficiency', transforming a somewhat prosaic civil debate on welfare and state procedural reform into a pseudo-scientific paradigm for divining British societal health.[11]

The national efficiency paradigm as a subversion of the Victorian status quo was best illustrated in the changing nature of scientific coverage from 1890 to 1914. As the years passed, newspapers and popular periodicals such as *Pearson's Magazine* dedicated less and less editorial space to the latest innovations; discussion itself reflected this shift as positive appraisals of Britain's technological and industrial prowess were supplanted by debates on eugenics and calls for a return to a simpler, pre-industrial existence.[12] As Henrika Kuklick argued, greater access to information did not necessarily lead to the emergence of a more scientifically informed reading public. This was framed against the rise of academic specialization in the 1880s with 'legitimate' science increasingly perceived as the factually-dull and inaccessible preserve of educated professionals. In the case of anthropology – and the study of foreign cultures like the South Slavs – this resulted in the creation of 'hierarchies of knowledge', wherein popular understanding nearly always lagged behind accredited advances in theory and practice by several years.[13]

Until the 1920s, public engagement with these scientific fields came mostly through works by amateur researchers and authors outside the academy. Besides a propensity for sensationalism, the types of study most readily available typically carried sub-commentaries on domestic or colonial problems. General understanding of scientific theory, meanwhile, was predetermined by non-contextualized cultural parallels that reinforced readers' worldviews, with publications on foreign cultures becoming a form of 'acceptable pornography' rather than an educational resource. Despite its author spending most of his life in academia, J. G. Frazer's *The Golden Bough* (1890), a wide-ranging comparative study of myth and religion, attracted a cult following with its 'eternal images of dying kings and parched fields'. The title's popularity only increased during the release of the twelve-volume third edition between 1906 and 1915 and the sense of social despondency accentuated by the Great War.[14] Evans, likewise, captured public interest with his excavation of the Minoan palace of Knossos on Crete from 1900 to 1905. His inconclusive suggestions as to why this once thriving Mediterranean civilization had seemingly collapsed sparked waves of excitable speculation characterizing the downfall of the ancient Minoa as a historical analogy for the industrialized West.[15]

Sub-textual references to declining national efficiency, articulated through fears that the populace had entered a state of 'degeneration', were brought to the public fore with the release, in 1904, of an inter-departmental government report linking 'physical deterioration' to the British Army's lacklustre military performance in the Boer War. A prevalence of poverty-related illnesses was cited as the root cause: the declining health and stricken social backgrounds of working-class army recruits were labelled as indicative of a long-term deterioration in the national physiology resulting from decades of industrialization. Among the reports more dire findings was a memorandum compiled by the Surgeon-General. Based on the Army Medical Service's own records, 37.6 per cent of all enlistees who had undergone medical inspection from 1893 to 1902 had 'proved to be unfit for military service'. The shock such figures aroused was made all the more evident by the fact that this didn't even factor in those would-be servicemen rejected outright at the initial stage of recruitment, failing to even reach the medical fitness exam.[16] Links between the contemporary state of public health and urban living conditions were seized upon by pundits who juxtaposed the image of the Boers as a 'virile race' of hardy farmers and pastoralists with that of Britain's 'degraded', predominantly English, working class.[17]

Nowhere were these anxieties more acute than in relation to the so-called 'East End crisis' that focused public attention on poverty and crime in those areas of London incorporated into the Metropolitan Borough of Stepney from 1900. While Charles Dickens and other prominent Victorian campaigners had highlighted these issues as a matter of social justice, depictions of the capital's slum districts had acquired a more sinister aspect by the 1860s. Investigative journalists like James Greenwood and social reformers such as Charles Booth and Charles Masterman, compared their findings to colonial explorations of sub-Saharan Africa, characterizing London's poorest residents as having degenerated into a primitive and dangerous Other.[18]

Although the hysteria surrounding the national efficiency debate quickly reached its zenith in the war's immediate aftermath, it continued to shape popular attitudes towards urbanization as a detriment to the 'national physique' or 'quality and quantity' of the British populace.[19] Writing in 1908, Rolfe Arnold Scott-James, one of the earliest commentators to adopt the term 'modernism' in reference to contemporary social norms, summarized the cultural displacement of scientific progress with a general sense of pessimism:

> the idea is being pressed in upon us that the men of the last century have brought things to such a pass for us that the world as it is, is almost intolerable. We have come to disbelieve in the success of our science, our improvements, our institutions, our civilization, and the literature and art which builds itself on all these [. . .]. Some, again, seek a refuge from the tumultuous scene by turning to other atmospheres of distant times or distant places [. . .], flying literally or in imagination to the peoples and cities of the Orient, or the wilds where primitive people and beasts still live in reverent terror of the unknown.[20]

Besides contributing to the Liberal Party's landslide victory over Arthur Balfour's unpopular Conservative-Liberal Unionist coalition in 1906, the conflict in southern Africa granted a sense of immediate political and cultural urgency to a plethora of domestic issues. The founding of the Parliamentary Labour Party in 1900 and the period of the 'Great Unrest', that saw a spike in industrial strikes and agitation from 1910 to 1914, ignited popular fears of radical Socialism as a political force at the ballot box and source of civil disruption within the burgeoning labour movement.[21] The Liverpool general transport strike, which took place in the summer of 1911, was the most explicit manifestation of this perceived trend. The strike paralysed much of Merseyside's commerce and culminated in a series of riots, police baton-charges and the fatal shooting of two striking workers as the then home secretary, Winston Churchill, ordered soldiers in to disperse the crowds. Industrial action consequently spread to other urban centres, inciting sympathy strikes as far afield as Belgium and the Netherlands.[22]

Fears of social unrest on the British mainland met with rising trepidation over the still unresolved question of Irish Home Rule. Even before 1902, these discursive currents were already perceptible in how British nationals formulated impressions of the South Slavic Balkans. During a family tour of southern and south-east Europe in 1901, Evelyn Wrench, a future editor of *The Spectator* and founder of the English-Speaking Union educational charity, lauded the Habsburg administration in Bosnia-Herzegovina for having created a working example of harmonious religious coexistence, using Ireland as his principal frame of reference. In contrast to the sectarian bellicosity and social division saturating the Irish Question, all major settlements under the occupation now appeared 'half Christian and half Mahommedan . . . it seems extraordinary how both sects live at peace with each other'.[23] Despite threads of continuity with the late 1800s, Wrench's approving reference to religious harmony, a subject rarely touched upon in previous accounts, presaged wider anxieties over perceived cracks in *Pax Britannica*'s once unassailable imperial edifice.

Direct parallels between underlying domestic anxieties were even linked to regional events, especially in cases depicted along narrative lines of victimhood. As Florian Keisinger notes in regard to Ireland, differing political interest groups appropriated the image of the region as an allegory for their specific interests, resulting in forms of representation that were not universally negative. By 1912, both the Unionist and Nationalist press presented the VMRO's guerrilla activities in Macedonia as a possible model for resolving the Irish political impasse through an embrace of more militant strategies.[24]

Intellectual disquiet and a revival of 'degeneration theory' coincided with the emergence of the international eugenics movement. In July 1912, less than three months before the outbreak of the First Balkan War, over 400 delegates gathered at the 'First International Eugenics Congress' in London to discuss various strategies for averting civilization's projected decline. These included programmes of enforced sterilization and schemes to promote selective breeding in order to 'raise the stock' of 'the lower social orders' and eliminate 'feeble-mindedness'.[25]

However, although certainly a recurrent feature in Victorian philosophical and scientific dialogues, racial notions of hereditary 'purity' or biological lineage as a determining factor in shaping national identities generally met with ambivalence or dismissal from British specialists. The fact that such ideas tended to be associated with German thinkers only strengthened this aversion. As attitudes towards the Irish demonstrated, the lack of any historical sense British nationhood and the populace's own ethnic ambiguousness, especially in England, tended to minimize race as a feature of domestic public life, in contrast to Germany or the United States. Although this certainly didn't equate to an absence of xenophobia, notably antisemitism, any systematic form of scientific racialist logic remained elusive, being subsumed, like eugenics, into much broader questions of poverty and social distinction.[26]

As Evans notes, while organized opinion and those with a direct interest in Balkan affairs sought to capture a middle-class public appetite for cultural titillation, the term 'race' was itself applied 'with startling inconsistency' and lacked any actual substance beyond its perceived suitability for denoting vague territorial, as opposed to ethnic, identities.[27] Conversely, environmental factors were regularly emphasized as determining many desirable psychological and physiological qualities now deemed to be lacking in urbanized Britons. Montenegrin tribesmen in their 'mountain fastness', or the peasant traders and labourers commonly encountered across Dalmatia and Serbia, were viewed as having been intrinsically moulded by a social remoteness that universally produced 'sterling stock'.[28] Couched in this eugenicist language, the Ottomans appeared in a particularly unfavourable light when compared to the 'virile' South Slavs.[29]

The relatively hollow and amorphous nature of these depictions contrasted with the greater scientific precision of South Slavic intellectuals, such as Cvijić, in their adoption of 'racial anthropology': the classification and stratification of human races or physical 'types'. This contributed towards crystallizing ideas of nationhood and a specific 'way of life' centred on rural traditions and cultural practices, equivocal to Western views of the 'noble primitive', providing the patina of scientific justification for political claims.[30] The Croatian archaeologist, and director of Sarajevo's *Landesmuseum* (National Museum), Ćiro Truhelka, was a particularly influential mediator of such ideas before 1914. Applying eugenicist theories to nineteenth-century racialist dogmas, Truhelka classified Croats as a superior, non-Slav, 'Nordic-Aryan type'. By virtue of blood, Bosnian Muslims, the alleged descendants of medieval Croat nobles who had converted to Islam, represented 'the flower' of the nation. This was juxtaposed with Bosnia-Herzegovina's Armenian, Jewish, Romani and Orthodox Serb communities. The latter in particular, were denigrated as the 'inferior, parasitic and violent' racial antithesis of the Nordic-Aryan Croats with Truhelka highlighting the Serbs' greater business acumen as indicative of an undesirable appetite for material gain.[31] As the custodian of one of Habsburg Sarajevo's signature cultural attractions, Truhelka's influence was also likely to have embellished certain aspects of British writing on Bosnia-Herzegovina. Percy Henderson, a former Indian army major, for instance, dismissed any suggestions of a future Southern Slavic union on ethnological and racial grounds. Beyond 'the Slav or Serbian tongue', and obscure tribal origins, Bosnia's Slav communities were judged to have held nothing in common.[32]

Nevertheless, discursive efforts to alienate specific groups who deviated from a territory's societal norms found allegorical resonance with the intensification of cultural antisemitism in Britain, stemming from an influx of Jewish migrants who had fled the wave of pogroms in Tsarist Russia during the 1880s. Rising discontent among working-class communities, notably in East London, and the growing prevalence of urban slums were blamed, in part, on the new arrivals, invoking pejorative, albeit reactionary, caricatures of Jews as a corrupting presence. This in turn culminated in the 1905 Aliens Act that sought to mainly restrict Jewish immigration from Eastern Europe.[33] From 1903, Jews in Macedonia attracted a similar antipathy as urban 'tax farmers', comparable to the 'shadowy Jewish financier' of late-Victorian and Edwardian popular literature and propagated by opponents of the Boer War.[34] Suonpää notes that British diplomatic sentiments also 'fitted in with the wider European and American pattern of distrust, envy and prejudice towards Jewish businessmen'.[35] However, such impressions ultimately represented an extension of Liberal and Radical political critiques rather than the deliberate targeting of a visible minority. Besides offering a link to Britain's own climate of causal antisemitism, animosity towards Balkan Jews was rooted in their conflation with Ottoman rule, and later German influence, as opposed to ingrained cultural hostility.[36]

Despite these analogous connections, South Slavic ethno-nationalism itself was more likely to draw disdain than admiration from British pundits. Here again, lingering associations with Ireland and India unconsciously manifested as a preference for maintaining the regional status quo. Henderson's dismissal of a future Yugoslavian polity also rebuked Croat and Serb claims to Bosnia-Herzegovina's Muslims, whom he argued as having come to effectively constitute a different race.[37] In 1906, Cvijić, seeking to bolster Serbia's contested claim to Macedonia, proposed that its Slav peasants represented an ahistorical 'amorphous mass' that could be effectively assimilated into either the Serbian or Bulgarian national cultures.[38] This proposition of a malleable ethnicity was conducive to British debates on the chaotic potential for conflating nationality with prescribed racial categories.

The extent of this ethno-nationalistic 'chaos' was brought to wider public attention in the aftermath of the Ilinden–Preobrazhenie uprising that broke out across Macedonia in August 1903, having been orchestrated by the VMRO after years of escalating political unrest.[39] 'Let me begin by correcting an almost universal fallacy', Evans stated, following the Ottoman's suppression of the main insurgent forces. 'There are no Macedonians.' The territory instead represented a meeting-point of the Albanian, Bulgarian, Greek, and Romanian nations with 'a large Spanish Jew population in Soloun [Thessaloniki]'.[40] The journalist George Abbott cast doubt on the assertion that ethnic lines could be so easily divisible. In 'one and the same household', individual family members might identify as Bulgarian, Greek, Serb, Russian, or 'simply Christian'. Rather than resolve the matter of identity, the imposition of the modern nation-state ideal only created

> a true comedy of errors in which no one knows who is who, but everybody instinctively feels that everybody is somebody else [. . .]. It may be described as a region peopled with new-born souls wandering in quest of a body, and losing themselves in the search.[41]

Regardless of this sensationalist discourse, as Christopher Prior has pointed out, national efficiency was always, at its heart, a question of how a fairer and more logical system of resource distribution might be achieved. In the regional press, concepts such as 'racial decline' were notable by their virtual absence.[42] Even attempts to build comparisons between London's working-class districts and those in other cities were likely to be vigorously refuted by local elites.[43] What ultimately sustained this heightened sense of anxiety in the Edwardian public sphere was less a fear of some encroaching decline then a sense of uncertainty regarding the future shape of the social status quo. Masterman's *The Condition of England*, published in 1909 and running into seven editions by 1912, encapsulated this ambiguity: 'We are uncertain whether civilization is about to blossom into flower or, wither in tangle [*sic*] of dead leaves and faded gold.'[44] Masterman appeared to align himself with the latter prediction, enflaming middle-class social sensibilities through his overly dismal portrait of Britain's economic climate – and demands for greater state welfare provision. Chief among these was the continuation of unplanned urbanization with Masterman warning that an English countryside in which stately homes merely existed as outposts of upper-class excess amid 'one vast wasteland' of 'decaying villages' and 'empty fields' threatened the very existence of the country's spiritual and cultural life.[45] This more specific concern served as the most direct point at which images of the South Slavic Balkans converged with Britain's domestic public discourse.

Echoes of the Long Depression

While the Boer War had further exposed the extent of Britain's domestic shortcomings to the wider public, it was the detrimental socio-economic legacy of the Long Depression that ultimately determined how these issues were culturally framed before 1914. The sensationalized fixation on national efficiency and collective national health prompted politicized calls to discard the country's Victorian-era trappings; both these factors fuelled much of the Liberal government's programme of welfare reform and progressive legislation after 1906. The national efficiency question also provided commentaries on the Balkans with a more concrete point of contrast. Since 1880, the British economy itself had slowly pivoted away from manufacturing and physical trade towards the increasingly lucrative service industries, particularly finance and logistics. By 1901, many 'traditional' manual industries, popularly perceived as the foundation of British global hegemony, accounted for only 40 per cent of national income while stiffening American and German competition saw the proportion of British-owned global trade shrink from 23 per cent in 1880 to 17 per cent in 1910. Correspondingly, on the death of Queen Victoria, British agriculture – the depression's primary victim and a popular metric through which pundits attempted to intuit the 'national vitality' – employed barely 7 per cent of the populace.[46] Although its impact was varied, with some specialist areas like dairying even enjoying a small boom, attention was inevitably drawn to the visible decline of grain cultivation and other socially prestigious types of farming tied to 'the ownership of great tracts of land'.[47] In contrast, a statistical survey of Serbia's population from 1900 to 1905 classified just over 87 per cent as 'agricultural' with 'a slight tendency to increase'.[48]

Neither had this sense of impending social crisis escaped the notice of foreign observers, including those from the South Slavic Balkans. '*Cela va sans dire* [That goes without saying]. We are a nation of peasants. We have scarcely any aristocracy', Serbia's ambassador to London, Sima Lozanić, quipped in a 1901 interview for *The Humanitarian*. Nevertheless, minimal industrial development did not necessarily assure a life of complete misery and hardship for the average Serb peasant. Life in a country that had yet to undergo a similar demographic transition to that of Victorian Britain also meant an absence of urban deprivation, 'submerged tenths' and 'proletarian discontent'.[49] There was 'no need of work houses or asylums' since poverty relief and mental health remained the preserve of the *zadruga* or village commune.[50]

Although Lozanić's political overtures garnered little sympathy among pundits, the sentiment he invoked increasingly informed the manner in which the South Slavic Balkans was presented within the cultural context of Britain's *fin de siècle*; authors were drawn to what they and their middle-class audiences presumed were moral virtues exclusive to its rural communities. As Victorian-era triumphalism receded, regional depictions increasingly framed the peasant village as integral to fostering a more comprehensive understanding of the territory under observation. The Scottish journalist John Foster Fraser, like Paton and Vivian, praised Serbia as 'the real peasant state of the Balkans'. The 'man who lives in London' might pity the peasantry for their material poverty, yet would find on encountering them a 'light-hearted and contented' people with little concern beyond acquiring the most basic necessities.[51] British visitors to other territories were no less approving in noting the absence of driving urban poverty or glaring social divisions.[52] Though often emphasizing customs, dress and agricultural practices, these accounts occasionally provided space for self-reflection, including meditations on contemporary 'civilization'. The sight of Christian peasants bargaining with Muslim shopkeepers in the northern Bosnian town of Maglaj convinced one photographer that an absence of industrialization assuaged human suffering by impeding the emergence of 'monied hierarchies'. One had to go 'to the very lowest rung of the social ladder to come across the squalid pauper class so common in the large cities of the civilized countries of the West'.[53]

Even contrasts in farming conditions and practices offered the potential for social allegory. Discussing his experience of travel in rural Herzegovina, one former Irish military officer lamented his countrymen's inability to match the province's 'stalwart shepherds and husbandmen' even in potato cultivation.[54] Moreover, in keeping with the popular turn against unbridled urbanization, external interference or the legacy of the 'degenerate Orient' were presented as incongruous to a 'natural' agrarian social order.[55] Writing in 1904, Vivian argued that successive Belgrade governments had, thus far, avoided this problem by minimizing the state's presence in rural Serbian life. This was correspondingly reflected in parliamentary elections at which the peasantry 'steadily' voted back into office politicians who promised only a continuation of the social status quo.[56]

Touristic literature also demonstrated a propensity for romanticizing the rural aesthetic. Discussing Habsburg Dalmatia's potential as a 'future' destination for British cultural tourism, the anthropologist Maude Holbach lamented that a rising prevalence of 'un-Dalmatian' practices and fashions in the coastal towns meant cultural authenticity could only be found in its outlying villages. While the peasants continued to distinguish themselves with their 'crimson turbans', 'twisted waist scarves' and 'sleeveless jackets of crimson cloth adorned with silver buttons or embroidery', their urban counterparts had abandoned their cultural heritage for the 'prosaic twentieth century'.[57]

Imagological scholarship tends to interpret such romanticism as further evidence of the historical othering that distanced these territories from the great European metropoles, resigning them to the status of picturesque, but backward, peripheries.[58] Although valid in some respects, it ignores a deeper conceptualization of the rural environment among Britain's constituent cultures that followed the advent of industrialization, especially in England. Before the 1870s, British travellers and commentators such as the Radical Liberal MP Richard Cobden extolled the benefits of a continental agrarianism based on smallholdings rather than landed estates – as had been the case in Serbia since the 1830s.[59] By the Edwardian era, even more cynical observers could conclude that in 'the Garden of the Balkans' (Serbia) even 'the untutored peasant can now make a living by antediluvian methods'. The fact that Austrians and Germans seemed to be the only foreign presence exploiting Serbia's agricultural fecundity appeared even more distressing as an overlooked opportunity for British investors.[60]

Romanticism in Britain was itself a reaction to Enlightenment rationalism and the Industrial Revolution's perceived societal ills. Early Scottish Romantics such as Robert

Figure 2 Peasants in the Market at Spalato (Split), photo by Otto Holbach, c. 1907. © Public domain.

Burns and Walter Scott leveraged what they viewed as a rising sense of social grievance to cultivate a cultural paradigm based on historical reverence for the Highland clan system.[61] South of the border, William Wordsworth and other artistic luminaries encouraged their English readers to perceive themselves as a 'people with immemorial rural roots'.[62] Such nostalgia promoted a belief in folk culture and rural tradition as the very basis for what had placed Britain at the forefront of Western civilization.[63] From the 1880s, a plurality of conservative, liberal and socialist cultural impulses attempted to revive, conserve or invent their own folk traditions while promoting outdoor pursuits as more wholesome forms of recreation. In larger cities, progressive town planners designed 'cottage style' dwellings, believing they would help improve the working class's psychological well-being. At the very extreme of this 'new pastoralism', new-age humanists advocated a 'return to the land' as a palliative for an urban society in danger of stagnation.[64] However, as Mandler argues in relation to England, this romanticizing of the countryside mostly remained 'the province of impassioned and highly articulate but fairly marginal artistic groups'.[65] Nevertheless, its manifestation was indicative of a cultural recalibration of Britain's constituent identities around abstract notions of moral resilience – qualities associated almost unconsciously with the perceived values of rural society.

This intellectual eulogizing of an idealized agrarian past percolated into wider concerns for the sustainability of the very urban society that began to supplant it from the mid-eighteenth century. In this regard, the rise of the Radical Liberal 'land reform movement' represented the most overtly political link between Britain and the region. In 1865, Cobden had even suggested that Serbia's social model of peasant smallholders be championed as an alternative to the landed estates of Britain's hereditary nobility. Travel in the country, as confirmed by his associate Humphry Sandwith, proved an illustration of contrasts 'between the sturdy Servian peasant with his self-respect, and our abject agricultural labourers!'[66] The perceived virtue of peasant proprietorship, frequently interpreted as a form of secular democratic piety, was also present in discussion of regional affairs. Prior to Berlin, Gladstone's parliamentary associate, George Campbell, echoed Cobden in proposing that Serbia's 'conservative peasant-proprietor sort of democracy' be replicated in the Ottoman's remaining Balkan territories as a viable means of guaranteeing free government and stability.[67]

By 1909, the Radicals' vision of a countryside of smallholders as a 'bulwark' against societal stagnation and organized Socialism had, as Paul Readman notes, moved beyond 'the sphere of rhetorical politicking and into the realm of practical policymaking'.[68] A 'healthy, vigorous and bold peasantry' was even perceived by some as a quantifiable state asset for the social shifts it might engender.[69] Consequently, land reform permeated every political facet of the 1909 constitutional crisis and the general elections of 1910, achieving a modicum of cross-party consensus. Radical MPs fashioned electoral campaigns around it, advocating working-class resettlement as a panacea for both rural and urban degradation.[70] In a comparative survey of British and Belgian land tenure in 1911, the anti-poverty campaigner Joseph Rowntree concluded that increasing the number of smallholdings represented the only tangible solution for English farming.[71] A second study on conditions in the English countryside reiterated this while stating that poverty in rural districts had since surpassed the more closely documented cities. This was exacerbated by the perception among agricultural labourers that much of the land on aristocratic estates was 'under-farmed'.[72] Even Durham, who rarely, if ever, displayed an interest in British domestic issues, echoed this popular zeal for reform in her description of the reactions of Serb peasants, whom she encountered outside the Orthodox monastery at Gračanica in east Kosovo, towards the plight of their distant British counterparts. '[T]he idea of paying rent amazed and shocked them. They regarded working for another as, under any circumstances, "*veliki zalum*" (great tyranny).'[73] Reviving Britain's agriculturalist classes was thus perceived as a crucial corrective to historical injustices in Ireland, Scotland and Wales while restoring 'lost or threatened continuities in the English national *telos*'.[74]

Reversing the decline of Britain's rural communities became enmeshed in foreign and colonial questions accentuated by the Boer War. In 1903, mainstream liberalism joined with British socialists in denouncing further 'vainglorious colonial adventurism' in Africa as antithetical to the drive for national well-being. The combined costs of recent pacification campaigns 'would have settled no less than 5000 cultivators on the land', George Lambert MP repeatedly told the National Liberal Federation's annual conferences from 1905 to 1907.[75] Some commentators took this theory even further by expanding it to the wider European context, with a nod to the south-east. Returning from a tour of Macedonia in 1905, Scott-James urged the Habsburg Monarchy to extend its occupation of Ottoman territory further south for the sake of reinvigorating 'our almost sterile Western civilization' with 'the new stock of vital force which the Balkans can offer'.[76] Such sympathies were conducive to a wider re-evaluation of South Slavic rural identity as displaying many of the qualities deemed intrinsic to the societal model increasingly idealized in popular discourses.

Peasants and the city

Despite living intermittently in the 'Austrian Littoral'[77] (where South Slavs formed a majority) from 1904 to 1915, the acclaimed Irish novelist James Joyce never expressed interest in the province, beyond the 'Italianized' capital of Trieste. '[I] hate this Catholic country with its hundred races and thousand languages', he complained in a letter to his aunt in December 1904 while serving as a language tutor in the Istrian port of Pula, where the Austro-Hungarian navy was also headquartered. For all its imperial trappings, Pula, according to Joyce, was little more than 'a back-of-God-speed place – a naval Siberia'. The cosmopolitan exoticism of Trieste that lent inspiration to *Dubliners*, *A Portrait of the Artist as a Young Man* and *Exiles*, found little resonance in provincial Pula: 'a long boring place wedged into the Adriatic peopled by ignorant Slavs who wear little red caps and colossal breeches'.[78]

Joyce's disparaging commentary seemed emblematic of the urban cultural lens through which Edwardian Britons tended to observe the Balkans. Indeed, at the beginning of the twentieth century, British and South Slavic social demography appeared as almost statistical inversions of one another. In 1911 for example, more than 78 per cent of the population of England and Wales resided in industrialized towns and cities.[79] By contrast, in December 1918, less than a quarter of interwar Yugoslavia's 12 million citizens resided in urban areas, with an appreciable portion being seasonal migrant workers from the countryside.[80] Moreover, while Britain's own agrarian past was very much a distant memory in the 1900s and 1910s, urban growth in the South Slav lands remained low, even by regional standards. Before 1918, Belgrade, Sarajevo and Zagreb were the only cities of the future Yugoslavia with more than 50,000 inhabitants; the former's growth from 69,000 residents in 1900 to over 100,000 in 1914 still lagged Athens, Bucharest and Sofia.[81]

As Norris and Mazower have observed, while Britain's cities emerged as centres of culture, economics and innovation, most of the urban Balkans had 'evolved under a Turkish Ottoman role model' into a series of localized commercial hubs oriented towards trade and provincial administration. Given their comparatively small scale and lack of distinguishing characteristics between neighbourhoods, earlier Western visitors often assumed their populations to be entirely Muslim and fundamentally alien to the region.[82] The later onset of European-style modernization had given way to the assumption that

Balkan cities had simply become pale imitations of their French and Central European counterparts.[83] Durham, for instance, described Belgrade in 1903 as having a veneer of prosperous modernity that masked the impoverished conditions to the immediate south.[84] Descriptions of Macedonia and Bosnia-Herzegovina conveyed similar sentiments, often noting how Sarajevo and other cosmopolitan urban centres appeared utterly detached from the religiously segregated villages where most of the populace resided.[85] According to Božidar Jezernik, by the mid-1800s, Western visitors could find 'nothing original about the Balkan towns, nothing individual. Everything was borrowed'.[86]

However, closer observance of these changes reveals a far more complex set of processes that sought to modify, rather than discard outright, pre-existing urban heritages in order to preserve them within more dominate European trends. In the case of Habsburg-administered Sarajevo, Mary Sparkes notes that between 1878 and 1918, elites, rural immigrants and private citizens actively engaged in redeveloping the Bosnian capital giving rise to an integrated 'Sarajevan' style that fused Islamic and Habsburg motifs, a point that was not lost on British observers.[87] The West may have 'won' in its battle for cultural dominance, commented Holbach, but when viewed from the surrounding hills, 'Austrian Sarajevo' and 'Turkish Sarajevo' had 'merged into one fair city'.[88] Her contemporaries were equally inclined towards a similar preference for this integrated style.[89] 'I have seen many cities renowned for their beauty', remarked a visiting anthropologist, 'but none of them excited within me such admiration as Sarajevo'.[90] This raises further questions as to how the relationship between the South Slavic city and its hinterlands was actually perceived in British accounts, particularly the latter's influence over the former.[91]

As the region's cultural image gained greater coherence in the British public sphere, discursive representations began to divine a general absence in the more rigid rural-urban divides prevalent in the industrialized West. Romantic or less critical voices presented the lack of urban capitalism as socially beneficial, praising the apparent absence of poverty while ignoring or interpreting its presence in rural districts as evidence of an unambiguous adherence to organic cultural traditions.[92] This was, often unconsciously, framed by British assumptions that the industrial metropolis represented the key point of socio-political divergence between European and non-European civilization. Neither rural nostalgia nor the anxieties of urban degeneration could diminish an appreciation of the city as a creative sight of urbanity: industry, scientific innovation, artistic refinement and a dynamic energy that drove socio-political change.[93] As mentioned, by 1900 Britain's convoluted patchwork of local identities had been mostly transplanted into its urban centres.

However, in keeping with the discursive turn from modernity as being a purely beneficial phenomenon, the lack of industrialization and urban sprawl in Balkan towns acquired many of the positive connotations associated with the rural environment. In the British case, this perspective was reinforced by the fact that most visitors tended to use London as their main point of comparison. As the centre of a global empire, and thus far more culturally detached from its respective geographical region than other English cities, while also being synonymous with Britain's prevailing social anxieties, this contrast only magnified the ostensibly peasant nature of London's south-east European counterparts.[94]

Geographical features were often deemed key to this notion of a less defined rural-urban divide. The Venetian grandeur of Adriatic coastal towns like Trogir or Zadar, several authors noted, belied their reliance on the rural economy and relative isolation within Austria-Hungary.[95] In the context of rising latent disillusion in the urban centre as a progressive space, however, this was not necessarily considered a negative; Zadar's lack of a railway station, one passing visitor concluded, simply reflected the citizenry's desire 'to live out of the world' (rather than a symptom of Vienna's financial neglect as claimed by local nationalists).[96] In some circumstances, division might appear non-existent such as western Istria, where it was observed that adverse in-land conditions obliged peasants to live in the cities themselves.[97] In these more exiguous coastal urban centres, greater cultural 'closeness' to the past blurred the distinction between peasant and town-dweller. Holbach argued that the authorities' encouragement of lace-making and other forms of 'native-industry', or new ones more congenial to Dalmatia's traditional intermingling of rural and urban such as the production of insect powder from wild chrysanthemums, could ameliorate economic problems without sacrificing the environment or local customs.[98]

Cities in the northern Croat lands, on the rare occasions they actually featured in British literature, were also indelibly linked to their hinterlands, despite displaying more outwardly 'European' facades. Having arrived in Zagreb anticipating the 'narrow, dark and odoriferous streets' of coastal Dalmatia, Henderson's professed surprise at being 'back in Western civilization'. This was somewhat attenuated, however, by the sight of peasants in national costume, appearing as a hybrid of Bosnian and Albanian dress, crowding the city centre.[99] Against the grandiose, Central European architectural simulacra of 'the Croat dream', such groups became 'near-mythical figures that might have stepped out of a picture book', their colourful outfits speaking 'of another race'.[100] Despite its appearance as a 'fervently Catholic capital', another visitor described Zagreb as possessing the cultural ambience of an Ottoman border town. The 'blue haze of the mountains of Bosnia', visible from the elevation of the upper town on a clear day, reminded foreigners that although Croats aspired to be 'European', they could not escape their fate as the 'Fringe of the Orient' with its socially integral agrarianism.[101]

This stylizing of the region's urban spaces as gateways to an authentic rural cultural sphere was not ubiquitous. In territories still under Ottoman administration, a revival in liberal anti-Turkish political sentiments increasingly characterized the towns as outposts of conservative Islamic repression, perpetuating socio-economic stagnation while stymieing the rural Christian populace's latent potential.[102] In Macedonia, where violent unrest in the countryside had produced one of the highest rates of rural to urban migration in the Balkans, cities were even construed as obstructions to socio-economic progress; excluding Bitola and the port of Thessaloniki, most were dismissed as 'dusty Turkish towns', important only for their strategic value or as microcosms of the Empire's festering domestic fault lines.[103] Abbott described Veles, 55 km south-east of Skopje, as epitomizing such tensions. Here a 'few weather-stained minarets stood in opposition to its more numerous church belfries', these being internally divided between 'Bulgarian' and 'Greek'.[104] Macedonia's social divisions also mirrored British contemporary anxieties concerning rural depopulation and urban impoverishment. Describing the situation in Prilep, 45 km south-west of Veles, in 1902, one Serb geographer warned that hundreds of internally displaced peasants 'sat idle' or joined the local 'political gangs', while 'the fertile Prilep fields weep for work-hands'.[105]

Conversely, the complete absence of a recognizable urban centre could also promote derision, with Montenegro serving as the principal example. Efforts to nurture industry in more readily accessible towns such as Kolašin, Nikšić and Ulcinj , as one correspondent sardonically remarked, did little to attenuate the country's reputation as 'a regal suburbia'.[106] Even the 'bravery, frankness, honesty, hardihood' and assorted virtues historically attributed to the Montenegrin national character conflicted with the risible international image of its diminutive national capital, Cetinje.[107] Arriving there for the first time in 1900, Durham's initial impressions were of 'the ugliest, oddest toy-capital conceivable'. The so-called seat of royal power might have passed for a colonial outpost 'at the end of the world or the other end of nowhere'.[108] Subsequent Edwardian comparisons to 'a South African township' or euphemistic descriptions of it as 'quaint in the extreme' implied the erosion of Montenegro's heroic reputation as some observers began to posit that its geographic inaccessibility, rather than its people's martial prowess, had actually been key to retaining political independence from the Ottomans.[109] Nevertheless, like other Balkan capitals, Cetinje's reputation as 'a big village' challenged post-agrarian British societal norms by blurring the received concept of a cultural rural-urban divide to the point of annulling it. The peasant mountaineers who congregated along its main streets appeared as social chameleons, with the potential for occupying the role of soldier, artisan, merchant, or even civil servant.[110]

This idea of the peasantry as the fulcrum of both urban and rural South Slavic identity was encapsulated in the 'peasant democracy' Fraser observed while attending an open sitting of the Serbian *skupština* (National Assembly). While delegates representing urban districts 'could pass for parliamentary deputies in Vienna or Budapest', the Belgrade parliament teemed with men 'in brown homespun zouave jackets, beflowered shirts, tight-fitting brown homespun trousers and rough rural-made sandals' or 'white trousers which look as though they have shrunk in the wash, and white shirts falling to their knees'.[111] This shift in attitudes was indeed a notable departure from the polarized characterizations of the 1870s. For Fraser, the peasant not only 'had presence' in the metropolis but occupied the seat of national politics at its heart. Even the parliament building's interior resembled 'the inside of a barn' with some deputies eschewing the formalities of the legislation chamber to debate outside in the shade of lime trees as though 'attending a village meeting'.[112] Rather than enforcing division, Serbia's urban sphere appeared to have amalgamated with its rural counterpart, much to Fraser's and many of his contemporaries' professed approval.[113]

Romancing remoteness

Throughout the nineteenth century, an emphasis on distance in imaginative geography, imagological historians have argued, created overarching impression of cultural remoteness and isolation.[114] Even after 1900, certain authors still described ostensibly European regions, such as Dalmatia, as lands of 'brigands, primitive travel and squalid fare'.[115] Finding a suitable analogy for this sense of cultural alienation, the *Westminster Gazette*'s foreign correspondent, Harry de Windt, seized on such historical tropes to portray his crossing of Montenegro's southern border as semi-metaphysical in its remoteness. A six-hour climb from Habsburg-ruled Kotor to the frontier signalled his arrival at what might as well have been a different worldly plain; the environment itself changed 'with the rapidity of a scene shift at a London theatre', exhibiting 'not a vestige of life or particle of verdure . . . more suggestive of a lunar than an earthly landscape'.[116] Although better disposed towards foreign tourism, lowland coastal Dalmatia retained a similar veneer of cultural obscurity, reinforced by an apparent lack of interest from British travellers. In 1908, Dubrovnik, Trogir and other coastal towns had been 'full of visitors speaking in German tongue', observed an itinerant female artist, but devoid of any Anglophone presence including 'the ever present American'.[117]

Prior to Ilinden–Preobrazhenie, such observations mostly followed the late nineteenth-century pattern of vague, semi-colonial or pseudo-scientific precepts. Durham's initial foray into the South Slavic lands typified this continuity. Landing on the Dalmatian coast in August 1900, her early correspondence described a 'bright dazzling land . . . flowing with maraschino and insect-powder', and populated by tall, dark peasants with 'aquiline features' who 'squat on their haunches just like savages'.[118] As imagological historiography argues, such tropes persisted even as knowledge of the region's history and culture expanded. Writing in 1908, the ex-Serbian diplomatic and Anglophile, Čedomilj Mijatović, admitted that the international opprobrium towards his country was not entirely unfounded when '82 per cent of the population' were beholden to a myriad of archaic shibboleths.[119]

As the Victorian era came to an end, imaginative distance became less a matter of geographical range and one of development. By 1900, thousands of kilometres of railway connected most of the Balkans' principal towns and cities with Vienna, Budapest and Istanbul; however, romantic notions of a most agrarian communities untouched by modernity persisted. Omer Hadžiselimović identifies Bosnia-Herzegovina as the primary exemplar of a ubiquitous 'east-meets-west' dichotomy underpinning such imagery.[120] Lionel James, *The Times*' long-standing war correspondent, described Sarajevo in 1909 as having been transformed from 'a ramshackle collection of wooden huts . . . almost submerging in the Marches of the East' into 'a military cantonment of the West, somewhat forbiddingly flaunting the virility of its Christian progress'. Yet, James did not have to venture far along the Miljacka River to discover 'as fascinating an intermingling of primitive Christian civilization with the mystery and lassitude of diluted Moslemism as is to be found in all Eastern Europe'.[121]

Nevertheless, growing public interest after 1903 also led to a measure of consensus around the belief that a clearer understanding could only be reached through a cultivated knowledge of local customs – or what British commentators understood them to be. In this regard, particular traditions and practices were increasingly portrayed as an integral, albeit esoteric, aspect of South Slavic culture, reflective of the attitudes which had accompanied the revival of interest in Britain's own agrarian past. The 'Balkan States Exhibition', held at Earl's Court in 1907, was illustrative of this trend. Organized, in part, through the collaboration of Bourchier, Durham, Seton-Watson and other regional experts such as the Liberal MP Noel Buxton, the exhibition included a replica of the 'typical Balkan village' as its centrepiece. Its Serb, Bulgarian and Montenegrin co-organizers hopes of showcasing their countries' recent advances in the arts, economics, sciences and urban planning were eclipsed by the displays of 'quaint houses', 'gypsy dancers' and 'peasant costume and crafts' prioritized by their British hosts.[122]

While the 1907 exhibition demonstrated a continuity in how rural South Slavs largely remained an essentializing cultural and ethnic motif in British imaginative geography, its emphasis on peasant communities rooted in their land and 'organic' rural customs offered a more positive reimagining of a formerly pejorative archetype.[123] The event's relative popularity with the middle-class public also granted momentum to a further wave of romantic and touristic literary interest in the regional aesthetic. The ubiquity of the 'Turkish fez' and 'embroidered sashes' worn by Bosnian peasant men, or 'the scarlet, gold-embroidered costumes' and 'small round hats' of Montenegro had already began to normalize peasants as envoys of an authentic cultural identity distinct to the eastern Adriatic and neighbouring Dinaric mountains.[124] Unsurprisingly, the political cognoscenti of organized opinion seized upon this receptiveness when presenting their own preferred national, or ethnic, groups while also seeking to establish historical pedigrees firmly tied to Western Christendom.[125]

Neither did a more positive reappraisal reduce the continued proliferation of sources emphasizing the region's most overtly outlandish cultural qualities. In his 1908 guide to Serbia, Mijatović dedicated a considerable portion to his homeland's national beliefs that he defined as a blending of Eastern Orthodoxy with pre-Christian pagan pastoralism. Concessions made by Christian missionaries in the sixth and seventh centuries meant that witches and nature spirits were still revered, alongside saints, in peasant folklore.[126] Even in the 'civilized' lands of Istria and Dalmatia, village festivals and defensive rituals still offered a glimpse into a pre-Christian era.[127] For Dalmatian farmers, firing 'three grains of corn and the Paschal wax-candle at the lightning before the thunder sounds' was believed to kill witches while throwing 'salt and shredded garlic' at the sky prevented summer hailstorms from damaging vineyards.[128] Further inland, Eastern mysticism influenced all such traditions observed in the hinterlands, regardless of their geographical position within Europe; 'amulets' were ubiquitous on both sides of the 'Turkish border' for warding off evil spirits with patterns of seasonal agriculture still determined through astrological divination.[129]

Indeed, in the opening years of the twentieth century the dissemination of information to a wider audience – especially those outside of London and south-east England for whom the Balkans were, at best, a remote curiosity – was often tied to a more general public fascination for the esoteric. In 1900, for instance, the *Hull Daily Mail* reported that Serbian state officials were resorting to the threat of collective prison sentences in order to stop peasant mobs from exhuming and mutilating the corpses of suspected vampires.[130] Two years later, the *Sheffield Evening Telegraph* mentioned that peasants in eastern Bosnia had poured water into the opened grave of a man who had committed suicide, believing it would alleviate drought.[131] Even contemporary politics were not entirely divorced from peasant superstition: three years after Serbia's 'May Coup', that had climaxed in the widely publicized assassination of King Aleksandar I Obrenović and his consort Queen Draga by nationalist military officer on 11 June

1903,[132] Bourchier wrote of the peasantry's growing discontent regarding 'the curse of blood-guiltiness'. Severe droughts in 1905, resulting in a shortage of basic staples, were interpreted as divine 'displeasure at the immunity accorded to the crime'.[133]

The irony surrounding this preoccupation with folklore and the supernatural was not entirely lost on some observers. Durham for example, discerned 'buried similarities' between Albanian and South Slavic peasant customs, and the vogue for spiritualism among her largely middle-class readership. Was the use of the 'breastbones of fowls to foretell the future' in Herzegovina and Macedonia so 'otherworldly' when 'palmistry and spiritualist societies' were flourishing in Edwardian London?[134]

Allusions to spiritualism and folklore were typically allied with discussions of religious observance. Imagological debate on the significance of religion has tended to focus on it as one of the few denominators of national and cultural identity. Todorova and Norris assert that Balkan Catholicism, unburdened by the 'cumbersome "Slavic" quality' of Orthodoxy or an Orientalized Islam, led to its Croat and Slovene adherents being viewed as historically closer to 'Western Civilization'.[135] Drapac contests this, arguing that a tendency to associate Orthodoxy with Protestantism, through a tradition of anti-Papal Erastianism, and the liberationist struggles against the Ottomans, left Catholics at a consistent disadvantage in British discourses.[136]

If Balkan Christianity's prescribed political function was shown to be unambiguous, its role as a system of spiritual belief was considerably less clear. Despite acknowledged ceremonial differences, portrayals of religious doctrine were underlined by an assumption that most South Slavs did not understand its higher purpose.[137] According to Mijatović, religious cultural sentiment and observance among the Serbian peasantry was 'neither deep nor warm', outside of family and church holidays.[138] Yet, from an allegorical perspective, these discursive representations of religion were themselves conducive to the decline of religiosity in British politics and public life since 1880. While the rhetoric of Victorian denominational fervour still proliferated within Edwardian politics, and was a prominent feature in organized opinion's own public campaigns, it had become an 'essentially figurative and metaphorical' means of emotively framing secular issues.[139] This did not necessarily mean, however, that faith was deemed an irrelevance, considering the continued reverence for Christianity as a foundational aspect in civilization's moral hierarchy.[140]

Unlike the romanticism attributed to their orientalized cultural trappings, Muslim Slavs, like Islam in general, remained an object of opprobrium, being mostly viewed as a political vestige of Ottoman rule with their faith symbolizing an innate secular allegiance to Istanbul. The legacy of the *millet* system – which categorized the Sultan's subjects by confession rather than ethnicity – compounded this by labelling all Muslims as 'Turks' regardless of ancestry.[141] Muslim conservatism in Bosnia-Herzegovina, in particular, was typically presented as an impediment to Austria-Hungary's modernization efforts.[142] Discussion of motifs and practices provided little analysis of its cultural intricacies while its 'inorganic' otherness appeared evident by an apparent absence of regional pagan influences.[143] This latent hostility was accentuated by the continued presence of Muslim land-owning *beys* in these territories.[144] Despite representing a small minority, their existence stiffened Liberal narratives of a culturally homogenous Christian peasantry repressed by an equally homogenous Islamic elite.[145]

Nevertheless, late-Victorian and Edwardian representations could also demonstrate more nuanced understanding of local cultural history. By 1900, Bogomilism, a medieval Christian sect believed to have been native to the Balkans, for example, was recognized as a possible precursor to the 'Eastern mysticism' prevalent within regional Islam.[146] This apparent contingency of history over dogmatic fidelity convinced Henderson that a network of state-run *madrasas* would sway temporal Muslim loyalties away from Istanbul towards Vienna, incorporating Bosnian Islam into a European cultural framework and neutralizing the 'Mohammedan fanaticism' reportedly rampant in Ottoman Macedonia.[147] In the aforementioned territory, however, the Islamic religion, Fraser claimed, had little social presence beyond the privileges Muslims enjoyed in matters of taxation.[148]

For the benighted Christian *rayah*, faith itself transcended liturgical practice as a euphemism for universal victimhood, a rhetorical motif popularized by Gladstone. The radical journalist Henry Noel Brailsford was largely responsible for reviving this concept as head of the 'Macedonian Relief Fund' (MRF) – a humanitarian aid mission operating out of the southwestern Macedonian city of Bitola (with Durham heading a mission in the municipalities of Ohrid and Resen) following Ilinden–Preobrazhenie. For five centuries, Brailsford claimed, the Slavic Christian peasant's inexpedient 'fidelity to his Church' made his historical lot 'one of continuous martyrdom'. Village communities near Bitola had even reportedly rejected the MRF's offer of relief aid in favour of financial assistance in restoring destroyed religious buildings and shrines. As 'the only free and communal life which the Turk permits', the Church was the peasantry's only source of identity, making it 'more or less secularized' and 'essentially a national organization':

> It reminds him of the greater past. It unites him to his fellow Christians throughout the [Ottoman] Empire, and in the free lands beyond the Empire. It is the one form of association and combination which is not treasonable. Its Bishops are the sole Christian aristocracy in Turkey, its synods and councils the only form of autonomy or representative self-government which the law allows.[149]

Similarly, non-religious parallels were to be found in Serbian Orthodoxy. 'A Church should be the soul of the nation and is so most emphatically in Servia', Vivian stated in 1904. That the peasants, in an effort to preserve their identity, were willing to endure generations of impoverishment and humiliation under Ottoman rule in order to maintain a successive line of ethnically Serb patriarchs, offered 'convincing proof of the identity of Servia as a Church and a State, as well as of the noblest and loftiest patriotism'.[150] According to Mijatović, however, the peasantry's ingrained pragmatism, a legacy of Ottoman subjugation, had actually reconciled the Church's role to that of a vehicle for national cohesion rather than the conservator of Serbian spiritual well-being. Upon commenting on this, a Scottish Presbyterian minister, who had accompanied Mijatović on an earlier tour of Serbia, was curtly informed by a local archimandrite (abbot) that the peasantry had been praying to God 'to deliver them from the Turks' for over four hundred years. What they had really needed was 'good education, good schools, good soldiers, good officers and good arms!'[151]

Along the Dalmatian coast, even the efforts of the Holy See's missionaries had apparently failed to dilute a raft of shared customs between Catholics and Orthodox. As in Serbia, where pagan idolatry was channelled towards saintly icons, Dalmatia's Catholic clergy were to be found leading their congregations before numerous shrines, in the hope of alleviating drought and illness.[152] This degree of overlapping liturgical tradition and secular function, performed at the peasantry's behest, led some to conclude that religious denominations were merely hypothetical. Amid a large crowd of Montenegrins and 'Christians from Bosnia-Herzegovina', one British visitor to Montenegro's famous Ostrog Monastery in 1903 observed 'a cavalcade of Turks . . . just arrived from Sarajevo' to pay homage at the monastic shrine to 'St. Vasili'. In this part of the Balkan lands, the author remarked, 'Moslems, Greek, Roman Catholics, even Protestants all journey to St. Vasili'.[153] Indeed, such ambiguity even prompted Seton-Watson and other campaigners to turn instead to Herder's theory of language as a more historically reliable precondition for Yugoslav nationhood by 1914.[154]

Unsurprisingly, these allusions to pre-Christian paganism, coupled with the South Slavs' ambiguous ancestral origins, evoked comparisons with Britain's own 'Celtic peripherals'. Even before 1900, British archaeology had already identified the South Slavic Balkans as a sine qua non in tracing the Celtic past; peasant clothing 'might pass muster among Scottish peasants', while the landscape brought to mind 'some of the more picturesque parts of our Scottish Highlands'.[155] Berber posits that despite Bosnia-Herzegovina having been recast as existing within the cultural orbit of 'Europe', its Muslims continued to be viewed as possessing a similar 'centre-periphery' relationship with Istanbul as the Catholic Irish did with London. In the hierarchy of civilized values, this invariably marked the Southern Slavs as falling beneath the Irish in their presumed readiness for political self-determination.[156]

Conversely, the South Slavs already appeared as a direct analogy to the contemporary Celtic nations (notably Ireland).[157] 'I pay them a great but well-deserved compliment, at the same time hinting at the weaker points of their psychological constitution', Mijatović remarked when summarizing the mentality of his fellow countrymen, 'they are – the Irish of the Balkans!'[158] This patronizingly Anglocentric conflation with Britain's own ascribed peripheries also inferred a sense of faded past glory. The Montenegrin village of Njeguši, 'the cradle of the Petrović dynasty', was described as resembling 'some squalid hamlet in the far north of Scotland', where peasants lived in stone huts 'more like cattle-sheds than human habitations'.[159] As its historic martial reputation waned in the 1890s, the wild desolation of the mountainous principality (proclaimed a kingdom in 1910) now indicated its 'under-development'.[160] On the approach to Cetinje, James commented that the royal capital retained as 'much [of] the appearance of a Cornish village' in the 1900s as it had done in the 1840s. Amid 'the lazy and good-for-nothing Montenegrins, lounging in their doorways, with interminable cigarettes, shedding ash across the fronts of their gaudy jerkins', the grandiose embassies of the Great Powers appeared as oases of Western civility.[161]

Yet, these discouraging comparisons were as likely to be dismissed as outdated nineteenth-century ignorance. Henderson complained that while Montenegro's Crown Prince Nikola Petrović-Njegoš had successfully eliminated most of his country's egregious traditions, an ill-informed British national press persisted in conflating the Black Mountaineers with Scottish 'caterans', synonymous with 'gangs of bandits, cattle-rustlers and other outlaws'.[162] The increasing plurality of opinion even prompted some to directly challenge more popularly ingrained tropes. Much of Durham's popularity as an anthropologist lay in her genuine conviction that proper understanding of the Balkans was obscured by derivative Victorian romanticism and a fixation on nationalist violence. The Montenegrins adherence to antediluvian codes of blood honour was dismissed as culturally picturesque but superficial. The principality exuded the qualities of 'a dream or cinematograph . . . safe as an Earl's Court show and many times more respectable'.[163] Even the 'clannish animosities' of Kosovo's Serb and Albanian communities were 'common to the childhood of all races' and would eventually fade as had happened in Scotland.[164] For the more romantically inclined, the appeal of cultural remoteness was its potential as a universal corrective to urbanized decline and capitalistic stagnation. Discussing the 'lake-dwellers' of Lough Neagh to the west of Belfast, Scott-James identified a 'primitive energy' contiguous with that of the Slavs whom he had encountered on the shores of Lake Ohrid in Macedonia. Through this association, he expressed vindication in categorizing Ireland as 'part of the Orient', believing such energy held the key to rejuvenating Western civilization:

> with something of the unchanging Orient it has combined an element of fire, energy unspoilt, the means within its own spiritual sphere, of perpetual revivification.[165]

Conclusion

While continuities with the previous century certainly remained in evidence, the heightening of latent anxiety and social unease that coloured post-Boer War discourses of national efficiency inadvertently affected the South Slavic peasant's image. By the 1910s, the positive connotations of an idealized rural simplicity imbued evolving cultural caricatures with an inherent moral virtue. Even if south-east Europe continued to be defined as a periphery, it existed in an era in which such a status was as likely to evoke positive sentiments. Furthermore, the allegorizing nature of Edwardian public rhetoric continued to entrench late-Victorian understanding of the region as an eastern parallel to Ireland. Although far from civilization's centre, by 1912, the South Slavic Balkans firmly 'orbited within the European cultural space' rather than outside it.[166]

This increasingly non-pejorative image not only afforded the peasant a presence in civilization's moral hierarchy, but highlighted a growing sense of precariousness towards Britain's place within it; unlike the ascribed values of the Slavic village community, the idea of Britain's own physiological and spiritual degradation as an outcome of urbanization raised questions as to how it might retain its once presumed superiority. Nevertheless, this intersection between representation and existential concern rehabilitated the South Slavic peasantry only in a cultural sense with understanding of modern Balkan politics still tarnished by the spectre of violence and chauvinistic nationalism. For those wishing to promote political engagement, success depended on how well their campaigns could be integrated into what were becoming the discursive formulations of Anglo-British identity.

3

The victimhood archetype?

Despite episodic spikes of interests that challenged the British public's 'front of ignorance', it was only after 1903 that the South Slavic Balkans assumed a more coherent form in the popular imaginary.[1] Nevertheless, this was still largely a consequence of developments in the previous decades where travel literature had proliferated, new channels of contact were established and the evolution of the press as 'a forum for the free exchange of opinion' had eroded the Foreign Office (FO) and diplomatic corps' status as arbiters of Britain's intercultural relations.[2] Indeed, since the 1850s, *The Times* or *Reuters* were often looked upon as considerably more reliable than the 'official sources'.[3] Growing public interest from 1903 also served to bolster the profiles of those specializing in regional affairs such as Bourchier, or were unconventional in their information gathering, *The Daily Telegraph*'s Russian correspondent E. J. Dillon being among the more innovative.[4]

While imagological historians have endowed such individuals, alongside the cultural figure of the late-Victorian and Edwardian traveller and publicist, with a historical significance in shaping the Balkans' international image, more recent studies have paid greater attention to their role as (would-be) political actors.[5] Particular emphasis has been placed on the politicization of regional knowledge and attempts at harnessing public interest as a form of leverage over foreign policymakers via a series of vocal lobbying campaigns. In this context, the significance of organized opinion as an alternative source of authority to the official channels can be attributed to the vigorous regional engagement of its members, their networks of local contacts and willingness to confront received opinion. This coincided with a succession of regional political crises from 1903 to 1913, leading to several didactic surveys linking culture, contemporary affairs and the recent past. Salient among these were Durham's *Through the Lands of the Serb* (1904), Brailsford's *Macedonia: Its Races and their Future* (1906) and Seton-Watson's *The Southern Slav Question and the Habsburg Monarchy* (1911). Besides broadening awareness, these texts foregrounded the peasantry as a determining factor in South Slavic cultural, social and political structures. This, in turn, gradually imprinted the concept of the peasant into the geographical imagination – not as an archetype, but as the region's social fulcrum. Michail notes, however, that these finer political details were usually submerged in sensationalized depictions of violent atrocities.[6]

Like domestic influences, the historiographical fixation on direct political representations presented in this literature, or the campaigning activities and ideological leanings of their authors, downplays the multifaceted nature of the British public sphere. While pro-Balkan publicists' efforts at stimulating political interest were met by a recurrent 'pattern of indifference', the allegorical resonance between British social anxieties and South Slavic rural culture proved conducive to shifting perceptions.[7] Central to this was the gradual revival of the victimhood narrative which emphasized the plight of the region's peoples, appealing to wider public sensibilities while bypassing the execrable realm of Balkan politics. This chapter considers how this narrative's intersection with Edwardian popular discourse reconfigured the peasantry's place in imaginative geography from benighted periphery-dwellers to victims of historical injustices, in conjunction with the gradual crystalizing of Anglo-British identity.

Organized opinion

Although the nineteenth century had seen the unprecedented growth and diversification of knowledge, a Victorian propensity to conflate overseas engagement with British foreign policy stances still inhibited the development of a more generalized interest, reflecting the elitist mentalities which continued to dominate at the FO. Unlike those involved in trade and enterprise, local issues and cultural context were rarely taken into account by diplomatists; missions to Belgrade and Cetinje were deemed a necessity for monitoring potential Russian, and later German, machinations while 'outlying' provinces such as Bosnia-Herzegovina and Dalmatia were simply a 'spill-over from the wider "Eastern Question"'.[8] In 1906, for example, Britain's consul-general in Budapest had broached the idea of a consulate in Zagreb: 'the capital of an autonomous country' and 'focus of South Slav aspirations'. This elicited no known response from London.[9] Tenuous diplomatic links were compounded by a paucity of economic interests, reinforcing preconceptions of the region as having already been 'claimed' as part of an Austro-German sphere of influence.[10]

The FO's limited interest in other countries' domestic affairs was compounded by parliament and the wider public's alienation from foreign policymaking: before 1914, only the prime minister himself could adequately restrict a foreign secretary's ability to act. Furthermore, in defiance of the ever-expanding middle-class influence at the Home Office and other Whitehall departments, the FO and diplomatic service remained dominated by a closed network of aristocrats with private incomes – and reflexively mistrustful of external 'expert' opinion. Consequently, Britain's consulates and embassies were often critically understaffed (by 1900, the overpaid, underworked diplomat was already proving to be a useful straw man when seeking to justify budget cuts), with little or no time for 'fact-finding' missions.[11] On the rare occasions that diplomatic personnel in south-east Europe ventured beyond their mission's immediate urban confines, a lack of linguistic proficiency and reliance on government escorts would dilute any informative value.[12] All of this was compounded by an innate aversion to Balkan postings; before and after 1918, Durham later wrote, any aspiring British diplomat would 'find it wiser not to learn the local language, lest knowledge of it should cause him to be kept for a lengthy period in some intolerable hole'.[13]

From a cultural perspective, before 1903, travel writing had remained largely derivative in content with authors often lifting anecdotes directly from Evans, Irby and Mackenzie.[14] Besides a discerning minority, exemplified by Bourchier, most British commentators typically differed towards the official narratives while logistical or safety concerns restricted access to certain areas and limited any scope for formulating more accurate impressions of the 'wider region'.[15]

The contemporary revival of the victimhood narrative found its genesis in the 'Hamidian Massacres': a series of anti-Christian pogroms directed against the Ottoman Sultan's Armenian and Assyrian subjects from 1894 to 1896.[16] Detailed reports by Dillon and other correspondents who managed to circumvent Istanbul's attempts at restricting the flow of information from eastern Anatolia provoked a resurgence of British Turcophobia and extensive historical revisionism. Negative traits previously ascribed to Armenians by earlier Victorian authors were omitted from later publication in order to accentuate their status as perpetual victims of 'villainous' Muslim rulers.[17]

While this narrative resonated with an increasingly desultory domestic climate, its revival was equally reflective of developments abroad. In July 1903, Buxton, taking his cue from a spirited pro-Macedonian campaign in France, proclaimed the formation of a 'Balkan Committee (BC)' that would operate as the nexus for British anti-Ottoman lobbying. In seeking to emulate the success of his Gallic counterparts, Buxton originally conceived of it as a conduit between the, hitherto closed, world of foreign policy activism and the wider public sphere.[18]

Despite drawing its membership from a relatively broad spectrum of the informed public, Radical Liberal politicians, with Nonconformist Protestant leanings (such as Buxton and his younger brother Charles), shaped and directed the BC's agenda.[19] As Perkins notes, its founding coincided with that of other liberal-humanitarian lobby groups, such as the Congo Reform Association, with Buxton and other leading members guided by the belief in a broader internationalist struggle against slavery and imperial misrule. Accordingly, its key political aim was to convince Whitehall to withdraw British support for the continuation of Ottoman rule in the Balkans, rectifying the perceived injustices committed at Berlin in 1878.[20]

In spite of this, the shape and orientation of this narrative vis-à-vis the South Slavic Balkans rested primarily on a small cadre comprising Bourchier, Brailsford, Buxton, Durham, and Seton-Watson with their knowledge being instrumentalized as a means of advancing political agendas through routine public engagement.[21] Individual motivation for involvement in Balkan affairs varied, although much of it stemmed from issues of personal identity. Like Bourchier, Durham originally travelled to southeast Europe for health reasons yet cultivated an imaginative connection to the region as a route to emancipation from a middle-class Britain still entrenched in Victorian attitudes towards older, unmarried women.[22] As she would later recant, on arriving in the Balkans for the very first time in August 1900 'the future stretched before me as endless years of grey monotony, and escape seemed hopeless'.[23] This offers some explanation for her coming to identify with the Montenegrin and Albanian national causes. '[O]ne senses at times', Hammond observes, 'that Durham's love is less for the country [Montenegro and Albania] than what she can personally achieve there'.[24]

Similarly, Brailsford and Buxton's interest in Macedonia represented an extension of their adherence to British Liberalism's Radical tradition, viewing their opposition to overseas despotism as one aspect of a much broader struggle against perceived socio-political injustices inherent in the domestic and international status quo.[25] Unsurprisingly, this standpoint overlooked the gulf between liberationist ideals and political pragmatism.[26] A Gladstonian absolutism coupled with attempts at construing the Macedonian cause as a Western crusade against Islamic despotism, proved especially detrimental. Buxton's demands for population and territorial transfers, for instance, while predicated on a secular hostility to Ottoman rule, demonstrated little consideration for the repercussions this could have for the area's Muslim and non-Slavic communities, later evidenced by the numerous atrocities of the Balkan Wars.[27]

Seton-Watson represented a notable exception in that his interests were focused on the Habsburg Monarchy, particularly its eastern Hungarian portion.[28] This, in turn, was guided by a more conservative perspective on ethnic self-determination, viewing it as a vicarious extension of British foreign policy goals.[29] A polarizing figure, historical criticism has tended to focus on his role in fermenting anti-Habsburg sentiment from 1908 and eventually advocating for Yugoslavia's creation during the First World War, as contradicting his liberal values regarding nativist self-determination by supporting a polity founded on elitist notions that minimalized, or even denied, historical identities. Despite being vehemently opposed to it himself, the unintended outcome of this stance, according to more censorious voices like Drapac, would be the aggrandizement of Serbian nationalist ambitions.[30]

While Seton-Watson and his peers were instrumental in advancing contemporary understanding of the region after 1903, their rise to prominence was itself reflective of the recent historical trend of stratifying knowledge into learned hierarchies and a tendency towards intellectual contrarianism; this gradual monopolization of representative channels was equally dependant on such experts possessing the means for independent travel, further accentuating an already entrenched social dimension. Nevertheless, a key measure of organized opinion's initial success was its members' ability to disseminate their opinions by appealing to a much broader audience than their Victorian predecessors. Durham, for instance, developed a reputation as a relatively popular travel writer. Her magnum opus, *High Albania* (1909), found favour with non-specialist readers, quickly becoming the preeminent English-language guide to a country that had remained obscure among even Balkan enthusiasts. In keeping with the Edwardian vogue for popular anthropology, a more informal narrative style – emphasizing her role as the lone female traveller exploring 'unknown' lands – proved successful in introducing British readers to areas such as Kosovo and Albania's northern highlands.[31]

These seemingly novel approaches were assisted by a wealth of connections. By 1908, Seton-Watson had one of the most formidable network of contacts in British journalism that included the tendentious Henry Wickham Steed, who had replaced Lavino as *The Times* Vienna correspondent in 1902, and leading personalities among the Monarchy's various nationalist movements.[32] Elsewhere, Bourchier, to the periodic irritation of the FO, continued to cultivate his reputation as Britain's 'voice' in the

Balkans while Durham could later boast of having gained the ear of Prince (later King) Nikola of Montenegro.[33]

Nevertheless, the overt political agendas underlying the BC's formation were indicative of organized opinion's inherent shortcomings. Seton-Watson, for example, characterized the Habsburg Monarchy's South Slavic question as one of political representation, ignoring the largely economic concerns of the wider populace.[34] Correspondingly, Durham regularly insisted that regional coverage adhere to an ethos of scientific impartiality, yet rarely applied this view to non-Albanians after 1908.[35] The BC itself was monopolized by a circle of 'professional' campaigners around Buxton who were 'arguably pro-Bulgarian and passionately anti-Ottoman', and fixated almost entirely on the Macedonian question.[36]

These discrepancies were evidenced by the relative success some experts had in carving out specific foreign policy niches before 1912. By virtue of their connections and public status as Britain's principle conduit for contemporary knowledge, neither the government nor the press could ignore their expertise completely.[37] However, their political raisons d'être were more often impeded by the FO's ingrained aversion to specialists. By 1910, officials were just as likely to challenge a 'self-proclaimed' authority's putative right 'to pronounce opinions on international affairs'. Prior to educational attainment becoming recognized as a suitable qualifying standard after 1918, the vagaries surrounding what actually determined one's status as an expert invariably brought substitute pejoratives such as 'crank', 'faddist' or 'propagandist' to the fore when discussions gravitated towards Balkan matters.[38]

This establishment antipathy was compounded by organized opinion's perpetual struggle against its members' bête noire: public indifference. Despite growing fascination for other cultures, interest in foreign politics had been declining since at least 1890.[39] Moreover, unlike the genuine emotive energy that galvanized the Congo Reform Association, dubious associations with nationalist violence deprived the Balkans of any credible cause célèbre for much of the early 1900s. Another limiting factor was its underlying sense of social exclusivity in relying on press organs marketed to middle- and upper-class audiences such as *The Times*, *The Manchester Guardian* and *The Daily News*, or niche specialist titles like *The Contemporary Review*. These publications were consistently outsold by the more popular tabloid press that paid 'greater attention to crime, sexual violence, sport and gambling' over politics while barely ever covering foreign or imperial affairs.[40]

The fact that the Balkans remained, at best, the most marginal of political and cultural oddities in the public sphere was only exacerbated by organized opinion's protracted fragmentation into rival factions that advocated for different national causes. The ensuing debates not only proved too recondite to gain traction beyond the more esoteric corners of the public sphere, but served to reinforce existing pejorative stereotypes.[41] Even, the BC's core message of Macedonian Slav liberation as a righteous moral cause was almost immediately undermined by lurid reports placing the blame for many of the atrocities on the VMRO and other anti-Ottoman paramilitary organizations.[42] *The Times*' foreign affairs editor, Valentine Chirol, articulated this sense of alienation in his correspondence with Britain's Russian ambassador:

in general, people are, I think, sick to death in this country of the Near Eastern Crisis, for few of them understand it and still fewer, of course, realise that behind it lies the much bigger question of the balance of power in Europe.[43]

Considering these political limitations, recasting the subject as a humanitarian issue by reviving the narrative of peasant victimhood represented one of the very few means of gaining a foothold in the public sphere. This was facilitated by a near ideological obsession with positivism, encapsulated in the cultural impact of philanthropic surveys into urban poverty during the 1890s and early 1900s, with discussion of the South Slavs and other foreign cultures requiring (pseudo)scientific verification via an 'evidence-based' narrative.[44] Regional contacts and direct interaction with local populations were now a prerequisite for legitimizing moralistic assertions while eyewitness accounts became integral as campaigners sought to shore up their claims with 'authenticated' evidenced-based knowledge rather than Victorian preconceptions. Relief work presented one potential avenue for this; writing in 1906, Brailsford claimed that aiding Macedonian peasants 'brought me into constant touch with people of every race . . . opportunities which rarely come to the European traveller for learning something of the realities of their daily life'.[45] Despite their limited success in instigating a sea-change in British foreign policy, at a popular level, organized opinion was instrumental in integrating discursive social factors into the South Slavic peasantry's representational subtext, transforming it into an object of sympathy rather than political derision. Like the Armenians, the South Slavs became another moral abstraction around which the new Anglo-Britishness could be further defined.

The 'civilizing mission'

The South Slavic peasantry's symbolic migration from Oriental primitive to virtuous victim did not, initially, signify a complete break with the pre-existing belief in modernization's 'civilizing' qualities. In popular Edwardian anthropological and colonial dialogues, 'progress' was still understood as an organic, linear process where minor cultural changes compelled societies to evolve into what were deemed as more advanced states. As with Ireland, this provided scientific justification for British socio-economic intervention in its colonies, where administrators and businesses presented themselves as being capable of improving local peoples' lives by guiding them along this evolutionary path at a more accelerated rate: the so-called civilizing mission.[46] By the late 1900s, however, popular understanding of this concept was enmeshed in the more emotive preoccupation of reviving Britain's (self-)image as a unique moral force. Colonialism would now be perpetuated 'on new moral grounds' with Britain as a purveyor of 'civilized values' in contrast to other countries' selfish pursuit of narrow political and economic interests.[47] In imaginative geography, the European imperial powers were themselves codified by their position in this new hierarchy of colonial benevolence that mirrored continental power relations. Unsurprisingly, the Ottomans, already framed as despotic Oriental oppressors, were automatically excluded. However, those perceived to have fallen into the German orbit, specifically Austria-Hungary, also drew suspicion as to their capability of implementing the civilizing mission in accordance with these new moral standards. In this regard, the South Slavic peasant's victimhood status was as much a reflection of the civilizing mission's changing meaning, indicating Britain's own conception of its place in what had become a largely static colonial sphere, following the partition of most of Africa.

As previously noted, by the end of the nineteenth century, caricatures of the South Slavic peasantry shared many of the core features associated with the rural Catholic Irish: a backward people awaiting guidance towards modernity by a more advanced society. The image of the victimized Macedonian Slav peasant became central to this by reinforcing the Ottoman Empire's ascribed status as the West's oppressive, culturally inert antithesis.[48] Michael Herzfeld and Thomas Gallant maintain that such a paradigm permitted Westerners to construct and assign specific identities to the Greeks and other southeastern Europeans as a means of quantifying their 'cultural (and by extension moral) qualities'.[49]

In January 1900, proponents of the post-Berlin status quo could still speak of southeastern Europe with a sense of political vindication. Central to this had been Austria-Hungary's administration of Bosnia-Herzegovina, a centre of modernization supposedly unrivalled in the South Slavic Balkans. Infrastructure projects drew particular praise, with over 3,000 km of roads and railway lines having been built by 1907.[50] Nevertheless, Edwardian discourse tended to laud the Monarchy's achievements by emphasizing the compatibility of these policies with the territory's pre-existing agrarian economy, rather than their potential to facilitate a future transition to urban-based industrialization. This appeared conducive to the notion that the civilizing mission's prescribed role was to improve the lives of local populations in accordance with existing social structures.[51]

As with most Balkan imagery, this representational trend had been established by late-Victorian commentators such as Miller, who lauded the Dual Monarchy's introduction of 'technical training' as the correct approach for an agricultural economy like Bosnia-Herzegovina. In the independent Balkans, by contrast, Miller noted that the 'evil effects of too much higher education' produced only 'a *Gelehrten-proletariat* which takes to politics as a means of getting a living', leaving agriculture underdeveloped and the majority impoverished. Reforms on land ownership and taxation, rather than a redistributionist 'agrarian revolution' (as had occurred in Serbia), alleviated the peasantry's fundamental grievances by addressing the root causes of existing social tensions without remedying 'an old wrong by committing a new one'. For these reasons, Miller concluded that 'the Bosnian *kmet*'[52] was better off at the close of the nineteenth century 'than the Dalmatian or Sicilian peasant', ignoring the fact that the former also lived under Habsburg rule.[53] Sympathetic Edwardian visitors to the province concurred. The question of redistribution itself, remarked a former Conservative MP, had made severing all vestiges of Ottoman rule a necessity since 'the Bosnians must themselves have a share in the responsibilities of making it by means of proper representative institutions', deliverable only under Habsburg supervision.[54]

The tangible presence of a proactive civilizing force in rural districts seemed all the more apparent through the irregular way in which the administration had implemented earlier development programmes. Wrench noted these inconsistencies while touring several villages in 1901. Following a visit to the state-run central Bosnian village of Bugojno, he reported that conditions were an 'outstanding example' of modern efficiency. Even the local slaughterhouse was 'spotless inside'. By contrast, Prisap, near Livno in northwest Herzegovina, was held up as an example of 'bad Turkish planning', little more than a collection of 'mere hovels' like 'those in the west of Ireland'. The only decent building, built with government funds, was 'dirty and run-down' through neglect. Being – like the Irish – 'all so natural and so like children', the peasants had never concerned themselves with its maintenance.[55] These comparisons to the Celtic nations, by mostly English authors, also implied caprice as an underlying trait in the regional psyche. As late as 1908, for example, the main road to Herzegovina's frontier with Montenegro was noted as stopping short of the border in the town of Gacko 'lest that warlike race [Montenegrins] should resent the familiarity and seize it, with almost Irish quickness, the chance of a fight'.[56]

The language of the civilizing mission was also an incorporated feature of the BC's anti-Ottoman campaign. In a pamphlet from 1907, Buxton argued that Istanbul's continued rule in Macedonia represented a form of psychological degradation that consigned its Christian Slavic peasantry to civilizational entropy. While Britain's own 'historic monster', the slave trade, 'affected but directly 700,000 . . . [T]hose whom Turkish rule degrades in body and in mind are many millions.'[57] The sight of peasants in Ohrid in 1903 had struck Brailsford as emblematic of this collective inertia, being 'a slight race that ages prematurely and clothes itself in a pathetic suggestion of childhood'; their costumes 'hardly have varied since the first Slavs invaded the Balkans'.[58] As late as the Second Balkan War, Buxton continued to inveigh against the Ottoman's, much reduced, territorial presence at Europe's geographical extremities. 'The record of Turkish rule in Europe is one not only of demoralisation, retardation and cruelty', he vented in *The Times*, 'but of menace to European peace and ruin to Turkey herself'.[59]

For all their romanticizing of rural tradition, Edwardian pundits often continued to yoke depictions of the pastoralist ideal to derogatory evaluations of the respective state or governing entity. 'While Servia earns the contempt of the civilized world as a State', commented one author, 'the Servian peasant sows in hope and reaps in peace' – a state of affairs deemed equally applicable to their kinsman in Habsburg Dalmatia.[60] Even Macedonia's *rayah* drew admiration in aspiring to the view that they would not be 'destined to drag the chain of slavery for ever'.[61] The apparent fortitude of villages where 'no one is idle' and communities expressed 'heroic virtue' through honest collective toil further accentuated their status as victimized captives of an Ottoman rule where everything 'material and social' had grown 'stunted and atrophied'.[62]

Neither was the alleged absence of civilizing qualities limited to critiques of the imperial hegemon. Excluding an expressed admiration for rural culture that typified liberal rhetoric, Seton-Watson had found little to enthuse him when visiting Serbia for the first time in 1908. Judging the post-1903 regime to be 'thoroughly corrupt and inefficient – worse even than the Hungarian', in October 1909, he sternly advised one Dalmatian political contact against pushing for secessionism if the 'sole alternative' was to be 'union with Servia and Montenegro'. Such a prospect 'would mean the triumph of Eastern over Western culture', made even worse by Cetinje's apparent willingness to achieve it 'by means of a general European War'.[63] Nevertheless, his subsequent observations on the condition of the Dalmatian peasantry provoked similar accusations that, like the Ottomans, the Monarchy was now in danger of falling short of its own civilizing aims.[64]

Less partial observers were more disposed towards theorizing that the prevailing cultural milieu was as much to blame as the legacy of Ottoman rule. James, for instance, posited that while emigration might refine the average Montenegrin into 'an industrious and reliable labourer on roads and in mines', such cultural metamorphosis always proved temporary. On returning to 'his own pastures', the former migrant typically reverted to 'an effeminate predilection for adorning his person in fancy vestments', stalling any potential for further betterment.[65] Following the outcry generated by Austria-Hungary's formal annexation of Bosnia-Herzegovina in 1908, Henderson defended the Monarchy's action along similar lines claiming it had 'rescued' the province from cultural inertia and decay. Drawing on established analogies with British Crown rule in India, which had granted 'equal rights before the law for protection of person and property, and liberty to all to worship as they please', he warned that the 'onerous' cultural attributes of Ottoman rule would reassert themselves in the future were the populace allowed to retain even nominal political links to Istanbul.[66] One American commentator even suggested to his putative British readership in 1906 that Macedonia might benefit from its own ongoing crisis. Despite their political motives, the Bulgarian and other nationalist-run schools still represented a 'civilizing presence' by offering impoverished peasant children opportunities for formal education and a degree of security.[67]

Austria-Hungary's perceived success in Bosnia-Herzegovina initially granted a measure of plausibility to the idea of intervention as a way of diffusing tensions. Following the 1903 regicide, Vivian warned that Serbia had 'been put back at least a century. . . . If I were Foreign Minister, I would counsel an occupation of Servia by the Powers, perhaps even a partition'.[68] Conversely, the Orientalist Alfred Stead, having grown infatuated with Serbian culture after visiting the country in 1904, petitioned the FO to restore its suspended diplomatic ties with Belgrade in the interests of reviving Britain's imperialistic instincts. In August 1905, influenced by the recent Moroccan crisis, Stead also presented the recently enthroned Petar I Karađorđević with a memorandum proposing that Serbia exploit its status as an international pariah by becoming a British economic satellite. Among his ambitious proposals were a loan of 87,500,000 French francs in exchange for mining and tariff concessions that would compel Britain to protect its new interests, as France had done in North Africa.[69]

As the victimhood narrative gathered momentum in the public sphere, Austria-Hungary's own treatment of its subjects and neighbours drew increased scrutiny. During the ongoing 'Customs War' with Serbia from 1906 to 1908, Buxton accused Vienna of seeking to impose 'economic slavery' on the Serbs and Montenegrins for 'the crime of rekindling freedom'. This course of action would, he predicted, exacerbate unrest and embolden Ottoman revanchism.[70] The, ostensibly, Germanocentric nature of the Monarchy's political institutions also worked to subvert its received image as a civilizing force. Indeed, from 1908 onwards, and in the absence of any viable alternatives, public discourse on Austria-Hungary was largely defined by the committedly anti-German Steed and anti-Hungarian Seton-Watson. While this did not convey the overt subtext of the victimhood narrative as in the Ottoman Balkans, it nevertheless sowed doubt as to the Monarchy's own capacity to act as the responsible imperial hegemon.[71]

The 1908 'Annexation Crisis' represented the first blow to the Habsburg's once infallible reputation, with both the liberal and conservative wings of the British press accusing Vienna of disrupting Europe's 'moral order' by deliberately 'tearing up' the Berlin Treaty.[72] Nevertheless, the immediate aftermath saw a more conservative-leaning current in British literary representations present the expropriation of Bosnia-Herzegovina's sovereignty as a necessary measure. Holbach opined that for the *kmetovi* good governance and economic stewardship mattered more than 'whether Bosnia be Austrian or Turkish'. Calls for a 'Greater-Servia' were also unappealing to the province's Orthodox Christians who held 'little faith in their kinsfolk' across the eastern frontier.[73] Those less willing to accept this official line at face value presented a more cynical picture. During a secret rendezvous in Sarajevo's old bazar, the city's Orthodox metropolitan bishop had implored Dillon to press for a British intervention. Having praised the annexation and Emperor Franz Joseph – at an officially moderated interview the previous day – the prelate had claimed that Austria-Hungary was actually seeking to 'crush' Bosnia's Serbs in order to placate the hated Muslim *beys*.[74]

Although never generating the vindictive hostility marshalled by the BC against the Ottomans, the political implications of the annexation fed into wider fears of the emergent spectre of 'pan-Germanism' with the suspected hand of Berlin overshadowing Habsburg efforts at countering nationalist agitation. Roy Bridge contests that this subversion of the Monarchy's image in Britain was itself informed by changing attitudes within the FO. Although quickly accepted as the new political reality, the annexation – informed by growing Anglo-French suspicion of German brinksmanship – undermined official faith in the Monarchy as a stabilizing or 'moral' force.[75] While press opinion generally framed regional change in diplomatic terms, perceptions of a rising pan-German chauvinism fed into the socio-political re-assessment of Habsburg rule. 'Austria's [new] mission', Seton-Watson later concluded in the *Southern Slav Question*, had to be the creation of a third 'trialist' South Slavic state entity, on equal political-footing with the Monarchy's German and Magyar portions. Only then could Vienna and Budapest hope to resolve 'Southern Slav aspirations' and curb the hardening potential for social unrest.[76]

By the 1910s, British consular correspondence had also grown less commendatory. Reporting on the administration's use of emergency powers in Bosnia-Herzegovina – several months after Serbia's success in the Second Balkan War – Britain's consul in Sarajevo, Edward Freeman, quoting a Croat observer, informed the foreign secretary, Edward Grey, that 'Austro-Hungarian rule in Bosnia-Herzegovina depends entirely on the power of the sword.' Any talk of political rights was now dismissed as 'only a make-believe' by the military authorities.[77] This pessimism was reflected in the wider critical assessment of the disjointed and uneven nature of the Monarchy's modernization programmes in its other South Slavic provinces. By the close of 1911, even Britain's consul in Dubrovnik was echoing local nationalist demands by suggesting that Vienna divert state investments into agriculture and infrastructure in order to assuage the Dalmatian peasantry's belief that it viewed them as 'an inferior race'.[78] This erosion in official confidence granted further validity to Seton-Watson's claims that localized autonomy represented the only feasible path to stability. Croatia-Slavonia, to the north of Dalmatia and Bosnia-Herzegovina, was touted as a model for achieving modernity through political empowerment. Development had only been 'ushered in' following the appointment of the 'Peasant Ban'[79] Ivan Mažuranić, in 1873, whose own rural upbringing had made him better attuned to the people's needs.[80]

This fluidity in attitudes was indicative of a realignment in British official perceptions of those imperial powers with a direct interest in the Balkans. Drapac contends that Seton-Watson and other foreign proponents of reform invoked 'increasingly harsh' anti-German sentiments to progressively demarcate the cultural and political contours of a future Yugoslavia.[81] Yet such a claim, stemming from an ambiguous conflation of political discourse with a vaguely defined set of transnational cultural relations, remains tenuous. Actual coverage of Austria-Hungary was far too sporadic for any consistent popular image to develop while anti-Germanism is equally too simplistic an explanation. As Richard Scully maintains, the bellicosity of British propaganda following the Reich's invasion of Belgium in August 1914, belied a latent sense of cultural Anglo-German kinship that had persisted throughout the Edwardian era.[82]

As with cultural discussions, the changing image of the peasant cannot be understood without an appreciation of the complex interplay in popular discourses that sought, in an age of presumed crisis, to define what civilization 'ought' to become. While the peasant remained an object for civilizing, the shift towards a form of hierarchy predicated on vaguely defined notions of morality also raised questions as to the motives of the civilizers. In the absence of 'British-style values', the only logical outcome appeared to be repression.

Women as metaphor

Among the roster of issues that dominated the Edwardian public sphere, few were as sensationalized or indicative of the currents shaping Anglo-Britishness as women's suffrage. Alongside organized labour and Irish Home Rule, Dangerfield identified female enfranchisement as the most significant challenge to the middle-class Victorian liberal order.[83] The critical period of Britain's suffrage debate even evolved in virtual parallel to events unfolding in the South Slavic lands, beginning with the founding of the Women's Social and Political Union in October 1903 – and its switch to more militant protest tactics in 1906 – that kept the issue in the public eye right up to August 1914.[84] While not necessarily drawing overt comparisons, its influence in relation to the internalization of the victimhood narrative became more overt as campaigning intensified.

In 1900, the concept of the British 'domestic woman' continued to be promoted as the feminine ideal, despite having only ever been historically applicable to the aristocratic upper classes; qualities associated with traditional femininity were themselves looked upon by Victorian writers and pundits as an articulation of British virtues, with Britain often personified in jingoistic ephemera as a protective and nurturing matriarch.[85] Sara Mills observes that those who deviated from this cultural conflation of the feminine presence with the middle- and upper-class domestic spheres were invariably associated with specific interests and modes of behaviour. By 1918, it was no coincidence that the more popular pre-war publications on foreign travel had been mostly authored by women whose personal lives embodied the Victorian literary stereotype of 'indomitable eccentric spinster'.[86] Goldsworthy and Hammond cite Durham's involvement in the Albanian national cause as this persona's obvious extreme: an unmarried British woman seeking personal emancipation through overseas causes.[87] Moreover, their status as wealthy foreigners elevated their social standing to a point that they would otherwise have never achieved in Britain, even leading them to engage in practices traditionally considered masculine.[88] Imagological historiography, however, has tended to overstate these direct parallels. Durham's experiences, for instance, were extraordinarily unusual among foreign travellers in general. Furthermore, any propensity to construct direct analogies with domestic matters such as women's suffrage was itself indicative of how British authors tended to ascribe similarities only after expounding on cultural differences.[89]

The British conceptualization of femininity as the personification of Anglophone spirituality and genteel moral virtue, requiring careful shielding, appeared to find its antithesis in the western Balkans. Bracewell notes that by the early 1900s, the region was often conceived of as a 'sort of museum of masculinity'; earlier orientalist portrayals of its inhabitants 'as feminized, unwarlike and subservient' had been superseded by images evoking 'physical toughness and violence, sexual conquest and the subordination of women, guns, strong drink and moustaches'.[90] As the 1900s progressed, however, negative impressions, while still present, carried an implied critique of Britain's own social failings in protecting women and children from abuse or neglect. In this regard, even descriptions of the South Slavic peasants' unedifying qualities could be relativized or reimagined as an aspect of their historical victimhood status.

While the figure of the South Slav was nearly always codified as masculine, the comparatively low social standing of peasant women was a recurrent pejorative. Travellers in Dalmatia and Bosnia-Herzegovina were often at pains to outline a culture of rampant male chauvinism in the remoter highland communities where birth rates remained 'uniformly high' and boys were 'held to be worth more than the women'.[91]

This motif found its fullest expression in Montenegro where, as late as 1913, a household's social value continued to be reportedly measured by the number of able-bodied males.[92] Even among the most sympathetic romantics, 'the treatment of women was the single worst mark' against the country.[93] In more isolated provinces, women were supposedly still expected to walk backwards when exiting the presence of men and kiss the hands of male relatives both in greeting and as a mark of subservience. Seeking to stem such customs, King Nikola had decreed that all clan patriarchs must first kiss his queen's hand at public events.[94] The extremes of patriarchy did appear to present some social advantages, however. Despite lives of toil and child-bearing, the rules governing Dinaric communal life were also noted as safeguarding against domestic and sexual violence. '[N]o woman in Montenegro is ill-treated, nor may man lift hand against her', concluded a more positive summation of Montenegrin gender roles.[95]

Jezernik notes that for foreign visitors, Dinaric Slav society's most egregious fault lay in an apparent absence of feminine beauty, notably in Montenegro and Herzegovina.[96]

Considering anything besides fighting as undignified, 'the opposite sex looks on' while peasant women in Cetinje performed work 'which, in other countries, is left to day-labourers', remarked a visiting diplomat in 1907.[97] This ostensibly confirmed the view that feminine beauty, as understood in the West, was an exclusive feature of modern civilization.[98] The treatment of women also appeared to highlight how modernization might fail to penetrate traditionalist attitudes or prove socially detrimental, echoing the popular late-Victorian belief in a degenerative urban underclass. Travelling from Niš to Zaječar in east Serbia, Durham was informed by her driver that 'there were always at least three women to one man working in the fields and that the "man" was usually a boy'. Heavy labour seemed pointless when one could find gainful employment in a nearby town as a 'pandur' (policeman). Those fortunate enough to have become the 'gazda' (head) of a household could spend his days 'elegantly in a kafana' (a local tavern or bistro).[99] The comparatively lowly standing of South Slav women in general could also provide a prism for ethnic contrast. Magyar peasants in the Hungarian lands 'honoured their womankind', noted one tourist, only calling upon female members of the household to assist in heavy labour when strictly necessary, presumably in contrast to their Slavic or Romanian counterparts.[100]

Such flagrant chauvinism did not necessarily preclude the existence of female agency with women often accused of reinforcing their own subservient status through retrogressive cultural conditioning. Brailsford found a notable allegory for Ottoman rule in the form of the 'silent and docile' Macedonian peasant woman who never asked 'for novelty and innovation nor rebelled against the conventions and monotonies of her lot'.[101] In Bosnia-Herzegovina, Christian as well as Muslim women were admonished for undermining Austria-Hungary's civilizing efforts by passively resisting state attempts to educate them (even with the approval of their male relatives).[102] Concurrently, those in Montenegro could appear equally guilty of perpetuating regressive customs. One itinerant artist, on encountering a woman bearing a heavy load while a male companion rode beside her on a pack-animal, noted that 'neither of them would consent to change their position, and put the load on the mule and make the man walk'.[103]

During her secondment with the MRF, Durham grew progressively resentful in her assessment of the Macedonian peasant refugees, the majority of whom were women and children, unable to find their rustic foibles 'in any way lovable or admirable'.[104] Writing in *The Monthly Review*, she described the crowds of women who insistently importuned the MRF as lacking any aesthetic quality. The ignorance and superstition displayed by her charges, demonstrated in their refusal of medical treatment and constant demands for food, money and clothing, only compounded a visible sense of degeneracy associated with rural Ireland and the industrial cities:

> They are stumpy, they are stout, they are heavily built and clumsy, they have faces like Dutch cheeses; they wear their hair in two draggly, skimpy pigtails which they prolong with wool and string . . . they tie their heads up in black handkerchiefs which cover mouth and chin in Mohammedan manner, and their costume is the most unlovely ever yet devised; they call me their 'golden sister'; the yard is full of them, and they are all unutterably filthy.[105]

Nevertheless, this fatalistic obstinacy was interpreted as another facet of the victimhood narrative, forged through the inter-generational trauma of Ottoman rule. 'Were it not for their extreme poverty and misery, my golden sisters would be intolerable', Durham concluded.[106] Their plight only seem to further clarify the Turks' inability, being a 'densely, crassly, hopelessly stupid people', to maintain basic civil order in their own dominions – 'one wants to chase the lot out of Europe'.[107] This further converged with ideas of cultural inertia as a by-product of Ottoman oppression. In Bitola's bazaars and 'quasi-European shops', the only female presence Brailsford could find was among parties of peasants, the streets being 'no place for a respectable Christian woman'.[108] Abbott noted, however, that the former were at equal risk of harassment from Ottoman military patrols and officials. In some districts, the kidnapping and forcing of peasant girls into Turkish harems was claimed to be so severe that parents tattooed their daughters with crucifixes as a form of legal identification.[109] Evidence of this practice in other South Slavic lands merited similar reactions with some commentators regarding the idea of 'branded' women as an enforced renunciation of their individuality. Holbach, however, dismissed tattooing among Catholic Herzegovinian women as the vestige of a 'simple superstitious religion of the Middle Ages'.[110]

Beneath these disparaging characterizations, the peasant woman came to embody the various overlapping metaphors that constituted and substantiated the victimhood narrative. A persistent degradation of femininity, with its associated spiritual and moral virtues, also echoed the hardening of domestic attitudes towards the suffrage issue as sensationalized acts of suffragette militancy, retaliatory police violence and the force-feeding of hunger-striking female inmates came to dominate public impressions from 1906 to 1913.[111] Against this, romanticized depictions of unchanging patriarchal peasant life could also evoke an image of an internalized social stability framed against the lengthening shadows of war, violence and impoverishment .

Reimagining violence

Since the 1870s, violence had been the dominant Balkan motif in British imaginative geography. 'Talking of war, there'll be trouble in the Balkans in the spring', comments a side-character in Rudyard Kipling's *The Light Fades* (1891), a phrase that soon became synonymous with Ottoman Macedonia.[112] By the turn of the century, notions of violent conflict were interwoven with narratives of Western decline. Demonstrating the *fin de siècle* fashion for framing these projections in ambivalently racial terms, one commentator warned that rising Slavic bullishness had made a 'great European war', originating in the Balkans 'one of the few political certainties of our time'.[113] Hulme-Beaman predicted an equally dismal fate for Macedonia as 'one of the great battlefields of Eastern Europe'.[114] The spike in violent guerrilla activities across the territory from 1903 to 1908 appeared to seal its reputation as 'that land of terror, fire and sword'.[115] By 1913, customs such as the 'law of vendetta' or headhunting, and a discursive preoccupation with individual incidents of violence were, according to Todorova, often conflated with social normalities, becoming 'frozen' into an archetype for the region at large.[116] Yet, this stance obfuscates the fact that violence 'was not always interpreted in the same manner, nor did it stand unchallenged' as an emblem of ingrained cultural animosity.[117] Popular reactions, such as the outpouring of opprobrium against Serbia following the 1903 regicide, for instance, were more a perfunctory disdain towards the specific nature of the act itself, often exposing a persistent dearth in British public knowledge as opposed to an instinctive prejudice.[118]

Following the events of 1903, violence was increasingly channelled into the allegorical motifs surrounding the victimhood narrative. Unsurprisingly, the Ottoman Empire's remaining Balkan territories were the primary focus for this dynamic with atrocity narratives involving an oppressed Christian populace construed as a blot on Britain's moral authority, owing to London's continued adherence to the Treaty of Berlin.[119] BC literature informing readers that a situation where 'men [had been] shot down in their fields, women outraged in their homes, and children stabbed at their mother's knee', and occurring 'within three days' of London' by railway travel, represented nothing less than a collective British failure to uphold civilization's most fundamental tenets.[120] Politically, however, this sensationalist rhetoric quickly lost its initial potency after 1903 as the question of who was actually committing these violent acts grew increasingly ambiguous.[121] What these developments did reveal, however, was a shift in perceptions of violence as a normative cultural trait among South Slavs to an aberrant manifestation of a malign form of modernity that victimized rural communities or, more egregiously, corroded their pre-industrial virtuousness through the corrupting influence of contemporary nationalism.

This incorporation of violence into thematic portrayals of victimhood was indicative of efforts among regional actors to influence the international political narrative. Seeking to capitalize on the resurgence of anti-Ottoman sentiment following the Hamidian Massacres, VMRO representatives and Balkan diplomats began circulating 'pro-memoria lists', detailing alleged atrocities, among Western journalists and editors. As in the 1890s, Istanbul's clumsy attempts at controlling this flow of negative coverage, exacerbated by its refusal to grant travel permits to foreign correspondents, unintentionally aided the enemy cause.[122] Consequently, as the political agitation entered its most intensive period in March 1903, correspondents such as Dillon reported on the rape and torture of Slav women and children by the Ottoman forces, based on mostly Bulgarian-supplied information.[123] British audiences were also informed of the cultural repercussions of these attacks; the loss of what an average Briton might consider a 'hovel' for instance, effectively signalled the Macedonian peasant's spiritual 'death' as an outcast from the village he once deemed 'his paradise'.[124]

In keeping with the new British propensity to arrange people into moral, rather than civilizational, hierarchies, popular fiction now appropriated Balkan violence in order to promote 'Britain's superior sense of justice' and explore qualities of 'self-mastery and volition'. Sallying forth into these suitably distant lands, Anglophone heroes discovered unknown depths of intrinsic genius as they aided, or assumed leadership over, 'noble primitive' peasant revolutionaries in the struggle against despotic rulers.[125] Neither was public moral triumphalism entirely complacent in its potential to intervene in matters outside the Edwardian domestic sphere. This was principally reflected in the tide of international condemnation directed against the brutal exploitation of the native Congolese under Leopold II of Belgium's Congo Free State, leading to it being politically wrested from him by the Belgian Federal Parliament in 1908.[126]

As Perkins notes, however, organized opinion's efforts to bring this moralistic energy to bear on the southern Balkans were constrained by the dubious presence of local nationalism.[127] Internecine violence between the VMRO and other paramilitary groups, as well as reported attacks on peasant communities, arouse as a counterpoint to calls for a political resolution favouring the independent Balkan states. 'The Turk is consistently held up as the personification of human devilry', observed one journalist in the immediate aftermath of the Balkan Wars, but whether his 'savagery' matched that of 'the Bulgarian "voivodes" [warlords]' was questionable in the extreme. Scenes of peasants lying dead in their fields, framed by burning villages, could not conceal the fact that the perpetrators were just as likely to have been Christian Greeks or Slavs.[128] By 1913, even fiction was at pains to highlight the Eastern Question's innate historical complexity for those 'who only see it from a distance'. Having chosen Macedonia as the setting for one of his popular 'Boy Scout' adventure stories, the children's author John Finnemore, most likely aware of reported violence against Muslim civilians, attempted to endow the plot with a degree of political nuance. The Turks may have been 'more than useless, as rulers' but a Macedonian Slav was still 'a long chalk off being the same kind of Christian that you may meet rambling to an English village church on a fine Sunday morning', comments the protagonist.[129]

From 1903, the appearance of Greek and Serbian fighters cemented Balkan-style nationalism's reputation as a catalyst for violence. The Macedonian philologist, Krste Misirkov, argued that it was not Ottoman misrule but the 'megalomania' of the independent states that had brought about the disastrous consequences of Ilinden–Preobrazhenie. Foreign encouragement only aggravated this situation, with Misirkov citing a campaign by several senior Anglican bishops as having awarded chauvinistic nationalism a veneer of political respectability.[130] While invariably framed as the principal victims of violence, peasants still occupied a subordinate position to the external forces that produced it. During her secondment with the MRF, Durham repeatedly clashed with the pro-Bulgarian Orthodox bishop of Ohrid, who took exception at her refusal to divert supplies to the VMRO. Incensed by her unwillingness to serve as a political accessory, the prelate had exercised his spiritual authority over the refugees, turning them against the mission and engendering her disillusionment with the anti-Ottoman cause.[131]

The peasantry's own potential for violence also raised the spectre of nationalist manipulation, paralleling latent fears over the possibility of renewed unrest in Ireland. In May 1903, *Reuters'* coverage of a wave of disturbances in Croatia-Slavonia and Dalmatia – in response to the trial of several Croatian Serb politicians charged on fabricated evidence – was seized upon by the Conservative and Unionist press as an appropriate parable for Dublin Castle's ostensible appeasement of republican agitators. Disputed allegations that rioting peasants had been lynched, or summarily executed in police retaliations, also served as a warning to the British authorities to exercise moral restraint.[132] Anti-German violence in Ljubljana in 1908 – attributed to the 'once passive' Slovene peasantry's 'corruption' by crude 'pan-Slavist chauvinism' rumoured to have been spread by Croat and Czech secessionists – was again cited as demonstrating modern nationalism's corrosive impact on the rule of law.[133]

Discussion of brigandage, and the culture surrounding it, demonstrated another angle in the ambiguous association between the peasant and localized violence. In his assessment of the Serbian regicide, Vivian dedicated an entire chapter to the subject, imbuing it with the medieval romanticism that had first attracted him to Serbia in the late 1890s. 'The real brigand', Vivian maintained, 'is usually a political refugee, who only desires to be let alone and is content if he can steal enough to keep body and soul together, or else a political emissary who travels about trying to force an unwilling peasantry into revolution'.[134] Centuries of repressive Turkish rule made Macedonia 'the headquarters of brigandage' where such individuals arose as avatars of the downtrodden. Vivian further contested, however, that the once noble figure of the brigand had been perverted through his appropriation by armed insurgents, such as the VMRO's *komitadji* bands.[135] Whereas the image of the Dinaric mountaineer evoked a heroic primitivism, through historical resistance to an exploitative and overbearing state, his contemporary successors in Macedonia practised a more insidious form of modern violence in the form of irregular warfare.[136] Claiming to have been held to ransom by the VMRO in 1905, one British businessman corroborated this assessment, describing his captors as little more than a provincial arm of the Bulgarian state apparatus. Its members' idolization in the international press only emboldened their criminal activities. According to Ottoman police reports, Bulgarian military officers were even known to lead VMRO bands in raids on Macedonian villages without even bothering to 'discard their uniforms'.[137]

Regardless of culpability, such violence provided a rare impetus for promoting political interest in the region. In early 1904, Aleksandar Jovičić, the chargé d'affaires to Britain's temporarily suspended Serbian ambassador, reported to Belgrade on a 'much discussed presentation' at the London residence of one Dr John Berry and his wife Dr Mary F. Dickinson Berry, who had cycled across Serbia 'in defiance of the boycott'. The 'simple and virtuous' lives of the peasantry had sufficiently impressed them into attempting to counter Western press sensationalism, based on information 'invented by Vienna'. Their audience had included senior parliamentarians 'frantically making notes' or gazing at photographs of rural Serbian life 'as if hypnotized' by a country of which they knew nothing beyond the 'intrigues of Belgrade'.[138] Unlike other attempts at encouraging engagement, these brief flurries of interest occasionally found resonance in the wider public sphere. A film depicting King Petar's coronation in September 1904 by the Yorkshire-based director Frank Mottershaw, for instance, played to sell-out audiences in Sheffield and London.[139] Another pioneering cinematographer, Charles Rider Noble, also enticed the public with a documentary on the 1903 Macedonian crisis, believed to have featured live footage captured during Ilinden–Preobrazhenie itself.[140]

Despite lingering ambiguities, the Edwardian period was revealing of the discursive separation of peasant culture from regional violence that was viewed as an almost exclusively modern phenomenon rooted in nationalism and state militarism. It was no coincidence that critiques of negative cultural stereotypes quickly gained prominence after 1903. 'For the West has a short term memory', Durham stated in rebuttal to the 'hysterical' yet 'insincere' reactions to the Serbian regicide. Only 'a few generations ago, when it, too, was young', discarded heads were public spectacle and executed criminals' corpses 'rotted and stank on wayside gibbets'. Dinaric highlanders would have baulked at such gruesome displays which were antithetical to their own 'primitive honour'.[141] The actions of the May conspirators, observed de Windt, seemed incongruous with the demeanour of their rural co-nationals who appeared completely detached from state politics.[142] Vivian, profoundly shaken by the regicide's exposure of an aspect of Balkan politics at odds with his chivalric idyll, rejected any association between the Serbian state and its rural hinterlands. Through the *zadruga*, Serb peasant virtues manifested in self-sufficiency, a preference for the communal and a 'natural capacity' for self-government. A 'constant craving to acquire more land' had nothing to do with a 'desire for power or ostentation, for they are essentially simple in nature. . . . It is only when they go abroad for their education, don black coats and a thin veneer of progress, that they invite criticism' in their embracing of a corrupt modernity. For this reason, Vivian wished 'to remember them as I have known them – admirable survivors of the age of chivalry'.[143]

Fundamentally, it was though this latter cultural and historical prism that the peasantry's image in British imaginative geography was recalibrated. Simultaneously, a continued emphasis on unrest, and its perpetrators' nationalist ties, found resonance in discursive ideas of moral contingency in the misappropriation of the state's assumed monopoly on violence.[144] The outbreak of the Balkan Wars provided clarity to these emerging tensions – while giving rise to some potential solutions.

Conclusion

Despite popular association with the sinking of the RMS Titanic, or the assassination of Archduke Franz Ferdinand itself, the outbreak of the First Balkan War in October 1912 arguably marked the end of the *fin de siècle*. While regional developments would eventually splinter organized opinion and further soured south-east Europe's political image in the public sphere, it also revealed the extent to which pejorative nineteenth-century archetypes had been subverted. Although the narrative of victimhood provoked vociferous public reactions during the 1820s and 1870s, their twentieth-century iteration proved more emotively enduring in harnessing the peasantry's plight as an allegory for the degraded condition of industrial civilization. In tandem with Britain's own climate of domestic unrest in the early 1910s, the excesses of the Balkan Wars became a logical manifestation of the moral decay at the heart of the modern age. The outcome of the Edwardian years was thus the convergence of historical victimhood with the figure of the peasant as a new cultural archetype. While this did not preclude pejoratives, the image of the victimized peasant would continue to grow in prominence as the cultural lens through which the British public came to view the wartime South Slavic Balkans.

Part II

The era of the Great War

4

The years of crisis

Despite the significance attributed to them by Todorova, few events in imagological historiography have been as subsumed into broader patterns of continuity than the Balkan Wars.[1] As with the First World War itself, the specific historical contingencies that determined events from 1912 to 1914 are also mostly absent from this discussion. Michail, for example, has explored the conflicts' relevance as a transnational event, promulgating a shift within Western internationalism towards an increasingly depoliticized emphasis on anti-militarist humanitarianism.[2] Nevertheless, this remains enmeshed within a still largely political and ideological framework, ignoring or minimalizing the influence domestic factors played in shaping such processes while overlooking the wider international context.

This chapter evaluates the singular historical moment October 1912 to the fatal summer of 1914 represented as a point of fracture and recalibration in Anglo-Balkan relations. Rather than symbolizing a sudden calamitous break with some placid nineteenth-century world, this brief period was the point at which competing and contradictory impulses were brought to a head, further accelerating the unraveling of a cultural, as well as political, status quo already on the verge of disintegration. For Britain, this would manifest in a convergence of its own simmering domestic tensions, heightening social anxiety even further. Conversely, it was in response to these crisis years that the cultural and intellectual strands of nascent Anglo-Britishness began to intersect.

The Balkan Wars through British eyes

While the Balkans Wars' long-term impact on British imaginative geography remains open to debate, it is difficult to refute that the events of 1912 to 1913 marked a historic turning-point, commensurate with the Great Eastern Crisis of the 1870s. Capitalizing on a resurgent public interest, anti-Turkish Liberal and Radical rhetoric hailed the founding of the Balkan League (comprising Bulgaria, Greece, Montenegro and Serbia) in March 1912, and its declaration of war on the Ottomans in October, as a culmination of the nineteenth-century liberationist struggles.[3] Writing from Sarajevo just before the outbreak of the First Balkan War, Evans declared the ratcheting up of regional tensions as the inevitable 'beginning of the end' for Turkey-in-Europe; since the 1875 uprising in Herzegovina, 'the chain of events is unbroken'.[4] Although opinion in Britain's more conservative-leaning press initially held to the government's 'official' pro-Ottoman line, this stance was shortly discarded as a wave of League victories forced Istanbul to relinquish its remaining Balkan holdings, with London obliged to quickly to realign its position.[5]

Despite appearing seemingly unrelated, the months leading up to the Balkan Wars coincided with a sudden escalation in Britain's own domestic tensions. While the unrest of the late-Edwardian era would eventually be overtaken by the First World War and events in the early 1920s, 1911 to 1914 saw much of this industrial conflict peak across western Europe. In Britain, the period immediately following the Liverpool general transport strike brought an unprecedented spike in the number of strikes, especially in the mining industry. By the outbreak of the First Balkan War, for instance, nearly 40 million working days had been lost through stoppages as the Great Unrest gathered momentum. By the end of the Second Balkan War in August 1913, many of those working in Britain's previously unorganized light industries and service sector 'from hotel workers to taxi drivers, cricket ball makers, and even newspaper boys' had joined their unionized peers or established their own pickets.[6]

Of greater political urgency, and a more direct point of comparison, however, was the consequences of the Third Home Rule Bill's introduction in April 1912. Along with the First World War, the resulting 'Home Rule Crisis' – precipitating the creation of rival loyalist and nationalist paramilitary formations – represented the pivot around which Anglo-British identity coalesced. Neither were these crises mutually exclusive as the Dublin lock-out from August 1913 to January 1914, mirroring the earlier violence in Liverpool, illustrated.[7] It was these twin developments that infused the Balkans Wars' reception in Britain with an unprecedented sense of social anxiety not witnessed since the conclusion of the Boer War.

At a representational level, 1912 also highlighted the extent to which perceptions of the region's people had grown increasingly fluid through their resonance with domestic concerns. While Pamela Sezgin notes a continuation in derogatory characterizations, these largely stemmed from unease over nationalist influence.[8] Dillon, for instance, presented Serbian leaders as 'both clever and nervous' in attempting to manipulate their countrymen's patriotic energy.[9] Another correspondent described the country's mobilization as 'wild and unrestrained' with those from even 'the most desolate farmsteads' and 'tiniest hamlets' accepting 'the call to the colours [. . .] as though it were an invitation to a national festival in which religion was mingled with merry-making'. Urged on by peasant women and 'village orators', Belgrade in October 1912 was described as having been flooded by excitable mobs 'without uniform and without arms, but with the look of men who were spoiling for a fight'.[10] As Sezgin further observes, from 1910, British war reporting tended to display a far higher degree of impartiality, with readers and contributors to the same publications often holding widely differing opinions. Pejorative Victorian stereotypes also continued to be challenged in the national and specialist press as the wars suddenly presented informed and organized opinion with an expanded national forum (and a briefly captive audience) in which to debate regional politics and interrogate cultural preconceptions.[11]

Even the subsequent revelation that widespread atrocities had been committed against civilians by the League's armies only reinforced the newly crystallized image of violence as stemming from an extreme form of modernity permeating into the Balkans, specifically from Germany. As the League's members attempted to construct the new nationalistic ideal of the ethnically homogenous nation-state in the former Ottoman lands they annexed, Western (and dissenting regional) commentators redefined the conflict as a 'war of extermination', demonstrating modernity's worst excesses.[12] In Britain's case, this was initially obfuscated, or relativized, by the exuberant response to the First Balkan War's outbreak, especially among those who had spent most of the previous decade championing specific countries. Early reports on the number of refugees were dismissed as commentators from niche periodicals to the major dailies rushed to proclaim the end of Ottoman rule in Europe. Dillon, having grown less interested in investigative journalism over voicing his own opinions, provided almost running coverage for *The Contemporary Review*, confidently predicting that peace was 'now in sight' as the 'long-awaited' conflagration promised a cathartic end to nearly ten years of unrest.[13] Nevertheless, Dillon caveated this by warning of a potential escalation in light of the recent 'Austro-Servian' dispute.[14] Brailsford further countenanced this anti-Turkish impulse in *The Nation*: 'Better an end with horrors than horrors without an end.'[15] Even the distinguished anti-militarist Norman Angell acknowledged that '"two opposed purposes" were present in the Balkans'. Despite being a leading proponent of the pacifist cause, Angell contested that the very nature of Ottoman rule amounted to 'peace' in name only, necessitating its forcible removal in the interests of European stability. However, uncertainty remained over whether 'the Balkan peoples prove Pacifist or Bellicist; adopt the Turkish or the Christian System?'[16]

This flurry of excitement quickly dissipated with the outbreak of the short-lived Second Balkan War in June 1913 that pitted Bulgaria – the historic darling of pro-Balkan Gladstonianism – against Greece, Serbia and Montenegro. The latter were soon joined by an oppurtunistic Romania and an Ottoman Empire eager to claw back those territories recently ceded to the Bulgarians. By this point, however, the majority of regional coverage had switched from political discourse to a stream of lurid vignettes describing arson, massacres, mass rape, mutilations and other atrocities – focusing on Montenegro and Serbia's campaigns in Albania and Kosovo in particular.[17] As with Istanbul's attempts at concealing its earlier persecution of the Armenians and Assyrians, or the suppression of Ilinden–Preobrazhenie, efforts at censure by the League's members only exacerbated their associated guilt while further diminishing any claims to territorial legitimacy. Following Macedonia's annexation by Serbia, for instance, a dispatch from Britain's consulate in Bitola in March 1913, estimated that 'less than 12,000' of the district's 149,000 inhabitants 'are Serbs, or rather the creation of Servian propaganda since the Austrian occupation of Bosnia and Herzegovina'. This was in spite of the 'scientific' evidence the new Serbian administration had presented to consular staff when pressed on complaints made by local civilians.[18]

The extent of these accusations even prompted an investigation by a commission of representatives from the United States and European Powers, on behalf of the recently founded Carnegie Endowment for International Peace. One of its witnesses, Raymond Fisher, the only Briton recorded as having served in an active military capacity as a volunteer in the Bulgarian army,[19] testified that 'Bulgarian' villages in east Macedonia were being subjected to a program of 'Serbianization'. Peasant women had died 'as the result of violation' while survivors were left to endure the misery of privation as the army forcibly requisitioned crops to be 'used in the trenches as bedding' and even levied taxes 'on burned houses'.[20] Another consular dispatch from Bitola in June 1914 observed that the bureaucratic mechanisms of the modern state were replacing outright military repression. Enforced taxation was used by the Serb authorities as a disincentive to drive Muslim peasants, including returning refugees, from their land. This was compounded by the new administration encouraging their Christian neighbours 'to terrorise them to such an extent that agriculture has in many cases been impossible'.[21]

Moreover, not even the Balkan Wars appeared entirely separate from Britain's own fractious socio-political climate. Even in October 1912, policymakers in London observed, with rising alarm, that elements in Ireland's loyalist and nationalist camps were already touting the use of insurrectionary violence, and soliciting direct foreign intervention, as prerequisites for achieving their own political ambitions.[22] Matters of colonial stability provided another touchstone for regional developments. Throughout the Balkan Wars, the India Office repeatedly issued press warnings that violence against Macedonian Muslims was inflaming hostilities across the subcontinent, with anti-European and anti-Christian chants becoming a feature of Islamic political rallies.[23] Following the end of the Second Balkan War, the Conservative MP Charles Hunter stressed that it had been 'peculiarly ill-judged' to sacrifice the loyalty of India's Muslims on the basis of 'false reports' claiming that the Ottoman authorities were persecuting Macedonian Christians. Having toured war-torn rural Macedonia himself, Hunter claimed that the truth had been quite the opposite.[24]

These revelations further marginalized organized opinion's members, with the BC itself fracturing along partisan lines. For Vivian, the war appeared to validate the extent to which Serbia had fallen under 'terrorist rule', its chivalric agrarian traditions and peasantry corrupted by the degenerate ideology of modern ethno-nationalism. Evoking the country's most successful medieval ruler, Stefan Dušan, Vivian urged Serbs to press for unification with Montenegro under the Petrović-Njegoš dynasty as a means of 'ending the regicide terrorism of the last nine years and restoring greater Servia, almost the Servia of Dushan, to her old place among civilised nations'.[25]

Appeals for a reversion to earlier tradition found little empathy among other critical voices such as Durham who, despite volunteering to serve in the Montenegrin Red Cross, grew increasingly hostile towards the 'pro-Slav' loyalties of her peers on the BC.[26] Her own one-sided account on the siege and eventual occupation of the northern Albanian city of Shkodër by Montenegrin forces from October 1912 to April 1913, followed in the wake of the Austrian publicist Leo Freundlich's *Albaniens Golgotha* (1913) and Leon Trotsky's coverage, all espousing a belief that liberationist rhetoric had masked localized campaigns of 'extermination' rooted in seditious nationalist ideology imported from the West.[27] Like Vivian, Durham also described earlier customs as having been twisted into macabre parodies, symbolized in the widespread use of facial mutilation. Evidence from the Montenegrin army's Spanish attaché and a Russian doctor serving in western Kosovo 'corroborated' her claims of the practice as having been encouraged as a terror tactic. By the end of 1912, Montenegrin soldiers had 'scarcely left a nose on a corpse between Berani and Ipek'.[28] This alleged nationalistic perversion of the country's mountaineer heritage was articulated in a recorded argument with a teacher from Podgorica who defended the practice as an 'old national custom': 'Of course we shall cut noses; we always have.'[29] Similar claims and counterclaims were exchanged across the public sphere's various discursive channels with growing enmity. Durham herself was rebuked by the Anglo-Irish novelist Joyce Cary, who had also served as a Red Cross orderly in Montenegro and had actually been present at the fall of Shkodër, maintaining that bands of Albanian irregulars bore responsibility for the mistreatment of Ottoman POWs, including mutilations.[30]

Neither did the belief that the wars' excesses might have reflected some deeper civilizational contagion produce a unanimous shift in the region's political image. As the First Balkan War came to an end, Durham had blamed the West for restricting local aspirations and escalating nationalist agitation. Attempts at restraining these forces had 'only made the final explosion more violent'.[31]

More general critiques, however, conceived of the violence as indicative of the region's cultural permeation by pernicious influences, reemphasizing the victimhood narrative. Contributors to the *Africa Times and Orient Review* and the conservative-leaning *National Review*, both of which had protested the wars at the outset, argued that the importing of European-style nationalism was always the true source of regional instability. The religious and moralistic rhetoric of Western commentators had facilitated this by only ever condemning violence when the perpetrators had been Muslim.[32] A pro-Turkish pamphlet urged British readers to overcome their prejudices and exercise public opinion 'against the atrocities' as a whole. It went on to accuse the British government and organized opinion of inadvertently enabling the current state of affairs by having treated every minor complaint made by Macedonian Christian Slavs 'as an international emergency'.[33] Suggestions of 'ancient' or 'tribal' hatreds, however, were usually dismissed as the simple ignorance of the uninformed. Blame lay solely with national governments and urban-based intellectuals, whose characterized duplicitousness further propagated the peasantry's enduring image as naïve but sympathetic victims of historical circumstance.[34]

The new humanism

In terms of historical engagement, the Balkan Wars marked a notable departure from previous patterns of British public reaction towards violent unrest. With the cessation of hostilities, overseas conflict had itself culturally metastasized into a conduit for expressing the slowly crystallizing, yet still suitably vague, sense of Anglo-Britishness as an active force on the world stage through humanitarian relief and medical provision. Such activities held a particular appeal for middle- and upper-class women, inspired by the popular mythology surrounding Florence Nightingale. In the Balkan context, a historical precedent had already been established during the Eastern Crisis. In 1876, Irby, herself an acquittance of Nightingale, had attracted press and parliamentary attention through her work in supervizing food distribution to Christian refugees in Bosnia-Herzegovina, alongside the author and nursing pioneer Emily Anne Beaufort's high-profile emergency aid mission to Bulgaria.[35] Alleviating wartime suffering thus became the moral pinion to which more engaged members of the public affixed their roles as representatives of Britain's superior standing in the hierarchy of civilization.

Aid work itself was envisioned as an expression of defiance against the prevailing spirit of cynicism perceived to be afflicting Western civilization.

Unlike the 1870s, however, humanitarian intervention in the Balkan Wars occurred on a far grander scale as volunteer missions from each of the major powers flocked to the region.[36] In Britain, this filtered into more philosophical discussions concerning the notional affirmation of moral worth through direct action. A campaign to expand the service remit of Red Cross volunteers elaborated on the organization's internationalist ethos as being equivocal to a 'unique sense' of British moral compulsion. Male and female volunteers even popularized the dispute as a moral confrontation between 'the medium of the benevolence of the British public' and the narrow-minded 'national limitations' imposed by their organization's governing charter.[37]

Beyond these evolutions in the victimhood narrative, the Balkan Wars also captured Western imaginations as a showcase for new military technologies and tactical innovations, such as surveillance aircraft, artillery bombardments, massed infantry charges and barbed wire entanglements, that later became synonymous with the First World War's Western Front.[38] Conversely, the campaigns in Albania and Kosovo retained much of the aesthetics of 'traditional' Balkan warfare.[39] In Cary's experience, King Nikola's army had possessed no medical corps and relied on Serbian ordnance while peasants who fought in 'sheepskin coats' comprised the rank and file. Battles had mostly consisted of chaotic infantry charges occasionally presaged by squads of 'bomb throwers': elderly men wearing 'the long white frock, blue breeches and white stockings of civil dress' who had volunteered for service 'because as they said it would not matter if they got killed'.[40] This apparent fatalism appeared to permeate the conflict as another facet of peasant victimhood. Writing from Montenegro in the winter of 1912, Durham described modern warfare itself as a form of social necrosis. Hospital wards were quickly overwhelmed by infectious diseases, spread via military and refugee columns, creating a state of perpetual misery for victor and vanquished alike: '"The Balkan land for the Balkan people." But the Balkan lands were but sparsely populated, and the victims innumerable.'[41]

The Balkan Wars also intersected with a formative shift in British altruism that would continue to develop throughout the twentieth century; the social reformer Eglantyne Jebb, for example, highlighted the suffering of Albanian and Macedonian children in 1913 as inspiring her decision to establish the *Save the Children Fund* in 1919.[42] The conflicts also marked a departure from the cultural and political ambiguities that had previously inhibited closer public interest, as volunteers conceived of their missions as directly analogous to domestic injustices. Mabel Ann St. Clair Stobart, an active suffragist and avowed humanitarian who led a 'Women's Convoy Corps' in Bulgaria and Macedonia, exemplified this turn. In a pamphlet authored on her return to Britain in 1913, Stobart argued for greater female participation in national defence in order to validate the right to political enfranchisement.[43] However, Stobart's commitment to suffrage was enmeshed in spiritualistic interpretations of humanitarianism, visualizing relief work as 'the militant arm' of anti-militarism. In an era blighted by moral decay, women should be compelled to limit war's destructive impact on the lives of soldiers and civilians 'regardless' of where or whom it affected.[44]

From Sarajevo to Cer

In the months following the Second Balkan War, discussion of the region was mostly subsumed into more general debates over how such conflicts might be prevented in the future. Explanations on its root causes, however, divided opinion between universalist and particularist interpretations. The limited disruption to Serbia's agricultural-based economy had been enough to convince Brailsford, as one of the Endowment's two British representatives, that moral collapse was a product of contemporary nationalism rather than industrial modernity or urbanization, and could manifest in any country. Nevertheless, given the Serbs' apparent lack of cultural restraints, which Brailsford still attributed to the legacy of Ottoman rule, he also proposed that 'those regions not ready to govern themselves' should have their sovereignty transferred to a supranational body (organized along democratic socialist principles).[45] Durham, by contrast, retreated from external explanations, attributing the wars' excesses to cultural deficiencies inherent in the Slav (specifically Serbian) racial psyche. Writing in her 1920 biography, the 'bestial experience' had, she claimed, convinced her that the 'Balkan Slav and his vaunted Christianity' was a uniquely disruptive force. An inherent propensity for violence necessitated that 'all civilisation should rise and restrain him from further brutality'. Conversely, she also claimed to have been equally convinced that such 'obscene' occurrences would never happen in enlightened 'West Europe'.[46]

However, the extent to which general British public interest in the Balkans had fallen away after 1912 was evidenced by the widespread indifference towards Archduke Franz Ferdinand's assassination on 28 June 1914 in Sarajevo.[47] Unlike the Annexation Crisis or the Balkan Wars themselves, the incident in the Bosnian capital appeared to have no tangible bearing on British interests. Speaking at Guildhall on 17 July, David Lloyd George dismissed 'any foreseeable diplomatic contretemps in Europe' as 'no more than a small cloud on the horizon'. The threat of 'a quarter of a million men under arms' and the 'implacable revolutionary ferment' in Ireland were of more pressing concern.[48] In the press, the Balkan origins of the unfolding July Crisis were quickly superseded by the convoluted diplomatic machinations playing out in the capitals of the Great Powers. It was only with Austria-Hungary's 'démarche' to Serbia, announced to the rest of the British cabinet by Grey during a meeting on Ireland, that events on the continent solicited official alarm.[49]

In the now fragmented academic and journalistic sphere of organized opinion, much of the outrage engendered by the Balkan Wars had given way to a sense of moral relativism. The Carnegie Endowment's final report into war crimes committed by the League's members went largely unnoticed owing to its publication coinciding with the escalating European crisis coupled with disparities in the investigation's findings and its inconclusiveness over how to apportion blame.[50] Reflecting on its lukewarm reception, Francis W. Hirst, the editor of *The Economist* and the Endowment's other British representative, speculated over whether the Balkan Wars had been forewarnings of what might transpire in future conflicts. Would 'the armies of civilised Europe . . . even the British Tommy' respect the edict of international law 'once the actual tide of war had swept away normal restraints'?[51]

Like the 1903 Serbian regicides, responses to the assassinations largely fixated on the act itself, provoking a familiar mix of shock, morbid curiosity and occasional, albeit less vehement, recourse to pejorative stereotyping.[52] By 30 June, the ever assiduous Steed could present readers of *The Times* with an established order of events, confirm the number of conspirators and substantiate Vienna's claim of 'a carefully laid plot' behind the murders.[53] Writing in an editorial the day after the event, he also contended that pro-government rallies held across Bosnia-Herzegovina were unlikely to quell Muslim and Orthodox unrest since both groups 'have always resented the annexation'.[54] Nevertheless, speculation continued to circulate regarding culpability. In mid-July, Horatio Bottomley, the demagogic editor of the populist magazine *John Bull*, announced that he had been made aware of an extensive plot devised by Serbian intelligence through the country's various embassies, including London. The magazine's incriminating 'evidence' took the form of an anonymously-authored document – conveniently detailing Belgrade's full complicity in the assassination. As 'a hot-bed of cold-blooded conspiracy and subterfuge' and perpetual 'menace' to European peace, Bottomley concluded that 'Servia must be wiped out'. Given its editor's public reputation for financial and political fraud, it came as no surprise that *John Bull* pre-emptively refused to verify any of its claims.[55]

Amid this sensationalist hyperbole and hermetic diplomacy, a lack of any obvious domestic or cultural hook curtailed the possibility of wider public interest. 'I knew nothing of European complications and cared less. The murder of an Archduke meant no more to me than some tale of an imaginary kingdom in Zenda,' wrote the children's novelist Mabel Dearmer, implying that fictional locales still offered a more palpable frame of reference.[56]

The Monarchy's formal declaration of war on 28 July 1914 was met with further indifference interspersed with occasional denouncements of Serbia as 'a nation of regicides and cut-throats', deserving punishment.[57] The Balkan theatre's presumed remoteness in the mind of the 'average British patriot' was seemingly articulated in a satirical poem appearing in *Punch* on 5 August, presented as a direct address to Serbia, Russia and Austria-Hungary. 'But why should I follow your fighting line, for a matter that's no concern of mine?' the author rhetorically asks the Serbs, to whom responsibility for the war is partially assigned.[58]

As Catriona Pennell notes, in July and early August 1914, Britain's enemies and allies were still 'very fluid concepts' within the public sphere.[59] Critical voices argued that a war against Germany amounted to a betrayal of the Western Enlightenment. 'Let us be perfectly clear at any rate,' stated the *London Daily News* on 28 July, 'what we are asked to do is to strike a blow at Western culture in order to bolster the infinitely lower culture of Eastern Europe.'[60] Scully's theory on the vagaries of Anglo-German antagonism was exhibited by the opposition's appeal to latent notions of cultural kinship.[61] A petition from nine Oxbridge academics, reprinted in *The Times*, contested that 'war upon her [Germany] in the interests of Servia and Russia would be a sin against civilization', as Europe's most rapidly modernizing nation 'leading the way in the Arts and Sciences . . . so near akin to our own and with whom we have so much in common'.[62] Angell also stressed Teutonic commonality as grounds against British intervention: would assisting Russia in the creation of 'a dominant Slavonic federation of, say, 200,000,000 autocratically governed people, with a very rudimentary civilisation, but heavily equipped for military aggression, be a less dangerous factor in Europe than a dominant Germany of 65,000,000 highly civilised and mainly given to the arts of trade and commerce [sic]?'[63] More popular media offered a less-considered response. Unperturbed by the threat of legal action its previous accusations had elicited from the Serbian embassy, *John Bull* remained stridently brazen, rhetorically declaring: 'TO HELL WITH SERVIA. *Why Should Britain Shed Her Blood to Save a Nation of Assassins?*' – four days after Germany's invasion of Belgium. This spectacular misreading of the reconfigured public mood (and an ill-timed publication schedule) prompted Bottomley to drop any further mention of Serbia in the following issue.[64]

Coupled with the Serbian army's unexpected victory at the Battle of Cer in mid-August, the earlier reimagining of civilization as a moral concept had created a domestic environment highly amenable to the notion of Anglo-Serbian solidarity. The relative obscurity that still surrounded Balkan politics, as well as ingrained public disinterest, allowed this arrangement to be easily construed as a natural outgrowth of the British wartime mission. The once lauded modernizing standards of Austria-Hungary – now little more than Germany's regional appendage – were swiftly reframed as a corruption of Enlightenment ideals by militaristic authoritarianism and the exploitation of a region as yet untainted by this modern degeneracy. This twisted reflection of progress was assigned the derisory epithet of 'Pan-Germanism' or *Kultur* with the Balkans becoming a microcosm of a far wider struggle. As the proclaimed moral standard-bearer of Western civilization, Britain's wartime duty was not towards Serbia per se, but the ideals it allegedly personified in opposing the spread of pan-Germanism. The figure of the Serbian peasant turned soldier quickly became the valiant avatar of democratic virtue; having once stood as the 'guardian' of Christendom against the Ottoman conquests, he now fought to preserve the legacy of the European Enlightenment.[65]

Denouncing the German army's adoption of trench warfare following the First Battle of the Marne in September 1914, Lloyd George warned that German advancements in science and art had been counterpoised by a loss of 'the noble human qualities'. Juxtaposing this with the Serbs' conduct against Austro-Hungarian forces at Cer, he concluded that, despite boasting the trappings of industrial civilization, 'Prussia cannot conceive of self-sacrifice in a righteous cause'.[66] Similarly, Serbia, which fell under the occupation of the 'tyrannical' Central Powers in November 1915, emerged as a kind of secular martyr to democratic freedom.[67]

This imaginative recalibration of the Serbian national image as a morally virtuous and capable wartime ally further legitimized earlier revisions of negative cultural stereotypes. Even before 1915, the 'nation of regicides' was easily recast as 'Gallant Serbia', its martial prowess presented in propaganda as a manifestation of a moral fortitude quintessential to the Serbian national character.[68] As Chirol gushed in a pamphlet published in October 1914, '[T]he splendid pluck with which her sons have faced the Austrian Goliath and smitten him hip and thigh' had removed any 'blots' from the Serbian national character. Although 'the worst pages of her history' might have framed British perceptions before the war, both countries had now found common ground in the 'shared cause of freedom'.[69] The first volume in Britain's official war history, appearing at the end of 1914, also sought to assuage any lingering public doubt by echoing Vivian's original hypothesis of a division between Serbia's 'false' imported urban culture and peasant authenticity. Pre-war 'globe-trotters' had seldom seen beyond 'the artificial gaieties of Belgrade', misconstruing the 1903 regicide as emblematic of the entire nation rather than the 'true Serbs' dwelling peacefully in the surrounding villages.[70] Seton-Watson reiterated these sentiment in an essay from early 1915 – informally signalling the beginning of Serbia's integration into wider British wartime propaganda narratives. The true 'spirit of the Serb' existed in rural traditions, attachment to the land and democratic peasant values, rather than the pseudo-Westernized cities that dominated the itineraries of Edwardian tourists and foreign correspondents.[71]

Conclusion

Although Winter's 'clarifying' effects of the Great War had yet to fully define the contours of Anglo-Britishness, public reactions to the Balkan Wars foreshadowed its emerging influence within imaginative geography. The greater plurality of contributing views, set against a far more culturally cynical domestic environment than that of the 1870s, meant Victorian-era prejudice held considerably less of an influence as reflected in the Endowment's coverage of violence against Muslims as well as Christians. They also exposed the obvious limits, and immutable decline, of politics and political opinion in determining the nature of regional representations in the public sphere.[72] Nowhere was this shift better illustrated than in subsequent reactions to Sarajevo. Beyond elite circles, the widespread indifference towards Franz Ferdinand's assassination demonstrated the extent to which such events had grown largely unmoored from any real sense of political meaning or consequence in the public consciousness.

The end of the Edwardian era also revealed a moralistic turn in how Britons perceived themselves within their own geographical imaginations. The 'shift of focus in the moral standards of the liberal camp from liberty to non-violence' after 1912 was conducive to this trend.[73] Organizations such as the Endowment, formed in 1910, implied a new spirit of humanism; in Britain's case this was interwoven with a re-imagined sense of identity predicated on an innate moral superiority – in place of a unifying idea of nationhood. Unlike the self-assuredness of the mid-Victorian era, maintaining or reviving this cultural virtuousness necessitated a need for continual renewal, lest British moral worth be eroded by materialistic complacency or the dehumanizing influences of industrial modernity. The First World War would further expedite this trend as Britain entered its most significant period of direct engagement with the South Slavic Balkans, transplanting many of its domestic social currents directly to the region.

5

The British and the Balkan front

Among the developments that stimulated British public interest in the modern Balkans, none were as pivotal as the First World War. Serbia's unanticipated military success over Austria-Hungary's invasion forces at Cer in August 1914 – the Entente's first decisive victory over the Central Powers – and subsequently the Battle of Kolubara from November to December resonated with the emotive rhetoric surrounding Belgium's resistance to the German army that same year. This heroic narrative of 'gallant little Serbia' was amplified with its eventual occupation by Germany, Bulgaria and the Dual Monarchy in November 1915.[1] Rather than surrender, the Serbian High Command ordered a mass retreat through Albania and Montenegro to the Adriatic coast from where approximately 155,000 military and civilian refugees were evacuated by British, French and Italian naval convoys to Corfu, Corsica and other Mediterranean outposts.[2]

Framed against these dramatic events, the war represented a critical moment in Anglo-Balkan relations as the apex of direct engagement. Throughout the conflict, over 400,000 British and Imperial subjects were deployed to Serbia and Macedonia in both a military and humanitarian capacity.[3] Furthermore, unlike previous conflicts, Britain's presence was distinguished by greater social diversity, comprising mostly women and working-class men. This granted a much wider cross-section of British society the potential to form their own impressions of the region's people and culture.

Like the Balkan Wars, imagological historiography has tended to adopt a broadly interpretative approach towards the Great War, typically subsuming it into a thematic chronology of recurrent Balkanist discourses or as an explanation for the evolution of certain paradigms, such as gender.[4] Drapac, for instance, highlights the significance of leading volunteers as 'informal diplomatists' whose aid work was expropriated by pro-Serb and pro-Yugoslav propagandists in Britain.[5] This form of assessment is typically restricted to a subset of prominent personalities while ignoring the diversity of British wartime experience, particularly that of military personnel. Despite the historically unique circumstances, the war undercut the niche debates and moralistic rhetoric characteristic of previous decades by facilitating a temporary space in which representational impressions were exposed to a greater plurality of viewpoints, rooted in social rather than narrow political concerns. It also promoted more proactive forms of engagement exemplified by the personal bonds between Britons and South Slavs – including peasants. These new criteria, revealed in both published and unpublished materials, reflect a complex set of observations framed, more than ever, by pre-existing domestic context and individual aspiration.[6]

As with the Balkan Wars, depictions of civilian trauma, emphasizing displacement, privation and human tragedy were instrumental in drawing British public attention to the war's southeastern theatre. Hammond observes that subsequent British memoirs produced a 'chain of counter-assertion' in representations from 1915 to 1939. This presented a clear break with earlier pejorative paradigms as a 'previously marginal cluster of [positive] motifs, images and evaluations' displaced older pejoratives but remained 'conditioned' by earlier preconceptions as well as the language of the civilizing mission.[7] Besides the fact this shift was already in evidence by 1912, such an approach typifies the historiographical tendency (inspired by Hobsbawm) to perceive 1914 as the definitive point of departure. In actuality, the Great War simply amplified and consolidated pre-existing trends while continuing to cement the peasants' status as perpetual victims, as well as public assuredness in an innate Anglo-British moral virtue.

This chapter explores the impact of the British intervention as a historical catalyst that further enmeshed representations of the peasantry within popular understandings of the wider war. It also considers how the war prompted a further evolution in the image of the peasant through the appearance of the 'peasant-soldier': a motif contingent on what Norris terms 'positive militarism'. Whereas violence was previously characterized as an egregious expression of an innate Balkan primitiveness, its wartime association with the Serb peasantry's resistance to the Central Powers integrated it within the victimhood narrative by aligning Britain and Serbia's war efforts as reflections of the same moral endeavour.[8]

'English sestre' and peasant soldiers

In a conflict that came to privilege the experience of the male combatant above all others, British intervention in the South Slavic Balkans was unique among the First World War's European fronts in being initially defined by a female civilian presence. Throughout its opening months, units of volunteers provided emergency relief aid to the Serbian army and civilians; besides the Red Cross and St. John's Ambulance, the most significant organizations involved were the Serbian Relief Fund (SRF), founded by Seton-Watson in August 1914, and the Scottish Women's Hospitals (SWH). By October 1915, some 600 British nurses and female doctors oversaw an expansive network of hospitals and clinics throughout Serbia, proportionally the highest among the war's military theatres.[9] Religious groups and private individuals, notably the Scottish tea merchant Thomas Lipton, also provided financial aid, logistical assistance or even organized their own units.[10] The relatively small numbers of trained and professional medical staff were also assisted by numerous non-specialist auxiliaries recruited in Britain, locally and from among the ranks of enemy POWs.[11] While the majority of volunteers remained in their postings following the occupation (or had already been relocated to other fronts), a determined minority, including a SRF unit commanded by Stobart, joined the columns of refugees fleeing to the coast.

What singled out this earlier period was its role in establishing a link between the British and Serbian war efforts through a uniquely gender prism.[12] The reported deaths of female volunteers during the evacuation, or from an aggressive typhus epidemic that broke out in early 1915, granted home audiences a window into the war's devastating impact on civilians. Serbia itself was believed to have suffered one of the highest death tolls among the war's participants.[13]

As Monica Krippner notes, within weeks of its outbreak, the First World War in the Balkans immediately eclipsed almost four decades of preceding British interventions in terms of scale and organization.[14] It also brought a far wider range of ideological convictions, in contrast to the Liberal-dominated Victorian and Edwardian eras. Like the Balkan Wars, however, a discernibly anti-militarist current, as espoused by Stobart in 1913, gradually developed among leading volunteers as an alternative form of patriotism, establishing much of the ideological tenor for organizations such as the SWH.[15]

When considering the implications of this sudden wave of direct engagement, these aid missions are frequently codified as part of an early-twentieth-century trend that saw woman seek out alternatives to domestic political campaigning.[16] Indeed, biographical texts on dominant personalities such as Stobart or the SWH's energetic founder, Dr Elsie Inglis, accentuate their ideological commitment to women's suffrage.[17] Imagological historiography has generally accepted such reasoning with women's 'righteous indignation' over a lack of political rights in Britain seemingly translating into support for the wartime plight of Europe's smaller nations.[18] Their actions have also been interpreted as echoing the late-Victorian ideal of the virtuous feminine caregiver that, according to Drapac, was instrumentalized in order to manipulate public sympathies.[19] While holding a degree of merit, such an interpretation, again, oversimplifies a far more nuanced picture. Although leading figures like Inglis played an influential role in publicizing wartime humanitarian aid, among the missions themselves, any pretensions of furthering concrete political agendas represented a very small minority.[20] Of greater significance was their ideological role as a conduit through which a myriad of social anxieties and dissatisfactions were projected directly onto the Balkans. Alleviating the Serbian people's plight was thus presented in propaganda narratives as one of multiple wartime objectives, falling within Britain's slowly conceived purview as civilization's moral arbiter.

Nevertheless, such developments remained emblematic of the First World War's salience in reframing cultural perceptions through the vigorous campaigning energy previously mobilized against urban poverty, gender discrimination and other domestic issues. Writing, in 1916, on her experiences of the Albanian retreat – and the estimated 140,000 deaths resulting from it – Stobart reiterated her claim that war represented 'maleness run riot'.[21] The Great War itself acquired the veneer of a crusade against 'retrogressive' concepts such militarism, materialism and the retreat from spiritual values. Women, by contrast, were conceptualized as embodying 'domestic order surrounded by turmoil and chaos'.[22] As Stobart surmised, 'primitive Woman' had been naturally motivated to defend 'an individual concrete life'. It was only logical that 'modern Woman must now, in an enlarged sphere, defend the abstract life of mankind'.[23] While few volunteers actually shared in Stobart's rhetorical grandiosity, her belief in women as the enablers of Anglo-British cultural and moral virtue served as the primary hook for public interest in the Balkan front. Harold Lake, a British logistics officer who, unusually, succeeded in completing and publishing his war memoirs before the fighting had officially concluded, reserved praise for nurses and medical staff as the only example of 'British worth' in an otherwise 'dismal' campaign. Only in honouring their sacrifice, through the eventual liberation of the Serbian homeland, would Britain's claim of being first among civilized nations have been vindicated.[24]

Britain's entry into the war in August 1914 had inflamed an already febrile domestic climate. Mawkish calls to 'keep the home fires burning' hardened the resolve of female volunteers seeking to contribute directly to the war effort.[25] Indeed, Inglis's inspiration for establishing the SWH was rumoured to have stemmed from the War Office's response to her initial proposition of using mobile units of female volunteers to bolster the logistical capacity of the Royal Army Medical Corps (RAMC), that she 'go home and sit still'. In spite of this, Inglis was careful to avoid overt political connotations during the SWH's founding, deliberately rejecting any reference to suffrage in the organization's title and mission statement.[26] Nevertheless, politics was an initial source of tension; younger and less politicized volunteers had expressed concerns that aid work would be subordinated to other agendas. Katherine Stuart MacPhail, a Glaswegian doctor in the SWH's first Serbian Unit from 1914 to 1915, later recalled the collective relief that more radical sympathies had been comparatively uncommon:

> We knew we were being sent out under the auspices of the 'Suffrage Societies' and each was afraid that every other was a strong supporter, but were much relieved to find that almost none of us was what might be called 'strong', and that Serbia was the common bond, not suffrage.[27]

For most participants, the compunction to volunteer came from more modest impulses. Katherine Hodges, a nurse who had accompanied Jebb to Macedonia in 1913, joined the SWH as a driver the following year, later recalling how she had succumbed to the 'naïve base euphoria' felt by those recruited into Herbert Kitchener's New Army. With 'no concept of what war actually was', the opportunity for a woman to serve on any military front had seemed 'a wonderful adventure', and remained so for many even in the jaded atmosphere of 1918.[28]

The overrepresentation of women obfuscated the fact that aid work was generally perceived as an alternative route to frontline participation among those for whom it was otherwise formally denied. Despite its name, the SWH, for example, was open to male and non-Scottish volunteers, the majority having also been rejected by the army or barred from serving in the RAMC. Hodges recalled its main London recruitment centre in September 1914 being 'swarmed' by men 'eager to get to any front, regardless of whose uniform they wore'.[29] Like their female colleagues, official rejection was usually the motivating factor. John Abraham, a surgeon assigned to a Red Cross posting in Skopje, claimed he had volunteered in protest at the War Office's rejection of his application to serve in France, being 'too old' at the age of 36.[30]

Volunteers with previous experience of the region such as Stobart or Louise Paget (the wife of Britain's then ambassador to Serbia) remained a small, socially exclusive, minority.[31] For most of those involved in relief work, Serbia itself had been a secondary importance. SWH and Red Cross orientation meetings often recorded how volunteers neither knew nor seemed especially concerned as to where they were about to be deployed.³² MacPhail later admitted that it was the RAMC's curt rejection of her service application, rather than 'a wild and barbaric people, living in a wild country', that led to her joining the SWH 'on impulse'. For the 'more adventurous' volunteers, the FO's nannyish warnings of 'dark intrigues and unknown subtleties', had only enhanced Serbia's initial allure as a wartime destination.³³

Despite general political apathy, questions surrounding the perceived wartime role of women proved instrumental in tying relief work to discursive domestic issues. Inglis, a trained surgeon, exemplified these converging priorities, having entered the war from a professional background and quickly rising to become one of the most high-profile figures associated with the Balkan front. Her approach to wartime service was typified by her formative years as a trainee doctor in Edinburgh and Glasgow. According to her biographer, repeated clashes with the male-dominated medical establishment and experience of practising in Scotland's most deprived working-class neighbourhoods had moulded her outlook into one of perpetual struggle against entrenched 'injustices'.³⁴ This was mainly reflected in her attitude towards poverty and illness among women, paralleling Stobart's views on war as a civilizational affliction necessitating intervention on behalf of its victims. Leah Leneman describes Inglis's political values as a mixture of 'Victorian virtues', Christian morality and suffragist dogma, reflected in the SWH's rigid hierarchy and 'austere military-styled uniforms'.³⁵ Like Stobart, her views on female-led humanitarian relief conjoined with a belief that social change could be achieved by having its advocates accrue patriotic credentials and aptitudes beyond regular 'peacetime' requirements. In Inglis's case, this would mean widening employment opportunities for women in medicine.

Continuity with pre-war travel writers was still evident in the public perception of wartime volunteers, where an idiosyncratic personality and lifestyle often played a salient role in soliciting public interest. Flora Sandes, whose recruitment into the Serbian army in 1915, was the preeminent example of this, garnering domestic fame as the only British woman known to have officially served as a frontline combatant. 'I seem to have just naturally drifted, by successive stages, from a nurse to a soldier', she blithely recalled in her autobiography, 'and for seven years lived practically a man's life'.³⁶ Rather than politics, Julie Wheelwright observes that Sandes's motives stemmed from social frustration, unable to join 'her male counterparts in the pursuit of life beyond the stifling confines of Edwardian Britain'.³⁷ In contrast to her peers who viewed their work as a wartime extension of the feminine sphere, Sandes's embrace of an active combat role, that saw her promoted to the rank of sergeant major after being wounded by a Bulgarian hand-grenade in 1916, symbolized the culmination of her desire to overcome these social limitations.³⁸

Like Inglis, MacPhail represented another personality drawn to overseas relief work through her dissatisfaction over employment rights.³⁹ However, she was equally unique in her continued engagement with South Slavic peasant communities following the war, with her priorities and immediate allegiances undergoing a partial metamorphosis from 1915 to 1918. Working among the peasantry, notably children, fostered a growing emotional and personal bond through which she came to associate with the Serbian, and later Yugoslav, national cause.⁴⁰ While Sandes represented a dramatic departure from accepted British feminine norms, the 'naturally pacifistic' MacPhail exemplified the wartime humanitarian ethos when separated from an overt political subtext. Her aversion to militaristic structures was demonstrated by her gravitating towards caring almost exclusively for civilians from late 1915. She subsequently made the unusual decision to remain in Yugoslavia after 1918, where she founded an 'Anglo-Yugoslav' paediatric ward in Belgrade.[41] The Serbs, she was later recorded as saying, were not 'wild savages as people had imagined', a dramatic volte-face to her stated motivations in 1914.[42]

Despite a multitude of privations and life-endangering risks, wartime Serbia proved ideal for those seeking personal or professional fulfilment. Free from 'rigid conventions', foreign women could be found 'carrying out complicated surgery and running entire hospitals and ambulance columns'.[43] Tangentially, volunteer leaders often found themselves exercising almost unprecedented influence and responsibility.[44] Dr Eleanor Soltau, who had been tasked with leading the first SWH mission to Serbia in December 1914, for instance, came to assume control over anti-typhus measures in the southern Serbian city of Kragujevac's surrounding rural districts.[45] Recurrent shortages in the number of trained medical staff also found volunteers undertaking responsibilities far exceeding the proficiencies of their training. Additionally, the epidemic and military evacuation in 1915, granted them a collective stake in British narratives of wartime heroism, turning the Balkan front into an informal space of resistance to traditional understandings of female subordination.[46]

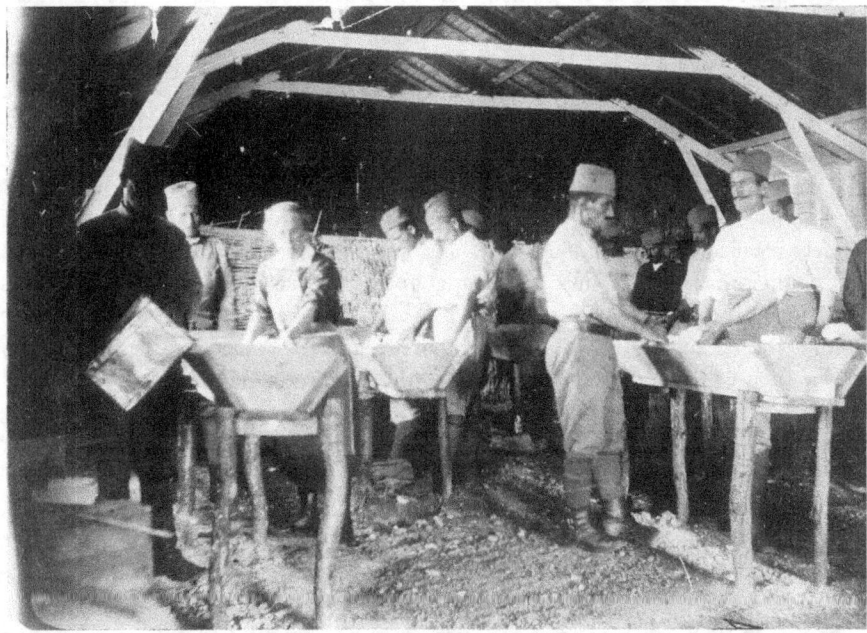

Figure 3 Miss Alice Tebbutt and members of the Serbian Army at large troughs or basins, Serbia, c. 1914–1915. © Courtesy of Imperial War Museum.

Romanticized depictions of female volunteers also brought the plight of Serbia's populace to the attention of the wider British public, integrating the existing victimhood narrative into the wartime context while allegorizing the country as partly akin to that of a sickly, impoverished child. The humanitarian activist Francesca Wilson described Serb amputees and convalescents evacuated to Egypt as having been 'child-like' in their bravery and cheerfulness, eager for the educational activities offered by relief organizations as preparation for their post-war return to civilian life. This was juxtaposed, however, with a quiescent despondency that their 'mother' Serbia lay under foreign occupation.[47] By 1916, such imagery coalesced around the caricature of the peasant-soldier – mobilized in the defence, and later reclamation, of his homeland – mirroring Belgium as a wartime casus belli and the Serbian populace's seemingly collective defiance. In contrast to Austria-Hungary or Germany, wrote Ellen Davies, a nursing volunteer in the SRF, 'the army is the people and every man is a born soldier'. Even the most indolent or pacifistic peasant marched willingly into battle for his country as if protecting a woman's honour.[48]

Certain cultural attitudes did merit occasional concern. Douglas Walshe, a British military transport officer, had found the Serb's patriarchal attitudes 'rather offensive to our ideas'. However, one 'never heard the least whisper of trouble with the women in the [Macedonian] villages': Serbs were 'a surprisingly moral race on Active Service'.[49] Indeed, female doctors even presented their status as caregivers as comparable to those of relatives with the Serbs typically referring to them as 'sestre' (sisters), or 'Maika' (mother) in Stobart's case.[50] As one of Soltau's associates opined:

> First, these simple peasant lads respect women, especially the mother figure, which, of course, given the special circumstances, we were. Second, they preferred us to the army doctors – they claimed that women surgeons were more gentle, never rough, and generally more tender and patient. After all, most women are, aren't they?[51]

This gendered contingency also received validation from Sandes who pointed out that peasant girls had been fighting in the Serbian and Montenegrin armies since 1912, usually making only token efforts to disguise themselves as men. One had even been serving in Sandes's regiment at the time of her recruitment. For the average Serb 'there was nothing particularly strange about a woman joining up.'[52]

For the public, Britain's humanitarian presence was the primary conduit through which the Balkans became a wartime showcase for Anglo-Britishness as a force of moral compassion. Nevertheless, this popular interest was mainly attributable to its uniqueness as a military theatre defined through the activities of female non-combatants. It also exemplified the war's placation of pre-existing domestic issues: despite drawing widespread praise, female volunteers' hopes of professional parity with their male counterparts remained as distant in 1918 as they had been in 1914.[53] Even individualized rebellions, such as Sandes, were 'unconnected to a broader social analysis of gender inequalities' in the minds of the general public.[54] The volunteer presence was therefore equally revealing of the transnational limitations of direct engagement, buoyed, as it was, by wartime propaganda.

Forgotten alliances at war

At the beginning of October 1915, Britain and France, facing the impending collapse of the Entente's Gallipoli campaign and the dismal prospect of a grinding and bloody stalemate on the Western Front, began deploying a vast expeditionary force in the Aegean port of Thessaloniki, Greece's most prized territorial acquisition from the Balkan Wars.[55] The initial aims of the 60,000-strong 'British Salonika Forces' (BSF), which included evacuees from Gallipoli, had been to provide strategic relief to the beleaguered Serbian army and deter the Bulgarians from advancing into then neutral Greece.[56] While Serbia's occupation abrogated the first objective, Britain's standing and commitments as a leading member of the Triple Entente inhibited London from redeploying its forces to other fronts.[57]

In contrast to the humanitarian relief missions, the wartime experiences of British military personnel in what was soon designated the 'Macedonian Campaign' remains largely overlooked outside of military history.[58] This itself reflects the First World War's somewhat limited place in British popular memory as 'an imagined space in France and Flanders'.[59] Lack of interest may also be attributed to contemporary perceptions of the French-led campaign as merely a 'sideshow' to the Western Front.[60] A persistent shortage of supplies, faulty or low-quality field equipment and inconsistent and disorganized tactical planning critically diminished the BSF's operational effectiveness. The only two major British-led offensives against Bulgarian positions near Lake Dojran in south-east Macedonia, both resulted in heavy casualties and ignominious defeat.[61] This abysmal campaign record was compounded by a near constant loss of manpower to various tropical diseases and environmental hazards. Rampant malaria proved particularly devastating, with a recorded infection rate of 75 per cent among British forces.[62]

From an imagological perspective, Michail contests that BSF personnel contributed little to Britain's evolving image of the Balkans. Unlike their counterparts in the relief missions, the number of veterans' accounts that reached publication was comparatively small, with most only appearing after 1918 and typically reflected the experiences of officers and administrative staff. This is compounded by the content of diaries and correspondence produced by rank-and-file soldiers on active service, which tended to be more concerned with complaining about illness, hygiene, the weather, inadequate rations, their living arrangements and conditions at the front, with only occasional observations on Thessaloniki or local flora and fauna.[63] In retrospect, BSF veterans could find comfort in knowing that they had been spared the horrors of the Western Front: when fighting in the remote mountainous terrain of the south Macedonian borderlands, as one Anglo-Greek military surgeon later remarked, ordnance and machine guns posed less of a threat to infantry while the topography rendered chemical weapons virtually useless.[64]

However, oppressive boredom, the desultory ambience and lengthy periods of military inaction, stemming from political indecision in London and Paris, led many soldiers to conclude that they had been denied the purported glory of having served on the Western Front. Later accounts recast this criticism as the British public's own wilful denial of the BSF's 'valid' sacrifices in the emerging post-war mythos.[65]

Although spared the worst excesses of industrialized trench warfare, Macedonia still presented the average BSF infantryman with myriad environmental dangers. Disease soon became a fact of everyday life, however, the greater risks, according to one nurse, were psychological, manifesting as a form of extreme neurosis dubbed 'the Balkan tap'. After three years of 'the same revolting food', 'the same dreary' mountain scenery and enduring the adverse after-effects of anti-malarial quinine issued to all personnel, the greatest surprise was how rare reported incidents of suicide had been.[66] The landscape, climate and even the local population intermingled into a singular context of boredom and discomfort that easily translated into indifference or even contempt for 'all the Balkan people'.[67] Popular depictions back in Britain exacerbated this antipathy and frustration, with the Macedonian Campaign often derided as an unnecessary drain on valuable military resources. 'If you want a holiday go to Salonika', ran a popular music-hall act at the time.[68]

Another point of contrast with the volunteers were the operational restrictions which, it was claimed, limited the BSF's ability to coordinate with most of its allies – specifically the reconstituted Serbian army following its redeployment to Thessaloniki in May 1916. The journalist Harry Owen, who edited the force's wartime newspaper, *The Balkan News*, lamented that the positioning of the Entente's main encampments had placed the French between the BSF and the Serbs.[69] Such frustrations were apparently reciprocated. Henry Fitch, a liaison officer at the Serbian headquarters, routinely

Figure 4 Serbian infantry marching to their camp at Mikra near Salonika (Thessaloniki) following the voyage from Corfu, 1916. © Courtesy of Imperial War Museum.

reported on the mounting anger towards the intransigence of the campaign's French commanders in their unwillingness to commit to a general offensive. 'And I don't blame them', he remarked in 1917.[70] Nevertheless, restrictions did not entail a complete absence of interaction. Outside of the main encampments, British and Serbian non-combat personnel routinely exchanged logistical, engineering and technical support, as shown in their joint management of the BSF Motorized Transport Unit as well as joint-police patrols, training exercises and periods of leave in Thessaloniki.[71] As a consequence, the dichotomy in how Britain's humanitarian and military missions were perceived, reinforced by accounts from ex-auxiliaries, further promulgated the Serb peasant-soldier as one of the campaign's defining motifs.

Although mostly absent in popular British travel literature, at an official level, one of the few overtly racialized forms of categorizing the South Slavic peoples lay in the assumption, originating in the 1850s, that they possessed a natural disposition for war. Seeking comparisons with the British Empire's own recruitment methods, observers in the latter half of the nineteenth century drew on 'martial races theory'[72] as a theoretical standard for evaluating different ethnic groups within the Habsburg and Ottoman Empires and later the independent Balkans. Montenegro's mountaineer tribes and the Croat and Serb regimental communities utilized in the defence of the Habsburg Military Frontier[73] had been a particular focus, being assessed as socially and racially conditioned for war through assumedly 'ancient' patrilineal family and clan structures.[74] In July 1914, this militaristic paradigm was seemingly still in evidence. In an interview with an American diplomat a few days prior to Austria-Hungary's first attempted invasion, the British military attaché in Belgrade confidently predicted, having observed the Serbian army first-hand during the Balkan Wars, that the Monarchy's forces would be repulsed without the assistance of Russia. Despite a paucity of equipment, weapons and ammunition, its peasant conscripts were near-perfect soldiers, able to live on 'next to nothing' and – like the British – in possession of 'a fund of common sense', frequently conducting field operations without officers.[75]

The motif of the Serb peasant-soldier might therefore be viewed as the perpetuation of a colonial stereotype within a non-colonial context. As Goldsworthy contests, its appearance in wartime British propaganda was a crucial point of divergence, further exemplifying how specific circumstances tended to exert greater influence than long-term preconceptions.[76] While not immediately apparent in late 1914, the First World War gradually reorganized British economic and civil life to serve a common goal: maintaining the country's military strength in the pursuit of victory. As earlier notions of a short, decisive conflict faded, meeting this objective through national mobilization overshadowed virtually all other concerns; duty and unity were elevated as societal ideals while the war itself was increasingly construed as a morally virtuous crusade with the British private, or 'Tommy', embodying a form of heroic masculinity.[77] The Macedonian Campaign and derisive public perceptions of BSF troops as parasitic idlers contravened this narrative, however. In lieu of a suitable British military presence, propagandistic energies were instead projected onto the Serbs whose hard-won victories in 1914, and the humanitarian tragedies of 1915, deemed them worthy of public adulation. Innate martial qualities were reinterpreted as features of a positive militarism commensurate to a shared Anglo-Serbian moral essence that reached beyond racial and cultural differences. Serbia's perceived culture of military stoicism, attributed to it being 'a peasant nation', evoked Britain's own innate sense agrarian virtuousness with the peasant-soldiers' 'simple love' of country, and cheerful willingness to endure privation and hardships, mirroring the image of the genial Tommy manning his trench on the Western Front.[78]

These qualities were presented as a composite of 'heroic' peasant idiosyncrasies and noted as being instrumental in the success of the Serbian-led 'Monastir Offensive' that retook Bitola in December 1916, the Entente's only significant military accomplishment in Macedonia prior to the Franco-Serbian-led 'Vardar Offensive' in September 1918.[79] Reports on air raids against Entente positions also referred to a propensity among Serbs on sentry duty to stand and shoot at aircraft during raids, with complete disregard for personal safety – traits described as ubiquitous among the region's Slavs.[80] Neither had the Serbian leadership been unaware of these admiring cultural perceptions; Serb generals boasted that the peasants' 'love for the Fatherland' guaranteed them an army that was always ready to fight at the shortest notice.[81] Even defeat in 1915, Fitch later claimed, had failed to dent an innate racial audacity for exaggeration:

> 'Why?' said a high Serbian officer to me, 'Why do you English and French fight in trenches? We Serbs don't fight in trenches, we attack all the time. If our enemy builds a trench we throw him out. If the Serbian army had landed on Gallipoli,' he added, 'we'd have been in Constantinople in three weeks'.[82]

Reconceiving the Serb peasant as a dauntless fighter and valued comrade did not necessarily negate earlier racial or cultural pejoratives. Walshe dismissed a 'circulating' caricature of the Serbs as a 'vengeful' people. Indeed, their treatment of Bulgarian POWs had, in certain respects, been superior to the other Entente armies, providing their captives with rations and accommodation identical to their own and even inviting them to partake in Orthodox holiday celebrations.[83] Nevertheless, like other such shifts, the adoption of positive militarist sentiments was neither consistent, nor universally shared. 'Undying enmity rules here', commented one SWH volunteer who accompanied the Serbian army during the advance on Bitola; the Serbs were recorded as being 'in a dangerous mood' with their planned engagement of the Bulgarians appearing to presage a 'racial fight' driven by a desire for revenge.[84] This impulse was reiterated in a less-sanitized account (that only appeared in the late 1930s) by an 'unprofessional soldier' who described a disturbing discovery shortly after crossing the, by then, deserted Bulgarian positions during the Vardar Offensive:

> The conduct of our fellows was exemplary but not so some of our allies. We soon came upon grim evidence of this, in the shape of blackened Bulgar corpses at an abandoned hospital. All of them were sitting up in their beds and rotting. Someone had got there before we did [. . .] (The Serbian Army was ahead of them.)[85]

Despite fewer opportunities for engagement, like their civilian counterparts the men of the BSF played an integral role in recalibrating the region's image through their own – unjustly maligned – characterization in British wartime cultural discourse. This provided a defining point of contrast with representations of the Serbs whose peasant rank and file emerged as a unitary body driven by a noble desire to reclaim their homeland. Whereas the Edwardian travellers had typically presented rural South Slavs as mostly passive, semi-ornamental figures, their wartime exploits resituated them at the centre of their respective national narratives.[86]

Peasant society in war and exile

The sheer scale of Britain's involvement in the wartime Balkans filtered the region's, specifically Serbia's, image through decidedly more intimate forms of engagement, largely removed from the alienating ambiguousness of political discourses. Depictions of volunteers working to relieve the afflictions of sick or wounded Serb soldiers during the typhus epidemic in particular, cultivated an empathetic link with circumstances on the Western Front.[87] Conversely, this sympathetic national portrait only gained traction in the public sphere as the epidemic started to abate from April 1915. Although localized outbreaks posed an occasional threat, many aid workers who had arrived in the country expecting a perpetual state of emergency and frenzied action suddenly found themselves 'surplus to requirement'.[88] Indeed, the delayed coverage in the British press 'months' after the infection rate had been brought fully under control, suddenly created problems of overstaffing as relief units became inundated with 'shoals of devoted Englishwomen . . . ready to risk their lives in a danger which no longer existed'.[89] Looking to alleviate the tedium of this 'waiting time', some volunteers seized the opportunity to better acquaint themselves with the local culture, allowing for a far wider cross-section of British society to gain first-hand experiences of regional life, previously restricted to mostly affluent tourists and diplomatic staff.[90]

Hammond postulates that this absence of conflicting political or foreign policy questions granted more visibility to areas of peasant life of which Britons were more inclined to approve. What Victorian-era diplomats and travellers had previously perceived as cultural backwardness now signified 'spiritual depth', with the Serbs essentialized as a naturally 'congenial' people, embodying all the positive virtues once associated with the Ottomans. The family-oriented village communities, among whom many volunteers worked, were extolled for their apparent disinterest in material possessions and semi-spiritual attachment to their land.[91] As already stated, this representational volte-face was itself the amplification of an established drift away from nineteenth-century pejoratives. The First World War served to further legitimize the bracketing of peasant customs into a perceived era of pre-industrial innocence. For the Red Cross doctor, Claude Askew, a lack of modernity meant 'the conditions of life in Serbia' resembled a societal 'ideal' that guaranteed a sustainable quality of life for that 'essential social element' – the peasantry. Echoing Edwardian-era accounts, limited urbanization and a preference for communal life meant a 'natural' absence of poverty and an organic stability.[92]

Similar to previous British visitors, wartime authors tended to invest the figure of the peasant with qualities derived from 'a distinct strain of [rural] Englishness' or 'the noble simplicity' projected onto the Celtic nations. Such romantic poeticism was also evident, albeit considerably rarer, among BSF personnel. In a series of articles for *The Balkan News*, one 'Private H. Sinclair' described the ritualized customs of Macedonian Slav peasants as akin to those he had witnessed in 'the remotest parts' of the Scottish Highlands and Outer Hebrides. Rather than symbolizing cultural alienation, Sinclair interpreted such practices as reflective of a universal human desire to rationalize the mysteries of the divine:

> 'East and West', thought I, yet how much akin! Children groping in the darkness for that which we know lies beyond. And for that instinct I thanked God.[93]

As the Entente's principal regional ally, this positive revaluation was typified by the conflation of 'Balkan' with 'Serbian'. Through the various memoirs and published journals that had started appearing in 1916, a more coherent image of the peasant was increasingly presented to the public. In both military and civilian life, Serbia's 'sons of the soil' possessed a range of qualities applicable to a mythic golden age of (mostly) English rural tradition, the ideal of which could even be discerned in the country's landscape.[94] Comparisons to Britain's Celtic heritage also remained in evidence alongside equally patronizing personal descriptions; one SRF nurse, for instance, likened the solemnity of the Serb soldiers' 'lovely voices' to the Welsh.[95] The long established Irish paradigm also continued to find cultural purchase:

> They are like the Irish in their gaiety, their depression, their mercurial temperament; tears and smiles all a-bubble; and in their carelessness of money, a real heart-free neglect of it when they have the necessaries.[96]

Life among the Serbian peasantry also strengthened, increasingly positive, impressions of an otherness separate from European modernity. One Red Cross nurse, who had previously served with the Greek army during the Balkan Wars, observed that, prior to October 1915, aid work in Serbia might have validated earlier public assumptions that war tended to exist in parallel to wider civil society. Even at the height of the epidemic, civilian life south of the front lines 'went on as normal'. Complaints about food, inactivity and the monotony of routine tended to dominate the average volunteer's experience as much as those of BSF personnel.[97] Even among those Britons who remained in Serbia following the occupation, the rural-urban divide even appeared to dictate responses to the new Austro-Hungarian military authorities. For the peasantry, occupation seemed little more than a perfunctory transition between near identical sets of governing social strata. Peasants, Davies observed, did not seem 'to feel the incongruity' of being under the dominion of the Habsburg army: 'it is "the Government" and that explains everything.' The installation of Bosnian Serbs in administrative positions made it seem all the more congenial while, aside from their uniforms, the manner and attitude of the 'Hungarian' rank and file were practically identical to that of the Serbs.[98]

As with organized opinion before 1912, wartime representations were quickly consolidated into a hierarchy of articulation that amplified certain individuals whose experiences conveyed a sense of intellectual authority, or eccentricity.⁹⁹ Nevertheless, this pre-existing pattern was quickly subsumed and modified within the context of the war. The artists Jan and Cora Gordon, who initially worked as part of a Red Cross unit organized by James and May Berry, exemplified this, eschewing pseudo-anthropology and partisan political commentary in favour of ironic humour and an astue sense of realism. Two subsequent accounts – *The Luck of Thirteen* (1916), detailing the less edifying realities of relief work and the human tragedy of the Serbian army's retreat through Montenegro, and *A Balkan Freebooter* (1916), the biography of a former Serb brigand interviewed by the Gordons, subverted previous modes of representation by forming their narratives around individual encounters.¹⁰⁰ This more intimate style amplified their writings' wartime significance. Initial public awareness of the extent of the retreat's death toll and the plight of Serb refugees, for example, originally came from material Jan Gordon submitted to *The Illustrated London News* that was then published in December 1915.¹⁰¹

The most significant point of representational divergence, itself linked to the shifting impressions of Serbian militarism, manifested in the gradual, and inconsistent, recalibration of the peasant's ascribed role as the social arbiter around which Serbia's political, as well as cultural, life revolved. Published accounts typically attributed Serbian military resistance to its 'thoroughly democratic' peasant society's lack of ingrained class division. A wealthier peasant may have possessed greater land and property holdings, yet his dress, mannerisms, habits and lifestyle would still be identical to his less affluent neighbours'. The Berry's described this as manifesting through a general indifference to social stratification that neutered the corrupting excesses of the modern state. Even among the elites, Western civilization was only 'skin-deep . . . many of them remained, in habit of mind, peasants'. A high-ranking general staying at their hospital, for instance, had elected to share his meagre living quarters with his daughter, as would 'a small farmer', despite there being no shortage of spare rooms.¹⁰² Correspondingly, Field Marshal Živojin Mišić, who commanded Serbia's forces during Kolubara and the Vardar Campaign, could have been mistaken for an 'elderly farmer' rather than a member of Entente High Command. When Owen attempted to interview Mišić's associate, Stepa Stepanović, he was shocked to discover that the former Minister of War spoke no foreign languages and nearly always wore a private's uniform, seemingly confirming '[h]ow much Serbs are a peasant race'.¹⁰³ This 'primitive habit of life' persisted as much within the country's political administration. Berry recounted rumours of older deputies in the *skupština* remaining illiterate, even after being elected, while civil administrators approached their duties with the insouciance of subsistence farmers.¹⁰⁴

Traditions, habits and virtues perceived as instinctive among the peasantry were framed as the guiding principles of their leaders. Within these positive revaluations, the Karađorđević monarchy, previously associated with the 1903 coup, enjoyed a reversal in its public image, as the recalibrated political manifestation of Serbia's national (peasant) spirit. Reports of King Petar picking up a soldier's rifle to fire on enemy positions during a visit to the front lines in 1915, for example, were equated with a peasant-doggedness that had repulsed the numerically superior Habsburg forces the previous year.¹⁰⁵ As the war progressed, however, the ageing Petar's leadership role was conferred onto his heir, Crown Prince Aleksandar, who had assumed most of his father's duties as Serbia's commander-in-chief in June 1914. In contrast to other wartime leaders, his record of recent military service and reputation as an active field commander projected the persona of 'warrior-king', thematically tying him to popular depictions of his obstinate peasant-soldiers. Moreover, admiration for his personal conduct – sharing in the 'Spartan lifestyle' of his men – upheld notions of a genuine national bond forged in the absence of a social class hierarchy.¹⁰⁶

Nevertheless, the Crown Prince's aloofness also set him apart from his compatriots. Owen remarked that even those with regular access knew little about Serbian heir apparent, who, from May 1916, spent most of his time at the front. This air of mystery granted him a sense of seriousness and maturity, whose declarative style of speech and frequent visits to convalescing soldiers conveyed a mixture of caring patriarch and responsible patrician.¹⁰⁷

Continuing the discursive retreat from negative stereotypes, the consolidation of the peasantry's social function also prompted a more concerted re-evaluation of the Balkans' more egregious cultural associations. Earlier perceptions of a culture permeated by violence were challenged as historically disingenuous, with volunteers asserting that brigandage and other such practices had been overstated by an uniformed British press.¹⁰⁸ Even those less enamoured with Serbian peasant life could discern a sense of poetic nobility in such traditions. *Balkan Freebooter* exemplifies this, with the Gordons presenting the protagonist's turn to banditry as born of the historical expediencies of Ottoman repression.¹⁰⁹

Direct engagement in peasant culture often served as a reflection of the immediate concerns and preoccupations of the British participants; unsurprisingly, eating and drinking, a universal theme in war literature, was a recurrent motif. Serbian 'Slavae' (*Slave*)¹¹⁰ and other 'prasnici' (holidays) soon became associated with lavish feasts that appeared 'from nowhere including clean cutlery and plates'.¹¹¹ When framed against the peasantry's seemingly limitless hospitality ('the most commendable of Oriental virtues') and the religious connotations surrounding such events, wartime Serbia's apparent abundance of food appeared comparable to an innocuous love of life's 'wholesome pleasures' and virtuous appreciation of seasonal produce popularly associated with 'old England'.¹¹² Invitations to participate in these celebrations furthered an underlying theme of cultural inclusivity, manifesting as a shared affinity between the Serbian present and an Edwardian cultural impulse to recapture the agrarian past. Female volunteers talked emphatically about dancing the *kolo*,¹¹³ interpreted as both ingratiation into the host culture and a metaphorical return to imagined rural origins.¹¹⁴

Deviations from this ambient communalism could incur criticism. One nurse recalled that the only time she ever felt contempt had been the sight of 'a fat prosperous-looking refugee' during the retreat who refused to share his abundant rations with three starving soldiers.¹¹⁵ Such disparities seemed equally apparent for those who remained in occupied Serbia. In contrast to the peasantry's quiet resignation, Davies remarked that 'the educated classes writhe under it', having been stripped of their privileges and placed under official suspicion as nationalist

Figure 5 British officer and Dr Katherine Stewart MacPhail of the Scottish Women's Hospital dancing the *Kolo* (the Serbian National Dance) at a Serbian Slava or regimental festival at Salonika, 1916. © Courtesy of Imperial War Museum.

agitators.[116] This perceived detachment from civilization was also construed as a moral carapace against modernity's less desirable influences. Following the Bolshevik seizure of power in Russia's October Revolution, one BSF chaplain opined that the Serbs would never resort to such a dramatic course of action. The utopia 'Mr Marx preached to the urban mass' had long since been achieved in the peasant village, 'without bloodshed'.[117]

Village or familial communalism was presented as defining the national psyche, with the Serb peasant conducting himself in war 'as he would in life', boasting of his nation, but regarding himself to be of little consequence. This was mirrored in his treatment of enemies, where hatred of an opposing country never translated into animosity for its people. In contrast, Berry described Habsburg POWs as a mixture of 'sheep and heroes' who followed orders without holding any passion or belief in the Austro-Hungarian cause.[118] While the Serb's had been compelled to defend a sense of national identity that rested on the 'living influences' of 'ancestors' and 'national heroes', the largely 'Croat' rank and file lacked any impetus to fight or appeared unwilling accessories in a punitive campaign against a people similar to their own.[119] Linguistic reciprocity and the assumption of shared rural traditions also saw non-Serbs portrayed as occupying the same broad peasant cultural milieu. 'Austrian' prisoners, many of whom were noted as being virtually 'identical' to Serbs in language, 'manner and custom', were often deemed exonerated through their recruitment as hospital orderlies.[120]

The veneer of Serbian cultural uniformity that initially greeted most volunteers, sequestered in Serbia's more ethnically homogeneous central and northern districts, found its antithesis further south. While passing through north-east Montenegro, the Gordons were bewildered to discover 'Turkish' shops whose 'turbaned-owners' sat cross-legged on the floor, 'but only spoke Serbian'.[121] A similar sense of dislocation was expressed by volunteers who discovered that Christian peasants often appeared to have more in common with Serbia's Albanian minority and Muslim 'Turks' than their own Orthodox Church.[122]

Such respect for peasant communal strength and preservation of tradition and heritage appeared to exert some influence in the otherwise disengaged memoirs of BSF personnel. On inspecting an 'abandoned' church during a patrol along Macedonia's 'Slav border', a former London infantryman recalled being humbled by the extent to which the peasants had gone to preserve the interior for their community's return. Reflecting on this episode '50 years or so' later, he considered this display of common humanity as leading him to rethink his initial animosities towards 'a front which nobody seemed to have heard of'.[123] However, attempting to establish any comprehensive impressions from among the BSF's rank and file, through memoirs often written decades after the war's conclusion, would be purely speculative. As the war progressed, British military commanders came to view the Balkans as more of a naval waypoint between the Western and Middle Eastern theatres, stymieing any deeper sense of empathy among a British force that was increasingly deployed on a temporary basis.[124]

Alongside the appearance of the peasant-soldier motif, the most notable outcome of these shifting wartime discourses was the appearance of a secondary caricature in the pre-existing victimhood narrative: the peasant exile. This was mostly established by those Britons who participated in the retreat, recounting harrowing scenes of death, starvation and widespread misery that were often infused with biblical or mythological allusions. *The Illustrated London News* highlighted descriptions of the refugee columns in Montenegro, with Jan Gordon having likened them to '[a] living snake with heads for scales'.[125] William Smith, a volunteer in the SWH, related an equally apocalyptic vision during the evacuation of Kragujevac:

> The road was a moving mass of transport [...] men, women and children all intent on escape [...] This procession had been passing continuously for days [...] it was the passing of a whole nation into exile, a people leaving a lost country.[126]

Combined with the chaos of the retreat, the loss of the Serbian homeland appeared as a collective psychological and spiritual trauma, summarized by Stobart as 'the tragedy of a nation wrenched by the roots from nationhood'.[127] Serbia's geography itself was said to resemble a nightmarish dreamscape, its barren, 'tortured' appearance seemingly reflecting the populace's suffering, ominously framed by the invading Central Powers.[128] This, in turn, invoked the possibility of a double tragedy: death outside a homeland considered indivisible from the national body. Within days of the Serbian army's arrival on Corfu, Sandes recorded the lack of burial plots as the most pertinent source of anguish: 'The Serbs are not a maritime nation, the idea of a burial at sea is repugnant to them.'¹²⁹ MacPhail even advised the French authorities on Corsica to rehouse refugees in abandoned mountain villages. To the culturally land-bound Serbs, she later wrote, life on the coast was anathema, the open sea evoking a constant sense of dread and visible distress.¹³⁰

The impact of the retreat clarified the degree to which the peasant's image had evolved beyond that of distant victim. In the case of Serbia, and by later extension all Southern Slavs, rural communities existed as both the nexus and progenitor of national culture and identity. Marvelling at the 'little Serbia' peasant evacuees had created on Corsica, the anthropologist Olive Lodge discerned a historical capacity for such societies to cyclically revive 'that intangible something which makes a nation'.¹³¹ This cultural endurance appeared to exist in opposition to the transience of contemporary statehood. Describing how an influx of refugees into the Kosovan capital of Priština in November 1915 had devolved into rioting, the American journalist, Fortier Jones, mused at the fragility of modern state trappings: 'The Government was crumbling, a nation was dying, and all such superfluities as courts of justice and police were a thing of the past.'¹³²

Like his British counterparts, however, Jones stressed that the loss of such institutions was irrelevant as long as the Serbian nation endured via the innate robustness of the peasantry.¹³³ Likewise, British accounts invariably voiced their own conviction in the peasantry's indomitable spirit with the preservation of rural tradition as a guarantor of Serbia's eventual return to independence.¹³⁴

Figure 6 Unit of the Scottish Women's Hospital during the Serbian military retreat, 1915. © Courtesy of Imperial War Museum.

Figure 7 A dead Serbian soldier lying on the side of the road during the retreat to the Adriatic Sea coast, November to December 1915. © Courtesy of Imperial War Museum.

The British panacea?

While these direct experiences continued to undermine late-Victorian pejoratives, the First World War also exposed the limitations of this process. Ultimately, the significance of the Great War lay in the creation of a concrete link between the plight of the South Slavs, and British self-perceptions as the archetypical purveyors of modernity's more positive qualities, a dynamic still generally associated with the colonial civilizing mission. In the context of wartime service, this became synonymous with the implementation of Western medical hygiene and logistical standards.

Although Britain's military, and arguably humanitarian, contributions to the Balkan campaign had diminished in importance after 1915, British nationals continued to exhibit a tendency to characterize their work as conducive to that of beneficent modernizers. While the Serbs' wartime image as heroic victims certainly allotted them a place in the new moral hierarchy, it did not prevent their allies from identifying a plethora of cultural deficiencies, evocative of Western colonial mentalities. Concurrently, the redefining of local peasant culture into a distinctive Serbian identity was itself expressive of the early-nineteenth-century attitudes that had previously underlined official depictions of other regional peoples such as the Ionian Greeks or Montenegrins.[135]

The initial remit under which most relief volunteers arrived in Serbia saw much of their day-to-day perception formed via the prism of medicine and medical hygiene.

As with Stobart's call for women to confront militarism through relief work, the focus on disease prevention imbued discursive ephemera with the implicit understanding that Britons, in remedying shortfalls in local practices, were vicariously disseminating superior moral, as well as practical, standards. Allusions to religious symbolism, such as the sobriquet of 'English *sestre*', added a quasi-spiritual dimension to their roles as medical staff.[136] Volunteers from devout or proselytizing backgrounds even defined aid dispensation as a secular version of overseas missionary work, with success measured in the acceptance of Western hygiene practices and preventative measures.[137] The Hippocratic Oath and the medical profession itself were almost recast temporal virtues, transcending the boundaries of nationality, language or ideology. Dearmer, who had volunteered to work in Serbia as an SRF medical orderly in early 1915, in spite of her stated apathy, disclosed that the head doctor of the 'Serbian hospital' in Kragujevac, where she had been assigned, was in fact an Austrian POW. Wartime political allegiances had 'never stopped his work of saving life – first as an officer of his own army, then as a doctor among the Serbs'.[138]

The initial preponderance of female volunteers was central to this moralistic subtext, finding an ideological genesis in the more esoteric currents of the suffrage movement. By 1900, anxieties over civilization's decline were interpreted by social campaigners, such as Ellice Hopkins, as symptomatic of a corrosion in moral standards. According to Hopkins, the duty of upper-class British women was to lead 'the crusade for restoring morality to the world' by pursuing sexual and political equality. In keeping with the intellectual inconsistencies of other late-Victorian and Edwardian movements, this was anchored in an earlier racialized belief that (Anglo-Saxon) femininity could be harnessed as a civilizing force.[139] Against this metric, societies such as Serbia's came to resemble something of a transitional phase. Cultural admiration for the village lifestyle and reverence for tradition was confounded by a lack or absence of the structures and amenities associated with Western modernity. Consequently, representations of the South Slavic Balkans continued to exist as a peripheral, albeit in closer proximity, to civilization's 'moral' Anglo-British centre.[140]

Direct involvement in an active war zone also afforded these women, and their marginalized male counterparts, a degree of cultural purchase in the crystallizing heroic narrative that soon defined the British war effort and provided the main ideological underpinnings for Anglo-British identity by 1918. Efforts to tackle typhus and other such diseases gave credence to this perception, characterizing aid work as an extension of the war, but waged against the 'enemy within'.[141] This was reinforced by the very real dangers volunteers increasingly faced. Writing in May 1915, Dearmer described how British nurses working in the hospitals surrounding Kragujevac had 'bathed and soaked in typhus' on a daily basis during the epidemic.[142] She herself died from typhoid fever less than two months later.[143]

Similarly, with the majority of British military forces concentrated in the malaria-infested Struma valley by 1917, many among the BSF's leadership came to view the Macedonian Campaign as a response to a series of medical emergencies. Under the command of officers drawn from the RAMC and Royal Engineers, entire infantry units were soon being redeployed to remote mountain districts and marshlands in order to implement anti-malarial initiatives. This often took the form of dramatic environmental measures including controlled 'prairie fires', rerouting rivers and streams and attempts at draining marshland in order to destroy mosquito breeding grounds.[144]

Indira Duraković argues that this insistence on disseminating Western medical and hygiene practices offers insight into continuing Balkanist narratives. Following the outbreak of the typhus epidemic, health experts classified the region as 'a menace to the health of the Western world . . . a synonym of death, starvation and disease'.[145] Enumerating the variety of diseases in early 1915, Berry mused that no other overseas posting could be 'so rich to the student in "interesting cases"':

> There were specimens of almost every known fever among the out-patients: measles, small-pox, scarlet fever, relapsing fever, malaria, typhus, diphtheria, whooping-cough, tuberculosis [. . .] All the terrible and often thought to be overdrawn pictures of the text books come to life. Neglected disease seldom seen at all in this country, [Britain], is there [Serbia] comparatively common.[146]

Generalizations concerning the Serbs' own 'crude' or 'medieval' attitudes towards sanitation were also prevalent, despite claims to the contrary.[147] Eyewitnesses related anecdotes of contaminated supplies, hospitals overcrowded beyond capacity and patients lying in garments 'foul and alive with vermin'.[148] Inadequate facilities and poor hygiene practices frequently obliged foreign staff to suspend all treatment while they worked to install 'disinfection plants': often rudimentary ovens used to 'bake' or 'boil' their patients' clothing as a basic means of sterilization.[149] This was compounded by reports that overcrowding and staffing shortages had caused conditions in wards to deteriorate to the point that patients regularly developed bed-sores from neglect.[150] Supply shortages and the stream of wounded soldiers presented the greatest challenge, becoming particularly acute as the conflict rapidly depleted Serbian medical strength, already diminished by the Balkan Wars.[151] Abraham's preliminary inspection of the Skopje military hospital in early 1915 illustrated this dire situation with the only visible staff having been a single Serbian medical officer:

> He was operating at great speed in a large out-patient department, surrounded by wounded, extracting bullets and pieces of shrapnel without any anaesthetic. We asked him why. He looked at us with lifted eyebrows. 'I haven't the time for anaesthetics,' he said in faltering German.[152]

The attitudes of the Serbs themselves were often deemed another obstacle to the British mission of instilling Western practices, especially in regard to hygiene. Outpatients who arrived at Berry's hospital would, according to the Gordons, often attempted to flee 'to avoid being doctored', especially when instructed to remove items of clothing.[153] Nurses based in military hospital wards were also prone to complain of the difficulties in maintaining (what they considered to be) a healthy atmosphere, against the Serbs' preference for unventilated buildings, where they could live 'in a good fug' of 'warmth and cigarette smoke'.[154] Serbian peasants inexplicably 'loathed, even feared, fresh air and ventilation', complained one SWH doctor. 'It was a constant struggle to keep the windows open to prevent the stuffiness they all loved.'[155] Nevertheless, by mid-1915,

British and other Western volunteers could observe a shift in peasant attitudes towards hygiene and sanitation. An American doctor noted, with satisfaction, that in their 'desire for communal preservation' village communities had started implementing their own 'crude and primitive' initiatives, such as constructing ovens for sterilizing clothing without having to first be instructed.[156]

The relief missions' success in subduing the typhus epidemic in six months was cited as affirmation of the irrefutable superiority of Western civilization.[157] In constructing a moral hierarchy with Britain at its head, these interpretations fed into the types of identity volunteers often assigned themselves in their own narratives. Stobart's efforts to alleviate suffering had, she later wrote, granted her the persona of crusader, maternal figurehead and military commander. These she ascribed to her empowered British femininity, a quality that had also guaranteed the survival of her entire party during the retreat.[158] Inglis and other prominent volunteers were equally adamant that only British women could demonstrate the inimitable sense of competence necessary to assist the Serbs.[159] Even Sandes, despite her unique position as an 'honouree Serb', stressed her Englishness as endowing her with an inherent moral virtue, extending 'to England's obligation to support the Serbs'.[160]

In the context of Britain's comparatively minor military role, veterans also looked to legitimize their presence by claiming an innate superiority over their allies. Owen argued that for all its squandered potential, the BSF had still left 'its mark' on the lives of Macedonia's inhabitants through infrastructural improvements and the spread of British cultural standards. Alongside roadbuilding, a 'straightforward' honesty and reputation for efficiency had made it the Entente's *Armée de Liaison* and standard-bearer for Western civility. Even the 'most mulish of the peasants – and they can be very mulish – began to realize that something new was abroad', Owen stated in 1919. After years of crisis, the average farmer came to realize that the presence of foreign troops did not always entail 'conquest, rape and looting'.[161]

Fraternization and cooperation with the multinational Entente forces also evinced a propensity to formulate cultural hierarchies of national character, as articulated by an anonymously-authored poem, appearing in *The Balkan News* in 1917, describing a joint military police patrol in Thessaloniki. Juxtaposed with the ostentatiousness and barely repressed excitability of his French, Greek and Italian colleagues, the British officer exudes natural confidence and authority in his simple khakis and equable demeanour. By contrast, his 'morose and moody' Serb compeer conveys even less natural authority, mirroring the 'booted Russian at his side'.[162]

Moral superiority was notably evident in the disdain often expressed towards the Serbian state and its representatives. The formulation of Serbia as a society of humble and honest peasants might itself be viewed as a partial response to the difficulties volunteers and military staff often faced when having to deal with Serbian (and Greek) officialdom. Systematic corruption was the most obvious point of criticism. Aid workers in Macedonia were reported to have regularly lodged complaints with the British and French authorities regarding the Serbian army's misappropriation of funds and supplies intended for refugees. This was compounded by an 'excruciating level of dishonesty' with promises 'made lightly without the slightest intention of keeping them'.[163] Berry even advised prospective volunteers to feign ignorance of the language or avoid officials altogether in the interests of expediency.[164] British accounts, Hammond notes, keenly stress their aid missions' autonomy from both the state and military authorities, despite many units having initially placed themselves under the purview of the government or Serbian Red Cross.[165] While female-run units could partly express this as symbolic of their gender's organizational and professional competency, expressions of managerial autonomy appeared interlinked with a latent suspicion of 'inferior' Balkan state structures.[166]

This also invited private and public criticism of the region's less reputable modern tendencies, notably nationalistic chauvinism. Following the recapture of Bitola, an SRF worker tasked with distributing aid to surrounding villages voiced disdain for the discrimination she encountered. The Serb corporal supervising her unit had insisted that Christian peasants receive preference over the 'Turks', of whom he was 'very scornful'.[167] Neither did engagement with rural communities completely ameliorate lingering negative preconceptions. Another relief worker who managed a refugee transit camp in Thessaloniki remarked that Serb refugees from Macedonia were 'for the most part I fancy minor officials'. In contrast to the 'blameless peasants' who had fled from Serbia proper, the former were no doubt escaping 'the vengeance of the Bulgarian population they had been oppressing!'[168] Even assertively pro-Serb voices were not inattentive to ulterior motives. Sandes observed that her recruitment into the army was as much a question of propaganda as it was the alleviation of personnel shortages. An upper-class British woman in a Serb regiment could be perceived as linking Serbia's wartime struggle to the wider Entente cause and serve as a pliable totem for attracting international sympathy, in the absence of tangible military aid.[169] A 'young Greek' who had also attempted to enlist at the same time had been rejected with the Serbian commandant stating that he 'would have no foreigners'.[170]

Neither were the peasants entirely beyond reproach. For all their vaunted courage in battle, among volunteers stationed in Thessaloniki Serb soldiers shared a reputation with the Greeks for being 'lazy', 'disorganized' and 'unscrupulous'.[171] Less critical voices also remarked that their predilection for lying or exaggeration could be interpreted as another unfortunate vestige of Ottoman rule.[172] Ernest Troubridge, who had commanded a token British naval detachment on the Danube, ranted in his journal of 'Slav incompetence', laziness and disorganization on receiving word of the government's plans to evacuate Belgrade in October 1915: 'It seems to me all are tired of effort, like all Slavs.' This, he further postulated, may have also signified a 'traitorous' desire to 'resume their normal Slav existence of idleness, plotting and dreaming while the virile Teuton colonises the country, bringing prosperity in his train'.[173] Accounts by BSF veterans offered equally unedifying portraits of the Macedonian peasantry, whose cultural and linguistic associations with Bulgaria inevitably aroused suspicion. Lake and Owen, for instance, attributed the success of German aerial bombing raids to information supplied by local peasants, influenced by Bulgarian nationalism and German promises 'which take form and substance in tangible rewards'.[174]

In this regard, the motif of the civilizing mission became interlinked with Britain's military intervention as a campaign to remove seditious external influences, specifically the Germans.[175] As one Red Cross nurse wrote, hostility was never expressed towards Austrian orderlies – 'that was reserved for the Germans'.[176] Military reports and testimonies from BSF soldiers also intoned this sentiment in the case of the Bulgarians. According to Ernest Jones, a former BSF infantryman, Bulgarian patrols were 'always commanded' by Germans who were rumoured to recruit from among the local peasantry. Recalling the ways in which these officers behaved, Jones mused that the former could have been mistaken for a German 'Foreign Legion' rather than a mutual ally.[177]

Such shortcomings, however, were easily dismissed as remnants of the Ottoman legacy or attributed to the faults of 'all young races'. Davies admonished her fellow volunteers who complained of undesirable working conditions, noting that Serbia was not to be judged against 'British standards' as these were 'inappropriate' for meeting the social needs of an agricultural society.[178] In some instances, perceived failings or weaknesses in the modern British character could be juxtaposed with that of the Serb peasant. Writing to the US chargé d'affaires in Sofia, Paget, who had been imprisoned by the Bulgarians following Serbia's occupation, spoke of her shame at the lack of decorum among the British POWs whom she had been permitted to visit. Their captors had even complained to her of laziness, fights, drunkenness and 'brazen demands' for better rations over the 'Spartan diet' that sustained the Serbian prisoners who bore their misfortune stoically 'without complaint'.[179]

Even in the war's aftermath, the idea of a civilizing mission in the Balkans retained a degree of influence over the popular imagination. Written by two BSF veterans, *Macedonia, a Plea for the Primitive* (1921) reiterated numerous pre-war tropes, theorizing that the territory had 'degenerated' from the glories of ancient Macedon to 'a vassal State with a hybrid population', echoing Brailsford's earlier claims of an isolation born of cultural inertia and religious fatalism.[180] Nowhere was this more evident than the native peasantry: 'the living negation of the aphorism "Tempora mutantur, nos et mutamur in illis" [Time changes and we change with them]'.[181] For Lake, Macedonia appeared ripe for a new kind of civilizing mission. If any lessons were to be learned from an 'unprofitable adventure' deemed 'unimportant by the British public', it was 'not unimportant that a fertile land should lie waste and be desolate'. The peasants, being 'so poor and depressed', were unlikely to help themselves. Yet, with Western aid, science and even emigration:

> a new Macedonia could be created [. . .] the present inhabitants learning in time that after all there is comfort in cleanliness, that it is not necessary to be ugly, and that an upstanding, well-built house is a better habitation than a hovel with mud-plastered walls.[182]

Conclusion

In terms of scale, the First World War remains a singularly unique historical moment in Anglo-Balkan relations. Rather than merely breaking with existing trends, experience of the wartime South Slavic Balkans brought about their culmination in bringing the peasantry into the immediate orbit of British public discourse. As illustrated by Inglis, MacPhail, Sandes and certain BSF personnel, alleviating or highlighting the plight of refugees, undertaking developmental work or confronting a perceived German insidiousness validated a British sense of place as a force for moral order.

The drift towards this representational apex further dismantled Edwardian cultural barriers by raising the imaginative status of the peasantry beyond that of mere victim. As the Serbian army crossed Greece's northern frontier in September 1918, the peasants who comprised its ranks, and those who had fled overseas as refugees, returned as arbiters of their nation's cultural and social identity. In conflating the Serb national movement with the virtuousness of peasant suffering and military defiance, the war also ameliorated any negative connotations once associated with it. This valorization of the Serbian peasant-soldier, mediated through the experiences of a mostly female humanitarian presence, integrated the Balkans into popular wartime narratives as another point of common reference against which Anglo-Britishness could be defined. As the exploits of the British volunteers gained public attention, this representational shift was projected into the domestic sphere and incorporated into broader propaganda narratives.

Nevertheless, such a process remained inconsistent and was frequently inhabited by the persistence of earlier stereotypes and attitudes. Despite venerating peasants as innately virtuous, wartime representations failed to advance beyond framing them as simplified caricatures, who could never be culturally equal to the British. Additionally, the solidarity formed through the wartime motivation to resolve peasant victimhood immediately revealed its limitations in being almost completely reliant on the social impetus created by the war itself.

6

Yugoslavia as British propaganda

For the majority of Britons, the creation of Yugoslavia would remain a footnote in the wider propaganda narrative of the Great War.[1] While Serbia was initially introduced to the public in late 1914 as a gallant, but distant ally, by the end of 1915 the campaign in the Balkans had come to be perceived as a largely humanitarian emergency through its association with female medical volunteers. Nevertheless, in keeping with the new pattern of Balkan war imagery, depictions of the South Slavic peasant as a victim of malign alien interferences galvanized public sympathy.[2]

British and French wartime propaganda has also been observed as an influential cultural factor in cementing the Western image of Serbia as a victim of external aggression.[3] While this latter role was nominally filled by Austria-Hungary, its integration into more mainstream propaganda currents cast both the Monarchy and Bulgaria as proxies of Imperial Germany – Britain's moral antithesis and the nexus of civilization's slide into militaristic nationalism. In relation to Yugoslavia, such propaganda has been noted for its overt historical revisionism. Drapac and Evans emphasize the role of British political activists in casting Yugoslavia's formation as predetermined. Wartime propaganda, overseen by pro-Yugoslav lobbyists, fed on ingrained Balkanist perceptions of linguistic reciprocity and distant tribal origins as a logical basis for unification, while cultural differences and political alternatives, specifically those excluding union with Serbia, were ignored.[4] The First World War also marked a discursive shift in how Balkan history was perceived among Britain's predominantly liberal intelligentsia. Rather than a heroic struggle against Oriental tyranny and colonial excess, by 1918, a less radical interpretation, championed by personalities like Seton-Watson and the historian Ramsay Muir, framed it in evolutionary terms as the 'rise of nationality' with the nation-state displacing Europe's multi-ethnic continental empires.[5]

However, this tendency to fixate on political tensions and maneuvering among elites once again minimizes the importance of ongoing social developments and the domestic function propaganda actually played in wartime Britain. While no formal state-propaganda apparatus existed at the outset of the war, by the end of August 1914, the public sphere was dominated by a series of campaigns organized by both government institutions and private groups, in direct service to the war effort.[6] As highlighted by Garth Jowett and Victoria O'Donnell, during the Great War British propagandists played a pivotal role in developing many of the psychological techniques used in contemporary forms of mass persuasion. Much of this rested on codifying the state's message via a range of subliminal and rhetorical appeals to attitudes, beliefs, values and societal norms perceived as holding an innate cultural resonance with the widest possible cross-section of the public. By 1916, this process had evolved into a near-total control of all major communication channels, obfuscating or censoring dissenting voices.[7] In relation to the war itself, Britain was presented as 'a standard for a new world order opposed to German values' with the conflict construed as a crusade against immoral and corrupting forces.[8] As Winter argues, it was this rapid expansion of the state as a source o social persuasion, alongside Ireland's ongoing political upheaval and the emergence of a 'cult of the fallen' emphasizing the veneration of the country's war dead from 1917, that ultimately defined the new Anglo-British identity.[9]

Previous studies also downplay the ways in which the domestic climate granted political actors from the region opportunities to influence the British public directly. Yugoslavia's very emergence in the public consciousness was itself instigated by South Slav politicians from Austria-Hungary. On 7 December 1914, with the Battle of Kolubara having turned in Serbia's favour, the coalition government of the long-serving prime minister Nikola Pašić proclaimed its official war aims. These would be 'nothing less' than the unification of all Serbs, Croats and Slovenes in a common state 'on the ruins of Austria-Hungary'.[10] In April 1915, a group of anti-Habsburg Croat, Serb and Slovene political secessionists led by the former mayor of Split, Ante Trumbić, gathered in Paris where they founded, with Serbian financial support, *Jugoslavenski odbor* (the Yugoslav Committee: JO). Its members quickly relocated to London, however, calculating that Britain was better placed to serve as a conduit for raising their cause's political profile within the Entente - as well as more pragmatic concerns over a potential German breakthrough on the Western Front.[11] By 1916, pressure groups such as the JO were freely utilizing Britain's wartime domestic climate to advance their post-war agendas. Identifying public opinion as a useful form of political leverage, attempts were made to appropriate the peasant victimhood narrative and place it within the wider context of a grand British wartime mission. Linguistic and cultural reciprocity, coupled with external threats, were also seized upon as preconditions for South Slav political union.[12] Humanitarian depictions of the Serbs as innocent victims of the Central Powers, with the fate of 'gallant little Serbia' paralleling that of 'brave little Belgium', reinforced the stated righteousness of the Entente cause, with support for Serbia, and later Yugoslavia, presented as paradigmatic of Anglo-British moral precedence and future role as a proactive global force.

This chapter assesses how the First World War – far from representing a discursive break with the past – signalled the apotheosis of Anglo-Balkan intercultural engagement in the modern period. Conversely, it also examines how the conflict further exposed the limitations of the region's shifting image in imaginative geography, with Yugoslavia's proclamation in December 1918 offering an apparent resolution to the victimhood narrative.

Draining 'Serbia's cup of sorrow'

Parallel to Britain's humanitarian and military interventions in south-east Europe, the war's most distinguishing feature was the opportunities for participation afforded to British audiences. While this was mostly conducted indirectly through a series of concerted (and heavily mediated) charity campaigns in support of the various relief missions, it represented something closer to a form of popular mass engagement than in previous decades. Fundamentally, it was the context of the First World War that projected the evolving discursive understanding of Anglo-British identity outwards onto military campaigns being (mostly) fought overseas.[13] Success in these conflicts prompted wartime propaganda narratives to foster a sense of moral solidarity with allied countries viewed as actively resisting German militarism. In the case of Serbia, such narratives were also deemed reflective of Britain's own inherent virtue as civilization's moral centre. Audiences were thus encouraged to become 'active' in the truest sense by contributing to the Serbian cause and attending public events as a patriotic demonstration of these moral values.

At a practical level, channelling support for the Serbian relief effort into an outward mobilization of public enthusiasm was a relatively simple task for groups such as the SRF, established in August 1914 under the patronage of several political and religious notables.[14] The emotive impulse engendered by the Serbian peasantry's ascribed victimhood status, as well as the obvious similarities with Belgium and the concrete affiliation the public could invest in the humanitarian missions, brought in a stream of donations. A letter of appeal from Sandes, published in the *Daily Mail* at the end of 1914, attracted over £2,000 worth of public contributions over three weeks while an SWH donation drive in March 1915 raised £1,165 in just two days.[15] Seton-Watson later boasted that the SRF alone had collected and distributed over £1,000,000 in emergency aid throughout the war.[16] By 1918, these efforts had expanded into other areas of provision such as education and housing for Serb refugees. Local governments and civic groups also launched initiatives or hosted charitable events, often competing to outdo one another in total donations as a demonstration of their community's patriotic zeal. Independent funds providing accommodation and scholarships for Serbian school children and students were even established in Aberdeen and Edinburgh.[17] The cultural impetus engendered by the public's experience of 'total war' also provided incentives for engagement at an intercommunal level. Following Serbia's liberation in October 1918, for instance, MacPhail's parents organized a vigorous campaign across Glasgow to provide funding and supplies for returning refugees.[18] Although it is difficult to evaluate the degree to which these efforts elicited a fully cross-societal response, their general success speaks of the extent to which the war facilitated wider public engagement by establishing direct, and often interpersonal, connections.

Nevertheless, while larger organizations like the Red Cross could secure funding and resources through size and name alone, smaller, specialized groups such as the SRF and SWH were obliged to disseminate propaganda as a means of retaining the public's divided attentions. Given its already politicized nature, ostensibly humanitarian appeals increasingly merged with pro-Serbian and, by 1917, pro-Yugoslavian efforts to promote political agendas by joining their message with pre-war victimhood narratives, paralleling British atrocity propaganda focused on Germany's occupation of Belgium. The South Slavic Balkans provided an ideal setting to illustrate the alleged German master plan for perpetuating its imperialist designs. *Serbia's Cup of Sorrows*, an introductory pamphlet to the war's impact on Serbia published by the SRF in 1915, presented both it and Belgium as a portent for the humanitarian disaster that might accompany a German invasion of the British Isles.[19] The Irish lawyer William Bailey offered a similar scenario in his depiction of Austria-Hungary's wartime regime in Croatia-Slavonia. '[For] the benefit of the State', all 'Serbo-Croats'[20] were branded potential subversives, a pretence by the war ministry to requisition food and property and leave them destitute, while the military openly abused its emergency powers to persecute peasants and other 'poor miserable hapless and ignorant folk'.[21] The psychological angle present in such imagery also offered a rhetorical challenge to the veracity of Britain's claims of moral superiority when it had mostly failed to support Serbia militarily; the public were now duty-bound to exonerate themselves through monetary and material assistance.[22]

Regardless of the extensive coverage afforded to Serbian victimhood, and a vaguely defined notion of shared values, the extent to which the First World War facilitated a popular sense of intercultural connection proved largely superficial. Notwithstanding the peasantry's newly conferred status as anti-German martyrs, wartime cultural revaluations did little to actively challenge pre-existing assumptions at a more popular level. One such example is presented in *An English Girl in Serbia* (c.1916), a children's adventure novel set during the Serbian army's Albanian retreat. Despite grounding its plot within the war's regional context, and the inclusion of a female lead protagonist, the text largely offers a continuation of Edwardian literary tropes. Serb soldiers now appear as Britain's 'noble savage' allies while the Bulgarian 'comitadji', sent to harass the retreating military columns, occupy the antagonistic role previously conferred on Albanians or the Ottoman authorities.[23]

More notable was the actual lack of acknowledgement of war crimes against the Serbian civilians, in contrast to refugees or those suffering from medical ailments, in British propaganda. Compared to the graphically stylized accounts concerning the German 'rape of Belgium', the German-Swiss forensic scientist Archibald Reiss's documentation of, alleged and confirmed, atrocities committed by Austro-Hungarian forces in 1914, for instance, was markedly absent from the narrative.[24] Reiss's later findings, pertaining to the Bulgarian occupation regime in eastern Serbia, were even corroborated by, somewhat dubious, testimonies from Entente POWs. Furthermore, reports from neutral American observers in the Balkans exposed a wartime blurring between the front and hinterlands in which civilians were deliberately targeted. The VMRO, who assisted the Bulgarians in annexing Macedonia, reportedly attacked and plundered with impunity.[25] Allegations against the Bulgarian authorities further asserted that Serbs in the eastern occupation zones had faced systematic violence that included the use of slave labour, reminiscent of the Congo Free State. British volunteers who accompanied Entente forces back into Macedonia and Serbia in 1918 also received testimonies detailing the use of mass killings in an effort to re-'Bulgarianize' the annexed territories, a 'grim repeat' of 1912 and 1913.[26] The American legation in Sofia had even informed Paget that the Macedonian peasantry had welcomed German soldiers who brought 'an influx of money and demand for labour' for which they paid 'liberally', in contrast to the Bulgarians' penchant for enslavement. Nevertheless, Macedonian Slavs continued to suffer as the Germans quickly commandeered even basic amenities. The resulting privations saw a proliferation of sexually transmitted diseases from prostitution and rising rates of suicide with claims of parents even murdering their children so as to 'save them from starvation'.[27]

While the veracity of Reiss's reports remain a matter of debate, the Balkans' absence from the grand atrocity narratives of British wartime propaganda was indicative of the contextual limitations in the evolution of the South Slav peasant's image. This included the seemingly indisputable concept of victimhood. Bastian Scianna contests that unlike subsequent conflicts, Reiss and his peers were still operating within an international legal and cultural framework that was only just beginning to redefine military attacks on civilians as a violation of 'a main component that had to be protected'.[28] Furthermore, while violence against non-combatants was certainly deemed abhorrent and worthy of condemnation, solutions for preventing such actions had yet to emerge as a wartime priority.[29] In this regard, the superficial portrayal of Serbia's plight in British propaganda signified the war's transient nature, being more a conduit for rationalizing what might otherwise have seemed an incongruous political and military alliance.

Visions of a Yugoslav nation

In contrast to Edwardian public ambivalence, the British Home Front proved far more amenable towards certain political agendas. Besides a febrile domestic climate, the increasingly sophisticated propaganda channels simplified the process of shaping and publicly disseminating one's narrative – on condition that it could be easily tailored in service to the Entente's general war effort. By extension, the image of the victimized peasant as a figure of resistance to pan-Germanism provided a useful conduit for directing public sympathy to the objective of a post-war Yugoslavian state, by characterizing its realization as fulfilling a moralistic duty that aligned with Britain's primary war aims. Conversely, as with relief aid to Serbia, the pro-Yugoslav propaganda campaign further illustrated the extent to which the success of such causes were always contingent on their immediate social context.

At its crux, the JO's narrative stipulated that Croats, Serbs and Slovenes represented the three distinctive 'tribes' that comprised a single Yugoslav race, legitimizing their homelands' political unification. Prior to 1914, this had manifested through 'Trialism': a political movement originating in elite Croat circles in the 1880s that called for the unification of all the Habsburg's South Slavic territories into a third constituent entity, on equal political-footing with the Monarchy's Austrian and Hungarian portions. Following the invasion of Serbia, however, Trumbić and other leading pro-Trialists, renounced their, already threadbare, loyalty to Emperor Franz Joseph in favour of union with Serbia and Montenegro as a single – federalized – Yugoslav entity.[30] In Britain, this rationale, which had also preoccupied regional observers since the 1870s, was brought to a head during the war.[31] Having warned that the death of Franz Ferdinand, a leading proponent of a tripartite Monarchy, should not serve as pretence for abandoning the liberal 'Habsburg mission' of promoting greater political freedoms, Seton-Watson soon discarded his previous support for it retaining its South Slav territories.[32] '[F]rom now on the Great Serbian state is inevitable; and we must create it', he confided in a letter to his wife following Britain's declaration of war on Germany. Trialism, 'the solution I have advocated for years', had been rendered 'dead' by a combination of Hungarian nationalism and pan-Germanist militarism. To preserve South Slav identity and 'save the Diet of Agram [Zagreb] . . . Dalmatia, Bosnia, Croatia, Istria must be united to Serbia'.[33]

By 1916, this perceived struggle for Yugoslavian freedom was enmeshed in broader narratives concerning the Entente's prescribed moral duty to secure the rights of 'subject peoples' in Central and Eastern Europe. *The New Europe* journal, instituted by Steed, Seton-Watson and other pro-Balkan advocates in October 1916, emerged as the main platform for a loose network of activists and diplomatic figures who championed this perspective, with the leading Czechoslovak secessionist Tomáš Masaryk's veneration of nationality and political self-determination as its ideological lynchpin.[34] Equally significant was the inauguration of the School of Slavonic Studies as a department of King's College London in 1915, with Masaryk as its 'spiritual' founder, and Seton-Watson as co-founder. Like *The New Europe*'s ascribed role as a mouthpiece for projecting Liberal internationalist ideas into the sphere of foreign policy decision-making, Seton-Watson envisioned the School as an academic training ground for preparing future generations of advisers to the FO.[35]

In contrast to their Czechoslovak and Polish counterparts, however, the JO faced greater international obstacles to its post-war state project. As Dragovan Šepić notes, while the former, especially the Poles, could claim that their homelands were under foreign occupation, the Yugoslavs faced the prospect of seeing theirs annexed by Italy in accordance with the secret 1915 Treaty of London. In exchange for Italy's entry into the war against the Central Powers, Rome had been promised extensive territorial gains including the Austria Littoral, most of Dalmatia and the western districts of the Duchy of Carniola, historically viewed as the Slovene national heartland. In order to countervail this, the JO's members needed to convince London and Paris that these lands represented part of a single allied nation, with a shared language and indivisible cultural and political borders.[36]

Promoting and normalizing the idea of a post-war Yugoslav state as an integral part of Britain's wartime mission thus became the cornerstone of the JO's efforts to legitimize their cause in the public sphere. Alongside pro-Serbian efforts, Yugoslavian propaganda stressed South Slavic independence as interlinked with Entente war aims while seeking to capitalize on the public's immediate anxieties regarding Germany. Much of this centred on constructing a narrative that presented the Southern Slavs as a 'bulwark' against a pan-Germanist strategy to subjugate continental Europe.[37] Since the early nineteenth century, so the argument ran, Austria-Hungary had employed 'every means in her power' to 'compromise', 'defame', and 'crush' the Yugoslav idea. This was compounded by a growing subservience to German imperialism that not only made the Monarchy responsible for war, but guilty of attempting to quash Serbian independence 'as Germany's vassal state and pioneer'.[38] Following the Serbian military victories in 1914 'the Jugoslav problem became a European problem', with a South Slav union now vital for overcoming pan-Germanism.[39]

In relating this to the region's peasants, Yugoslavian propagandists construed western Balkan history as a cycle of repression and resistance. The Croat writer Srdjan

Tucić, who edited the JO's news sheet, the *South Slav Bulletin*, defined the Second Reich and Dual Monarchy as the historical heirs of the Ottoman Empire. In contrast to the latter, however, Teutonic repression had been more insidious by attempting to render the Southern Slavs down into a race of slaves. Whereas the brutality of the Turks 'steeled the hearts of the Slavs they oppressed ... Austrian captivity has cankered them and made them effete'.[40] Across this narrative the peasant predominated as the embodiment of South Slavic cultural consciousness and an emblem of Christian and democratic martyrdom. Resistance to Ottoman rule was itself cast as an exclusively rural phenomenon promulgated by outlaws, peasant revolutionaries and the *Grenzer* (frontiersmen) who had garrisoned the former Habsburg-Ottoman military frontier.[41]

While Croat and Serb nationalists had recurrently depicted their respective nations as guarding Christian Europe against the spread of Islam, the war heralded a shift in emphasis onto the Germanic powers. Tucić even framed acts of military aggression against Serbia as a direct continuation of the Ottoman conquests, or a 'latter day *Prussian Islam*'.[42] The Southern Slavs had simply continued to fulfil their role in defending Christian Europe by opposing an Austria-Hungary 'that had strayed away from its European and Christian heritage'.[43] This stance was reiterated as the logical conclusion to Serbian history in the former army chaplain Robin Laffan's treatise, *Guardians of the Gate* (1918), with the country's wartime plight representing a continuation of a centuries-long spiritual, as well as martial struggle. Serbia had finally met its ultimate antagonist in the form of pan-Germanism, a statist rejection of the Christian moral ideals which the Serb peasantry had sacrificed their own national freedom to protect.[44]

A similar attempt at spiritual and moral vindication was promulgated by the Anglophile Orthodox bishop of Ohrid and Žiča, Nikolaj Velimirović, who arrived in Britain in 1915 under the pretext of providing religious instruction to refugee seminarians.[45] Winning the support of the Anglican Church's ecclesiastical establishment, and touring England (and later the United States) extensively, his sermons and lectures stressed the Southern Slavs' role in history as comparable to a grand religious mission. Dubbing Serbia 'Europe's America', Velimirović presented its early revolutionary struggle for independence as a counterblast of the 'downtrodden' against a degenerative slide into 'political nihilism' that pitted the 'humble' against the 'unjust and brutal'. Playing to religious philosophical critiques of Nietzsche's 'godless Superman', he proposed that it was the peasant who embodied it's pious and altruistic inversion, the 'All-man'. While the Superman selfishly sought individualistic domination, the All-man stood for the collective, offering democratic equality and stability. A political union of Croats, Serbs and Slovenes was thus essential for preserving this ideal; British Christians wishing to defeat the 'scientific perfidy' and 'atheistic brutality' of Berlin, or the 'Turkish Nietzscheanism' of the Ottoman Young Turk movement, should therefore be compelled to seek 'Jugoslavia's realisation'.[46]

This wartime mantle of South Slavic linguistic and cultural unity even transcended the impasse of contemporary political ideology. At the third Zimmerwald Conference in Stockholm, organized by Europe's anti-war socialist movements, Bosnian and Croat delegates argued the case for Yugoslav unification along much the same lines as the JO and Velimirović. From a Marxist perspective, the economic potential of the Habsburgs' South Slavic provinces had been squandered through their treatment as 'African colonies'. Forty years of 'civilisatory activity [sic]' had not only failed to resolve widespread rural illiteracy and impoverishment, but equated to little more than safeguarding the feudal privileges of Muslim landowners and capitalist exploitation by the Monarchy's surplus of 'squires and priests'.⁴⁷ As with the Macedonian unrest, discernible parallels were also extrapolated in relation to Britain's own pre-war domestic troubles. Writing in *The New Europe* at the end of 1916, Henry Hyndman, the pro-war 'veteran of English Socialism', stressed that Europe could never achieve universal human rights without the Monarchy's partition. Hyndman caveated this, however, by noting that demanding regional independence while London continued to deny Ireland and India the right to home rule 'lays us open to the charge of hypocrisy'.⁴⁸

As demonstrated by organized opinion's previous efforts, foreign policy lobbyists had always been at a disadvantage when trying to sustain public interest in their cause. From its inception, cultivating a presence through which a more targeted, as opposed to a mass, audience could acquire a basic understanding of South Slav history and politics was considered essential to the campaign's overall effectiveness. Like the humanitarian groups, it also sought to capitalize on the wave of pro-Serbian sympathies and the state's growing wartime monopoly over public information. *The New Europe*, for instance, while only achieving a circulation of 5,000 at its height, still managed to establish itself as the authoritative voice in continental affairs among policymaking circles, with many of its regular contributors already holding key positions at the FO. Consequently, information presented in the journal filtered through into Britain's mainstream propaganda channels without it having to necessarily became a 'household name'. In his new capacity as foreign editor for *The Times*, a position he had assumed only months before Franz Ferdinand's assassination, Steed proved a pivotal figure, granting the Yugoslavs regular access to the paper's powerful proprietor, Viscount Northcliffe (Alfred Harmsworth). Despite having little knowledge, or interest, in Balkan affairs, Northcliffe's own vehement anti-Germanism was easily directed towards a pro-Serb, and by extension pro-Yugoslav, stance that was expressed, albeit loosely, in his more widely read title, the *Daily Mail*.⁴⁹ In this manner, a more sympathetic image of the South Slavs acquired the potential to directly reach a mass audience.

Besides media coverage, spectacle and public visibility proved to be of equal, if not greater, importance. This was most explicitly conveyed through the Yugoslavist Croat 'peasant-sculptor', and JO affiliate, Ivan Meštrović's *Kosovo* exhibition held at the Victoria and Albert Museum in the summer of 1915. Through a romanticized pastiche of South Slavic rural mythologies, Meštrović sought to articulate a coherent Yugoslavist vision tied to the cyclical narrative of peasant martyrdom. The sculptures, originally exhibited at an international event in Rome in 1911, were in reference to the Serbian 'Kosovo Cycle': a series of epic poems recounting an attempt by a medieval pan-Christian alliance, led by the Serbian ruler Prince Lazar Hrebeljanović, to check the advancing Ottomans at the Battle of Kosovo in June 1389.⁵⁰ Although only attracting a somewhat exclusive audience, the exhibition proved effective as a cultural reference point from which the wider public could derive an understanding of modern Yugoslavism's core philosophical tenants. Although an amalgamation of Croat, Serb and Slovene folk traditions, its themes of peasant sacrifice and cultural

Figure 8 Victoria and Albert Museum's West Hall during Ivan Meštrović's *Kosovo* exhibition, June to July 1915. © Courtesy of V&A Images.

custodianship were presented by Meštrović as quintessential 'Yugoslav' values. This depiction also contravened the idea of the 'Serbian soldier' as Yugoslavia's symbolic essence, focusing instead on the more pacifistic qualities of the peasantry.[51] The positive critical response to *Kosovo* was itself informed by pre-existing social tensions which the war had served to amplify. Reflecting on the exhibition's philosophical subtext, the historian Arnold Toynbee echoed Scott-James in praising the 'primitive' traditions underlining Meštrović's work. At a time when belief in modern progress was under threat from German militarism, the culture and values of the South Slavs could offer a vital remedy.[52]

It was, however, the work of Britain's pro-Serbian organizations specifically the 'Kossovo Day Committee' – headed by Inglis, with Seton-Watson as secretary and Berry, Paget, Stobart and Velimirović as cultural advisers, that became the campaign's focal point from 1916 to 1917. Blurring humanitarian sermonizing with political lobbying, the Committee disseminated Yugoslavist literature and organized a range of events aimed at fostering a political dimension to wartime Anglo-Serbian solidarity. A specialized bookshop in London, for example, was set-up to sell Serbian literature with Seton-Watson estimating that over 30,000 copies of the country's national anthem had been purchased.[53] Central to the Committee's strategy, however, was a week-long nationwide series of civic and religious observations commemorating the Serbian national holiday *Vidovdan* (St. Vitus Day) in June 1916.[54] Across some 12,000 British schools, children were taught folk songs and introduced to a mythologized version of Serbian history in the form of a 'school address' – also composed by Seton-Watson. *Vidovdan* itself drew extensive coverage in the national and local press (with over 400 articles covering the Committee's activities alone) while a series of public processions and enthusiastic religious ceremonies eulogized Serbia's aspirations as indicative of the new moral international vision being pursued by Britain. This message was further disseminated to a mass audience through cinema and public events; the *Punch* cartoon 'Heroic Serbia', epitomized the moment, equating the medieval Serb's resistance to the Ottomans at Kosovo Polje to the stand made against the invading Central Powers in 1915. This striking image was subsequently reproduced and displayed in public spaces around the country throughout the summer of 1916.[55]

The sudden kindling of interest in Serbian and Kosovan history was seized upon as sharing historical significance for all South Slavs.[56] As with Meštrović's *Kosovo*, the JO representative Bogumil Vošnjak elaborated on medieval Serbia's 'sacrifice' as a mnemonic for the wider South Slavic impulse towards unity, accentuating the fact that Bosnian and Croat armies had also fought at Kosovo. Since both territories were subsequently conquered by a 'German Empire', Kosovo represented the historical

Figure 9 'Heroic Serbia', poster promoting 'Kossovo Day', June 1916. © Public domain.

blueprint for collective South Slavic suffering at the hands of alien rulers.[57] In conjunction with Velimirović, the JO's propaganda rhetoric repeatedly challenged the British to prove their claims of superior moral virtue by intervening on behalf of all Southern Slavs still living under Habsburg dominion. 'What we people without home wish to see', Vošnjak pontificated in the transcript to one of his public lectures, 'is the stern, imperturbable will of English public opinion to destroy this despair of an Empire [Austria-Hungary]'.[58] Identifiable similarities in Serb, Croat and Slovene rural traditions were also accentuated as evidence of a dormant national consciousness with the peasantry's naturally 'democratic instincts' repressed by the 'autocratic tendencies' of their Austrian and Hungarian rulers.[59]

Discursive portraiture of a repressed peasantry created a shared reality between the Habsburg and former Ottoman territories steeped in a tradition of systematic persecution by outsiders.[60] In substance, however, these appeals were ancillary to more contemporary fears of Italian irredentism. The JO's own literature made no secret of the potential fate awaiting those Southern Slavs inhabiting areas claimed by Italy, warning the British public that acquiescing to Rome's territorial demands would represent a historical betrayal by perpetuating the cycle of South Slavic victimhood.[61] British pro-Yugoslavs also warned of the repercussions facing Dalmatia's Slavic peasantry if London continued to treat their homeland as 'disposable' in its dealings with Italy.[62]

The success of the 1916 *Vidovdan* commemorations drew equally positive commentary from British pundits as an interpretive display of spiritual and moral humility, only conceivable in a pre-industrial society. The most impassioned of these plaudits was articulated by G. K. Chesterton in an opinion piece for the *Daily News* that conceptualized Serbia as the ideal nation, derived from the people's collective historical memory. Amalgamating this rhetoric with the doctrines of Catholic social teaching, notably distributism,[63] Chesterton expounded that this could only be realized in a society structured around agricultural smallholdings.

> We must be content to tell the Prussian, well knowing that he will not understand us, that we are fighting to give him a Kosovo Day to make a man of him, that he may someday be as civilised as a Serbian peasant . . . the chief fruit of this philosophy is the national idea itself, the sacramental sense of boundary, the basis in an almost religious sense of agriculture, the idea of having a home upon this earth, which the Arab armies out of the deserts can hardly even be said to have violated, having never begun to understand.

Against 'that ancient ideal . . . Serbia must be called the eldest brother of the Alliance [Entente]'.[64]

Detoxifying public spectacle fell in tandem with the ongoing revision of recent Serbian history. Seton-Watson's school address, for example, argued that following the deaths of the last two Obrenović rulers (agents to Germany's 'baggage porter', Austria-Hungary), King Petar's reign had marked 'the Serbian national revival'.[65] This was granted further validation by his conduct in 1914 and 1915: humbly releasing his men from their oath of loyalty to him in 1914, only for them to 'unanimously' renew it, was presented as indicative of the 'brotherhood' that existed between king and peasant-soldier. Crown Prince Aleksandar was venerated along much the same lines; reported acts of selflessness during the retreat, such as refusing to be evacuated from the Albanian coast before his fellow Serbs despite having recently undergone emergency surgery, were emphasized as exhibited traits of a modern 'warrior-king'.[66] *Punch*'s widely syndicated 'Heroic Serbia' represented this process's wartime apogee by casting the Crown Prince as the embodiment of martial resistance, presenting the public with a point of individual reference onto which collective ideals could be projected. Vošnjak linked his role in the Albanian retreat as harking back to that of his predecessors at Kosovo, choosing 'exile, poverty, and death' as a basis for Serbia's 'national resurrection', framed as synonymous with the notion of a future Yugoslavia.[67] The heir apparent also invited praise as a post-war unitary figure. 'The prince', Askew opined, 'is the apostle of progress as well as a knight paladin'. An eagerness to 'develop the capabilities of his land' by improving agriculture appeared as a remedy to previous centuries of Ottoman neglect and the Habsburg's inconsistent modernization programmes.[68]

The limits of propaganda

Regardless of its success in garnering public attention and sympathy throughout 1915 and 1916, by 1917, it was evident that the Yugoslavs' propaganda campaign had failed to make any significant political headway among policymakers in London or Paris. Indeed, from 1916, the JO had already entered into talks with Serbia's government-in-exile on the prospect of joint war aims. Events in early 1917, notably Russia's February Revolution and America's entry into the war in April, accelerated this process; the US president Woodrow Wilson's Gladstonian commitment to national self-determination in Eastern Europe aroused particular excitement among secessionist movements increasingly frustrated at Anglo-French reluctance to back their proposals for Austria-Hungary's partition. In the case of the JO and Serbian government, this culminated in the Corfu declaration on 20 July: a statement of joint intent committing both parties to the creation of a Kingdom of Serbs, Croats and Slovenes. More direct forms of political action had, so it appeared, started to supersede international propaganda.[69]

The limitations of these activities were further illustrated by the ingrained tensions between the JO and Pašić, who viewed the former as 'an ancillary of Serbian foreign policy'.[70] Trumbić and the JO's Croat members increasingly complained of an 'Orthodox exclusivism' in how their British hosts appeared to conflate Yugoslavia with Serbian national interests. Its Slovene members, in turn, voiced their own concerns that their native territories were being almost entirely ignored, even as the Italian military continued to amass on the Carniolan border.[71] Seton-Watson, Steed and other leading campaigners were themselves prone to viewing Pašić with suspicion, stemming mostly from pre-war aversion to narrow Serbian nationalism. Behind the scenes, campaign planning was often dominated by frequent quarrels over the Serbian ambassador Mateja Bošković's hostility to the JO and unacknowledged allocation of SRF funds, prior to his eventual replacing in 1916.[72]

The post-war ramifications for the rest of the South Slavic Balkans were another point of contention. In a report to the SRF's Montenegrin counterpart, also established in 1914, its most proactive member, the educationist Alexander Devine, voiced concerns that Montenegrin and Serb refugees were being treated as 'one and the same' by Entente officials.[73] As the campaign expanded, Devine's apprehensions only increased over Montenegro's narrativized subordination to Serbia:

> The Serbian propagandists are so active and avail themselves of funerals and the fashionable columns in the *Morning Post* at every possible occasion that turns up to advertise themselves. I don't mind that, but I do mind their doing so to the detriment of their sister country.[74]

Anti-Serb elements of organized opinion also endeavoured to voice their opposition, with Brailsford and Durham vociferously protesting to *The Manchester Guardian* and other sceptical publications, while Buxton and Bourchier warned of post-war instability.[75] Their failure to produce a counter-narrative not only revealed an inability to resonate with the wartime atmosphere but presaged the resumption of the Balkans' continued drift from the public consciousness after 1918.

Neither were the campaign's apparent successes entirely uncontested. Despite rallying public opinion, the FO's upper echelons remained mostly aloof from calls for the Monarchy's partition, viewing Steed and Seton-Watson's attempts to informally influence foreign policy with the same mixture of irritation and suspicion as the rest of organized opinion before 1914. In March 1917, the latter even found himself being drafted into the RAMC after his exemption from military service was raised in the House of Commons by the Liberal MP Joseph King, a member of the Union for Democratic Control that opposed external influence in government. He subsequently spent several weeks performing menial duties at an officers' training camp in Blackpool, his political lobbying temporarily suspended. Regardless, this disruption to the campaign belied its diminishing importance.[76] Indeed, the 1916 *Vidovdan* commemorations had already revealed the extent to which even emotive propaganda could only sustain popular interest for so long. Similar celebrations organized for 1917 and 1918 failed to attract public notice as attention gravitated towards achieving victory on the Western Front.[77]

Besides the whims of an ever-fickle public, the propaganda campaign's relative success in legitimizing Yugoslavia within the British (and French) popular imagination, failed to translate into an effective form of psychological warfare. Following a Cabinet-level intervention by the author John Buchan in his capacity as director of the Department of Information's Intelligence Bureau, Seton-Watson was transferred from the RAMC to the Bureau's Balkans division. Here he remained from May 1917 to March 1918, before joining Steed in Northcliffe's Enemy Propaganda Department at Crewe House in Mayfair, while continuing to edit *The New Europe*. Despite Evans's observation that this brought Britain's two leading anti-Habsburg voices much closer to the levers of FO decision-making, it greatly overstates British propaganda's actual role in the war against the Dual Monarchy.[78] As Mark Cornwall demonstrates comprehensively, the Entente campaign to undermine Austro-Hungarian morale was dominated by Italy at almost every level with the coordinated psychological offensive launched in April 1918 'a largely Italian enterprise'.[79] Even the independent efforts of the JO and Serbian government yielded greater tangible results in swaying South Slav POWs to the Yugoslav cause. Like Northcliffe's own highly publicized activities,

Britain's exaggerated role was the product of a wider mythologizing process that saw different actors attempting to enshrine themselves as the war's universal protagonists.[80]

Conclusion

For Yugoslavia's British and South Slavic advocates, the outbreak of the First World War had occurred at the most opportune historical moment. In contrast to the Edwardian period, the war provided the only real instance in which Balkan affairs could be aligned with Britain's domestic priorities. Those seeking to further humanitarian or political aims found in British propaganda narratives a pliable rhetorical mechanism that could be used to shape the resolution of the South Slavic peasantry's now crystallized status as victims of history, achieving wider resonance with a persistent public desire for moral vindication. Representations of the peasant crossed the imaginative threshold from a mere analogy on the shortcomings of modern industrial society, to a symbolic justification for British regional intervention within the parameters of a broader wartime mission. Thus, the Great War's importance lay in the extent to which it afforded South Slavic actors a measure of agency in conditioning Britain's geographical imaginary as it reformed to accommodate the Anglo-British turn.[81] A process handily articulated through domestic wartime propaganda.

Nevertheless, the adoption of the peasantry as an object of moral intervention, based on the established precedence of a noble rural underclass victimized by an amoral iteration of modernity, was again illustrative of the extent to which all such developments generally relied on the specific context in which they were conceived to retain relevance. As discussed, even before December 1918, a fixation on victimhood had revealed the limited possibilities for sustaining an acute level of public empathy or promoting closer cultural ties to the region once the motif around which it was maintained was politically resolved. Furthermore, as its junior position in both the Macedonian and anti-Habsburg propaganda campaigns demonstrated, the war had once again exposed how narrow Britain's mythologized role in the Balkans was in actual concrete terms.

Not only did Yugoslavia's creation provide a logical conclusion to popular understandings of the South Slavic question, it effectively ended over a century of debate concerning Britain's geopolitical stake in the region. This sense of finality was further cemented in 1919 with the Eastern Question itself having been ostensibly resolved: the Entente's Vardar Offensive had brought Bulgaria into compliance in just two weeks while leaving the Ottoman Empire politically moribund. In the wider international context, fears that the newly proclaimed Russian Soviet Federative Socialist Republic might continue the expansionist policies of its imperial predecessor had largely dissipated with the outbreak of civil war in November 1917. For the public, the disintegration of Austria-Hungary and the expunging of Berlin's influence from the region appeared to bring closure to the victimhood narrative, with Southern Slavs having seemingly triumphed in liberating themselves.[82] Without the Great War's cultural impetus, the prospect of further repression in Adriatic coastal areas annexed by Italy – or within Yugoslavia itself – could no longer be construed as a British political concern.[83]

Part III

The era of the 'New Europe'

7

Yugoslavia in the 'Anglo-British' mind

With the end of the First World War, Yugoslavia almost immediately disappeared from the British public sphere, even as ratification of its national borders continued to be debated at Versailles from January 1919 to June 1920.[1] While Michail interprets this as indicative of a broad process of public 'interwar disengagement', it was largely a reassertion of pre-war trends, compounded by even greater apathy and disenchantment with foreign affairs. Such sentiments were also present at the official level, with the collective trauma of the Great War strengthening official aversion to overseas entanglements. Moreover, throughout the 1920s and 1930s, successive foreign secretaries and diplomats found themselves burdened by a heighted sense of public weariness and mistrust.[2]

Although a far more balanced picture of the first Yugoslavia's cultural and socio-political climate has begun to emerge since 2010, imagological historiography remains broadly focused on overarching themes deemed applicable to the entire Balkans.[3] Historians of the cultural-colonialist perspective generally trace the West's creation of a distinctive Balkan image to these interwar years. As Beaven argues in Britain's case, this was the era in which a genuine national mass culture of commercialized leisure finally 'came of age'.[4] Unpreceded access to books, magazines and newspapers, coupled with a continual rise in cinema-going and radio-ownership, popularized many Victorian-era tropes later associated with Balkanism. By 1939, Goldsworthy postulates, even imaginative geography resembled that of the late nineteenth century, with the Balkans once again appropriated as a setting for ahistorical escapism.[5] Besides the media's enduring fixation on political violence, Britain's shrinking and isolated pool of cognoscenti remained equally dispirited by the manner in which regional information was now mostly disseminated to the public as 'ephemera'. These 'short-lived pieces of news', arising from the ever-present need for editorial copy, presented Balkan events as consumable short-term spectacle that tended to not 'engage its material in an interpretive way', more often fixating on trivial details.[6] As a report by the *Political and Economic Planning* think tank revealed in 1938, royalty, politicians' personal lives and high-profile scandals commanded far greater public interest than foreign countries, or politics in general.[7]

Nevertheless, these developments did little to negate the ever-present domestic influences. Indeed, among vague, and inconsistently applied, clichés alluding to regional backwardness, southeastern Europe increasingly served as a cultural sounding board in which evolving political and social trends could be deconstructed and critiqued to a degree previously unknown, as shown in Graham Greene's *Stamboul Train* (1932).[8]

This chapter explores the nature of the first Yugoslavia's representation in the changing context of British interwar society and social life. As illustrated in the prevalence of commercialized leisure and the geographic imaginary's recalibration around, supposedly inconsequential, ephemera, the defining theme of the interwar years manifested in a shift away from social and political ideals, to newer forms of engagement predicated on consumption and commodification. Rather than a regression back to more Balkanist Victorian ideas, these developments were reflective of a new phase in the British domestic climate created by the war and the gradual resolution of Edwardian-era tensions, most importantly Ireland: the cultural manifestation of Anglo-British identity.

An Anglo-British paradigm?

When considering the domestic allegories that afforded the South Slavic peasantry a place in late-Edwardian public sympathies, the socio-economic context of the 1920s ostensibly promised continuity. Having been artificially buoyed by the war and efforts to reintegrate demobilized soldiers back into the workforce, by 1921, rapidly changing global economic conditions had left Britain's staple industries of steel, textiles, shipbuilding and heavy engineering on the verge of collapse. Changing patterns of demand, notably declining coal exports and competition from more efficient manufacturing countries like Japan, exacerbated these trends.[9] The resulting social tensions – focused in entrenched pockets of unemployment and deprivation in Northern Ireland, south Wales, central Scotland, and northern England – initially appeared to be a realization of pre-war anxieties.

Like the Great Unrest of the 1910s, these anxieties were granted some vindication after 1918. The most significant development was the Irish War of Independence that broke out in January 1919, amid a still heavily militarized post-war social atmosphere. Seizing on mounting public unrest, particularly in Belfast, Dublin and Munster, the Irish Republican Army launched a paramilitary campaign of assassination, property destruction and guerrilla warfare while fashioning itself as an anti-imperial insurgency resisting a foreign occupation. This new style of warfare, amalgamating political and military objectives, pushed the outworn parameters of British rule far beyond their tolerances, evoking the Ottoman Balkans following Ilinden–Preobrazhenie.

By mid-1920, the authority of the British state had effectively collapsed as forces loyal to the new *Dáil Éireann* (Assembly of Ireland) systematically wrested political control away from the Dublin Castle administration.[10] This deterioration of Britain's civil legitimacy was only hastened by London's declaration of martial law later that year and the deployment of the Royal Irish Constabulary's own paramilitary Auxiliary Division and notorious Special Reserve units, the 'Black and Tans'. Both organizations' lack of discipline and violent counterinsurgency tactics, including reprisals against Catholic civilians involving arson and extrajudicial killings, quickly alienated moderate public opinion in Ireland and mainland Britain. As the violence escalated during the spring of 1921, opponents of Lloyd George's post-war coalition even compared Ireland to the former Ottoman-ruled Balkans, denouncing the Black and Tans as 'a force of bashi-bazouks'.[11] Critics needn't have looked to the nineteenth century for political parallels. Across much of Central and Eastern Europe, insurgent and transgressive violence remained widespread, including in southern Yugoslavia where the Serb-dominated army and gendarmerie attempted to subdue a still active VMRO and the anti-unionist, pro-Petrović-Njegoš, 'Greens' in Montenegro.[12]

Neither was the British mainland entirely free of unrest with the army being deployed on the streets of Glasgow following major riots, labelled by the Secretary for Scotland as an attempted 'Bolshevist rising', in January 1919.[13] Although these searing class tensions had receded following the 1926 General Strike, the stagnate economic climate that characterized interwar life for many of the lower-middle and working class defined much of the new era's political tone. Later acts of protest – notably the Hunger Marches of the 1930s and agitation by more radical MPs and organized labour, brought the ongoing plight of regional working-class communities to wider public attention, fostering a progressive turn in social attitudes similar to that inspired by late-Victorian social reformers.[14]

Continuity was also present in the cultural and social spheres. Despite the sociological challenges created by the war, Britain's general proclivity for rural nostalgia intensified during the interbellum, precipitating a greater interpenetration between town and country. Villages previously portrayed as facing imminent extinction, were gradually repopulated by influxes of former city dwellers; 'rural industries' were retooled for urban consumption as bespoke 'local crafts', often prompting producers of said crafts to abandon their 'traditional' working methods in order to meet rising demand; and town planners distinguished areas of countryside from urban sprawl as an essential social amenity for working-class neighbourhoods.[15] Even an appreciable number of artists and intellectuals remained in thrall to the still active pastoralist movement, predicated on a belief that 'a new rural civilisation' would soon arise to usurp the decadent urban one.[16]

Yet, these developments ultimately signified Britain's transition away from the Edwardian era, as the country, ironically, started to internalize the notion of Anglo-Britishness. Central to this was Ireland's effective departure from the union, with the establishment of the Irish Free State in December 1922 – and full independence in December 1937 – removing what had been its main political impediment. This fell in tandem with the state's appropriation of the populace's wartime experiences as an expression of a new pan-British identity. Beginning with the founding of the Imperial War Graves Commission in May 1917, the inauguration of Armistice Day in 1919 and the accompanying wave of local memorialization initiatives, lasting into the 1930s, conflated collective grief with the mythologized Anglo-British ideal. In this instance, the figure of the fallen soldier emerged as its cornerstone, personifying the British state as the world's moral arbiter and a latently shared object of public aspiration. The attendant glorification of military institutions, or individuals drawn mostly from the ranks of the officer class, such as T. E. Lawrence, further strengthened these popular cultural affiliations to the state.[17]

However, this did not equate to the emergence of a unitary British nation. Regardless of wider Anglo-British associations with duty and sacrifice, the majority of war memorials continued to exist as markers of local identity, with their funereal and allegorical nature allowing individuals to freely interpret their specific meaning.[18] Beaven observes a similar process regarding local communities' relationship to the empire. Although instituted in 1905, it was only after the British Empire Exhibition of 1924 that Empire Day became a major annual event, being promoted as a patriotic holiday focused on education and public spectacle. However, as with the period prior to 1914, 'imperial identity' was always understood through its relationship to local concerns, indicated by the inconsistency of its adoption among civic authorities.[19] In contrast to the unitary nationalism underpinning Irish independence, localism became an enduring aspect of a new 'Anglo-British' paradigm that now threaded through society.

The continued primacy of location deprived Anglo-Britishness of any substantive political aspect that could not be directly filtered through a local context. To the majority of Britons, bodies associated with the central state, such as the FO, remained almost nonentities. Despite the press's fixation on the Paris Peace Conference, the political apathy of the early 1910s, already in evidence by 1917, promptly reasserted itself through a general public extrication from foreign affairs. To a broad extent, this was the logical outcome of a system that had come to rely upon the socio-political conditions created by the war. Discussions among those employed at Crewe House of turning the department towards the creation of 'peace propaganda', for example, were abruptly dashed. Northcliffe's sudden resignation on 12 November 1918, following an acrimonious split with Lloyd George, brought Steed and Seton-Watson's involvement in decision-making to an immediate end. Lingering hopes of a possible return were put to rest with their former head of department's death in 1922.[20]

Moreover, despite the exceptional degree of influence *The New Europe* still exerted over British delegates and regional envoys during the Paris Peace Conference, excitable speculation among activists, diplomats and foreign policy punditry belied a 'widespread acceptance that Balkan liberationist movements had reached the end of their road'.[21] The rhetorical accentuation of the Yugoslavs as heroic architects of their own national destiny only magnified these assumptions, quelling any apparent need for further British involvement.[22] This proved no less detrimental to the efforts of those still sequestered in the region: travelling through southern Yugoslavia as an envoy for the Red Cross in the summer of 1919, Stobart warned that withdrawing wartime aid had resulted in the rate of typhus cases (already aggravated by the 1918 influenza pandemic) returning to levels comparable to 1915.[23]

However, the critical difference to the Edwardian years lay in the disappearance of the domestic ecosystem on which organized opinion had previously relied in order to maintain a public presence. By the late 1920s, most of those who had once been received as leading regional authorities found their former channels of communication to have either closed or been drastically curtailed. Writing to Steed in October 1920, Seton-Watson admitted that *The New Europe*'s impending liquidation was simply the logical outcome of 'deadened public opinion'. Such circumstance had even forced him to shoulder the journal's printing, editing and circulation costs, estimating to 'have lost £7,500 on this enterprise'. With an ever diminishing public willingness to engage in issues outside of immediate domestic concerns, he glumly predicted that private individuals would be 'less and less likely to embark unaided upon such a venture as *The New Europe*' in the future.²⁴ The School of Slavonic Studies met with equally limited success in fulfilling his grand vision of cultivating a dedicated cadre of foreign policy expertise, similar to that in France. Even its nominal objective of promoting the teaching of East European languages in British higher education was not fully realized until the 1960s.²⁵

Even committed exponents of Balkan causes who had been bolstered by the febrile atmosphere of the Edwardian and Great War years found themselves publicly, and often professionally, marginalized. Despite numerous accolades, including honorary doctorates from the universities of Zagreb and Belgrade, mounting financial difficulties in the 1920s forced Seton-Watson to dedicate more of his time to academic teaching obligations.²⁶ Those who had advocated for less fashionable causes fared considerably worse. Dismissed in 1919 as a Montenegrin 'agent' and propagandist 'probably in the pay of King Nicholas', Devine's vehement support for the Green's short-lived anti-unionist uprising and incessant repetition of the illegality of Montenegro's union with Serbia found only a 'wall of public indifference'. 'This campaign . . . has been a very hard and lonely fight for me' he confided in a letter to Herbert Gladstone in 1924.²⁷ The reality of post-war politics and the often rancorous discourse surrounding it, notably Durham and Seton-Watson's prolonged feud over Serbian culpability for the war, promulgated this sense of alienation with most campaigners abandoning the Balkans or withdrawing from the public sphere entirely by 1930.²⁸

The slow disappearance of Britain's entire body of regional expertise added a further degree of pathos to these sharp vicissitudes of fortune. Seton-Watson's efforts to replicate his earlier success as an independent political adviser and state propagandist, for example, proved entirely incompatible with the stringent intelligence posts he occupied during the Second World War. Unable to access policymakers or have any contact with the press, he resigned from his position in 1942 and finally withdrew from public life in 1946, dying in relative obscurity in 1951.²⁹ His fate mirrored the rest of Edwardian organized and informed opinion. Beginning with Bourchier in 1920 and concluding with Brailsford in 1958, the cohort of personalities who had once 'expanded the uses and channels of public knowledge of the region, bringing it to academia, to politics and to the centre of the public sphere' passed away without any intellectual successors to replace them.³⁰

This gradual dissolution of British expertise was equally contingent on the fact that the consolidation of Anglo-British identity from 1912 to 1922 had negated or stripped away much of the domestic social context that originally imbued the plight of the South Slavic peasantry with allegorical meaning. In August 1914, for instance, the Liberal-led Land Campaign had 'simply fizzled out. Ending not with a bang but a whimper' when the government suspended it before any agreement had been reached. Despite Buxton's efforts to revive it in his capacity as Minister for Agriculture and Fisheries under both of Ramsay MacDonald's interwar Labour governments, the ensuing European financial crisis of 1931 rendered it moribund as a serious policy issue.³¹

Public disengagement was compounded by the obvious disparities between the expectations for Yugoslavia nurtured in wartime propaganda and the post-war reality. Institutional corruption, official incompetence, economic instability and antagonistic nationalist politics only furthered British cultural disenchantment.³² Politically, the FO judged the kingdom's value as mostly contingent on its membership of France's 'Little

Entente': a regional alliance designed to check Hungary's revanchist ambitions and serve as a *cordon sanitaire* against the Soviet Union that echoed British relations with Serbia in the early nineteenth century.[33] As Dragan Bakić contends, despite the vestigial influences of Seton-Watson and the 'New Europe Group', official support for the successor states was quickly tempered by prevailing 'Edwardian' attitudes that viewed them dispassionately as unstable and lacking permanence. Until the appearance of Nazi Germany, a prevailing sense of non-commitment defined British regional policy, reflecting wider public ambivalence.[34]

Such attitudes were perhaps equally indicative of continuities in the oligarchic nature of Britain's foreign policy establishment. The Royal Institute of International Affairs, established in 1920 by former delegates to the Paris Peace Conference and more commonly known as Chatham House after 1923, exemplified these shortcomings. From the outset, its stated aim of broadening public engagement with foreign policy issues was encumbered by its founder Lionel Curtis's elitist Edwardian conception of 'public opinion'. Despite paying lip service to the idea of expanding its outreach, in practice this simply meant 'the opinion of those in the City, Parliament, the universities and the press, and, of course, in London's gentleman's clubs', in contrast to the egalitarianism that had driven Buxton to establish the BC in 1903.[35] Indeed, by the early 1930s even veteran members were urging for direct co-operation with the trade union movement, in hopes of bringing in working-class voices; a staff list published in *Hansard* in November 1939, consisted almost entirely of senior academics and ex-diplomats, with Seton-Watson and Laffan as in-house specialists for southeastern Europe.[36]

Of equal significance was the FO's diminishing status in British foreign policy. Associations between the outbreak of the Great War and a lack of political accountability among senior diplomats saw its independence gradually reduced. Despite retaining exclusivity in the recruitment and training of diplomatic staff, by the 1930s, the FO found itself ever more reliant on the good graces of other departments and institutions, notably the Treasury and the Bank of England, to fulfil much of its remit.[37] Finney and Miklós Lojkó regard this as characteristic of London's subsequent lack of diplomatic or cultural capital that stymied its Balkan re-engagement efforts after 1933. Throughout the 1920s, lofty assumptions that Britain's 'moral' standing commanded universal respect among small, independent countries became an affective substitute for traditional diplomacy and economic interests, depreciating any later scope for cultivating a unified regional front against the Third Reich.[38] This was reflected in the failure of Yugoslavia's Anglophile institutions, such as the Anglo-American-Yugoslav Club[39] or the *South Slav Herald*, a newspaper marketed to an Anglophone readership, in promoting cultural and economic ties.[40] As the paper's economic correspondent reported in early 1939, British and French unwillingness to build or sustain business links had left Yugoslavian exporters almost entirely reliant on German markets.[41]

The appearance of Chatham House was no less suggestive of the pre-war holistic trends that had seen 'legitimate' expertise grow ever more professionalized, hierarchical and remote from general concerns. Ironically, the growth in educational opportunities after 1900 also normalized expectations that incoming generations of scholars would embark on more standardized paths of specialist attainment. Consequently, organizations dedicated to promoting knowledge-based disciplines were increasingly reliant on the university for members with the now requisite academic credentials. The Royal Anthropological Institute (RAI), of which Durham had been affiliated since 1908, was a microcosm of this process. Before the 1930s, anthropology's drift towards greater professionalism was partly offset by a still significant amateur presence among the RAI's membership, many of whom held political connections or whose involvement in public affairs had attracted a more non-specialist audience. However, this appeal was soon eroded by an influx of academics, of which the RAI's leadership was almost entirely comprised by 1938, and professionalized field researchers working in colonial postings. As the RAI's scholarly profile pivoted towards investigating more 'esoteric problems', much of its lay membership started to arrive at the conclusion that anthropology held 'little practical value' for society at large.[42]

M-O's founding – and the decision to originally headquarter it in the industrial Lancashire town of Bolton – was in part viewed as a reaction to the wider citizenry's perceived alienation from 'public opinion', a term easily dismissed as the 'products of editorial invention' that allowed Britain's elites to evoke the views of the masses while continuing to exclude them.[43] Although predicated on press responses to the abdication of King Edward VIII in 1936, the rapid deterioration of international relations shortly after its formation, stimulated concern among M-O's staff that an absence of dialogue 'between leader and led, between published opinion and public opinion, between Westminster chatter and Lancashire talk has built an invisible barrier, and that is dangerous in our democracy'.[44]

Nevertheless, these broader trends did not equate to a latter-day form of splendid isolationism. For the politically engaged minority who aspired to proactively involve themselves in internationalist causes, the period proved something of a high-water mark. The League of Nations Union, formed in October 1918 to promote humanitarian principles and the ideal of collective security, arguably represented one of the most influential lobby groups in interwar Britain. Boasting well over 400,000 members at its peak in 1931, the Union's pacifistic agenda, educational programmes and vigorous campaigns, including the Peace Ballot of 1935, proved instrumental in galvanizing public opposition to militarism.[45] Like the FO, however, this fixation on international collaboration further diminished the perceived relevance of foreign relations. Even the Spanish Civil War, arguably the most high-profile example of non-state intervention before 1945, occurred along similar lines. Interactions between Left-wing British and Yugoslav volunteers within the International Brigades were also framed by an internationalist context that sought to de-emphasize cultural and national difference.[46] It was through a similar Anglo-British paradigm that Yugoslavia ultimately manifested in the interwar British imagination, confining politics to a distant margin.

Commodifying the 'New Europe'

Despite largely disappearing as a subject of political discussion in the public sphere, the interwar decade did not equate to complete disengagement with what could now be termed the Yugoslav Balkans. Indeed, the 1930s were marked by a brief revival in cultural and scientific interest, somewhat echoing that of 1903 to 1912. As later demonstrated with *Black Lamb and Grey Falcon*, the flurry of artistic, literary and scientific representations this produced was anything but divorced from domestic influence or popular allegory. Nevertheless, even West's two-volume magnum opus was a product of one of British travel writing's most demonstrably elitist and contradictory phases. Central to this was an overall narrowing of the scope of Anglo-Balkan engagement, both in the imaginary and literal sense.[47]

Nevertheless, this sudden return to a restricted and elitist regional presence did not represent a break with the previous twenty years. Indeed, Yugoslavia's remoteness as a foreign policy concern left it more open to the influences of British domestic culture than at any point in history. Whereas earlier imagological shifts had resulted from a process of engagement shaped by, and often seeking to form parallels with, more immediate socio-political factors, the cultural revival of the 1930s was a product of tourism – itself an offshoot of rising consumerism and an Anglo-British cultural mentality of commodification.

While the degree to which the interwar period witnessed the crystallizing of an Anglo-British 'common culture' remains a matter of debate and conjecture among social historians, an undeniable factor was the spread of consumerism as a form of standard social practice.[48] As well as representing the amplification of embedded, long-term socio-economic trends, many of which originated in the advent of the Industrial Revolution itself, the progression of this development rested on a general stability that permeated much of the British political and economic landscape between the wars. Indeed, by international standards, Britain's political system proved unusually resilient to both forms of Left- and Right-wing ideological extremism, in stark contrast to its earlier failure at stymieing Irish republicanism.[49] The National Government, an electoral coalition formed in August 1931 as a response to the collapse of the Second Labour Administration, the Great Depression and the impending devaluation of the pound sterling, established itself as a de facto centrist hegemon until 1940. Combined with a softening of Labour's earlier radical stances, a growing cross-party embrace of domestic reform and a decline in trade union militancy after 1926, the social instability of the early to mid-1920s was considerably less pronounced during the so-called 'Devil's Decade' of the 1930s.[50]

Of equal, if not greater, significance was the Depression's relatively mild, albeit unevenly segmented, socio-economic impact. The stagnation and decline of the old staple industries masked Britain's emerging economic diversification, predicated on a flourishing service sector and lighter industries focused on mass produced consumer goods; a private housing boom, fuelled by lower interest rates following the pound's devaluation; and, unlike the United States and Germany, a domestic banking system unscathed by the Great Crash of 1929. Stephen Constantine argues that despite the unemployment rate more than tripling to over 3 million by 1933, its impacts was far from uniform. While cities and towns that still relied on mining or the staple industries bore the brunt of the recession, its impact in southern England and much of the Midlands – where the majority of newer industries were concentrated – was comparatively marginal, beyond already established pockets of historical deprivation.[51]

The outcome of this was the heightening of a pre-existing transition towards what could be described as a form of Anglo-British 'national' lifestyle oriented towards consumerism. This in turn generated an explosion in the public's appetite for the printed word: the number of published books alone rose from 8,666 in 1914 to 14,904 in 1939, yet total sales nearly quadrupled from 7.2 million to 26.8 million between 1928 and 1939.[52] Early research by M-O, however, revealed that most of this seemed to have been driven by escapist genre fiction unlike 'the classics' which were 'read by few' and 'more serious modern authors' even less.[53] Later surveys, notably those compiled under M-O's expansive empirical study of public reading habits during the Second World War, further revealed that while demand for 'serious non-fiction' increased, access to such reading material was often out of reach for many.[54] This was framed against a background in which cinema-going had become the country's most popular leisure activity by 1935, with radio competing with print to be the dominant form of British household entertainment and information in 1939. As George Orwell observed, during the Depression cinema and 'access to a radio' remained an integral part of community and regional identity across northern England, even for those living 'on the verge of starvation'.[55]

Contrary to West's later assertions of a complacent insularity, this intensive commercialism, the state's still relatively limited presence and Britain's unique status as a true 'mass society' actually made its interwar cultural orientations far more international than those of most other European countries. Although this predominately came in the form of a ubiquitous American influence (via Hollywood and popular swing music), new media organizations such as the British Broadcasting Company strove to introduce listeners to a range of cultural alternatives, including Eastern European music.[56]

It should be acknowledged that such efforts were unlikely to have met with any major success. Furthermore, unlike Yugoslavia, a strain of cultural insularity did remain evident in British public attitudes towards international spectator sports – the only such forum with a genuine mass appeal. Despite participating at every Summer and Winter Olympic Games from 1920 to 1936, Britons proved to be fairly mediocre athletes on the world stage; the home audience for these interwar games was itself limited owing to their elitist nature. In contrast, Yugoslavia was brought to wider international attention as the youngest national squad to participate at the inaugural FIFA World Cup in 1930, cementing the country's long-standing reputation in European association football.[57] Although Britain's own national and club teams also took part in international matches, these tended to be viewed as less significant to the Home Championships: a 'friendly' between England and Yugoslavia in May 1939, for example, mostly garnered interest from the kingdom's immediate neighbours.[58]

Tourism and literary depictions therefore remained the only medium for substantive cultural engagement between the wars. Such social exclusivity, however, did not disqualify Yugoslavia from being subjected to the consumerist trends shaping British domestic cultural habits, in which travel became increasingly prominent. More structured patterns of education and employment meant 'traditions of popular holiday-making' were already an established part of national life by the 1930s. Even recreational visits to continental Europe existed in a growing capacity for more 'enterprising' working-class holidaymakers. At the beginning of the 1930s, broader cross-sections of British society were already a familiar presence in more readily accessible locations, such as the Belgian resort of Ostend, while those affiliated to the 'Workers' Travel Association' were beginning to view Spain as a more adventurous, yet still affordable, destination.[59] Coupled with a continual stream of ephemera discussing the more exclusive travel-habits of the rich and famous, Britain's interwar consumer culture marked the true point of departure in how the wider public perceived and framed engagement with foreigners. While this certainly did not imply an end to national or cultural stereotyping, it nevertheless signalled an important transition through which overseas travel was normalized as a distinctive form of leisure. This, in turn, promoted more utilitarian preconceptions of foreign interactions as commodities, or potential commodities, rather than something wholly alien. It was this Anglo-British mentality of commodification that determined Yugoslavia's popular image.

Before 1930, the Balkan lands continued to exude a similar patina of remoteness to that of the Edwardian era. Despite a reputation for unearthing scandal across Europe's 'playgrounds of the rich', the popular gossip columnist Charles Graves could casually dismiss the 'Austrian Riviera' as 'too far away' from London to be worth visiting in the 1920s.[60] By the late 1930s, however, this veneer of inaccessibility had largely faded. Although marred by political in-fighting, Yugoslavia's peace delegation to Paris in 1919 had successfully outmanoeuvred its equally fractious Italian counterpart to retain sovereignty over most of the Dalmatian coast, one of the few regional enclaves with an established tradition of international tourism.[61]

While an 'enduring genre' of British Balkan travel literature still proliferated in Orientalist idioms of 'quaintness' and picturesque poverty, by the early 1930s, it had also begun to codify Yugoslavia's coastline as a destination ideally suited for the budget-conscious middle classes, perpetuating a vogue for travel in the east Adriatic.[62] Mary Ann Dolling, who first visited Dalmatia in 1930, later credited herself with having brought about this increased public interest through the success of her romantic novel *Illyrian Spring* (1935), written and published under her famous pen name 'Ann Bridge'.[63] While presented from the perspective of an upper-class heroine, Dolling's semi-feminist subtext and emphasis on Dalmatia's genteel remoteness as a cultural palliative for modern social pressures offered lay readers a more intimate introduction to the region's heritage without the imperiousness of earlier non-fiction. The novel's secondary function as a vicarious tourist guide even lampoons the derivative, Anglo-centric perspectives of earlier British visitors. In response to the heroine's complaints of there being 'more guide-books for the Sahara' than Dalmatia, Dolling's male lead suggests she (and the audience) consult foreign publishers, rather than relying on outdated Victoria-era texts.[64] Nevertheless, in contrast to other titles such as Oona Ball's *Dalmatia* (1932), a more traditionally styled travelogue offering précis of local history and geography alongside bespoke travel advice, *Illyrian Spring* heralded an important imagological turn through which Yugoslavia came to be understood within a more generalized public cultural milieu.[65] Dolling's glamorizing of the Dalmatian coast was granted further impetus by Edward VIII, who visited the province with Wallis Simpson in August 1936. The presence of Britain's increasingly troubled sovereign, only a few months before his abdication, further situated Dalmatia within a series of semi-commodifiable spaces that formed a newly emerging imaginative geography predicated more on ephemera than contemporary knowledge.[66]

While political pundits and a shrinking number of academic authors continued to present Yugoslavia through the lens of socio-political conflict, this was more often overshadowed by newer depictions that deliberately appealed to consumerist inclinations. Literary endorsement, coupled with promotional campaigns by travel companies, soon undermined Dalmatia's projected image as an undiscovered corner of the Mediterranean; between 1936 and 1938, Yugoslavia recorded almost 41,000 British tourists, its coastline being the primary attraction.[67] Eugene Fodor's highly discursive *1938 in Europe* encapsulated this trend, highlighting reasonably low prices as integral to the country's value as a 'novelty' destination. Pitching Yugoslavia as a land tailored for 'that vast mass of middle-class people who are in need of a real change but must watch the cost', this was complimented by an exhaustive list of romantic cultural selling-points – including the 'picturesque costumes and interesting customs' of the local peasantry.[68]

Besides the innate romanticism of cultural obscurity, local actors were equally keen to continue fostering this less egregious international image. 'Putnik', Yugoslavia's official tourist agency, that served as one of the *Herald*'s principal advertising sponsors and boasted its own branch in London by 1939, was quick to latch onto the Anglo-British consumerist mind-set as a means of further expanding into one of Europe's more lucrative markets. Its own officially approved guide also drew attention to Yugoslavia's cheapness, when compared to Italy, yet it was far less subtle in its commercial leanings. The kingdom itself was defined almost exclusively by its material offerings, being a land 'rich in spas', 'new hotels', outdoor pursuits, classical architecture and picturesque remoteness. Aspiring scholars were even promised opportunities to pursue amateur anthropological field studies of 'traditional festivals' and though various 'authentic' cultural encounters in and around Yugoslavia's major towns and cities.[69]

Nevertheless, this commodified image exposed the limitations of the peasantry as a tangible or desirable point of interaction owing to the unwillingness of most British tourists to venture into the country's hinterlands. Anecdotes concerning discomfort, poor hygiene and the embarrassment of communication difficulties discouraged Britons from leaving the familiarity of the coast and larger towns, subconsciously restricting their itineraries to a distinguishable 'tourist zone' centred on Dalmatia, Zagreb and established resort areas like Bled in north-west Slovenia.[70] Even for the more adventurous, any commitment to wholly interact with the 'native' culture was rarely sustained. An account by the Gordons describing life in the South Slavic 'heartland' of Bosnia-Herzegovina post-independence, based on impressions from a three-month sketching tour in the summer of 1921, was dominated by a preoccupation with procuring food that wouldn't test their commitment to 'live frugally'. Even on the Adriatic islands, where they concluded their sojourn in the hopes of a more 'agreeable' Mediterranean diet, travellers were obliged to partake in 'stringy and gelatinous' mutton, consumption of which evoked 'the infantile joys of sucking a sponge'.[71] This underlying disappointment with 'authentic' Yugoslavian peasant life was later inferred in depictions of Islamic or non-Slavic heritage, which even guidebooks suggested as a more culturally engaging experience.[72] Beginning their tour in Sarajevo, the Gordons exposited on how the captivating musical talents of the city's ubiquitous

Romani entertainers seemed far removed from the heroic ballads they'd 'endured' in wartime Montenegro.[73] Fifteen years later, Stephen Graham, *The Times*'s former Russia correspondent, concurred, finding the whirling dervishes and 'gentle dream-like melody' of Ohrid's 'Turkish music' a 'sweet relief' to the 'trying moroseness' of the local Christian peasantry.[74]

Despite Britain representing a far from insignificant share of the interwar tourist market, Yugoslavia did not emerge as a mainstream destination until the 1950s. Of the two largest British travel agencies in 1939, Thomas Cook and the Polytechnic Touring Association, a mere three pages were dedicated to it in the former's expansive European travel catalogue while the latter's didn't even have Yugoslavia listed.[75] An article in the *Herald* from September 1933, discussing the growing importance of tourism to Yugoslavia's inland economy, cited the Herzegovinian town of Trebinje, just over 30 km north-east of Dubrovnik, where it had accounted for nearly a third of all local traders' profits in 1932. This welcome injection of foreign capital was apparently tempered, however, by the fact that the majority of visitors had been parsimonious Austrians, Czechs and Germans – unwilling to concede when haggling over prices; despite previous forecasts that 'Anglo-Saxons' would form the majority of Yugoslavia's annual tourist trade, the 'English', according to one disgruntled Muslim merchant, had been 'disappointingly scarce' that year.[76]

Uncovering the 'Yugoslav type'

Patterns of disengagement in the 1920s, and cultural commodification in the 1930s, did not equate to a complete abandoning of pseudo-scientific representation. Throughout the interwar years, touristic literature continued to indulge in cultural, and even political, speculation – specifically the ambiguous and highly contested nature of Yugoslavian identity. Recounting a motoring tour of Croatia and Bosnia-Herzegovina in the mid-1920s, one anonymous author deemed this self-evident upon leaving Zagreb:

> The soil was fertile and the farming intensive – one realized the whole country was a land of peasants and small holders [. . .] There are no Middle Class, no châteaux, no manor houses, only miles of peasantry.[77]

Tourism's supplanting of diplomacy and political lobbying as the primary means through which Britons directly engaged with the South Slavic Balkans did little to redirect the popular literary onus away from the habits and lifestyles of rural communities. This was aided by the now ingrained fascination for the countryside through positive cultural associations and a resumption of the, much understated, reversal in Britain's own rural demographic decline. The 1921 census for England and Wales, for instance, revealed an increase of approximately 4.3 per cent in districts classed as 'rural', a trend set to continue well beyond 1945.[78] As with the Edwardians, this cultural milieu coalesced around ingrained generalizations that 'rural people were different', with village and farming communities perceived as moulding a type of individual possessing a clarity of vision and purpose.⁷⁹ Among the more esoteric, reviving country life was once again equated to the resurrecting of a pre-industrial democratic spirit that found analogies in Yugoslavian peasant society. Unlike the latter, however, the British, more specifically English, countryside appeared far more open to permeation by unwanted 'town influences'.⁸⁰

This persistent ideal of rural society as representative of an organic 'national' character remained widespread in more 'serious' travel writing, which still characterized the Balkans 'as the Volksmuseum of Europe'.⁸¹ The war's immediate aftermath, for instance, saw a wave of publications featuring translated peasant folk poetry, songs and stories that had been collected by activists, relief volunteers and even BSF veterans during the Balkans campaign.⁸² This continued fixation on folkloric customs might be explained by the fact that it remained one of the few areas of specialist interest still accessible to those outside Britain's hierarchies of academic learning. Any aspiring American scholar in the 1940s, the influential folklorist Richard Dorson later wrote, would have been bewildered by the absence of academic rigour among their English (and Welsh) counterparts. In 1939, the Folklore Society, Britain's principle organization, could have been an inversion of the RAI with its leadership adhering to a Victorian amateurism centred on unearthing and cataloguing old 'customs and usages', often presenting them without any historical context. Conversely, these depictions of folklore, or just obscure local traditions, held far greater resonance with lay audiences as representative of an 'authentic' culture.⁸³

Such an ethos also permeated research on Yugoslavia. Throughout the 1930s, the new country's enhanced profile attracted a coterie of academics and amateur enthusiasts who emphasized positivist approaches based on accumulating empirical evidence. These included Lodge, who returned to the Balkans as an anthropologist in 1938, and the *Le Play Society* – a research organization dedicated to engaging in overseas geographical and sociological fieldwork – that conducted an extensive cultural survey of northern Slovenia's remote Upper Savinja valley in 1932.⁸⁴ Tourist guidebooks and articles on Dalmatia also urged travellers to venture away from the amenities of the coast in search of spiritually healthier alternatives in the form of 'rural hospitality' and 'rustic country inns'. These efforts were often prefaced with introductory language guides, often accompanied by warnings on the difficulties of communication outside of the main urban centres.⁸⁵

Although the 1930s mostly represented a depoliticized revival of previous trends, as with the Edwardian period, this was foreshadowed by developments in the 1920s. The Gordons, for example, described their return visit to the Balkans in 1921 as having been conditioned by a desire to fashion narratives around 'the life of simple folk which is denied to the ordinary tourist'.⁸⁶ Despite food poisoning and general discomfort, the subsequent record of their experiences in Bosnia-Herzegovina and Croatia provided rare insight into the poverty and political dysfunction of the new state.⁸⁷ A more established precedent among the romantically inclined, who gravitated to Yugoslavia from 1930, was to be found in the work of the Slavophile Scottish linguist Fanny Copeland. Having served as a translator for the JO, her vicarious role in Yugoslavia's creation, decision to take up residence in Ljubljana from 1921 as an adopted citizen and reinvention of herself as an expert authority, placed Copeland in a similar 'spatial

Figure 10 'Serbo-Turkish Villages', by Cora Gordon, 1921. © Courtesy of Ken Bryant.

and temporal junction' to that of Durham. This perception of expatriate life as a 'route to personal emancipation', following the end of an unhappy marriage in 1912, also led her to identify with a semi-liberationist cause, namely the recorded persecution of South Slavs in the territories annexed by Italy at the Paris Peace Conference.[88]

The accentuation of peasant customs as authentically Yugoslavian reinforced existing assumptions that similarities between the traditions of its constituent territories equated to a nascent national culture. Echoes of the 1907 Balkan States exhibition were evident at a Yugoslav art show held in Liverpool and Glasgow in 1939: visitors were once again presented with ethnological displays of 'national costume', dances, and recitals of ballads and epic poetry described as symbolizing Yugoslavia's 'spiritual and temporal quintessence'.[89] Even after the outbreak of the Second World War, West hailed the peasant as the source of Yugoslavian artistic creativity and spontaneity rather than an 'aspiring middle class'. Native peasant art was 'not a plaything; but a necessity [. . .] a cup into which life can be poured and lifted to the lips and be tasted'. From this, she predicted that a Yugoslav national conscience would eventually be given shape.[90] The *Herald*, to which Copeland became a regular contributor, repeatedly projected this notion of a unitary identity onto a mosaic of overlapping village traditions, a sentiment echoed in the British national and specialist press.[91]

The Yugoslavian state itself was keenly interested in drawing foreign attention to statistics that reinforced this distinctly agrarian national character, buttressed by an intellectual establishment that incessantly glorified the 'tillers of the soil'.[92] Meštrović – the kingdom's only cultural figure with an established international presence – continued to attract almost unfettered praise for his efficacious blending of modernism and peasant folklore, depicted as being integral to Yugoslavism.[93] Despite the country's nationalist divisions, the leading Croat, Serb and Slovene political parties all espoused some form of agrarianist ideology that valorized the peasant as the 'moral hypostasis' of their respective nations. Party and state propaganda only reinforced this by aggressively designating Yugoslavia as 'primarily a "peasant country"' founded and sustained exclusively on the customs, religious beliefs and 'self-sufficiency' of the village. Politicians who preached fidelity to these values were equally vigorous in denigrating urban culture and society.[94] Even in the more industrialized Slovene lands, the governing Slovene People's Party regularly placated its core voters with Catholic dogma that effectively equated capitalism with Marxism. 'A rich man', argued the leading Catholic daily *Slovenec* in 1920, 'is as abnormal a sight in the SLS, as is a small peasant in the party of [the] capitalist bourgeoisie [the main Liberal opposition]'.[95]

This was even lent credence by prominent scientific figures; Yugoslavia's delegation to Paris in 1919 included its own 'ethnographic section' – led by Cvijić – who presented findings from his recently published ethnographical survey on Balkan personality types, *La Peninsule Balkanique* (1918), as evidence in disputes over the kingdom's borders. Although placing greater emphasis on historical and environmental metrics, Cvijić's approach, originating in the earlier folkloric tradition of Karadžić, partially offered a psycho-analytical extrapolation of Victorian-era 'customs and usages' in the form of 'folk mentalities'. These would subsequently be invoked by other Yugoslavian ethnographers as a means of determining ethnicity and ethnic behaviours.[96]

In keeping with Britain's own colonial tradition of applying a geopolitical dimension to anthropological research, interwar depictions of Yugoslav peasant customs followed in a similar pattern. Writing in the early 1920s, Durham interpreted the prevalence of bird motifs in Albanian folklore as indicative of cultures in its surrounding territories. This, she argued, appeared most notable in Bosnian iconography such as the 'bird chariot of the sun', surmising that such 'bird traditions' had been assimilated into a Slavicized culture – and casting doubt on the populace's true ethnic origins.[97] Lodge's work on folk traditions along Yugoslavia's eastern border ran counter to this by stressing a purely Slavic cultural continuum extending westwards. The plethora of 'semi-pagan' rituals honouring the rites of spring in eastern Serbia (an areas dismissed by Durham as 'distinctly Bulgar') were claimed by Lodge to exist in vestigial form as far west as the environs of Zagreb. Agricultural communities in both Macedonia and Slovenia, meanwhile, displayed variations in the practice of grooms symbolically 'chasing' their brides during wedding ceremonies.[98] Copeland hypothesized that geographical remoteness 'inevitably resulted' in a set of 'base attributes' becoming ubiquitous to highland communities. In the Yugoslavian context, these qualities manifested in areas as disparate as Lower Carniola in southeastern Slovenia and Montenegro's coastal Brda region. Methods of construction, the use of landscape for viticulture and common design patterns in the national costumes (now mostly worn by older women) appeared evident of a 'common Slav heritage'.[99] For less attentive observers, historical precedence for Yugoslavia could merely be extrapolated from common cultural legacies. Planning an expedition into central Bosnia-Herzegovina or Macedonia in hopes of viewing 'Oriental dress' or meeting peasants who still lived in fear of 'the evil eye' was unnecessary, remarked one diplomat: such encounters where no less common when travelling the direct route from Zagreb to Belgrade.[100]

At a more popular level, however, academic speculation on ethnological commonalities had minimal influence. Press coverage and travel literature tended to regard the country through a narrative of differentiation that characterized Yugoslavia as a collection of historic polities and provinces bound by language, rather than a single national entity. As Wolff notes, West's own text routinely contradicts its professed support for a unitary Yugoslavian identity by presenting each constituent people as historically distinct.[101] Moreover, identifying peasant commonalities did not prevent political discourses from bracketing the country's constituent peoples into hierarchies or distinct cultural spheres. Hostile or disparaging voices spoke of a receding Western influence as one travelled from Zagreb to Belgrade, where Serbs and politicians of 'peasant stock' were overrepresented in the Yugoslav government and parliament.[102] Reports sympathetic to the new status quo also stressed this fractious divide, yet were inclined to attribute it to historical divisions. The Serbs, wrote the former spy R. H. Bruce Lockhart, possessed 'little to no culture' and were prone to being 'rather lazy'. However, this made them no less ambitious, innovative, willing to endure hardships, or 'stubbornly independent'. By contrast, the cultured countenance of the Croats obscured a 'servile' temperament for mimicking their non-Slavic neighbours, despite also including 'illiterates from the villages' within their political leadership.[103]

Slovenia, viewed as a virtually self-contained national entity by the 1920s, resembled a contradiction of sorts: contiguous to its geography, visitors noted that the social sphere was dominated by skiing and outdoor pursuits.[104] Copeland extrapolated upon this as the crux for the Slovene's own internalized struggle to craft a cultural identity independent of hegemonic external influences. This was comparable to how Montenegrin and Serb peasants had historically safeguarded their own identity through fealty to the Orthodox Church and the oral traditions of the wandering *guslari*.[105] The Slovenes' redefining of activities such as mountaineering and skiing as 'mass pursuits' were thus deemed an act of cultural resistance to elitist perceptions of these pastimes in Austria or Italy, comparable to the Serbs' refusal to submit to Islam in the fourteenth century.[106]

Images of placid defiance also inferred continuing notions of civilization's cultural and moral hierarchy. 'The Slovenes are excellent Jugoslavs. I think they have the makings of the backbone of the country,' Copeland enthused in a letter to the Belgian publicist Charles Saroléa in 1922. Unsurprisingly, the 'national' Slovene mentality was frequently equated to that of her native Scotland where 'they contrive to make a situation work, instead of grousing about it to each other and to the Universe'.[107] Indeed, the creation of Yugoslavia itself initially reassured some pundits that the spirit of the Habsburg's *mission civilisatrice* would, in fact, continue in the Balkans. As the once sceptical Miller argued, '[T]he formation of Jugoslavia has made the people look westward . . . and should tend rather to Europeanise the Serbs than to Balkanise the Croats and Slovenes.'[108] Any difficulties in reconciling their 'higher plane of European civilization' with 'a land of peasant proprietors without an aristocracy' would, in time, be resolved.[109]

Nevertheless, even more sanguine observers detected the obvious geographical disparities. In Yugoslavia's southernmost provinces, Copeland observed, the easy conflation between culture and ethnicity found in the Slovene lands gave way to the 'ambiguous Orient' with its racial and religious intermixing rendered any clear division or boundaries void.[110] The *Le Play* survey was even more explicit. Slovenia's links might have historically been 'with the south', yet they now exemplified a case of geographic isolation eclipsing ethnic traditions, mirroring Cvijić's interpretation of Dinaric society as one determined by environmental factors.[111] Among the villages of Upper Savinja, the racial characteristics of the 'Tall, broad headed . . . dark and muscular . . . Dinaric type' was completely absent. Like the environment, this had supposedly occurred far back in history, resulting from Slovenes having not inter-mixed with non-Slavs:

> It [Slovenes] is not so muscular nor active as the Dinaric mountaineer; nor so steeped in folklore nor so temperamental and imaginative. The original settlers came here without having lived in the Dinaric region to the south [. . .] The absence of the zadruga clan organisation of society, together with the marked isolation of the region, have happily left it quite free from the feuds of the southern region.[112]

Ingrained heterogeneity was not universally perceived as an inherent weakness, however. Some commentators even discerned Yugoslavia's 'variety of types, costumes, culture' as intrinsic to its nascent national character.[113] Photographic montages and other ephemera were regularly featured in the *Herald*, normalizing diversity as a defining aspect of Yugoslavian national life. As one historian observed, the sight of 'the Latin inhabitants' of Zadar 'jostling with the Slav peasants of the interior' illustrated that cultural coexistence need not be antagonistic.[114] Multi-ethnicity was even promoted by Putnik as a touristic selling-point in the 1930s. Ironically, it was Yugoslavia's much maligned cities, notably those unique in 'oriental and western contrasts' such as Belgrade and Sarajevo, rather than its vaunted rural society that purportedly offered a glimpse of the country's hoped-for future. Only in these cultural melting pots would foreigners uncover the kingdom's potential 'to create what could only now have been created: the new Yugoslav type'.[115]

Conclusion

Whereas 1914 facilitated the transition to a more culturally positive image of the South Slavic Balkans in Britain, Yugoslavia's entry into the Second World War in

April 1941 resembled an official attempt to replicate the propagandized adulation for the Serbs of 1915 and 1916. This was certainly reflected among British officialdom; the politically charged atmosphere arising from the failure of Neville Chamberlain's Appeasement policy, reconfigured the interwar years as a time of stagnation and international short-sightedness. 'They stand together . . . Jugoslavia's polyglot peoples united against tyranny!' the Secretary of State for India and Burma, Leo Amery, declared in *The Illustrated London News*, less than a week before the Yugoslavian army's unconditional surrender to the Axis. Having attempted to avoid conflict by joining the Tripartite Pact that March, Belgrade had, like London, simply been seeking to maintain an unsustainable status quo. The 'true threat of annihilation', Amery predicted, would overcome the country's internecine bickering and meld the Southern Slavs into a democratic bulwark against the Third Reich's 'drive to the East'.[116]

Shades of this characterization can be found in imagological historiography that typically defines British interwar (and even Cold War) engagement as either following earlier patterns of disparagement or diverging along wartime loyalties. While these assessments are not wholly inaccurate, they're prevalence masks a more nuanced, and highly contradictory, episode in Anglo-Balkan relations. For a significant portion of those who developed an interest in Yugoslavia, or simply curious members of the wider public, the 1920s and 1930s were their introduction to the culture and politics of the South Slavic Balkans. Consequently, in the absence of a more obvious frame of historical reference, the imagery surrounding the lands and people of Yugoslavia was, like the British Empire, filtered through the myriad trends that defined notions of Anglo-Britishness between the wars. This was most definitively revealed in the fixation on Dalmatia and the east Adriatic as a promising new destination for the emergent tourist market; while easy to dismiss as superficial and materialistic, these consumerist attitudes were arguably far closer to the general character of British mass society than the political allegory of the Edwardian years.

As with the First World War, this period represented another evolutionary phase, rather than an implied break with the past. Indeed, growing middle-class awareness of Britain's regional economic divide in the 1930s appeared to carry over into perceptions of Yugoslavian identity as Victorian cultural assumptions continued to fall away. Neither did Britain's apparent political stability after 1922 equate to an absence of latent anxiety or cultural pessimism.

8

The shape of things to come?

Unlike the Edwardians, interwar British impressions of the first Yugoslavia were distinguished by a far greater propensity for exaggeration and cultural embellishment. Richard Overy asserts that while Britain, discounting Ireland, had been largely spared the socio-political turbulence experienced across much of the continent, like the 1900s and early 1910s, a potent sense of cultural pessimism continued to influence popular understanding of ideas in the abstract. Regardless of domestic stability, a more heightened awareness of international trends and entrenched belief in a state of decline characterized much of the political and intellectual spheres of the 1920s and 1930s. The international presence of ideological extremism, and growing evidence of capitalism's social failings, set the timbre for this 'Morbid Age'; riven by an ever pervasive cynicism and morbidity, Western civilization had seemingly entered a stage of 'terminal crises'.[1] This was most acutely illustrated by the prevalence of pacifism in political, civic and intellectual life. Only with the recognition of fascism as an actively aggressive threat was the prospect of a second war welcomed as a means of finally resolving the contradictions and anxieties that had arisen as a result of modernity.[2]

Galvanized by this cultural disenchantment, British authors often presented accounts of their overseas travels as a necessary rectification of the disingenuous pejorative imagery created by their Victorian forebears, encapsulated in West's *Black Lamb and Grey Falcon*. Although originally conceived over three separate trips to Yugoslavia from 1936 to 1938, her extensive commentary did not reach publication until the height of the London Blitz in 1941 – an appropriate time for proffering some historical meditation on the decay of European civilization. The agrarian world of the South Slavs not only provided solace from an ailing Britain ostensibly afflicted by cultural 'idiocy', but offered insight into the essence of humanity when stripped of its modernistic trappings: 'I had come to Yugoslavia because I knew that the past had made the present and I want to see how the process works.'[3] Other late-interwar visitors were no less adamant in framing the act of travel as, what Hammond terms, an 'escape from decadence', fleeing a culturally degenerate West for the 'spiritual relief' and 'social comprehensibility' of Europe's more rustic peripherals.[4]

Yet, even proponents of this professed desire to rediscover some pre-industrial society found their enthusiasm tempered by the very modernity they imagined themselves to be fleeing – politically as well as socially. Prior to their arrival in Belgrade, West professed excitement that they were to experience the symbolic pinnacle of Yugoslavian peasant culture, or another 'barbaric village' as her husband had apparently quipped. What they instead discovered (to her spouse's probable relief) was a rapidly expanding urban metropolis boasting most of the amenities and services one could find in Budapest or Paris. After visiting its capital, West had 'felt a sudden abatement of [her] infatuation for Yugoslavia'.[5]

In this regard, latent disappointment, parallel to the dissipation of political pacifism in the 1930s, gradually began to colour Yugoslavia's image. This chapter concludes the study by assessing how the failings of Yugoslavia as a political entity were accompanied by a gradual recognition that even the supposedly timeless South Slavic peasantry was beginning to succumb to the encroachment of modernity.

Allegories for a 'Morbid Age'

When situated within historical patterns of Anglo-Balkan interaction, the interwar years represented, after a fashion, a secondary phase in the allegorizing process that began in the wake of the Boer War. However, unlike the more positivist mentalities of the Edwardian years, in which social allegory was as much a conduit for enhancing public knowledge, the Balkans' diminished presence in the public sphere appeared to partially reverse this transnational dynamic. This was evident in travel literature that re-emerged as the most readily accessible source of contemporary information. Here too, as Hammond maintains, the interwar decades witnessed a return to the cultural 'self/other dichotomy' of the nineteenth century but with the Balkans, and the East in general, representing this binary's 'positive pole'. Agrarian Yugoslavia now offered cultural 'relief' for middle-class British travellers jaded by the war and societal change through 'comprehensible' village social structures and 'colourful' aesthetics; a stark contrast to the supposedly drab realities of life in the industrialized West.[6]

To a certain extent, the imagological trajectory of the interwar period corresponded to that of 1890 to 1914. The Gordon's observations of Bosnia-Herzegovina in 1921 for example, while far from enamouring in portraying the realities of persistent rural poverty, foreshadowed the more metaphysical leanings of later commentaries. Notable among these had been the sight of Catholic peasants spontaneously gathering to perform a *kolo* in the northern Herzegovinian town of Konjic, 60 km south-west of Sarajevo:

> we were struck by the curious effect of solidarity given by this circle of men and women . . . there was something metallic, something more permanent than flesh in its construction. It was an ancient rite rather than a dance; and by thus linking themselves the dancers had merged their beings into both the past and the future.[7]

The Gordons' record was itself an early example of a backlash against the perceived social outcome of the Great War in British travel literature, returning to a more romanticized portrait of Europe's less industrialized regions. Such accounts typically adopted the 'national' customs of countries such as Yugoslavia as allegories for vehiculating their frustrations with the adjudged decadence, mediocrity and social aimlessness of urban modernity. In keeping with what was, by then, a tradition of British writing

The Kolo.

Figure 11 'The Kolo', by Cora Gordon, 1921. © Courtesy of Ken Bryant.

that could be traced back to Kinglake, such travelogues were less concerned with conveying political or socio-economic realities as they were with introspective cultural interrogation. The photographer E. O. Hoppé's meditations on post-war Romania, *In Gipsy Camp and Royal Palace* (1924), for example, evoked Vivian's earlier praise of late-nineteenth-century Serbia as a land of 'feudal harmony' and 'rustic pleasures', sentiments later conveyed in Patrick Leigh Fermor's *Between the Woods and the Water* (1986).[8] Likewise, the Anglo-Russian surgeon George Sava's *Donkey Serenade* (1940), recounting travels in his father's native Bulgaria in 1938, framed the experience as a joyful odyssey of pre-modern discovery and refuge from the insidious modernity driving Europe towards another major war.[9]

In this context, West's own record appears curiously derivative in its subtext, yet transcendental in having been constructed around a series of recurring allegorical devices and interventionist philosophical intentions. Her fascination with peasant culture and the theme of sacrifice focus its narrative climax on Yugoslavia's less developed southern territories. The Serbian defeat at Kosovo, following Prince Lazar's decision to sacrifice his 'earthly' kingdom for a 'heavenly' one, was, in West's mind, emblematic of

Western civilization's apparent acquiescence to communism and fascism: epitomized in the sacrifice of the titular 'Black Lamb' at a fertility rite in Macedonia. Among the assumed rural fastness of the peasantry, however, West discerned a historical rejection of this fatalism in favour of the 'Grey Falcon' of social and spiritual revival. Croats and Muslims were thus implored to reject the 'crude' Habsburgs and 'alien and indecipherable' Ottomans in favour of their native rural milieu. Unsurprisingly, the peasantry's 'preference for life' offered a possible beacon for her pessimistic notions of Britain's monotonous consumerist hedonism and Europe's presumed political nihilism, articulating the spirit of apprehension, melancholia and vexation that informed many interwar British intellectuals.[10]

Having previously drawn criticism as textual apologia for Serbian nationalism, characterized by anti-Croat and anti-Muslim prejudices,[11] *Black Lamb and Grey Falcon* has since been re-evaluated through this historical subtext. The 'presentiment of impending disaster' that premises her own journey was, according to Hammond, symbolic of 'an intervention into the Balkanist tradition' by a British woman wishing to challenge the cultural derision and political disenfranchisement perpetuated 'by male journalists, historians and travel writers'. For all the decades of ridiculing the Balkans as historically paralyzed, it was European civilization that had locked itself into a spiral of stagnation and decline.[12] This finds expression in her preoccupation with sacrifice and the hope of rebirth as analogous with Western civilization's contemporary degradation through destructive modern impulses. Her patronizing eulogies to a 'a land where everything is comprehensible, where the mode of life is so honest that it put an end to [modern] perplexity' harkened back to the late-Victorian and Edwardian obsession for Britain's own agrarian past; by rejecting Prince Lazar's 'betrayal', in desiring martyrdom, West espoused the need for a new moral crusade against the evil's that had grown inherent to modernity. 'The difference between [Kosovo] in 1389 and England in 1939', she observed, 'lay in time and place and not in the events experienced'.[13]

For some, Europe's agrarian south-east was more cathartic than revelatory. Dismissing criticism of its lack of modern development, Graham lauded the simple delights to be found in 'a somewhat backward State which has not tamed Nature with many roads and railways'.[14] Like West, his own disdain for interwar British society was articulated in the opening of his travelogue that distanced his own preference for outdoor pursuits from modern 'tourism'. The 'shallow metropolitanism' and consumerist ethos the term evoked had made it a 'word to be fought'.[15]

Even more popular literature was not entirely averse to offering critiques, usually through satirizing the escapist wish-fulfilments of Victorian and Edwardian authors. Ethel Lina White's *The Wheel Spins* (1936) opens on a comedic depiction of its upper-class heroine's efforts to seek directions from a bemused local peasant in 'a remote corner of Europe', likely to be Yugoslavia.[16] The dramatic Orientalist sense of Western disassociation and disquiet is snidely undercut, however, when White briefly switches to the perspective of the foreign Other:

> In his turn, the man heard only a string of gibberish. He
> saw a girl, dressed like a man, who was unattractively
> skinny – according to the local standards of beauty [...]

She was a foreigner [...] worked up to a pitch
of excitement, and was exceptionally stupid.¹⁷

Regardless of these revisionist undercurrents, this allegorical revival remained firmly niche, both as literature or as part of the cultural mainstream. Combined with an already narrow audience, and no mitigating strata of organized opinion to propose a counter-narrative, literary depictions remained submerged in a flood of escapist fiction solidifying Yugoslavia's image as Dolling's distant backwater rather than West's allegory for the condition of civilization.

The 'east end of Europe'

Besides widespread indifference towards the minimal and sporadic coverage Yugoslavian politics were afforded in the British press, interwar perceptions of the kingdom as a state entity typically conformed to earlier pejorative associations. By the end of the 1920s, these characterizations were not only ubiquitous to the region, but construed around broader narratives of dysfunction and the failure of the post-Versailles international order to achieve stability. Domestically, the popular conceptualizing of international relations around socialism or liberal-oriented pacifism found little common ground with the reactionary nationalism deemed to have permeated Eastern European politics. Neither had the sense of wartime Anglo-Serbian solidarity successfully dispelled nineteenth-century fixations on violence and the Balkans presumed dysfunctionality. West herself admitted as much: '[v]iolence was indeed all I knew of the Balkans, all I knew of the South Slavs.'¹⁸

The re-emergence of negative perceptions stemmed as much from the socio-political fatigue of the Great War's closing months. Within weeks of the Armistice, abstract notions of Britain's ascribed duty as civilization's moral arbiter had already become subject to the mandates of realpolitik and London's aloofness towards further Balkan entanglements. Such an approach was in evidence during Montenegro's 'Christmas uprising' in January 1919: a short-lived revolt launched by the Italian-backed Greens in support of the recently dethroned King Nicholas against the proposed unification with Serbia. Italian hopes of restoring the House of Petrović-Njegoš to power, however, were frustrated by a British Adriatic squadron. The Montenegrins 'should be permitted to retain their inalienable right to murder each other, as and when they considered it necessary, provided that no inconvenience to the Allies is caused thereby' the squadron's commander stated in a subsequent emergency dispatch to the FO.¹⁹

As well as generating a wave of hostile coverage from Durham and other anti-Serbian pundits, Montenegro's annexation marked a new phase of representation predicated more explicitly on the political tensions surrounding the duty and functions of the state. Similar to the domestic concerns which had dominated Edwardian public discourse, support or opposition for Yugoslavia and the other successor states appeared as much an echo of the presumed shortcomings of interwar British politics.

Yugoslavian domestic politics, however, only accentuated existing negative stereotypes; Serbian domination coupled with over-expenditure on the police and armed forces and their use in repressing the Macedonian Slavs and Kosovar Albanians revived pre-war motifs of corruption and victimhood among some critics. These incriminations only intensified with the proclamation of a 'Royal Dictatorship' in January 1929 by the then King Aleksander, in response to the ongoing political crisis triggered by the popular Croat leader Stjepan Radić's assassination in August 1928.[20] At a popular level, however, it was the king's own assassination by a VMRO operative, during a state visit to France in October 1934, that brought Yugoslavia briefly back into the wider public conscience. Apart from historical parallels with June 1914, much of this stemmed from the event being captured vividly on newsreel.[21]

Imagological historians have tended to extrapolate on this as indicative of a propensity to automatically juxtapose images of daily life in the Balkans with that of Britain. This intrinsic dichotomy not only focused attention onto the overt lack of mass society or materialistic modernity, but codified south-east Europe as existing in a perpetual state of what Michail terms 'under-modernity'.[22] Under this paradigm, the lack of urbanization and industrial development, as well as ineffectual state institutions, accentuated Balkan cultural alienation – particularly in its urban spaces. Belgrade, according to West, presented itself through a modernistic façade of European metropolitanism that poorly masked its derivative backwardness.[23] Unsurprisingly, notions of under-modernity played no small role in the diplomatic sphere and London's (cautious) welcoming of the dictatorship in 1929.[24] A few months before Radić's assassination, Britain's ambassador, Howard Kennard, attributed Yugoslavia's seemingly unending political chaos, and the ongoing crisis in its relations with Italy, to the Croat leader's 'disconnected' and 'childishly' incoherent approach to every policy issue. The Serb-dominated government, meanwhile, was led by men of a 'primitive race' driven by an incongruous rationale that the state's principle duty was to engage in perpetual struggle 'with a stronger power'.[25]

However, in contrast to its Balkan neighbours, Yugoslavia's place in this pejorative regional continuum was considerably more ambiguous. A British propensity to conflate the country with centralizing authority figures, such as King Aleksandar, and later Marshal Tito; the inclusion of distinctly 'un-Balkan' territories, specifically Dalmatia and the Slovene lands by way of Zagreb; and the presence of a large and aggressively hostile threat in the form of Fascist Italy represented a more obvious link to wider European tensions and a decidedly modern source of external disruption.

Among Yugoslavia's British observers, consensus could mostly be found regarding the kingdom's political systems and state institutions, deemed to do nothing but proliferate inept bureaucrats and belligerent nationalist ideologues – to the detriment of the peasantry. In 1921, the critical challenge facing Herzegovinian peasants, observed the Gordons, appeared to stem from the disorderly transition of sovereignty that had taken place less than three years earlier. Despite 'Southern Slavia' appearing to be 'a much governed country', its political class had been quick to fulfil their committed aim of redistributing the lands of the former Muslim aristocracy without providing the requisite educational or infrastructural framework. Consequently, peasants who were already inclined to be mistrustful of government were now 'being led to distrust liberty, because too much is given to them before they have been taught to use it', a situation exacerbated by the state's 'lack of diplomacy' in dealing with 'complex social problems'.[26] Based on his examination of ministerial records, Graham later concluded that, alongside the murders of King Aleksandar and Radić, the gravest error had been to allow politicians like Pašić, who had died in 1926, to waste parliamentary time by fuelling intrigue. A much needed 'five-year plan for agriculture' had been rendered all but impossible by routine sackings and resignations at its respective ministry, which was rarely allocated more than 1 per cent of the national budget. '[L]ess was done for the peasants than any class of the community'; by the 1930s, even the average Serb farmer 'had not improved his position since the days of Kara George'.[27]

News of the dictatorship's proclamation saw Laffan and other pro-Yugoslavs echo the FO's claim that a 'benign authoritarianism', overseen by apolitical military men, was needed to remedy the 'parliamentary chaos' and nationalistic grandstanding of the 1920s. To restore national confidence and protect his people from the 'predations of Rome and Moscow', the King was returning to a 'traditional' brand of paternalistic authority, similar to a patriarchal *zadruga*.[28] Anti-Yugoslav voices, whose opposition was often an extension of a more general criticism of the Paris peace settlements, were less than enthused, construing Yugoslavia as a diplomatic affectation for Greater Serbian expansionism. Durham had earlier refuted any cultural associations as

Figure 12 Vox Populi (*Evening Standard*, 29 January 1929). The cartoonist David Low's take on the proclamation of King Aleksandar's Royal Dictatorship. The king's 'mistress' (Yugoslavia) has been forcibly restrained and silenced; a 'chorus' of other European dictators informs the League of Nations that 'It is officially announced that she welcomes the new regime, she remains quiet.' © Courtesy of Solo Syndication.

obfuscating the reality of the Serb's mission to subjugate their fellow Southern Slavs. Pointing to Montenegro's fate, she accused Yugoslavia's monarch of having categorically contravened and disregarded the codes and practices of the Dinaric mountaineer.[29] Aleksandar, who ascended to the throne in 1921, had proceeded to strip his ancestral homeland,[30] a 'once independent state dry' after deposing 'his own grandfather', King Nikola. 'No peasant can have aught but contempt and horror for the King [Aleksandar] who acted so impiously' against someone traditionally revered in the patriarchal Serb and Montenegrin household as 'the great man of the family'.[31]

Claims and counterclaims of repression and torture prompted efforts to re-invoke the earlier narrative of peasant victimhood. From 1918 to 1924, Devine reiterated the view, across multiple books and pamphlets, that the descision to depose the House of Petrović-Njegoš had amounted to nothing less than an outright war crime.[32] Following in the wake of Austria-Hungary's occupation, the Serbian army had plundered what remained 'including the glass from the windows in schools' with the treatment of the rural Montenegrin populace resembling 'colonial savagery' masquerading as progress.[33] Vivian was equally fervent in accusing the Serbs of atrocities equivocal to those of the Balkan Wars: 'Every day a fresh village destroyed'.[34]

The repressive measures implemented under the dictatorship intensified these condemnations, even among its proponents. By the early 1930s, Seton-Watson, based on his own observations and correspondence with Yugoslavia's banned opposition parties, warned that the situation had grown so untenable that even anti-government 'Orthodox bands' had reportedly grown active along the Bosnian-Croatian border. Outlining these concerns in an unpublished memorandum to the Royal government, Seton-Watson stated that the suppression of political rights would only amplify the 'allure of Marxism' and invite 'foreign interference'.[35]

King Aleksandar's assassination marked a departure from these more explicitly regionalized political concerns as the subsequent deterioration of international relations prompted others to interpret them as reflecting a more generalized European problem.[36] Touring the Balkans again in 1935, Wrench, for example, despaired at the sight of 'goose-stepping soldiers' in Split and other Dalmatian towns as an unwelcome reminder of Europe's transformation into 'a simmering cauldron. Every man fearing his neighbours'.[37] These anxieties over external hostilities manifested in late-interwar imagery as, what Hammond terms, a form of 'frontier psychosis'.[38] Describing her experience of passing through Italian-controlled Rijeka into the town of Sušak on the Yugoslavian side of the border, West discerned the rigid use of bureaucratic and police control, implemented by the Fascist authorities, as a form of cultural defilement upon an otherwise placid Mediterranean landscape:

There we found a town that has the quality of a dream, a bad headachy dream. . . . And at places where no frontiers could possibly be, in the middle of a square, or on a bridge linking the parts of a quay, men in uniform step forward and demand passports.[39]

The contemporary menace of Fascist Italy served as the main antagonistic undercurrent in Copland's writing. The defining of 'unnatural' political frontiers such as that between

Italy and Yugoslavia with 'barbed wire tangle', 'cement pillars' and the presence of border posts in western Slovenia's remoter alpine districts was an ominous reminder of the 'Italianization' occurring across the border.[40] This aggressively militaristic presence drove Copeland towards openly champion enterprises such as the Slovene Alpine Society *Skala* (which she had joined shortly after its formation in 1921). The organization's altruistic ethos, with a membership lacking in class-distinction and gender discrimination, appeared as both the vanguard of a Slovene national awakening and a direct challenge to its more elitist, and often chauvinistic, Italian and Austrian counterparts.[41]

In contrast to earlier iterations on the victimhood narrative, however, this imagery of repression was more often associated with bureaucratic measures and forced assimilation, rather than suppression through outright violence. Modern bureaucracy's repressive potential was illustrated in Italy's aggressive educational policies and selective use of surveys as a form of demographic warfare against its Yugoslav minority.[42] Critics reflected these anxieties back onto the actions of the Yugoslavian state, before and after January 1929. Durham claimed that the conscription and deployment of Croat peasants to uphold martial law in the Serbian 'colonies' of Kosovo and Macedonia was indicative of the 'divide and rule' by which Belgrade sought to retain control over its non-Serb subjects.[43] A 1932 report for 'the House of Commons Balkans Committee' by the Labour MPs Rhys Davies and Ben Riley described the Croat territories as having become 'practically an armed camp' with peasants 'held down at the point of a bayonet' through constant police surveillance and monitoring of political gatherings.[44]

Regardless of these isolated voices, a more deeply entrenched culture of public indifference and the framing of persecution as a transnational phenomenon, tended to dilute the victimhood narrative's once resonate emotive impact. Unlike the Edwardian and wartime periods, the absence of a definitive aggressor, in a European political climate that increasingly disregarded notions of democratic accountability, left the figure of the peasant stranded as a victim of contemporary circumstances, rather than under-modernity, to which there seemed no tangible solution.[45]

Nowhere did this sense of transnational alienation appear more apt than in Britain's official attempts at reviving its regional presence in the opening years of the Second World War. From the early 1930s, the Secret Intelligence Service had started to operate several spy networks out of various British consulates, the Passport Control Office and under the guise of commercial interests. The latter of these included the *Herald*'s editor, Terence Atherton, who was later killed in 1942, following an abortive attempt at opening official contact with Tito's headquarters in eastern Herzegovina.[46] Rising German belligerence in 1936 also saw British operatives attempting to establish informant networks among rural communities along the Italian and Austrian frontiers. However, with the outbreak of the so-called 'Phoney War' in western Europe, concerns that Yugoslavia might drift into the Axis camp refocused the attentions of the FO and recently founded Special Operations Executive back onto Belgrade. This did not necessarily preclude official efforts at swaying grassroots public opinion. A month into the war, the entomologist Malcolm Burr, another Belgrade operative who had served in the Macedonian Campaign, was instructed to tour Serbian village communities in an effort to counter suspected German subterfuge. A short-lived plan to promote the moral benevolence of the Allied cause among the Croatian peasantry (via a mobile cinema unit) was also proposed in January 1940 but was quickly abandoned.[47]

Despite these relatively ambitious objectives, and intensifying anti-Axis propaganda, on 27 March 1941, the Yugoslavian government, seeking to avoid exacerbating its own internal divisions in the aftermath of France's surrender in June 1940, followed Hungary, Romania and Bulgaria in joining the Axis Tripartite Pact as a defensive precaution. Two days later, British public interest in the region was briefly rekindled with news that a group of pro-Allied Yugoslav military officials and civil servants had successfully staged a coup d'état, elevating Petar II, the adolescent heir apparent, to the throne. In London, the coup was hailed as a moral and propaganda victory with Churchill announcing that Yugoslavia had 'found its soul'.[48] 'At last the tide is turning', Seton-Watson stated in a radio message broadcast to the Yugoslavian public, 'a whole people has risen up in protest against those who sought to barter its independence'.[49] Neville Henderson, Britain's ambassador from 1929 to 1935, greeted the announcement by reading out a list of congratulations from veterans of the former Balkan Front, most of whom equated the coup with Serbia's resistance to the Central Powers in 1914 and 1915.[50] Events in Yugoslavia even appeared as banner headlines in the provincial press, mostly declaring the end of Adolf Hitler's 'war through diplomacy'.[51]

This jubilant reception was rendered moot by the Axis invasion and partition of Yugoslavia in early April. Stark contrasts soon began to arouse, demonstrating how British involvement in the Balkans during the Second World War failed to replicate the transnational solidarity of the First. Central to this was the lack of a relatable civilian element. While some British operatives would later indulge in their own self-mythologizing, the conflict failed to produce an equivalent to Inglis or Sandes, whose depiction as the embodiment of Anglo-British virtue had captured the triumphal sense of the country's emergent self-image. From 1940 to 1944, Britain's presence in the region was mostly sequestered behind a wall of official secrecy, restricted almost exclusively to military and intelligence personnel of whom the majority were deployed to Greece – the only country in south-east Europe that had held any consistent historical value in London's geostrategic calculations.

Moreover, the inability of many of those who remained active voices in political debates, or developed an interest in the region after 1918, to adopt a less partisan stance remained an ever-present lightning rod for criticism. Reviewing some recent travel publications on Bulgaria and Yugoslavia in the American weekly *Outlook and Independent* in 1930, one anonymous critic decried the ongoing 'craze' of Anglophone authors wanting to present themselves as 'bit-part political players' by becoming 'propagandists for their favoured governments'.[52] By the Second World War, this rising hostility towards the elitism surrounding international relations prompted accusations of a cultural as much as political failing. Writing in the aftermath of Yugoslavia's surrender and partition by the Axis, *The Evening News*'s diplomatic correspondent, Cecil Melville, surmized that London's past failures in the region were indicative of a broader reflexive trend in how foreign affairs were viewed by the wider public. Rather than seeking to educate and promote clearer understanding through speaking to lay concerns, national favouritism and an imbued sense of clannishness had codified interwar dialogue on foreign policy as the hermetic preserve of diplomats, petty academic rivalries and middle-class 'drawing-room politics'. While those 'more frivolous sought escape in the night clubs' the more serious-minded satiated their intellectual narcissism 'by meddling in the affairs of other countries . . . to salve our consciences for neglecting the unpicturesque poor of the East End of London by taking an interest in the picturesque poor of the East End of Europe'.[53]

Witnesses to 'the passing of Arcadia'

In keeping with interwar British intellectualism's defining motifs of disillusion and cultural morbidity, it is perhaps unsurprising that depictions of Yugoslavia after 1934 increasingly evoked a sense of historical passing. This was indicative of broader socio-economic realities, the growth of Yugoslavia's nascent tourism industry being the most obvious. Nevertheless, as with previous trends such a change was as much a projection of Britain's own domestic climate.

Like the Edwardian period, the 1920s and 1930s had exposed the cumulative impact of modernistic changes at a societal level. While commentators such as Orwell popularly associated this with economic stagnation and the impoverishment of areas reliant on mining and the old industrial staples, as discussed in the previous chapter, life in Britain between the wars was as much defined by the transition to a consumer-oriented mass society. One notable outcome of this was a partial reversal of the aggressive urbanization of the 1860s to 1910s that saw interwar Britain emerge as the world's first 'post-urban country' by 1939. Urban growth slowed as suburbanization saw London, Birmingham, Glasgow and other major cities experience outflows of wealthier residents into rural hinterlands and satellite towns. This once virtually unknown phenomenon brought with it a new form of public interest in the countryside predicated on its practical utility as a space for leisure and the promise of a more relaxed lifestyle. For the urbanized consumer, and much to the dismay of cultural nostalgics, the appeal of the rural environment lay in its lack of social conflict and supposed 'emptiness'; suburbia, despite its ostensibly rural setting, was always recognized as an extension of the urban residential network.[54] This 'return' of the town to the countryside and the spread of urban influence and values through the commodification of the latter was best illustrated by the growing presence of service and white-collar workers in former agricultural communities.[55]

The impact of these changes was easily perceptibly in the frustrations expressed through romantic travel literature and reactionary impulses discernible in anthropological research. The founding of the *Le Play Society*, for instance, was ostensibly in protest at the growing prevalence of economic and sociological theory in the geographical sciences, to the perceived detriment of direct fieldwork. This dovetailed into assertions that 'adult amateurs' had been marginalized by the growth of academic professionalism and fewer studies accessible to lay readers.[56] In the context of the peasantry, Lodge's *Peasant Life in Jugoslavia* (1941) provided something of a coda to this popular tradition. Focusing on rural custom and domestic economy in districts 'away from Western influences and civilization', her research invoked the importance of history and environment alongside a belief that researchers should adhere to a lifestyle similar to their subject of study.

Having sought to present the 'simple and wild', Lodge placed her research in direct contention with British suburbia's 'ever-encroaching blanket of ordinariness' and a 'machine-made' outlook.[57]

Conversely, by the 1930s, this quietly dreaded sense of a prosaic urban milieu had percolated into depictions of rural Yugoslav life. Despite remaining the least industrialized country in Europe after Bulgaria and Albania, with no obvious alternatives to agriculture like the Greek shipping and Romanian petrochemical industries, the interwar period was defined by what Ehrlich termed the 'proletarianization' of the Yugoslavian peasantry.[58] Although lacking any clear linearity, changes in rural employment patterns, the state's progressive regulation of religious institutions and the undermining of conservative gender roles had already eroded the rural social fabric of more developed areas. Even in the 'old-style' patriarchal villages of Montenegro, Bosnia-Herzegovina and Macedonia, traditional hierarchies had also 'begun to decay' with improving access to education and the spread of new political ideas. Economic migrants returning from North America propelled these changes along by aspiring to establish themselves as private smallholders, hastening the decline of the *zadruga* as a social-economic institution. Ehrlich would later attribute the success of her 1937 survey to it having given voice to the peasantry's own sense of impending cataclysm and irreparable social change:

> They felt that they were storing up treasures before it was too late. They were anxious to record their knowledge of old ideas and traditional attitudes before they all were lost. Already Nazis were on the march.[59]

This sense of fatalistic immediacy found expression in the shifting focus of the *Herald*. By 1937, the paper's attempts at enticing English-speaking tourists to visit Dalmatia or the Julian Alps had partly given way to more introspective coverage of the country's considerably less-visited inland provinces, notably Europe's last 'true Orient' of Bosnia-Herzegovina.[60] Moreover, prior to 1939, Atherton had even started petitioning its expatriate readership to emulate M-O's approach in Britain by recording scenes of everyday Yugoslav public life.[61]

Besides an ambient disenchantment with modern society, late-interwar British dialogues elicited anxieties that the cultural trappings of Yugoslavia's peasant society were beginning to disappear. Encounters with anything that might suggest 'modernity', or intimations of its encroachment, could induce a sense of loss and nostalgia, particularly for those with memories of the region before 1914. Revisiting Montenegro in 1935, Wrench expressed dismay at their being 'very few people in costume left' with most of the customs and ceremonies witnessed in his youth having long since disappeared.[62] Lodge and Copeland further corroborated this, noting that most rural traditions in 1930s Croatia, Slovenia and northern Serbia were only observed by older peasants or at weddings and funerals.[63]

Even the diffusion of modernistic trappings across interwar Yugoslavia was more likely to evoke a measure of distain. The sight of younger peasants shunning traditional dress in favour of Western clothing, for example, was decried by Wrench as signalling 'the end of uniqueness'.[64] Lodge painted a less, albeit still despondent, picture of 'simple communities invaded by the civilization of European capitals'. While national costume, alongside numerous superstitions and customs, continued to flourish as a 'protestation of strong individuality', these would doubtless be 'doomed to vanish altogether' over the coming decad. Already 'materials made in factories and brought in shops' had started to usurp the peasantry's once enshrined principle of (relative) self-sufficiency.[65]

Anticipation of this creeping modernity often followed on from the initial impressions foreigners formed by typically beginning their excursions in the most developed areas of the country – usually Zagreb or Belgrade. In the case of the latter, this was further accentuated by a series of urban redesigns in the 1920s that gradually demarcated most of the city centre as the preserve of Yugoslavia's burgeoning metropolitan elites, as had happened in London, Paris and Berlin. This perceivable narrowing of cultural experience between the Yugoslav capital and its counterparts in other European countries was mirrored in a new urbanized middle class whose appetite for Western fashions and entertainment triggered the creation of socially exclusive leisure and commercial zones.[66] For British romanticists, and pre-war nostalgics, the Belgrade of the mid- to late 1930s seemed to allegorize this Balkan retreat from history. Wrench dismissed the city as little more than a 'European Washington ... grand while also charmless' and devoid of any 'historic character'.[67] As she travelled further south, West continued to concur with this sentiment, being enamoured more by Yugoslavia's Ottoman architecture and Islamic cultural heritage, while carefully divorcing it from any political or religious associations. The imposition of perceived European homogeneity, such as Sarajevo's Habsburg-era City Hall 'stuffed with beer and sausages down to its toes' or the replacing of a 'beautiful mosque', that had dominated Skopje's skyline 'for three centuries', with 'an Officer's Club which is one of the most hideous buildings in the whole of Europe', quickly became her principle object of scorn.[68]

Paradoxically, close proximity to an urban centre did not guarantee infiltration by these reviled modernistic influences. Following the Axis invasion, Louisa Rayner, the British wife of a Bosnian fuel merchant, found herself obliged to seek refuge in the village of Rušanj, 'twelve miles' south of German-occupied Belgrade. Her post-war memoir described the community as a virtual 'City State' with the peasant's chief loyalty being to the land they worked, a scenario which, she suspected, existed across much of rural Serbia where 'there had been little change for centuries'.[69] In the eyes of the peasantry, urban-based authority was almost entirely superfluous and regarded with a mixture of disdain and general indifference. Besides the village clerk, Rayner recorded Rušanj as having operated before the war without need of officials, *gendarmes* – or even a priest! Indeed, before 1944, when the KPJ's military success in Bosnia-Herzegovina refocused its leaders' attentions back towards Serbia, the war had passed almost unnoticed besides some 1,800 refugees whom the peasants accommodated '[w]ithout apparent fusses'.[70]

British preoccupations with juxtaposing urban modernity against the conceived virtue of a comprehensible agrarian past belied the shifting realities recorded by a more politically sceptical generation of scientific observers, such as the Croat economist Rudolf Bićanić and the Serb ethnographer Milenko Filipović. Notable among these studies was Bićanić's *Kako živi narod* (1936) that documented the grim realities of rural poverty in the remote 'passive' or 'depressed' regions of Dalmatia and Bosnia-Herzegovina's mountainous borderlands in the mid-1930s. Environmental hardships, minimal infrastructure and the peasantry's own financially ruinous adherence to what Bićanić termed the 'tyranny of custom' had created a society that would condemn itself to starvation without state intervention.[71]

Against these contradictory metrics, Copeland's writing on the pastoralist culture of Yugoslavia's alpine Velika Planina in December 1939 appeared as a more accurate précis of the interwar period's essential themes concerning the insurmountable conflicts between modernity and tradition. In contrast to West, her more measured summation discerned the encroachment of change as neither wholly positive nor negative, having achieved discernible equilibrium in north-west Yugoslavia:

> I sit on a corner of the hearthstone in a hut, waiting for the owner to give me a drink of new warm milk. His pail is of spotless new enamel. An electric torch hangs by his couch of hay and horseclothes besides the massive silver watch he was given for his confirmation, many years ago. In the evenings he comes up to the hostel, swallows his dram strikes a light for his cigarette with flint and steel, and listens to the wireless before he goes to sleep in a hut more familiar perhaps to Atilla's warriors or even to prehistoric man than to the modern tourist.[72]

However, this acceptance of the inexorable advance of modernity was punctuated by Copeland's resignation that the region's eventual 'discovery' by Western tourism would signal the end of its rural identity, as industrialization and suburbanization had done in Britain. Through the peasantry's gradual embrace of modernity, and its material comforts, another remnant of pre-industrial Europe would soon become 'lost, indeed and forever. We shall have seen the passing of Arcadia'.[73]

Conclusion

Although the spectre of cultural and political change had haunted Edwardian Britain during its own 'age of crisis' in the early 1910s, these fears had been mitigated by the belief that a return to an (imagined) past of social comprehensibility was still achievable. The excesses of 1914 to 1918 had shattered this illusion. In this context, the archetypical image of the Yugoslav peasant remained an idyll yet no longer appeared interminable. Change, be it the detested intrusion of modernity, the disruption of war, or what Evans had first described in the 1870s as the abandoning of 'customs and costumes', effectively become its own form of cultural motif.[74] Regardless of the limited revival in cultural interest during the 1930s, the interwar period exposed the extent to which any resonance in the public sphere had always been contingent on a sense of domestic cultural reciprocity. The Great War had brought this to its apex while neutering any future potential for it to be sustained.

At a broader societal level, the attitudes and ideological mentalities that dominated Britain's interwar domestic climate proved far less conducive to the sorts of cultural and allegorical factors prevalent in the era of the First World War. The socio-economic and political changes facilitated by the war not only undermined but eroded cultural narratives pertaining to Anglo-Britishness as a moral construct, coupled with the rise of a more domestically oriented mass society. What Michail defines as the 'fragmentation' of the Balkans' nineteenth-century image after 1918 could just as well be interpreted as the fragmentation of the late-Victorian ideals and iconography that had underpinned the emerging concept of Anglo-British identity.[75] The final 'critical assault on nineteenth-century certainties', beginning in the late 1920s, left such notions intellectually dead by 1939.[76]

By 1943, following the Churchill war ministry's decision to abandon support for the exiled government of Petar II in favour of the more proactive Partisan forces of the KPJ, wartime ephemera directed public sentiment towards the figure of Tito himself. Despite heading an insurgent communist movement, his record of active leadership and open appeals for British support in the liberation of his homeland, made him a popular symbol of anti-Fascist resistance underwritten by a sense of certainty more conducive to the wartime climate. With the onset of the Cold War, Tito effectively came to inhabit that space in the British geographical imaginary previously occupied by the peasantry.[77] Within the South Slavic lands themselves, the peasant's social prevalence only continued to diminish as Yugoslavian society resumed its pre-war cultural transition. The country was set to play an integral part in the 'flowering' mass tourism boom of the 1960s and 1970s, signifying its incorporation into an increasingly post-urban European sphere. Foreign visitors who chose to venture inland, away from the oversaturated Adriatic resorts, now encountered 'the commodification of traditional national costumes, festivals, music, and dance . . . the re-packaging of the Ottoman legacy in Bosnian towns', and '"folkloric" tourist presentations' of a cultural heritage that had been consigning itself to history long before 1945.[78]

Conclusion

By the beginning of the twentieth century, it seemed increasingly evident that for a country as historically multifaceted, yet lacking a sense of unitary 'nationhood' as Britain, questions of identity would only become more prevalent in the face of rising domestic pluralism and challenges to its status as the world's industrial and colonial hegemon. This was, at its heart, a distinctly post-Victorian issue on matters of self-perception, yet one that existed within a transnational context. Besides more blatant influences, be it the French-inspired tradition of radical agitation seen in the unrest of 1911 to 1926 or the American-style consumerism of the interwar decades, the various cultural impulses and social tensions surrounding a concept as pliable as 'Anglo-Britishness' shaped and was shaped by perceptions of the Other. To this end, the South Slavic Balkans, and subsequently Yugoslavia, represented almost an ideal parallel. In an era in which social anxieties lingered perpetually within the public sphere, the identification of the South Slavic Balkans as a partially 'European' space, transformed what had once been pejorative leitmotifs into a form of allegory for an uncertain and shifting set of domestic conditions. Fundamentally, Yugoslavia evolved as one of many allegorical concepts used to clarify and redefine British society's material and intellectual relationship with the British state.

In adopting this conceptual framework, that determines the regions' place in imaginative geography by its ability to resonate with the domestic debates and the creation of Anglo-British identity, the study has sought to move discussion past more direct forms of cultural comparison. The focus on allegorical meaning, in particular, looks to steer imagological historiography's focus away from how images of differing cultures are created to the role they play in assigning and rationalizing identities at a specific point in history. In adopting this angle, it hopes to enhance understanding of how the Southern Slavs were perceived outside the elite minority capable of actively engaging with the region for most of this period. What emerged was a process of gradual modification whereby cultural representations of these western Balkan territories became an allegory to fit into the changing social dynamics of British self-perception before 1945.

By conjoining the Edwardian, First World War and Interwar periods into a single chronological focus, the study has also considered how historical contingencies converged at an unusual point in British (and South Slavic) history. Unlike the 1800s, the rapidity of events in the early twentieth century elevated them to allegorical points of reference for changes impinging upon the lives of the wider public. Both the beginning and end of this period were bookended by British involvement in conflicts with socially (and psychologically) traumatic repercussions. The Boer War accentuated anxieties by drawing public attention to a broad spectrum of pre-existing domestic tensions, heightening an existing sense of cultural disillusion, unease and vulnerability. The growing presence of societal divisions were compounded by active displays of unrest, mirroring – what was sensationally presented as – a period of protracted upheaval in the South Slavic Balkans.

Unsurprisingly, it was the peasant that existed at the heart of this paradigm as sympathetic victim and a historically recognized emblem of the region's culture. However, as this study has also demonstrated, throughout the early twentieth century, Britain and the South Slavic lands existed in a state of accelerating, albeit uneven, economic and socio-political change that persistently redefined perceptions. This, in turn, made efforts to construct a coherent body of public knowledge far more susceptible to the tides of historical contingency. Nowhere was this more apparent than from 1912 to 1918, which catalysed and defined these processes on a, quite literally, transnational scale.

At a popular level, which the study has endeavoured to reflect as accurately as possible, the transnational context in which Yugoslavia was shaped in British imaginative geography was not rooted in cultural prejudice. While pejorative stereotypes, the rhetoric of imperialism, or even outright xenophobia regularly featured in representations, with the onset of the *fin de siècle*, the Victorian ideas of a scientific and cultural 'modernity' previously used to justify them were increasingly contested. Dynamic new forces such as organized labour, the women's suffrage movements and Irish nationalism not only posed direct challenges to the existing status quo, but represented alternative, or divergent, visions for society. Accompanying discussions on national efficiency inflamed the cultural anxieties surrounding these visible conflicts, feeding, by extension, into matters of Empire and Britain's global status in general. Correspondingly, modern urbanization was reimagined as a social model in need of 'moral recalibration', centred on increased state intervention against potential stagnation, decline and social fragmentation.

The intersection of this milieu with contemporary depictions of the South Slavic peasantry, especially in Macedonia, thus found some resonance with a rising belief that both local communities and the state were morally obliged to intervene on behalf of those deemed openly vulnerable. While building upon nineteenth-century legislative action to regulate the conditions of industrial employment, notably in relation to child labourers, the twentieth century saw the rapid expansion of this trend under the Liberal welfare reforms of 1906 to 1914.[1] Notions of a renewed rural England, free of urban poverty and morally invigorated by a new progressive social transparency, found a suitable point of reference in the village communities of the future Yugoslavia as positive allegories for the revival of British society's collective vigour and spiritual health.[2]

Against this context, the recurrent leitmotif of victimhood also found popular resonance by establishing the peasant's status as an allegory for contemporary domestic problems and their potential solutions. The discursive currents which gave this form in the public sphere came from a sprawling, and often contradictory, miscellany of cultural, religious and ideological notions that elucidated notions of an active citizenry as an expression of 'moral character', integral to the 'public spirit'. By 1914, this had fused with the narrative that an ingrained heroism constituted the true essence of Anglo-British identity but necessitated that it be demonstrated rather than merely implied. Impetus for this shift was as much in evidence among groups like the suffrage and labour movements, both of which regularly framed their campaigns and actions in moralistic terms.[3] This rhetorical trend became more precipitous as unrest in Ireland and suffrage and labour militancy were ratcheted upwards from 1910 to 1914, with seemingly no obvious cultural or political resolutions.

Against these converging historical factors, popular attitudes towards the creation of Yugoslavia in December 1918 appear far less surprising . Indeed, when analysing the changing nature of peasant representation against the discursive currents that gave rise to Anglo-British identity during the Great War, the transnational concept of a South Slavic union carried as much a cultural as political rationale. This further challenges the use of the Balkanist thesis as an interpretative framework for why the country received British support. Drapac and Evans, for instance, present Yugoslavia's formation as a product of elite ideologies and the diplomatic machinations of the Western powers. Reference to those outside of policymaking circles, such as female relief volunteers in Serbia and Macedonia, limits them to informal political functionaries without considering the influence of deeper factors besides vestigial Victorian-era prejudices. Interconnections between gender, civic duty and social justice, and the reception of such individuals back in Britain, appear almost invisible next to their extremely minor roles in the creation of a country over which British influence was profoundly exaggerated.[4]

While the concept of a Yugoslav polity only acquired recognition in the public sphere from mid-1915, the cultural basis for its legitimacy in imaginative geography was mostly established through the recalibration of the South Slavic peasantry's image as commensurate with the cultural reshaping of British identity. This confluence of representative trends and the intersecting of the victimhood narrative with aspects of Britain's social climate was accentuated by the collective trauma of the Balkan and First World Wars. Depictions of disease, privation, human displacement, violence against civilians and environmental destruction, attributable to the actions of external forces, were easily positioned in relation to an Anglo-British heroic ideal as force of international arbitration. With the outbreak of the Great War, peasant victimhood was no longer an unfortunate product of historical circumstance or callous foreign policy failure, but the violation of a 'protected' group by an extraneous evil, echoing much of the rhetoric that had previously framed the Edwardian Liberal reforms.[5]

Forging this sense of allegorical equivalence allowed the JO and other pro-Yugoslav campaigners to legitimize their political cause by denoting it as innately moral and symbiotic with Anglo-British identity. Despite propaganda claims that a Yugoslavian national entity had historical precedence, its actual realization proved to be of secondary importance to its presence as a symbolic public reminder of the need to continue supporting Britain's war effort. While moulding knowledge to suit agendas was paramount, British and South Slavic political actors recognized the need to harness popular sentiment by appealing to idealized self-perceptions. The wartime atmosphere thus allowed a complex territorial reconfiguration to be conceptualized as analogous to the restoration of civilizational morality on behalf of a historically repressed people. Regardless of fading popular interest after 1916, this temporary amalgamation of moral identity and regional victimhood narrative sealed the South Slavic Balkans' transformation in British imaginative geography, with Yugoslavia as the final, logical outcome.

Nevertheless, this ideal of a morally grounded British identity only ever existed in a state of perpetual flux as well as being in tension with a more prosaic sense of consumerism. For the majority, the Great War's conclusion also symbolized the narrative end to what could be described as a 'Long Eastern Crisis' that earlier diplomatic or military efforts had failed to solve. Consequently, this resolution removed any sense of Britain possessing a direct stake, political or otherwise, in southeast Europe. Yugoslavia remained as an aspect of the geographical imaginary but not one in which Britain could effectively, or had an imperative to, interact in any further meaningful capacity.

The erosion of this Edwardian sense of Britain as a moral actor on the world stage, particularly in the 1930s, was itself indicative of the country's transition into a modern mass society having effectively reached its end. While this certainly did not foreshadow the region's complete disappearance, the receding of Yugoslavia, and the Balkans, from the public consciousness were indicative of a post-war shift away from earlier patterns of Britons projecting their latent social anxieties onto other cultures. Having opened itself to greater international influence after 1918, creating what could be described as an internalized form of consumer-based modernity, the 'British Imagination' grew less constrained by the need to define Britain's transnational relationships through parallels or allegories. Even Yugoslavia's 'discovery' as a tourist destination led to it being mostly viewed as a novel extension of Britain's commodified cultural sphere, all while many of its historical peasant customs were being discarded or appropriated for nationalist iconography.

The end of the Great War, and the twenty-year interregnum that followed, not only signified the death of Edwardian cultural mentalities, but exposed the latent class divide within the Anglo-British paradigm. As a proscribed form of identity, Anglo-Britishness was an inherently elitist concept that largely built upon understandings of duty and deference to the institutions of state. Any true sense of belonging remained localized or restricted to one's constituent nation. Ireland's dramatic departure from the union in 1922, mirrored by Yugoslavia's own political dysfunctionality, demonstrated the degree to which such state systems could potentially engender alienation, division and resentment in an age of nation-states. The repeated failure of organized opinion and other forms of expert authority to promote closer political ties merely emphasized this divide. Nowhere was this clearer than in the self-mythologizing of figures like Durham, Seton-Watson or even West, all of whom overstated their roles as individual actors rather than as products of a singularly unique moment in British history.

The purpose of this study has not been to repudiate or overturn the concept of Balkanism or other analytical models previously used by imagological and non-imagological scholars. Throughout this early-twentieth-century period, it was undeniable that the patronizing mentalities and negative cultural stereotypes of the Victorians still exorcized a strong rhetorical and literary hold. The events of the 1990s and all that has transpired since demonstrate the pressing and urgent need to confront such essentialist thinking and the proliferation of falsehoods. Yet, even systems of belief that appear as fixed as national and ethnic stereotypes will rarely remain unchanged within a transnational context. By paying greater attention to these phases of engagement between cultures, scholars can assist in shedding light on those who remain at the margins of history. Regardless of the time or place in which they lived.

Notes

Introduction

1. Rebecca West, *Black Lamb and Grey Falcon: A Journey through Yugoslavia in 1937 [Vol.1]* (London: MacMillan, 1941), 70.
2. Officially the 'Kingdom of Serbs, Croats and Slovenes' until 1929. For the sake of brevity, this study will refer to it as Yugoslavia throughout.
3. Edward W. Said, *Orientalism* (London: Penguin Books, 2003 [1978]), 49.
4. Pamela J. Dorn Sezgin, 'Between Cross and Crescent: British Public Opinion towards the Ottoman Empire in Resolving the Balkan Wars, 1912-1913', in M. Hakan Yavuz and Isa Blumi (eds), *War and Nationalism: The Balkan Wars, 1912-1913, and their Sociopolitical Implications* (Salt Lake City: University of Utah Press, 2013), 423.
5. Henrika Kuklick, *The Savage Within: The Social History of British Anthropology, 1885-1945* (Cambridge: Cambridge University Press, 1991), 5-6.
6. A form of patriarchal family cooperative that had once been common across the South Slavic Balkans.
7. Karl Kaser, 'Anthropology and the Balkanization of the Balkans: Jovan Cvijić and Dinko Tomašić', *Ethnologia Balkanica* 2 (1998): 91-5; Natascha Vittorelli, 'An "Other" of One's Own: Pre-WW1 South Slavic Academic Discourses on the Zadruga', *Spaces of Identity* 2, no. 3 (2002): 37.
8. West, *Black Lamb [Vol.1]* 3, 21.
9. Barbara Jelavich, 'The Abuses of Ottoman Administration in the Slavonic Provinces', *The Slavonic and East European Review* 33, no. 81 (1955): 396-413. See also Emmet B. Ford (Jr), 'Montenegro in the Eyes of the English Traveller, 1840-1914', *Südost Forschungen* 18 (1959): 350-80; Stevan K. Pavlowitch, 'Early Nineteenth-century Serbia in the Eyes of British Travellers', *Slavic Review* 21, no. 2 (1962): 322-9.
10. Sanja Potkonjak, 'In Women's Arms: Croatian Ethnography between 1945 and 1990', in Aleksandar Bošković and Chris Hann (eds), *The Anthropological Field on the Margins of Europe, 1945-1991* (Zürich: Lit Verlag, 2013), 239. See also Vera St. Ehrlich, *Family in Transition: A Study of 300 Yugoslav Villages* (Princeton: Princeton University Press, 1966).
11. A movement within the academic humanities and social sciences emphasizing culture and meaning as its central analytical focus.
12. Said, *Orientalism*, 12.
13. William L. Chew (III), 'What's in a National Stereotype? An Introduction to Imagology at the Threshold of the 21st Century', *Language and Intercultural Communication* 6, nos. 3-4 (2006): 180-1; Joep Leerssen, 'Imagology: History and Method', in Manfred Beller and Joep Leerssen (eds), *Imagology: The Cultural Construction and Literary Representation of National Characters – A Critical Survey* (Amsterdam: Rodopi Press, 2007), 16.
14. Benedict Anderson, *Imagined Communities: Reflections on the Origins and Spread of Nationalism, Revised Edition* (London: Verso, 2016), 5-6, 46; Michael Herzfeld,

Anthropology Through the Looking-Glass: Critical Ethnology in the Margins of Europe (Cambridge: Cambridge University Press, 1987), 2–4; Jill Dubisch, 'Europe through the Back Door: Doing Anthropology in Greece', in Susan Parman (ed.), *Europe in the Anthropological Imagination* (Upper Saddle River: Pearson Education, 1998) 35; Ger Duijzings, 'Changes in the Social Roles of Western Anthropologists and Indigenous Ethnologists', *Xenopoliana (Iaşi)* 11, nos. 1–2 (2003): 11–12.

15 Wendy Bracewell, 'Opinion-Makers: The Balkans in Popular Literature', in Petar Kačavenda (ed.), *Jugoslovensko-britanski odnosi/ British Yugoslav Relations, 1856-1876* (Belgrade: Institut za savremenu istoriju, 1988), 92–3.

16 Allcock had first outlined this concept in 1989 with Maria Todorova admitting to 'numerous incidents' of her research having 'coincided' with his original analysis. John B. Allcock, 'Constructing the Balkans', in John B. Allcock and Antonia Young (eds), *Black Lambs and Grey Falcons: Women Travellers in the Balkans* (Bradford: Bradford University Press, 1991), 217, fn 223–9; Maria Todorova, *Imagining the Balkans* (Oxford: Oxford University Press, 1997), 192, fn 16.

17 Maria Todorova, 'The Balkans: From Discovery to Invention', *Slavic Review* 53, no. 2 (1994): 461.

18 David Norris, *In the Wake of the Balkan Myth: Questions of Identity and Modernity* (London: Macmillan Press, 1999), 14.

19 Milica Bakić-Hayden and Robert M. Hayden, 'Orientalist Variations on the Theme "Balkans": Symbolic Geography in Recent Yugoslav Cultural Politics', *Slavic Review* 51 (1992): 4–5.

20 Larry Wolff, *Inventing Eastern Europe: The Map of Civilization on the Mind of the Enlightenment* (Stanford: Stanford University Press, 1994), 5–6.

21 Todorova, *Imagining*, 15–19, 188.

22 Ibid., 88; Vesna Goldsworthy, *Inventing Ruritania: The Imperialism of the Imagination* (New Haven: Yale University Press, 1998), x.

23 Eugene Michail, *The British and the Balkans: Forming Images of Foreign Lands 1900-1950* (London: Continuum, 2011), ix; Diana Mishkova, *Beyond Balkanism: The Scholarly Politics of Region Making* (Abingdon: Routledge, 2018), 211.

24 See Robert J. Donia and John V. A. Fine, *Bosnia and Herzegovina: A Tradition Betrayed* (London: C.Hurst & Co., 1994); Misha Glenny, *The Balkans: Nationalism, War and the Great Powers, 1804-1999* (London: Granta Books, 1999); Mark Mazower, *The Balkans: A Short History* (London: Weidenfeld & Nicolson, 2000).

25 Norris, *In the Wake*, 27–8.

26 Ludmilla Kostova, *Tales of the Periphery: The Balkans in Nineteenth Century British Writing* (Veliko Tŭrnovo: Universitetsko izd-vo Sv. sv. Kiril i Metodii, 1997), 14; Goldsworthy, *Inventing Ruritania*, x.

27 Mika Petteri Suonpää, *British Perceptions of the Balkan Slavs: Professional and Popular Categorizations before 1914* (PhD Thesis, University of Hull, 2008), 21.

28 K. E. Fleming, 'Orientalism, the Balkans, and Balkan Historiography', *The American Historical Review* 105, no. 4 (2000): 1232–3.

29 Patrick Finney, 'Raising Frankenstein: Great Britain, "Balkanism" and the Search for a Balkan Locarno in the 1920s', *European History Quarterly* 33, no. 3 (2003): 318; Suonpää, *British Perceptions of the Balkan Slavs*, 21.

30 See Dušan I. Bjelić and Obrad Savić (eds), *Balkan as Metaphor: Between Globalization and Fragmentation* (Cambridge, MA: MIT Press, 2002).

31 Mishkova, *Beyond*, 4–5.

32 Andrew Hammond, *The Debated Lands: British and American Representations of the Balkans* (Cardiff: University of Cardiff Press, 2007), 252.
33 Albert Meier, 'Travel Writing', in Beller and Leerssen, *Imagology*, 446–7.
34 Suonpää, *British Perceptions of the Balkan Slavs*, 2.
35 See Florian Keisinger, *Unzivilisierte Kriege im zivilisierten Europa?: Die Balkankriege und die öffentliche Meinung in Deutschland, England und Irland, 1876-1913* (Paderborn: Ferdinand Schoeningh, 2008); Neval Berber, *Unveiling Bosnia-Herzegovina in British Travel Literature* (1844-1912) (Pisa: Pisa University Press, 2010).
36 Michail, *The British and the Balkans*, 46; James Perkins, 'Peasants and Politics: Re-thinking the British Imaginative Geography of the Balkans at the Time of the First World War', *European History Quarterly* 47, no. 1 (2017): 60–2.
37 Vesna Drapac, *Constructing Yugoslavia: A Transnational History* (Basingstoke: Palgrave Macmillan, 2010), 10–14, 34–45.
38 James Evans, *Great Britain and the Creation of Yugoslavia: Negotiating Balkan Nationality and Identity* (London: I.B.Tauris, 2008), 5–6.
39 Michail, *The British and the Balkans*, 6–7.
40 J. M. Winter, 'British National Identity and the First World War', in S. J. D. Green and R. C. Whiting (eds), *The Boundaries of the State in Modern Britain* (Cambridge: Cambridge University Press, 1996), 262.
41 Tom Nairn, *The Break-up of Britain: Crisis and Neo-Nationalism* (London: NLB, 1977), 17–18; Anderson, *Imagined Communities*, 155–6.
42 Colin Kidd, *Subverting Scotland's Past: Scottish Whig Historians and the Creation of Anglo-British Identity, 1689-c.1830* (Cambridge: Cambridge University Press, 1993), 1.
43 Linda Colley, *Britons: Forging the Nation, 1707-1837* (New Haven: Yale University Press, 1992), 5–6. For a contrasting perspective, see David Edgerton, *The Rise and Fall of the British Nation: A Twentieth-Century History* (London: Penguin 2018).
44 Winter, 'British National Identity', 262.
45 Krishan Kumar, *The Making of English National Identity* (Cambridge: Cambridge University Press, 2003); Peter Mandler, *The English National Character: The History of an Idea from Edmund Burke to Tony Blair* (New Haven: Yale University Press, 2006); Brad Beaven, *Visions of Empire: Patriotism, Popular Culture and the City, 1870-1939* (Manchester: Manchester University Press, 2012).
46 Glenda Sluga, 'Narrating Difference and Defining the Nation in Late Nineteenth and Early Twentieth Century "Western" Europe', *European Review of History: Revue européenne d'histoire* 9, no. 2 (2002): 186–8.
47 Peter Mandler, 'Against "Englishness": English Culture and the Limits to Rural Nostalgia, 1850-1940', *Transactions of the Royal Historical Society* 7 (1997): 158–61; G. R. Searle, *A New England?: Peace and War, 1886-1918* (London: Methuen, 2004), 87.
48 Beaven, *Visions*, 208.
49 William Wallace, *The Foreign Policy Process in Britain* (London: George Allen & Unwin, 1977), 107.
50 James Thompson, *British Political Culture and the Idea of 'Public Opinion', 1867-1914* (Cambridge: Cambridge University Press, 2013), 35.
51 Gerald A. Hauser, *Vernacular Voices: The Rhetoric of Publics and Public Spheres* (Columbia: University of South Carolina Press, 1999), 57–64.
52 See John Narayan, *John Dewey: The Global Public and Its Problems* (Manchester: Manchester University Press, 2016).

53 George Dangerfield described the Edwardian era as one of 'general crisis' that was only assuaged by the outbreak of the First World War. David Powell, *The Edwardian Crisis: Britain, 1901-1914* (Basingstoke: Palgrave, 1996), vii–viii, 9; Daniel Pick, *Faces of Degeneration: A European Disorder, c.1848-c.1918* (Cambridge: Cambridge University Press, 1989), 189–92.

54 While a pan-Balkan union had been a talking point since the 1800s, it is doubtful whether the Yugoslav project would have gained any political traction without the contingency of the First World War. Dennison Rusinow, 'The Yugoslav Idea before Yugoslavia', in Dejan Djokić (ed.), *Yugoslavism: Histories of a Failed Idea 1918-1992* (Madison: University of Wisconsin Press, 2003), 12–14.

Chapter 1

1 Ivana Živančević-Sekeruš, 'Balkans', in Beller and Leerssen (eds), *Imagology*, 106–7.
2 Kiril Petkov, 'England and the Balkan Slavs 1354-1583: An Outline of a Late Medieval and Renaissance Image', *The Slavonic and East European Review* 76, no. 1 (1997): 86–8.
3 Hammond, *Debated Lands*, 8.
4 The geostrategic considerations of the European Great Powers towards the Ottoman Empire's political and economic instability from the late eighteenth to the early twentieth centuries.
5 Barbara Jelavich, 'The British Traveller in the Balkans: The Abuses of Ottoman Administration in the Slavonic Provinces', *The Slavonic and East European Review* 33, no. 81 (1955): 412.
6 Bracewell, 'Opinion-Makers', 96.
7 A Western intellectual movement advocating Greek independence and the promotion of Hellenic cultural studies.
8 Mazower, 'Travellers and the Oriental City', *Transactions of the Royal Historical Society* 12 (2002): 59–60; Kostova, *Tales*, 14.
9 Kuklick, *Savage Within*, 11–13; Kostova, *Tales*, 15.
10 Friedrich Engels, 'The Magyar Struggle, 1849', in Karl Marx and Friedrich Engels, *Collected Works, Volume 8, 1848-9* (London: Lawrence & Wishart, 2010), 235.
11 Arden G. Hulme-Beaman, *Twenty Years in the Near East* (London: Methuen & Co., 1898), 121.
12 Todorova, *Imagining*, 114–15; Norris, *In the Wake*, 15–22.
13 Hammond, *Debated Lands*, 38.
14 Vojislav Mate Jovanović, *An English Bibliography on the Near Eastern Question, 1481-1906* (Belgrade: The Government Press, 1909).
15 Thomas Jackson's three-volume guide to Dalmatian architecture and history, originally published in 1887, was being marketed to British tourists as late as the 1930s. Božidar Jezernik, *Wild Europe: The Balkans in the Gaze of Western Travellers* (London: Saqi Books), 31–2; Sonia Wild-Bićanić, *British Travellers in Dalmatia 1757-1935* (Zagreb: Zaprešić Fraktura, 2006), 28–9. See also, T. G. Jackson, *Dalmatia: The Quarnero and Istria*, 1–3 Vols (Oxford: The Clarendon Press, 1887).
16 Michail, *The British and the Balkans*, 139.
17 A mountain range in the Eastern Alps running through north-east Italy and northern Slovenia. Petkov, 'England and the Balkan Slavs 1354-1583', 92.

18 One such example appeared in the *Itineraries* of the Anglo-Irish friar Symon Semeonis from 1322 to 1324 which described the Slavs he encountered as possessing significant political and economic leverage in the east Adriatic; speaking a language that conformed 'in great part to the Bohemians (Czechs)'; following 'the Greek rite (Eastern Orthodoxy)'; and being mainly 'rustics and common folk'. Eugene Hoade, *Western Pilgrims (1322-1392)* (Jerusalem: Franciscan Printing Press, 1970 [1952]), v–vi, 8–9.
19 Petkov, 'England and the Balkan Slavs 1354-1583', 91–2.
20 Catherine D. Carmichael, 'Two Gentleman Travellers in the Slovene Lands in 1737', *Slovene Studies* 13, no. 1 (1991): 21.
21 See, for example, Bernadette Andrea and Linda McJannet (eds), *Early Modern England and Islamic Worlds* (Basingstoke: Palgrave Macmillan, 2011).
22 See Henry Blount, *A Voyage into the Levant* (London: Andrew Crooke, 1636).
23 The arresting Ottoman's defeat at Vienna in 1683 may have also played a role in this dissipation of interest. Berber, *Unveiling*, xiii.
24 In 1700, an account by the Norwich physician Edward Browne was the nearest equivalent to an English travel guide still in circulation. Carmichael, 'Two Gentleman Travellers', 20; Mazower, 'Travellers and the Oriental City', 62. See Edward Browne (MD), *A Brief Account of Some Travels in Divers Parts of Europe* (London: printed for Benjamin Tooke, 1685).
25 Wolff, *Inventing Eastern Europe*, 5–7.
26 Carmichael, 'Two Gentleman Travellers', 19.
27 Robert Adam, *Ruins of the Palace of Diocletian at Spalatro in Dalmatia* (London: printed for the author, 1764), 2–3.
28 Earlier works such as Frederik Calvert's *A Tour to the East, in the Years 1763 and 1764* (1767) were lambasted as examples of how 'a man may travel without observation, and be an author without ideas'. Horace Walpole and Thomas Park, *A Catalogue of the Royal and Noble Authors of England, Scotland, and Ireland, Volume 5* (London: John Scott, 1806), 278–9.
29 Todorova, *Imagining*, 22–3.
30 Cathie Carmichael, 'A People Exists and That People Has Its Language', in Stephen Barbour and Cathie Carmichael (eds), *Language and Nationalism in Europe* (Oxford: Oxford University Press, 2002), 286; F. M. Barnard, *Herder on Nationality, Humanity, and History* (Montreal and Kingston: McGill-Queen's University Press, 2003), 134.
31 *Morlaci* was an exonym originally applied to the Romance-speaking communities (Vlachs) of eastern Dalmatia. Larry Wolff, *Venice and the Slav: The Discovery of Dalmatia in the Age of Enlightenment* (Stanford: Stanford University Press, 2001), 13, 86–7, 126–7; Pavle Sekeruš, 'Serbs', in Beller and Leerssen, *Imagology*, 234–5. See (Abbé) Alberto Fortis, *Travels into Dalmatia* (London: printed for J. Robson, 1778).
32 Evans, *Great Britain and the Creation*, 34–51.
33 Despite coming under nominal Ottoman suzerainty in the late fifteenth century, the embryonic Montenegrin state emerged as an autonomous Orthodox enclave, centred on the monastery at Cetinje, gaining de facto independence in the 1690s. Kenneth Morrison, *Montenegro: A Modern History* (London: I.B. Tauris, 2008), 17–18.
34 L. S. Stavrianos, *The Balkans since 1453* (London: Hurst & Company, 2000), 269.
35 Davide Rodogno, *Against Massacre: Humanitarian Interventions in the Ottoman Empire, 1815-1914* (Princeton: Princeton University Press, 2012), 66–74, 83–9.
36 Andrew Archibald Paton (Esq.), *Servia, The Youngest Member of the European Family* (London: Longman, Brown, Green & Longmans, 1845), 136–41.

37 Ibid., 3, 16.
38 Alexander William Kinglake, *Eōthen, or, Traces of Travel, Brought Home from the East* (London: John Oliver, 1844), v–ix.
39 For a comparatively early example, see Mary Adelaide Walker, *Through Macedonia to the Albanian Lakes* (London: Chapman & Hall, 1864). Gary Kelly, *Revolutionary Feminism: The Mind and Career of Mary Wollstonecraft* (Basingstoke: Macmillan, 1992), 2–4; Todorova, 'The Balkans: From Discovery to Invention', 462–3.
40 See G. Muir MacKenzie and A. Irby, *Travels in the Slavonic Provinces of Turkey-in-Europe* Vol. 1, 2nd edn (London: Daldy, Isbister & Co.,1877 [1867]); Arthur J. Evans, *Through Bosnia and Herzegovina on Foot during the Insurrection* (London: Longmans, Green & Co., 1876); idem, *Illyrian Letters: A Revized Selection of Correspondence* (London: Longmans, Green, & Co., 1878).
41 Members of the tax-paying lower classes in Ottoman society. Although Jews and Muslims also fell within this category, by 1900 the term was synonymous with Christians. Jelavich, *The British Traveller*, 413; Todorova, *Imagining*, 97–8.
42 James Creagh, *Over the Borders of Christendom and Eslamiah, Vol. II* (London: Samuel Tinsley, 1876), 136–7, 255; Bracewell, 'Opinion-Makers', 98–105.
43 Evans, *Illyrian Letters*, 189.
44 A series of violent measures employed by the Ottoman military in its efforts to subdue the uprising that broke out in Bulgaria in April 1876. These events were pivotal in mobilizing British public opinion against the Conservative government of Benjamin Disraeli and its pro-Ottoman stance on the Eastern Question.
45 W. E. Gladstone (M.), *Bulgarian Horrors and the Question of the East* (London: John Murray, 1876), 15–17.
46 Idem, 'Preface', in Mackenzie and Irby, *Travels in the Slavonic Provinces*, vii–xiv.
47 Rodogno, *Against Massacre*, 3.
48 Jonathan Parry, *The Politics of Patriotism: English Liberalism, National Identity and Europe, 1830-1886* (Cambridge: Cambridge University Press, 2006), 340.
49 Perkins, 'Peasants and Politics', 61.
50 The Treaty of San Stefano between Russia and the Ottoman Empire in March 1878 offered similar terms but proposed a 'Greater Bulgaria' that included the entirety of Macedonia. This was rejected by the other powers with its terms being superseded by Berlin several months later.
51 Cathy Gere, *Knossos and the Prophets of Modernism* (Chicago: University of Chicago Press, 2009), 62–3.
52 Stevan K. Pavlowitch, *Anglo-Russian Rivalry Russian Rivalry in Serbia, 1837–1839: The Mission of Colonel Hodges* (Paris: Mouton & Co, 1961), 160; David Steele, 'Three British Prime Ministers and the Survival of the Ottoman Empire, 1855-1902', *Middle Eastern Studies* 50, no. 1 (2014): 43–60.
53 Winter, 'British National Identity', 265.
54 Suonpää, *British Perceptions of the Balkan Slavs*, 12.
55 Bruno Naarden and Joep Leerssen, 'Russians', in Beller and Leerssen, *Imagology*, 227; Sekeruš, 'Serbs', in ibid., 235. See also, Živančević-Sekeruš, 'Balkans', 103–8; Gregory Paschalidis, 'Greeks', in ibid., 166–71; Dennis Deletant, 'Romanians', in ibid., 223–6; Bruno Naarden, 'Slavs', in ibid., 237–42.
56 William Miller, *Travel and Politics in the Near East* (London: T. Fisher Unwin, 1898), 118.
57 Ibid., 100–18.

58 (Sir) Lepel Griffin, 'England and France in Asia', *The Monthly Review* 34, no. 201 (1893): 673.
59 'Mowatt to the Foreign Office (22 December 1893)', FO32/658; 'Law to Egerton (20 January 1898)', FO32/708.
60 (Lieut.) G. Arbuthnot, *Herzegovina; Or Omer Pacha and the Christian Rebels* (London: Longman, Green, Longman, Roberts & Green, 1862), 62.
61 Hulme-Beaman, *Twenty Years in the Near East*, 91; Ipek K. Yosmaoğlu, *Blood Ties: Religion, Violence and the Politics of Nationhood in Ottoman Macedonia, 1878-1908* (Ithaca: Cornell University Press, 2013), 27–31.
62 Goldsworthy, *Inventing Ruritania*, 42; Keisinger, *Unzivilisierte Kriege*, 159.
63 Kostova, *Tales*, 113–14.
64 Berber, *Unveiling*, xv.
65 Sevtap Demirci, *British Public Opinion towards the Ottoman Empire during the Two Crises: Bosnia-Herzegovina (1908-1909) and the Balkan Wars (1912-1913)* (Istanbul: Isis, 2006), 9.
66 Toni Weller, *The Victorians and Information* (Saarbrücken: VDM Verlag, 2009), 157–8.
67 Slobodan G. Markovich, *British Perceptions of Serbia and the Balkans, 1903-1906* (Paris: Dialogue, 2000), 29.
68 (Lady) E. Grogan, *The Life of J.D Bourchier* (London: Hurst & Blackett, 1926), 93–4.
69 *The Times* (22 January 1996). Cited in Michael Foley, 'James David Bourchier: An Irish Journalist in the Balkans', *Irish Communication Review* 10, no. 1 (2007): 58–62.
70 Ibid., 63.
71 Berber, *Unveiling*, 99–101.
72 Suonpää, *British Perceptions of the Balkan Slavs*, 192–3.
73 Berber, *Unveiling*, 107. Thomas Gallant observes a similar paradigm under the Britain's protectorate of the Greek-inhabited Ionian islands from 1815 to 1864. Greek islanders were presented as a hybrid of Western and Eastern cultures or 'Mediterranean Irish'. Thomas Gallant, *Experiencing Dominion: Culture, Identity, and Power in the British Mediterranean* (Notre Dame: University of Notre Dame Press, 2002), 35–9.
74 Keisinger, *Unzivilisierte Kriege*, 35–8, 142.
75 Michael de Nie, *The Eternal Paddy: Irish Identity and the British Press, 1789-1882* (Madison: The University of Wisconsin Press, 2004), 22–5.
76 Andrew Gamble, 'The Conservatives and the Union: The "New English Toryism" and the Origins of Anglo-Britishness', *Political Studies Review* 14, no. 3 (2016): 362.
77 Suonpää, *British Perceptions of the Balkan Slavs*, 12.
78 Ibid., 85, 231–7.
79 Ibid., 123; Pick, *Faces of Degeneration*, 36–8; Richard A. Soloway, *Demography and Degeneration: Eugenics and the Declining Birthrate in Twentieth-Century Britain* (Chapel Hill: University of North Carolina Press, 1990), 39. See (General) William Booth, *In Darkest England and the Way Out* (London: Funk & Wagnalls, 1890); B. Seebohm Rowntree, *Poverty: A Study of Town Life* (London: Macmillan & Co., 1901).
80 Suonpää, *British Perceptions of the Balkan Slavs*, 185.
81 Herbert Vivian, *Servia: The Poor Man's Paradise* (London: Longman, Green & Co., 1897), vii–ix; Radmila Pejić, 'Herbert Vivian: A Late Nineteenth-Century British Traveller in Serbia', *Balcanica* 44 (2013): 257–61.
82 Vivian, *Servia*, 147.
83 See W. E. Gladstone, *The Irish Question* (London: John Murray, 1886).

84 Stjepan G. Meštrović, *The Coming Fin de Siecle: An Application of Durkheim's Sociology to Modernity and Postmodernism* (London: Routledge, 1991), 2.
85 Pick, *Faces of Degeneration*, 38; Kostova, *Tales*, 18.

Chapter 2

1 Todorova, *Imagining*, 116.
2 Hammond, *Debated Lands*, 109–13; Evans, *Great Britain and the Creation*, 115–18.
3 Searle, *A New England?*, 545.
4 Alan Lee, *The Origins of the Popular Press in England, 1855-1914* (London: Rowman & Littlefield, 1976), 52–4. See also, Joel H. Wiener, *The Americanization of the British Press, 1830s-1914: Speed in the Age of Transatlantic Journalism* (Basingstoke: Palgrave Macmillan, 2011).
5 Sluga, 'Narrating Difference', 184–7, 190–2.
6 Ibid., 191.
7 Hammond, *Debated Lands*, 93; Perkins, 'Peasants and Politics', 57. Hammond's proclivity for periodization leads him to associate this development with the interwar rather than Edwardian years.
8 Suonpää, *British Perceptions of the Balkan Slavs*, 235.
9 See C. F. G. Masterman, *The Condition of England* (London: Methuen & Co., 1909).
10 Powell, *Edwardian Crisis*, 89; J. B. Priestley, *The Edwardians* (London: Heinemann, 1970), 55.
11 See, for example, E. P. Hennock, 'Poverty and Social Theory in England: The Experience of the Eighteen-Eighties', *Social History* 1, no. 1 (1976): 67–91; G. R. Searle, 'The Politics of National Efficiency and of War', in Chris Wrigley (ed.), *A Companion to Early-Twentieth Century Britain* (Oxford: Blackwell, 2002).
12 Peter Broks, 'Science, Media and Culture: British Magazines, 1890-1914', *Public Understanding of Science* 2, no. 2 (1993): 123–39.
13 Kuklick, *Savage Within*, 152–5.
14 Ibid., 5–13.
15 Gere, *Knossos*, 75–9.
16 It was speculated that up to 60 per cent had been medically unfit to serve. *Report of the Inter-Departmental Committee on Physical Deterioration: Vol. 1 Report and Appendix* (London: H.M. Stationery Office by Darling & Son, 1904), 23–41, 95–6.
17 Alun Howkins, 'The Discovery of Rural England', in Robert Collins and Philip Dodd (eds), *Englishness: Politics and Culture, 1880-1920*, 2nd edn (London: Bloomsbury, 2014), 88–91; Searle, *A New England?*, 283; Paul Readman, *Land and Nation in England: Patriotism, National Identity, and the Politics of Land, 1880-1914* (Woodbridge: Boydell Press, 2008), 73–4.
18 See, John Marriot, *The Other Empire: Metropolis, India and Progress in the Colonial Imagination* (Manchester: Manchester University Press, 2009).
19 Kuklick, *Savage Within*, 152; Suonpää, *British Perceptions of the Balkan Slavs*, 233. Press hysteria was further aroused by a string of highly publicized rugby tours between 1905 and 1912 that saw local British teams lose heavily to squads from Australia, New Zealand and South Africa. See Timothy J. L. Chandler and John Nauright (eds), *Making Men: Rugby and Masculine Identity* (Abingdon: Routledge, 1996).

20 R. A. Scott-James, *Modernism and Romance* (London: John Lane, 1908), 31–2.
21 See Lewis H. Mates, *The Great Labour Unrest: Rank-and-File Movements and Political Change in the Durham Coalfield* (Manchester: Manchester University Press, 2016).
22 Searle, *A New England?*, 441–3.
23 'Diaries of John Evelyn Wrench, Vol 1. The Tour in 1901, 31 Aug.–2 Oct. 1901', *Wrench Papers. Vol. XVI*, BL Western Manuscripts: Add MS 59556, 33, 40.
24 Keisinger, *Unzivilisierte Kriege*, 159–71.
25 'First International Eugenics Congress', *The British Medical Journal* 2 (1912): 253–5.
26 See, for example, Douglas A. Lorimer, *Science, Race Relations and Resistance: Britain, 1870–1914* (Manchester: Manchester University Press, 2013).
27 Evans, *Great Britain and the Creation*, 15.
28 R. A. Scott-James, 'The Austrian Occupation of Macedonia', *The Fortnightly Review* 84 (1905): 902–3.
29 Reginald Wyon and Gerald Prance, *The Land of the Black Mountain: The Adventures of Two Englishmen in Montenegro* (London: Methuen & Co., 1903), 50; (Lieut.-Col.) J. P. Barry, *At the Gates of the East: A Book of Travel among Historic Wonderlands* (London: Longmans, Green & Co., 1906), 245; Roy Trevor, *Montenegro: A Land of Warriors* (London: Adam & Charles Black, 1913), 88; G. E. Mitton, *Austria-Hungary* (London: Adam & Charles Black, 1914), 73–4.
30 Kaser, 'Anthropology and the Balkanization of the Balkans', 91–5; Duijzings, 'Changes in the Social Roles', 9–10.
31 Ćiro Truhelka, *Hrvatska Bosna (Mi i 'oni tamo')* (Sarajevo: Tiskara Vogler, 1907), 24–9, 37–41; Nevenko Bartulin, *The Racial Idea in the Independent State of Croatia: Origins and Theory* (Leiden & Boston: Brill, 2014), 52–5.
32 Percy E. Henderson, *A British Officer in the Balkans* (London: Seeley & Co., 1909), 105–6.
33 See Todd M. Endelman, *The Jews of Britain, 1656 to 2000* (Berkeley: University of California Press, 2002).
34 Goldsworthy, *Inventing Ruritania*, 227; Perkins, 'Peasants and Politics', 65.
35 Suonpää, *Perceptions of the Balkan Slavs*, 170–1.
36 Andre Liebich, 'The Antisemitism of Henry Wickham Steed', *Patterns of Prejudice* 46, no. 2 (2012): 204; Perkins, 'Peasants and Politics', 65–6.
37 Henderson, *British Officer*, 106.
38 Jovan Cvijić, *Nekolika promatranja o etnografiji makedonskih Slovena* (Belgrade: Štamparija 'Dositije Obradović', 1906), 5.
39 Michail, *The British and the Balkans*, 7–8.
40 Although insurgent activity persisted until November, the principal revolts had been suppressed by the end of September with most of the populace remaining apathetic in the face of VMRO propaganda and coercion. Arthur J. Evans, 'The Policy of Extermination in Macedonia', *The Times* (1 October 1903), 10.
41 G. F. Abbott, *The Tale of a Tour in Macedonia* (London: Edward Arnold, 1903), 80–1.
42 Christopher Prior, *Edwardian England and the Idea of Decline: An Empire's Future* (Basingstoke: Palgrave Macmillan, 2013), 107–9.
43 Beaven, *Visions*, 59–60.
44 Masterman, *The Condition of England*, 304.
45 Ibid., 190–3.
46 Peter Mathias, *The First Industrial Nation: An Economic History of Britain, 1700-1914* (London: Methuen, 1969), 478; Richard Soloway, 'Counting the Degenerates: The Statistics of Race Deterioration in Edwardian England', *Journal of Contemporary*

History 17 (1982): 137–40; Simon Mollan and Ranald Michie, 'The City of London as an International Commercial and Financial Center since 1900', *Enterprise and Society* 13, no. 3 (2012): 539–40.

47 L. C. B. Seaman, *Victorian England: Aspects of English and Imperial History, 1837-1901* (London: Methuen, 1973), 263–4.

48 G. Diouritch, 'A Survey of the Development of the Serbian (Southern Slav) Nation: An Economic and Statistical Study', *Journal of the Royal Statistical Society* 82, no. 3 (1919): 299.

49 The fraction of England's population estimated to be living in 'permanent poverty' at the end of the nineteenth century. Booth, *In Darkest England*, 22–3.

50 'Servia – the Peasant Kingdom'. Interview with Simeon 'Sima' Lozanić, *The Humanitarian*, XVIII (1901): 382.

51 John Foster Fraser, *Pictures from the Balkans* (London: Caswell & Co., 1906), 60.

52 [William Le Queux], *An Observer in the Near East* (London: T. Fisher Unwin, 1907), 126–9; Agnes Ethel Conway, *A Ride through the Balkans. On Classic Ground with a Camera* (London: Robert Scott, 1917), 171.

53 Victor Goedorp, 'With a Camera in Bosnia', *The Wide World Magazine* VIII (1901–1902): 498.

54 Barry, *At the Gates of the East*, 236–7.

55 Noel Buxton, *Europe and the Turks* (London: John Murray, 1907), 60–1; T. Comyn-Platt, *The Turk in the Balkans* (London: Alston Rivers, 1904), 10–13; Geoffrey Drage, *Austria-Hungary* (London: J. Murray, 1909), 596–603; Henderson, *British Officer*, 106–8.

56 Herbert Vivian, *The Servian Tragedy, with some Impressions of Macedonia* (London: G. Richards, 1904), 236.

57 Holbach, *Dalmatia: The Land where East Meets West* (London: John Lane, The Bodley Head, 1908), 88–90.

58 See Todorova, *Imagining*; Goldsworthy, *Inventing Ruritania*; Fleming, 'Balkan Historiography'; Norris, *In the Wake*; Hammond, *Debated Lands*.

59 See Anthony Howe and Simon Morgan (eds), *The Letters of Richard Cobden: Volume IV* (Oxford: Oxford University Press, 2015), 596–7.

60 Henry de Windt, *Through Savage Europe* (London: T. Fisher Unwin, 1907), 173–4.

61 See Leith Davis, Ian Duncan and Janet Sorensen (eds), *Scotland and the Borders of Romanticism* (Cambridge: Cambridge University Press, 2004).

62 Julian Moynahan, 'Pastoralism as Culture and Counter-Culture in English Fiction, 1800-1928: From a View to a Death', *Novel: A Forum on Fiction* 6, no. 1 (1972): 20; Howkins, 'The Discovery of Rural England', 63; Paul Ward, *Britishness since 1870* (London: Routledge, 2004), 56.

63 Pick, *Faces of Degeneration*, 202; Kuklick, *Savage Within*, 101–5.

64 Readman, *Land and Nation*, 72–7, 82.

65 Mandler, 'Against "Englishness"', 170.

66 'Letter to Potter (18 March 1865)', in Howe and Morgan (eds), *Letters of Richard Cobden*, 596.

67 George Campbell, 'The Resettlement of the Turkish Dominions', *Fortnightly Review* 23 (1878): 550.

68 Paul Readman, 'The Edwardian Land Question', in Matthew Cragoe and Paul Readman (eds), *The Land Question in Britain, 1750-1950* (Basingstoke: Palgrave Macmillan, 2010), 185–7.

69 Hugh Aronson, 'Rural Housing: A Lesson from Hertfordshire', *The Contemporary Review* 557 (1912): 713.
70 Ellis W. Davie, 'The Break-up of Landed Estates', *The Contemporary Review* 558 (1912): 4–6.
71 B. Seebohm Rowntree, *Land and Labour: Lessons from Belgium* (London: Macmillan & Co., 1911), 542–7. See also, B. Seebohm Rowntree and May Kendall, *How the Labourer Lives: A Study of the Rural Labour Problem* (London: T. Nielson, 1913).
72 Ibid., 302–7, 319–20.
73 M. Edith Durham, *High Albania* (London: Edward Arnold, 1909), 285.
74 Readman, *Land and Nation*, 137.
75 National Liberal Federation, *Annual Reports*, card 27 (1905); card 29 (1907). Cited in ibid., 82.
76 Scott-James, 'The Austrian Occupation of Macedonia', 902–3.
77 A Habsburg crown land comprising Trieste, the Istrian peninsula and the county of Gorizia and Gradisca. After 1918, it was divided between Italy and Yugoslavia.
78 John McCourt, *The Years of Bloom: James Joyce in Trieste 1904-1920* (Madison: University of Wisconsin Press, 2000), 8–13.
79 *Census of England and Wales, 1911* (London: H.M.S.O, 1915), 11.
80 *Kingdom of Yugoslavia 1919-1929* (Belgrade: Central Press Bureau, 1930), 3.
81 Belgrade and Sarajevo had experienced severe demographic decline until the 1860s while Zagreb's population only exceeded 10,000 inhabitants at the beginning of the nineteenth century. John R. Lampe, *Yugoslavia as History: Twice there was a Country* (Cambridge: Cambridge University Press, 2000), 77–81, 86–7.
82 The Aegean port of Thessaloniki was a salient example. Despite its uniqueness within the Empire for having been 40 to 50 per cent Jewish since the seventeenth century, Westerners frequently cited it as an archetypical Ottoman city. Norris, *In the Wake*, 89–90; Mazower, 'Travellers and the Oriental City', 65–6.
83 Goldsworthy, *Inventing Ruritania*, 168.
84 M. E. Durham, *Through the Lands of the Serb* (London: Edward Arnold, 1904), 143–4.
85 Abbot, *Tale of a Tour*, 135; Henderson, *British Officer*, 93–107; Maude M. Holbach, *Bosnia and Herzegovina: Some Wayside Wanderings* (London: The Bodley Head, 1910 [1909]), 140.
86 Jezernik, *Wild Europe*, 227.
87 Mary Sparks, *The Development of Austro-Hungarian Sarajevo, 1878-1918: An Urban History* (London: Bloomsbury Academic, 2014), 181.
88 Holbach, *Wayside Wanderings*, 89–90.
89 Roy Trevor, *My Balkan Tour: An Account of some Journeyings and Adventures in the Near East* (London: John Lane, 1911), 87–9.
90 Robert Munro, *Rambles and Studies in Bosnia-Herzegovina and Dalmatia*, 2nd edn (Edinburgh: William Blackwood & Sons, 1900 [1895]), 16.
91 See Joel M. Halpern, 'Peasant Culture and Urbanization in Yugoslavia', *EKISTICS: Review of the Problems and Science of Human Settlements* 21, no. 122 (1966): 21–3; Andrei Simić, *The Peasant Urbanites: A Study of Rural-Urban Mobility in Serbia* (New York: Seminar Press, 1973).
92 Hammond, *British Literature and the Balkan: Themes and Contexts* (Amsterdam: Rodopi Press, 2010), 180–1.
93 See Christopher J. Ferguson, *Inventing the Modern City: Urban Culture and Ideas in Britain, 1780-1880* (PhD Thesis, Indiana University, 2008).

94 Beaven, *Visions*, 65.
95 Holbach, *Dalmatia*, 31; F. Hamilton Jackson, *The Shores of the Adriatic, The Austrian Side* (London: John Murray, 1908), 138–9, 206–7; Mrs E. I. Russell Barrington, *Through Greece and Dalmatia* (London: Adam & Charles Black, 1912), 151–5, 202–4.
96 Robert Hichens, *The Near East: Dalmatia, Greece and Constantinople* (London: Hodder & Stoughton, 1913), 8.
97 Jackson, *Shores of the Adriatic*, 128.
98 Holbach, *Dalmatia*, 23–5.
99 Henderson, *British Officer*, 293–4.
100 Trevor, *Balkan Tour*, 7–8.
101 Ibid., 9.
102 Jezernik, *Wild Europe*, 207–9; Perkins, 'Peasants and Politics', 65–6.
103 Abbott, *Tale of a Tour*, 9; H. N. Brailsford, *Macedonia: Its Races and their Future* (London: Methuen & Co., 1906), 29; Fraser, *Pictures*, 156–7.
104 Abbott, *Tale of a Tour*, 10.
105 Jovan Hadži-Vasiljević, *Prilep i njegova okolina:istorijsko-geografska izlaganja* (Belgrade: Štamp. P. Jockovića, 1902), 44.
106 (Col.) Lionel James, *Times of Stress* (London: John Murray, 1929), 179.
107 Ford, 'Montenegro in the Eyes of the Traveller', 355–6.
108 M. E. Durham, 'Letter to Mother (10 September 1900)', *Durham*, RAI: MS 43.
109 [Le Queux], *An Observer*, 23; Suonpää, *British Perceptions of the Balkan Slavs*, 101.
110 Trevor, *Montenegro*, 21.
111 Fraser, *Pictures*, 38.
112 Construction of the current Serbian parliament building was only completed in 1936.
113 Fraser, *Pictures*, 37–9; [Le Queux], *An Observer*, 21–8, 101.
114 Kostova, *Tales*, 10–12; Fleming, 'Balkan Historiography', 12; Hammond, *Debated Lands*, 112.
115 de Windt, *Savage Europe*, 69.
116 Ibid., 38–9.
117 (Mrs.) E. R. Whitwell, *Through Bosnia and Herzegovina with a Paint Brush* (Darlington: William Dresser & Sons, 1909), 44.
118 M. E. Durham, 'Diary (10 September 1900)', *Mary Edith Durham 'Collection'*, RAI: MS 42; eadem, 'Letter to Mother (20 August 1900)', *Durham*, RAI: MS 43.
119 Chedo Mijatovich, *Servia and the Servians* (London: Sir Isaac Pitman & Sons, 1908), 236.
120 Omer Hadžiselimović, *At the Gates of the East: British Travel Writers on Bosnia and Herzegovina from the 16th to the 20th Centuries* (New York: Columbia University Press, 2001), xxvii.
121 A river that passes through central Sarajevo. James, *Times of Stress*, 172–3.
122 J. Steward, '"The Balkans in London": Political Culture and the Cultural Politics of Exhibitions at Earl's Court, 1906-1908', *Balkan Studies (Études Balkaniques)* 44, no. 4 (2008): 77–82.
123 The 1900 Paris *Exposition Universelle*'s Austrian pavilion set a precedent by featuring regional embroidery and 'folklore traditions' among its displays. Philippe Jullian, *The Triumph of Art Nouveau: Paris Exhibition, 1900* (London: Phaidon Press, 1974), 71–2.
124 Believed to be Byzantine in origin, despite becoming an Orientalist cliché, the fez had been adopted by the Ottoman army in the 1820s as a Westernizing measure. Mitton, *Austria-Hungary*, 192; Trevor, *Montenegro*, 22–3.

125 Seton-Watson, for instance, pointed to a prevalence of spoken English among the Croat peasants of the Pelješac peninsula and island of Korčula, many of whom had served on British merchant ships, as evidence of a cultural receptiveness to Western mores. R. W. Seton-Watson, *The Southern Slav Question and the Habsburg Monarchy* (London: Constable & Co., 1911), 5.
126 Mijatovich, *Servia*, 38.
127 Barrington, *Greece and Dalmatia*, 203.
128 Jackson, *Shores of the Adriatic*, 14–16.
129 Ibid., 17–18. The ostensibly less parochial Slovenes were no exception in this recourse to the supernatural. Well after 1900, travellers noted that the services of 'counterwitches', female mystics able to nullify witches' curses and predict the future, remained in high demand. Mirjam Mencej, 'Witchcraft in Eastern Slovenia and Western Macedonia – A Comparative Analysis', in Zmago Šmitek and Aneta Svetieva (eds), *Post-Yugoslav Lifeworlds: Between Tradition and Modernity* (Ljubljana: Univerza v Ljubljani, 2005), 45–6.
130 'Manacled by Superstition', *Hull Daily Mail* (29 August 1900), 4.
131 'Superstition in Bosnia', *Sheffield Evening Telegraph* (18 August 1902), 7.
132 The Julian calendar was still officially used in Serbia until 1918, placing the date of the assassination on 29 May.
133 J. D. Bourchier, 'The Situation in Servia', *The Times* (9 February 1906), 8.
134 John Hodgson, 'Edith Durham: Traveller and Publicist', in Allcock and Young, *Black Lambs*, 10. Mijatović had only come to press attention after it was revealed that he had been present at a clairvoyance ceremony where the Serbian regicide had allegedly been foretold. W. T. Stead (ed.), 'A Clairvoyant Vision of the Assassination at Belgrade', *Review of Reviews* 28 (1903): 31.
135 Todorova, *Imagining*, 11–12, 131; Norris, *In the Wake*, 12–13, 50–8.
136 Drapac, *Constructing Yugoslavia*, 38–40.
137 Goldsworthy, *Inventing Ruritania*, 75–6; Suonpää, *British Perceptions of the Balkan Slavs*, 73; Evans, *Great Britain and the Creation*, 54–5.
138 Mijatovich, *Servia*, 51.
139 Simon Skinner, 'Religion', in David Craig and James Thompson (eds), *Languages of Politics in Nineteenth-Century Britain* (Basingstoke: Palgrave Macmillan, 2013), 112–13.
140 Sluga, 'Narrating Difference', 186.
141 [Charles Eliot], 'Odysseus', in *Turkey in Europe* (London: Edward Arnold, 1900), 321–3.
142 [Eliot], *Turkey in Europe*, 158; Henderson, *British Officer*, 99–101; Holbach, *Wayside Wanderings*, 33.
143 Munro, *Rambles and Studies*, 22–3.
144 A Turkish title originally used to denote tribal chieftains. Under the Ottomans, it evolved into a formal term of address associated with the political and military elites.
145 [Eliot], *Turkey in Europe*, 379–80.
146 M. E. Durham, *My Balkan Notebook Vol. II: Montenegro* [1940], Mary Edith Durham 'Collection', RAI: MS 41/1, 11; Berber, *Unveiling*, 86.
147 Henderson, *British Officer*, 106–7.
148 Fraser, *Pictures*, 259–60.
149 Brailsford, *Macedonia*, 60–2.
150 The head of an autocephalous, or independent, Orthodox Church. Vivian noted similar trends in Macedonia and Bulgaria whose Slavic adherents 'until quite recently

...were commonly supposed throughout Europe to be Greeks'. Vivian, *Servian Tragedy*, 227–8.
151 Another of Mijatović's British friends was equally shocked to discover that Serbian religious education involved debates on the implausibility of biblical scripture in favour of scientific rationalism. Mijatovich, *Servia*, 51–2.
152 Jackson, *Shores of the Adriatic*, 54; Holbach, *Dalmatia*, 41.
153 Wyon, *The Balkans from Within*, 260.
154 Evans, *Great Britain and the Creation*, 36–42; Drapac, *Constructing Yugoslavia*, 50–3.
155 Munro, *Rambles and Studies*, vi, 45–9.
156 Berber, *Unveiling*, 106.
157 Keisinger, *Unzivilisierte Kriege*, 143–4; Berber, *Unveiling*, 93–5.
158 Mijatovich, *Servia*, iv.
159 de Windt, *Savage Europe*, 40.
160 Wyon and Prance, *Land of the Black Mountain*, 219; [Le Queux], *An Observer*, 22.
161 James, *Times of Stress*, 174–6.
162 Henderson, *British Officer*, 56.
163 Durham, 'Letter to Mother (24 August 1900)', Durham, RAI: MS 43.
164 Eadem, *The Burden of the Balkans* (London: Edward Arnold, 1905), 8; 'Folk Tales from the Balkans' (unpublished, c.1908), 1–2, Durham, RAI: MS 45.
165 R. A. Scott-James, *An Englishman in Ireland: Impressions of a Journey in a Canoe by River, Lough, and Canal* (London: J. M. Dent & Sons, 1910), 262.
166 Berber, *Unveiling*, 107.

Chapter 3

1 Kostova, *Tales*, 170–5; Todorova, *Imagining*, 62–4; Michail, *The British and the Balkans*, 4.
2 Demirci, *British Public Opinion*, 7–8.
3 Weller, *The Victorians and Information*, 23.
4 As well as speaking multiple languages, Dillon had few reservations about integrating himself into local cultures, often through the use of disguises, when covering events. These included first-hand reports on the Hamidian Massacres (1894–6), the Greco-Turkish War (1897) and the Great Power's suppression of the Boxer Rebellion in China (1899–1901). David Ayerst, *Garvin of the Observer* (London: Croom Helm, 1985), 36; P. W. Johnson and Joseph O. Baylen, 'Dillon, Dr. Emile Joseph, 1854–1933', in Joseph L. Wieczynski and George V. Rhyne (eds), *The Modern Encyclopaedia of Russian and Soviet History [Vol. 9]* (Gulf Breeze: Academic International Press, 1994), 106.
5 See Drapac, *Constructing Yugoslavia*; Michail, *The British and the Balkans*; Larry Wolff, 'The Western Representation of Eastern Europe on the Eve of World War I: Mediated Encounters and Intellectual Expertise in Dalmatia, Albania and Macedonia', *The Journal of Modern History* 86, no. 2 (2014): 381–407; James Perkins, 'The Congo of Europe: The Congo of Europe: The Balkans and Empire in Early Twentieth-Century British Political Culture', *The Historical Journal* 58, no. 2 (2015): 55–77.
6 Michail, *The British and the Balkans*, 11–12.
7 Ibid., 10.

8 In 1862, Britain had established a consulate in Dubrovnik for the sole purpose of monitoring unrest along Montenegro's border with Herzegovina. It closed in 1885 following the Habsburg's pacification of the area. Robin Okey, 'British Impressions of the Serb-Croat Speaking Lands of the Habsburg Monarchy – Reports to the Foreign Office 1867-1908', in Robert Evans, Dušan Kováč and Edita Ivaničková (eds), *Great Britain and Central Europe 1867-1914* (Brastislava: VEDA, 2002), 62.
9 Ibid., 63.
10 Before 1912, 12.25 per cent of Serbia's imports came from Britain but never exceeded £110,000 per annum. By contrast, Romania accounted for more than half of British trade in southeastern Europe. Products from the Habsburg territories were marketed as Austrian or Hungarian, while Montenegrin goods were restricted to tourist purchases from traders in Kotor and other coastal market towns. British demand for Macedonian commodities had also declined following the completion of the Suez Canal in 1869. Chedomille Mijatovich, 'Servia', in *The New Volumes of the Encyclopaedia Britannica, Tenth Edition* 32 (1902). Cited in Markovich, *British Perceptions of Serbia*, 159; Michael Palairet, *The Balkan Economies c.1800-1914: Evolution without Development* (Cambridge: Cambridge University Press, 1997), 143; John R. Lampe and Marvin R. Jackson, *Balkan Economic History, 1550-1950: From Imperial Borderlands to Developing Nations* (Bloomington: Indiana University Press, 1982), 168–76, 280–8.
11 Michael Hughes, *Inside the Enigma: British Officials in Russia, 1900-39* (London: Hambledon Press, 1997), 31–2; Zara S. Steiner, *The Foreign Office and Foreign Policy, 1898-1914* (Cambridge: Cambridge University Press, 1969), 17; eadem and Keith Nielson, *Britain and the Origins of the First World War*, 2nd edn (Basingstoke: Palgrave Macmillan, 2003), 136–7.
12 Hughes, *Inside the Enigma*, 34; Suonpää, *British Perceptions of the Balkan Slavs*, 187–8.
13 Wrench's diary from 1901 notes that the British Consul in Sarajevo, Edward Freeman, had been in post since before 1878. *Wrench Papers*, XVI, 22; M. E. Durham, *The Serajevo Crime* (London: G. Allen & Unwin, 1925), 11.
14 Barrington, *Greece and Dalmatia*, v; Jezernik, *Wild Europe*, 31–2.
15 During her secondment with the MRF, Durham wrote that Brailsford 'was not allowed to move without an officer and five cavalry', while the Fund's benefactress, Lady Annie Thompson, always travelled in the company of 'a major and twenty cavalry'. M. E. Durham, 'Letter to Mrs Seymour (7 January 1904)', RAI: MS 43.
16 Named after Sultan Abdul Hamid II, whose reign from 1876 to 1909 came to be associated with accentuated decline. Jo Laycock, *Imagining Armenia: Orientalism, Ambiguity and Intervention* (Manchester: Manchester University Press, 2009), 111.
17 Seeking to excise previous antisemitic associations between Armenians and Jews, the Liberal MP James Bryce claimed that the former were a peasant rather than an urbanised merchant-based society despite population data suggesting that more Armenians lived in western Anatolia than Armenia proper! Roy Douglas, 'Britain and the Armenian Question, 1894-7', *The Historical Journal* 19, no. 1 (1976): 114–15.
18 Robert Vogel, 'Noel Buxton: The "Trouble-Maker" and His Papers', *Fontanus* 3 (1990): 138–9; Michail, *The British and the Balkans*, 14; Rodogno, *Against Massacre*, 234–5.
19 These included several Anglican bishops, the editor of the radical *Daily News*, A. G. Gardiner, its proprietor George Cadbury and the future Labour prime minister

Ramsay MacDonald, under whom Buxton later held a cabinet post in the 1920s. Vogel, 'The "Trouble-Maker" and His Papers', 136–8.
20 Perkins, 'The Congo of Europe', 568.
21 Evans, *Great Britain and the Creation*, 7; Wolff, 'The Western Representation of Eastern Europe on the Eve of World War I', 381–3; Michail, *The British and the Balkans*, 33–8; Perkins, 'The Congo of Europe', 568–9.
22 On Durham, see Hodgson, 'Edith Durham', 9–31; June Hill, 'Edith Durham as a Collector', in Allcock and Young, *Black Lambs*, 32–7; Marcus Tanner, *Albania's Mountain Queen: Edith Durham and the Balkans* (London: I.B. Tauris, 2014).
23 M. E. Durham, *Twenty Years of Balkan Tangle* (London: George Allen & Unwin, 1920), 9.
24 Hammond, *Debated Lands*, 96–7.
25 On Buxton and Brailsford, see Mosa Anderson, *Noel Buxton: A Life* (London: Allen & Unwin, 1952); F. M. Leventhal, *The Last Dissenter: H.N. Brailsford and His World* (Oxford: Clarendon Press, 1985).
26 Ibid., 304–6.
27 Yosmaoğlu, *Blood Ties*, 139–40.
28 See Hugh and Christopher Seton-Watson, *The Making of a New Europe: R.W. Seton-Watson and the Last Years of Austria-Hungary* (London: Methuen, 1981).
29 Péter Lásló, 'The European Balance of Power and R. W. Seton-Watson's Changing Views on the National Question of the Habsburg Monarchy', in Evans, Kováč and Ivaničková, *Great Britain and Central Europe*, 98–100.
30 Nicholas J. Miller, 'R.W. Seton-Watson and Serbia during the Reemergence of Yugoslavia, 1903-1914', *Canadian Review of Studies in Nationalism* 15, nos. 1–2 (1988): 69; Lásló, 'R.W. Seton-Watson's Changing Views', in Evans, Kováč and Ivaničková, *Great Britain and Central Europe*, 101–2. See also, Stjepan Matković, 'Ivo Pilar i Robert W. Seton-Watson (Dva pogleda na južnoslavensko pitanje)', *Pilar: časopis za društvene i humanističke studije* 1, no. 1 (2006): 21–45; Drapac, *Constructing Yugoslavia*, 11–12, 19; Evans, *Great Britain and the Creation*, 184.
31 See Durham, *Through the Lands*, 263–345; Michail, *The British and the Balkans*, 30–2.
32 Notably the Czech philosopher Tomáš Garrigue Masaryk. Miller, 'Seton-Watson and Serbia', 59.
33 M. E. Durham, 'Letter to Sister Ellen ("Nellie") Durham (2 April 1912)', RAI: MS 43; Foley, 'An Irish Journalist', 60–1.
34 Wolff, 'The Western Representation of Eastern Europe on the Eve of World War I', 382.
35 Hammond, *Debated Lands*, 123–6.
36 Rodogno, *Against Massacre*, 237; Perkins, 'The Congo of Europe', 577.
37 Michail, *The British and the Balkans*, 41–5.
38 In 1912, Seton-Watson, possibly aware of these derogatory stereotypes, rejected a Slovak contact's request for him to edit an English-language quarterly covering the political aspirations of 'small nations'. Seton-Watson, *Making of a New Europe*, 98–9; Michail, *The British and the Balkans*, 30.
39 In 1892, Bourchier's elevation to the post of *The Times* Balkan correspondent came with that caveat that 'as a rule the British public only care for one thing at once and two things in the Balkans would be more than they could stand'. Quoted in Markovich, *British Perceptions of Serbia*, 92–3.
40 Based on the Advertiser's Protection Society's estimates, by 1910 *The Times* and *The Manchester Guardian* were among the smallest of Britain's national dailies in terms

of press circulation at only 45,000 and 40,000 respectively. Other broadsheets fared considerably better such as *The Daily Telegraph* (230,000 in 1910) and the *Daily News* (150,000 to 200,000), yet these remained permanently dwarfed by their mid-market competitors, the *Daily Mail* (900,000) and the *Daily Mirror* (630,000 and the first British daily to reach a circulation of over 1 million in 1911). Figures cited in David Butler and Gareth Butler, *British Political Facts*, 10th edn (Basingstoke: Palgrave Macmillan, 2011), 573; John B. Thompson, *Ideology and Modern Culture* (Cambridge: Polity Press, 2007[1990]), 178.
41 Perkins, 'The Congo of Europe', 583–4.
42 Robert B. McCormick, 'Noel Buxton, The Balkan Committee and Reform in Macedonia, 1903-1914', in Nicholas Charles Pappas (ed.), *Antiquity and Modernity: A Celebration of European History and Heritage in the Olympic Year 2004* (Athens: Institute for Education and Research, 2004), 156.
43 'Chirol to Nicolson (19 January 1909)', (Sir) Arthur Nicolson, *Miscellaneous Correspondence*, FO 800/342.
44 Kuklick, *Savage Within*, 92–3.
45 Brailsford, *Macedonia*, xi.
46 Kuklick, *Savage Within*, 75, 93.
47 Sluga, 'Narrating Difference', 196–8.
48 Laycock, *Imagining Armenia*, 93.
49 Herzfeld, *Anthropology through the Looking-Glass*, 11–15; Gallant, *Experiencing Dominion*, 55–6.
50 Peter F. Sugar, *The Industrialization of Bosnia-Hercegovina, 1878-1918* (Seattle: University of Washington Press, 1963), 71–3, 233.
51 [Eliot], *Turkey in Europe*, 356–7, 363; Drage, *Austria-Hungary*, 335–42, 449–52; Mitton, *Austria-Hungary*, 191; Gallant, *Experiencing Dominion*, 59.
52 Indentured peasants who worked the land on Muslim-owned estates, akin to serfs or tenant share-croppers.
53 Miller, *Travel and Politics*, 100–7.
54 Drage, *Austria-Hungary*, 617–18.
55 'Diaries of John Evelyn Wrench', *Wrench Papers. Vol. XVI*, 40.
56 Trevor, *Balkan Tour*, 187.
57 Buxton, *Europe and the Turks*, 119–20.
58 Brailsford, *Macedonia*, 76–7.
59 Noel Buxton, 'The Turks and Adrianople', *The Times* (14 August 1913), 5.
60 Drage, *Austria-Hungary*, 662.
61 Abbott, *Tale of a Tour*, 148.
62 Comyn-Platt, *Turk in the Balkans*, 19–20.
63 'R.W. Seton-Watson to Ivo Lupis-Vukić (17 October 1909)', *Seton-Watson Collection*, SSEES, SEW/1/1/8.
64 Seton-Watson, *Southern Slav Question*, 6–7.
65 James, *Times of Stress*, 176 ff.
66 Henderson, *British Officer*, 106.
67 Frederick Moore, *The Balkan Trail* (London: Smith, Elder & Co., 1906), 155–6. This perspective on the so-called Macedonian question seemed less feasible among British commentators: 'It is easy to tell from his [Moore's] narrative that he belongs to a country which has no active share in the problem,' ran an anonymous review in *The Spectator*. 'He does not attempt to sketch any solution.' 'The Balkan Trail* [Review]', *The Spectator* (22 September 1906), 401.

68 Herbert Vivian, 'A "Glorious" Revolution in Servia', *The Fortnightly Review* 75 (1903): 75. Were it not likely to provoke a Russian counter-occupation of Bulgaria, Bourchier even suggested that a Habsburg military occupation presented 'the best cure for Servia'. Quoted in Markovich, *British Perceptions of Serbia*, 178.
69 A. Stead, *Memorandum o odnosima između Engleske i Srbije*, ASANU. NO. 12880/3. For all their nationalist bellicosity, Montenegrin and Serb politicians continued to pursue foreign economic patronage. Between 1903 and 1914 for instance, Prince Nikola, with Serbian backing, had agreed to allow a Venetian consortium to undertake development projects in Montenegro including the proposed 'colonization' of its uninhabited coastal districts by Italian settlers. Palairet, *The Balkan Economies*, 240.
70 Buxton, *Europe and the Turks*, 48.
71 Since 1906, Seton-Watson had repeatedly outlined what he perceived as the repression of non-Hungarian ethnicities in the Monarchy's Hungarian portion (Transleithania). 'First Impressions of Transylvania, dated 1906', SEW/1/1/1. See also [R. W. Seton-Watson] 'Scotus Viator', *Racial Problems in Hungary* (London: Archibald Constable & Co., 1908). Steed's own anti-Germanism stemmed from his time as *The Times*' Vienna correspondent from 1902 to 1914. See Henry Wickham Steed, *Through Thirty Years 1892-1922: A Personal Narrative [Vol.1]* (London: Heinemann, 1924); Liebich, 'The Antisemitism of Henry Wickham Steed'.
72 Demirci, *British Public Opinion*, 30-1.
73 Holbach, *Wayside Wanderings*, 20-1.
74 (Dr.) E. J. Dillon, 'Foreign Affairs', *The Contemporary Review* 513 (1908): 382.
75 Roy Bridge, 'The British Foreign Office and National Questions in the Dual Monarchy', in Evans, Kováč and Ivaničková (eds), *Great Britain and Central Europe*, 45, 60; Demirci, *British Public Opinion*, 33.
76 Seton-Watson, *Southern Slav Question*, 343-4.
77 'Freeman to Grey, No.6 (6 October 1913)', *Austria-Hungary*, FO 371/1575.
78 'Lucas-Shadwell to Cartwright (29 December 1911)', FO371/1296.
79 A Croatian aristocratic or military title denoting a local or provincial ruler. Under Hungarian rule, its usage in Croatia-Slavonia held a similar meaning to viceroy.
80 Seton-Watson, *Southern Slav Question*, 91-2.
81 Drapac, *Constructing Yugoslavia*, 35-62.
82 Richard Scully, *British Images of Germany: Admiration, Antagonism & Ambivalence 1860-1914* (Basingstoke: Palgrave Macmillan, 2012), 316-17.
83 Dangerfield, *The Strange Death of Liberal England* (London: Constable & Co., 1936), 138; Powell, *Edwardian Crisis*, 68.
84 Ibid., 68. See also Martin Pugh, *The British Women's Suffrage Campaign 1866-1928, Revised*, 2nd edn (London: Routledge, 2009 [1998]).
85 Kostova, *Tales*, 15-17; Powell, *Edwardian Crisis*, 69-70.
86 Sara Mills, *Discourses of Difference: An Analysis of Women's Travel Writing and Colonialism* (London: Routledge, 1991), 27.
87 Goldsworthy, *Inventing Ruritania*, 165; Hammond, *Debated Lands*, 208.
88 Ibid., 152.
89 Michail, *The British and the Balkans*, 150.
90 Wendy Bracewell, 'New Men, Old Europe: Being a Man in Balkan Travel Writing', in Wendy Bracewell and Alex Drace-Francis (eds), *Balkan Departures: Travel Writing from Southeastern Europe* (New York: Berghahn Books, 2009), 137-8.
91 Drage, *Austria-Hungary*, 461-2; Trevor, *Montenegro*, 55-6.

92 Wyon and Prance, *Land of the Black Mountain*, 192.
93 (Rev.) W. Denton, *Montenegro: Its People and Their History* (London: Daldy, Isbister & Co., 1877), 124–7; Trevor, *Montenegro*, 299; Ford, 'Montenegro in the Eyes of the English Traveller', 365.
94 This also applied to children and male servants. Wyon and Prance, *Land of the Black Mountain*, 196–7.
95 Trevor, *Montenegro*, 45–7.
96 Jezernik, *Wild Europe*, 109–10.
97 [Le Queux], *An Observer*, 23.
98 Jezernik, *Wild Europe*, 111–12. The inferior status of women in Montenegro had long been noted by South Slav intellectuals. Writing in the 1830s, the influential Serb philologist Vuk Karadžić had observed that even the term 'woman' was deemed an insult. Cvijić later explained that, besides shepherding or fighting, manual labour was considered degrading to a mountaineer's honour. Vuk Stefanović Karadžić, *Crna Gora i Crnogorci*, ed. Golub Dobrašinović (Cetinje: Obod, 1975 [1837]), 89; Jovan Cvijić, *La Péninsule Balkanique: Geographie Humaine* (Paris: Librairie Armand Colin, 1918), 288–9.
99 Durham, *Through the Lands*, 193–4.
100 Adrian (& Marianne) Stokes, *Hungary* (London: Adam & Charles Black, 1909), 14.
101 Brailsford, *Macedonia*, 76–7.
102 Henderson, *British Officer*, 77–8.
103 Jackson, *Shores of the Adriatic*, 391; Jezernik, *Wild Europe*, 111.
104 Edith Durham, 'My Golden Sisters: A Macedonian Picture', *The Monthly Review*, 15 (1904): 76.
105 Ibid., 76–8.
106 Ibid., 73.
107 Durham, 'Letter to Mrs Seymour (7 January 1904)', RAI: MS 43.
108 Brailsford, *Macedonia*, 182–3.
109 Abbott, *Tale of a Tour*, 171. Durham later rejected such explanations theorizing it as predating both the Slavs and Ottomans. E. M. Durham, 'Albania Past and Present', *Journal of the Central Asian Society* 4, no. 1 (1917): 12–13.
110 Munro, *Rambles and Studies*, 46–7; Holbach, *Wayside Wanderings*, 62.
111 Searle, *A New England*, 456–70.
112 John L. C. Booth, *Trouble in the Balkans* (London: Hurst & Blackett, 1905), vii–viii.
113 T. W. Legh, 'A Ramble in Bosnia and Herzegovina', *New Review* 5 (1891): 479–80.
114 Hulme-Beaman, *Twenty Years in the Near East*, 137.
115 Statistics compiled by Britain's consulates in Bitola, Skopje and Thessaloniki reported 66 'violent assaults' between 1894 and 1900, climbing to over 3,300 'known murders' from 1903 to 1908. [Le Queux], *An Observer*, 6; Basil C. Gounaris, 'Preachers of God and Martyrs of the Nation: The Politics of Murder in Ottoman Macedonia in the Early Twentieth Century', *Balkanologie* 9, nos. 1–2 (2005): 37.
116 Jezernik, *Wild Europe*, 127–32; Todorova, *Imagining*, 7, 144.
117 Michail, *The British and the Balkans*, 79.
118 Sensationalist speculation was not restricted to the European presses. *The New York Times* dedicated an entire column to analysing the cultural iniquitousness of defenestration among the 'Slav' race. The fact that the assassins had thrown the royal couple's bodies out of a palace window was ascribed to their being descended from 'forest dwellers living in square-built log houses'. Centuries of 'indulgences in vodka and brandy' had made 'the window habit' a racial instinct. 'Out the Window', *The*

New York Times (24 June 1903). Cited in Markovich, *British Perceptions of Serbia*, 192–3.
119 D. M. Mason, *Macedonia and Great Britain's Responsibility* (London: T. Fisher Unwin, 1903), 4–12.
120 Victoria de Bunsen and Noel Buxton, *Macedonian Massacres: Photos from Macedonia* (London: The Balkan Committee, 1907), 6–9.
121 The BC's attempt to sensationalize events in Macedonia through an illustrated pamphlet in 1907, for example, was undermined by it admitting that 'Christian bands' were just as likely responsible for the atrocities depicted. De Bunsen and Buxton, *Macedonian Massacres*, 5–6.
122 International outrage over the Armenian massacres migrated to the Balkans in September 1902 when European newspapers reported on the Ottomans' suppression of the Gorna-Djumaya revolt in eastern Macedonia. Rodogno, *Against Massacre*, 231–2.
123 E. J. Dillon, 'The Reign of Terror in Macedonia', *The Contemporary Review* 447 (1903): 313.
124 Comyn-Platt, *Turk in the Balkans*, 100–1.
125 Hammond, *Debated Lands*, 77. See, for example, Tom Bevan, *The Insurgent Trail: A Story of the Balkans* (London: T. Nelson & Sons, 1910); John Finnemore, *A Boy Scout in the Balkans* (London: W. & R. Chambers, 1913).
126 See Dean Pavlakis, *British Humanitarianism and the Congo Reform Movement, 1896-1913* (London: Routledge, 2016).
127 Perkins, 'The Congo of Europe', 584.
128 W. H. Crawfurd Price, *The Balkan Cockpit: The Political and Military Story of the Balkan Wars in Macedonia* (London: T. Werner Laurie, 1913), 14.
129 Finnemore, *A Boy Scout*, 12.
130 Krste P. Misirkov, *Za makedonckite raboti* (Sofiā: Pečatnica na 'Liberalnij Klub', 1903), 1–2, 34.
131 Durham, 'My Golden Sisters', 79.
132 'Race-Riots in Croatia. Railways Torn Up: Mob Fired on by Troops', *St. James's Gazette* (22 May 1903), 15; 'The Rising in Croatia', *Edinburgh Evening News* (23 May 1903), 4; 'The Rioting in Croatia: A Tragedy', *Belfast News Letter* (25 May 1903), 8.
133 'Anti-German Riots in Austria', *Belfast News Letter* (21 September 1908), 8; 'Mob Charged by Military', *The Irish Times* (21 September 1908), 7; 'Serious Riots', *The Western Times* (21 September 1908), 4; Keisinger, *Unzivilisierte Kriege*, 141–2.
134 Vivian, *Servian Tragedy*, 254.
135 Ibid., 263–6.
136 Keisinger, *Unzivilisierte Kriege*, 118–21.
137 P. L. M. Wills, *A Captive of the Bulgarian Brigands: Englishman's Terrible Experiences in Macedonia* (London: Ede, Allom & Townsend, 1906), 6–7.
138 Arhiv Srbije, *Ministarstvo inostranih dela, Političko odeljenje* (1904), Fascikla – III, Docije – IV, I/9 Pov.br. 2191, Jovičić-Pašiću, 2/15. XI (1904).
139 Besides Bourchier, the only known British attendees at Petar's coronation in September 1904 were believed to have been, Mottershaw, a few 'curious tourists' and Serbia's 'honorary counsel in Sheffield', Arnold Muir Wilson. Srdya Knezhevich, 'Pochasni konzul Srbiye Arnold Myuir Vilson', *Istoriyski chasopis* 39 (1992): 171–2.
140 Peter Kardjilov, '"Cinematograms" of a Balkan Conflict: Charles Rider Noble in Bulgaria, 1903–1904', *Film History: An International Journal* 24, no. 3 (2012): 302, 313–14.

141 Durham, *The Burden*, 336. While visiting Cetinje in 1839, the archaeologist Henry Leyard claimed that his welcome reception had been hosted in a fort decorated with 'Turkish heads'. A later game of billiards was interrupted by a band of mountaineers returning from a successful raid on the Albanian city of Shkodër. More heads had been among their spoils, including those of children. (Sir) Henry Layard, W. N. Bruceand and A. Otway (eds), *Autobiography and Letters from His Childhood until His Appointment as H.M. Ambassador at Madrid* (London: John Murray, 1903), 127–33.
142 De Windt, *Savage Europe*, 146.
143 Vivian, *Servian Tragedy*, 247–52.
144 Sluga, 'Narrating Difference', 190–1.

Chapter 4

1 Todorova, *Imagining*, 3.
2 See Eugene Michail, 'Western Attitudes to War in the Balkans and the Shifting Meaning of Violence 1912-91', *The Journal of Contemporary History* 47, no. 2 (2012): 219–39.
3 Keisinger, *Unzivilisierte Kriege*, 120–1; Michail, 'Western Attitudes', 220–1.
4 Arthur J. Evans, 'The Drama of the Balkans and its Closing Scenes', *The Contemporary Review* 564 (1912): 766.
5 Despite officially retaining their support for the post-Berlin status quo, British diplomats had secretly encouraged Greece's entry into the League in order to diminish its suspected potential as a vehicle for Russian pan-Slavism. Demirci, *British Public Opinion*, 42–3.
6 Yann Béliard, 'Introduction: Revisiting the Great Labour Unrest, 1911-1914', *Labour History Review* 79, no. 1 (2014): 1–2.
7 See Gabriel Doherty (ed.), *The Home Rule Crisis, 1912-14* (Cork: Mercier Press, 2014).
8 Dorn Sezgin, 'Between Cross and Crescent', 428.
9 Dillon, 'Foreign Affairs', *The Contemporary Review* 563 (1912): 726.
10 Philip Gibbs and Bernard Grant, *The Balkan War: Adventures of War with Cross and Crescent* (Boston: Small, Maynard & Co., 1913), 17–20.
11 Dorn Sezgin, 'Between Cross and Crescent', 429–31.
12 Western depictions of broad public support for the wars within the Balkan countries obscured a complex reality. Even in 1912, the outbreak of war had met with opposition from elements of Serbia's agrarian and socialist movements while much of the rural population resisted nationalist overtures. Michail, 'Western Attitudes', 223–5; Mark Biondich, 'The Balkan Wars: Violence and Nation-Building in the Balkans', *Journal of Genocide Research* 18, no. 4 (2016): 397–8; Samuel Foster, 'Reviving the Völkerabfälle: The South Slavic Left, Balkan Federalism and the Creation of the First Yugoslavia', *Socialist History* 53 (2018): 59.
13 'Relief Appeals', *The Times* (26 October 1912), 5; Dillon, 'Foreign Affairs', *The Contemporary Review* 563 (1912): 734–7.
14 Dillon, 'Foreign Affairs', *The Contemporary Review* 564 (1912): 873–6.
15 H. N. Brailsford, 'Politics and Affairs: The War and the Concert', *The Nation* 8, no. 2 (12 October 1912): 88.

16 Norman Angell, *Peace Theories and the Balkan War* (London: Horace Marshall & Son, 1912), 13. See also idem, *The Great Illusion: A Study of the Relation of Military Power in Nations to their Economic and Social Advantage* (London: William Heinemann, 1910).
17 Both sides sought to control the flow of information by restricting access to the front. One British correspondent wrote that he and a colleague had been detained by the authorities in Belgrade for several days without explanation. On arriving in Macedonia, both were treated by their respective Bulgarian and Ottoman hosts 'not as war-correspondents, but almost as prisoners of war – not as friends, but as enemies of dangerous character' with access to the front lines being prohibited. Gibbs and Grant, *The Balkan War*, 1; (Sir) Adam Block, *Come Over to Macedonia and Help Us* (Constantinople: Le Comité de Publication D.A.C.B, 1913), 1–6, 19–24; Michail, 'Western Attitudes', 226.
18 'Creigh to FO; Despatch 16 (27 March 1913)', *Monastir (Political)*, FO 294/51.
19 In contrast to other foreign nationals, British military engagement was modest; Fisher's own Macedonian Volunteer Legion, for example, mostly consisted of returning American émigrés.
20 *Report of the International Commission to Inquire into the Causes and Conduct of the Balkan War* (Washington, DC: The Endowment, 1914), 318.
21 'Creigh to Crackanthorpe; Despatch No.48 (24 June 1914)', *Foreign Office: Embassy and Consulates, Turkey (formerly Ottoman Empire): General Correspondence*, FO 195/2457.
22 Keisinger, *Unzivilisierte Kriege*, 159–71.
23 'Macedonian Atrocities', *The Times* (22 February 1913), 5.
24 Charles R. Hunter, 'Three Weeks in the Balkans', *The National Review* 62 (1913): 375.
25 Herbert Vivian, 'After the War', *The Fortnightly Review* 93 (1913): 320.
26 Durham, *Twenty Years*, 3–4.
27 See Leo Freundlich, *Albaniens Golgatha: Anklageakten Gegen die Vernichter des Albanervolkes* (Vienna: J. Roller, 1913); Leon Trotsky, *The War Correspondence of Leon Trotsky*, trans. Brian Pearce (New York: Monad Press, 1980).
28 Britain's attaché, by contrast, had fully believed the official Montenegrin line, according to Durham. *My Balkan Notebook Vol. II*; eadem, *The Struggle for Scutari (Turk, Slav, and Albanian)* (London: Edward Arnold, 1914), 236–7.
29 Ibid., 185.
30 In mid-1913 for instance, Buxton entered into a prolonged dispute with pro-Turkish campaigners in the letters section of *The Times* claiming that allegations of anti-Muslim atrocities had been fabricated by Istanbul. Noel Buxton, 'Faked Atrocities', *The Times* (9 April 1913), 7; Aubrey Herbert, 'Faked Atrocities', *The Times* (10 April 1913), 5; A. Majid, 'Faked Atrocities', *The Times* (29 May 1913), 7; Buxton, 'Faked Atrocities', *The Times* (30 May 1913), 7.
31 Joyce Cary, *Memoir of the Bobotes* (London: Weidenfeld & Nicolson, 2000), 48.
32 E. M. Durham, 'The Soul of the War', *The Nation* (16 November 1912), 695.
33 Dorn Sezgin, 'Between Cross and Crescent', 463.
34 Block, *Come Over to Macedonia and Help Us*, 29.
35 'The Atrocity Campaign', *The Times* (18 January 1913), 5.
36 Richard C. Hall, *The Balkan Wars 1912-1913: Prelude to the First World War* (London: Routledge, 2000), 63–6; Igor Despot, *The Balkan Wars in the Eyes of the Warring Parties: Perceptions and Interpretations* (Bloomington: iUniverse, 2012), 172–80.
37 Cary, *Memoir of the Bobotes*, 119.

38 M. E. Durham, 'Miseria', *The Nation* (21 December 1912), 528.
39 Edward A. Freeman, 'Bosnian and Herzegovinian Refugees', *The Times* (3 July 1876), 6; Gladstone, *Bulgarian Horrors and the Question of the East*, 32; Todorova, *Imagining*, 98–9. During the Romanian War of Independence (1877–1878), an 'English' military hospital was opened in Bucharest under the directorship of a 'Mrs. E.B. Mawer' who, with the support of Florence Nightingale, later established a Romanian nursing society. See E. D. Tappe, 'Florence Nightingale and Rumanian Nursing', *The Slavonic and East European Review* 49, no. 114 (1971): 125–7.
40 Despot, *The Balkan Wars in the Eyes of the Warring Parties*, 181–91.
41 *The British Red Cross in the Balkans* (London: Cassell & Co., 1913), v–vi; Samuel Foster, 'The Balkan Wars and "the Macedonian Question" through the Eyes of British Nationals', in Natasha Garrett (ed.), *Macedonia 2013: 100 Years after the Treaty of Bucharest* (Ottawa: Legas, 2017), 105.
42 This also convinced Jebb to abandon her mission's non-partisan ethos and gather Albanian testimonies on the actions of the Serbian army, which she passed on to Buxton. Clare Mulley, *The Woman Who Saved the Children: A Biography of Eglantyne Jebb, Founder of Save the Children* (Oxford: Oneworld Publications, 2009), 154–65.
43 Jenny Gould, 'Women's Military Service in First World War Britain', in Margaret R. Higonnet (ed.), *Behind the Lines: Gender and the Two World Wars* (New Haven: Yale University Press, 1987), 115–16.
44 M. A. St. Clair Stobart, *War and Women: From Experience in the Balkans and Elsewhere* (London: G. Bell & Sons, 1913), xiv–xvi.
45 Leventhal, *The Last Dissenter*, 105–7.
46 Durham, *Twenty Years*, 238.
47 See Christopher Clark, *The Sleepwalkers: How Europe Went to War in 1914* (London: Allen Lane, 2012); T. G. Otte, *July Crisis: The World's Descent into War, Summer 1914* (Cambridge: Cambridge University Press, 2014).
48 A. J. A. Morris, *The Scaremongers: The Advocacy of War and Rearmament 1896-1914* (London: Routledge & Kegan Paul, 1984), 355.
49 D. C. Watt, 'The British Reactions to the Assassination at Sarajevo', *European Studies Review* 1, no. 3 (1971): 235–6.
50 This was due the war's participants' unwillingness to cooperate with the investigation and the openly contradictory witness testimonies. *Report of the International Commission to Inquire into the Causes and Conduct of the Balkan War* (1914), 280–1.
51 Francis W. Hirst, 'The Balkan War Enquiry', *The Economist* (18 July 1914), 106.
52 An article appearing in *The Manchester Guardian* on the 29 June even stated that the assassins' motives were 'unknown and unimportant' when compared to the human tragedy. 'The Assassination of the Austrian Heir Apparent', *The Manchester Guardian* (29 July 1914), 1.
53 A few days later, Serbia's London envoy reported to the prime minister, Nikola Pašić, that through the concerted efforts of Austrian officials, 'nearly all the English newspapers attribute the Serajevo outrage to the work of Serbian revolutionaries'. No. 7, 'M.M.S. Boschkovitch, Minister in London to M.N. Pashitch, Prime Minister and Minister for Foreign Affairs, London (June 18/July 1, 1914)', *The Serbian Blue Book* (New York: American Association for International Conciliation, 1915), 9.
54 'The Tragedy of Serajevo', *The Times* (29 June 1914), 9.
55 When the Serbian embassy threatened legal action, the FO was obliged to intervene informing the Serbs that Bottomley and *John Bull* were already facing multiple defamation claims from their previous targets. Julian Symons, *Horatio Bottomley: A*

Biography (London: The Cresset Press, 1955), 162; Alan Hyman, *The Rise and Fall of Horatio Bottomley: The Biography of a Swindler* (London: Cassell, 1972), 143–4. See also Harry Hanak, *Great Britain and Austria-Hungary during the First World War* (London: Oxford University Press, 1962).

56   Dearmer had confused the town in which Hope's popular novel is set with the fictional kingdom of Ruritania. Similarly, she had only volunteered as an orderly in order to accompany her husband, a Red Cross chaplain, to Serbia. Mabel Dearmer, *Letters from a Field Hospital* (London: Macmillan & Co., 1915), 46, 60–2.
57   Catriona Pennell, *A Kingdom United: Popular Responses to the Outbreak of the First World War in Britain and Ireland* (Oxford: Oxford University Press, 2012), 26.
58   Quoted in Irene Cooper Willis, *England's Holy War: A Study of English Liberal Idealism During the Great War* (New York: Knopf, 1928), 10–11.
59   Pennell, *A Kingdom United*, 26–7.
60   Quoted in Hanak, *Great Britain and Austria-Hungary*, 39.
61   Scully, *British Images of Germany*, 319–20. A similar view was present among critical voices in Germany, particularly within the Social Democratic Party. See, for example, Stefan Berger, *The British Labour Party and the German Social Democrats, 1900–1931* (Oxford: Clarendon Press, 1994).
62   'Scholars Protest against War with Germany', *The Times* (1 August 1914), 6.
63   Norman Angell, 'The Menace of War: Dominance of Russia or Germany', *The Times* (1 August 1914), 6.
64   Despite being later highlighted by Yugoslavia's critics as evidence of the British public's reluctance to ally with Serbia, the article's actual stance was ambiguously inconsistent. While the author (presumably Bottomley himself) opposed any involvement in the Balkans, they refrained from backing continued neutrality by advocating a blockade of the North Sea and pre-emptive raids on Germany's naval bases. Hyman, *Rise and Fall*, 145–51.
65   (JO), 'Manifesto', *South Slav Bulletin* 3 (1915): 7.
66   'A Great Speech', *The Times* (21 September 1914), 9. A subsequent letter from Mijatović thanked the Chancellor of the Exchequer for tacitly lending support for a future 'Yugoslav union'. Chedo Mijatovich, 'Serbians and Mr Lloyd George', *The Times* (23 September 1914), 9.
67   'Serbia's Sacrifices', *The New Europe* 1, no. 1 (1916): 32.
68   Hammond, *Debated Lands*, 126; Evans, *Great Britain and the Creation*, 88–98, 125; Drapac, *Constructing Yugoslavia*, 71–6; Michail, *The British and the Balkans*, 85–6.
69   (Sir) Valentine Chirol, *Serbia and the Serbs* (London: Oxford University Press, 1914), 3, 18.
70   H. W. Wilson and J. A. Hammerton, *The Great War: The Standard History of the All-Europe Conflict [Vol. 1]* (London: The Amalgamated Press, 1914), 11.
71   R. W. Seton-Watson, *The Spirit of the Serb* (London: Nisbet & Co., 1915), 13–19.
72   Dorn Sezgin, 'Between Cross and Crescent', 489–90.
73   Michail, 'Western Attitudes', 227.

Chapter 5

1   Although Bulgaria had remained neutral in July 1914, it joined the Central Powers in September 1915 after Berlin offered more than half of the territory acquired by Serbia since 1877.

2   See Andrej Mitrović, *Serbia's Great War 1914-1918* (London: C. Hurst & Co., 2007). Montenegro also fell under Austro-Hungarian occupation in January 1916. Srdja Pavlović, *Balkan Anschluss: The Annexation of Montenegro and the Creation of the Common South Slavic State* (West Lafayette: Purdue University Press, 2008), 68, 76.
3   Krippner, 'The Work of British Medical Women in Serbia during and after the First World War', in Allcock and Young, *Black Lambs*, 77; Alan Wakefield and Simon Moody, *Under the Devil's Eye: Britain's Forgotten Army at Salonika, 1915-1918* (Stroud: Sutton Publishing, 2004), 230–1.
4   See Hammond, *Debated Lands*; idem, *British Literature*; Michail, *The British and the Balkans*.
5   Drapac, *Constructing Yugoslavia*, 81.
6   Perkins, 'Peasants and Politics', 56.
7   Hammond, *Debated Lands*, 129–31. See for example, A. Goff and Hugh A. Fawcett, *Macedonia: A Plea for the Primitive* (London: John Lane, 1921).
8   Norris, *In the Wake*, 34.
9   Monica Krippner, 'The Work of British Medical Women', 77–9.
10 As one SRF nurse speculated, Lipton's arrival may have also had a commercial motive. Following each of his supply deliveries, 'Lipton's tea was on sale in every town and village we passed through'. 'The Mad Escapades of a War Nurse, unpublished', *Private Papers of Miss A.J. Pinniger*, IWM Documents: 2320, 57.
11 The exact numbers of non-medical staff who served in these units is difficult to ascertain since volunteers frequently transferred between organizations and military fronts, and POWs were recruited on an ad hoc basis in response to shortfalls in staffing. For discussion on the use of enemy-combatants as orderlies, see, for example, James Berry, F. May Dickinson Berry, W. Lyon Blease [& Other Members of the Unit], *The Story of a Red Cross Unit in Serbia* (London: J. & A. Churchill, 1916); J. Johnston Abraham, *My Balkan Log* (New York: E.P. Dutton & Co., 1922); I. Emslie Hutton, *With a Women's Unit in Serbia, Salonika and Sebastopol* (London: Williams & Norgate, 1928).
12 Michail, *The British and the Balkans*, 59.
13 Although Serbia's war losses are believed to have been proportionally among the highest of the war's participants, the exact numbers are contested due to a lack of records: estimates range from approximately 450,000 to over 1 million. See Slobodan G. Markovich, 'Serbia's War Losses during the Great War Reconsidered', in Dragoljub R. Živojinović (ed.), *The Serbs and the First World War 1914-1918* (Belgrade: The Serbian Academy of Sciences and Arts, 2015), 369–81.
14 Krippner, 'The Work of British Medical Women', 76–7.
15 Ellen Chivers Davies, *A Farmer in Serbia* (London: Methuen & Co., 1916), 1–3; (Dr.) Caroline Matthews, *Experiences of a Woman Doctor in Serbia* (London: Mills & Boon, 1916), 2–3; Eva Shaw McLaren (ed.), *The History of the Scottish Women's Hospitals* (London: Hodder & Stoughton, 1919), 1–4.
16 See Angela K. Smith, *The Second Battlefield: Women, Modernism and the First World War* (Manchester: Manchester University Press, 2000); Alison S. Fell and Ingrid Sharp (eds), *The Women's Movement in Wartime: International Perspectives, 1914-19* (Basingstoke: Palgrave Macmillan, 2007). See also Angela K. Smith, *British Women of the Eastern Front: War, Writing and Experience in Serbia and Russia, 1914-20* (Manchester: Manchester University Press, 2016).
17 See (Lady) Frances Balfour, *Dr Elsie Inglis* (London: Hodder & Stoughton, 1918); M. A. St. Clair Stobart, *Miracles and Adventures: An Autobiography* (London: Rider

& Co., 1936); Leah Leneman, *In the Service of Life: The Story of Elsie Inglis and the Scottish Women's Hospitals* (Edinburgh: Mercat Press, 1994).
18 The SWH, for example, was founded in 1914 with extensive financial backing from several suffrage groups. Evans, *Great Britain and the Creation*, 7.
19 Michail, *The British and the Balkans*, 60.
20 McLaren, *The History of the Scottish Women's Hospitals*, 5–8.
21 M. A. St. Clair Stobart, *The Flaming Sword in Serbia and Elsewhere* (London: Hodder & Stoughton, 1916), vii–viii. The exact number of deaths endured by Serbia remains a matter of debate and contestation. 'Introduction by Mark Cornwall', vii, 152.
22 Smith, *British Women of the Eastern Front*, 155–6.
23 Stobart later speculated that this had manifested as a series of 'miracles' which enabled her to escape death several times, including execution by a German firing squad in Belgium, where she had been managing another field hospital at the beginning of the war. Stobart, *Flaming Sword*, vii–viii; 3–4; eadem, *Miracles and Adventures*, 158–65.
24 Harold Lake, *In Salonika with Our Army* (London: A. Melrose, 1917), 226–8, 284.
25 The title of a patriotic British music hall song that appeared in October 1914. Monica Krippner, *The Quality of Mercy: Women at War in Serbia 1915-18* (London: David & Charles, 1980), 28.
26 The ban on allowing female doctors to serve in the RAMC was only lifted in 1916, owing to wartime expediencies and mounting casualty rates among male personnel. Balfour, *Elsie Inglis*, 156–62.
27 Furthermore, despite Inglis's efforts to present her organization as apolitical, the 'National Union of Women's Suffrage Societies' continued to appear in the SWH's letterhead and on the sides of its vehicles throughout the war. MacPhail also later claimed that these unresolved tensions between politics and humanitarian ideals were behind her decision to resign at the end of 1915. 'Letter dated September 1916', *Private Papers of Dr. K.S. MacPhail*, IWM Documents: 6767.
28 'Unpublished Memoir, dated 1934', *Private Papers of Miss K. Hodges*, IWM Documents: 1974, 5.
29 'Unpublished Memoir', *Hodges*, IWM Documents: 1974, 6.
30 Assuming an enlistee was able to pass all prerequisite health checks, the maximum age for recruitment into the British army's operational formations was thirty-eight. J. Johnston Abraham, *Surgeon's Journey* (London: Heinemann, 1957), 3.
31 *Dr Elsi Inglis memorijal-bolnica za žene i decu* (Belgrade: Štamparija 'Jovanović', 1929), 25; Krippner, 'The Work of British Medical Women', 73.
32 Leneman, *Service of Life*, 33.
33 Bray, 'The Extraordinary Ambassador', *MacPhail*, IWM Documents: 6767, 1.
34 Once 'she had won the vote', quoted her biographer, husbands who disrupted their family life through excessive drinking would be publically 'horsewhipped' until they had 'learnt to behave'. Balfour, *Elsie Inglis*, 41–64.
35 Leneman, *Service of Life*, 3–4, 38–9, 81.
36 Flora Sandes, *The Autobiography of a Women Soldier: A Brief Record of Adventure in the Serbian Army, 1916-1919* (New York: Frederick A. Stokes Co., 1927), 9–12. See also eadem, *An English Woman-Sergeant in the Serbian Army* (London: Hodder & Stoughton, 1916). As the only British woman known to have undertaken active military service in the First World War, Sandes has attracted a considerable degree of attention. See Louise Miller, *A Fine Brother: The Life of Captain Flora Sandes* (Richmond: Alma Books, 2012).

37 Julie Wheelwright, 'Captain Flora Sandes: A Case Study in the Social Construction of Gender in the Serbian Context', in Allcock and Young, *Black Lambs*, 91. See also idem, *Amazons and Military Maids: Women who Dressed as Men in the Pursuit of Life, Liberty and Happiness* (London: Pandora, 1989); Janet Lee, 'A Nurse and a Soldier: Gender, Class, and National Identity in the First World War Adventures of Grace McDougall and Flora Sandes', *Women's History Review* 15, no. 1 (2006): 83–103.
38 Ibid., 85.
39 Bray, 'The Extraordinary Ambassador', *MacPhail*, IWM Documents: 6767, 2–3.
40 Precedence for this, according to her biographer, was shown in her work among Glasgow's impoverished Irish and Polish immigrant communities 'in their grim hovels [. . .] often with families of eight or ten to a house'. Ibid., 3.
41 Other SWH volunteers like the former suffragette Evalina Haverfield, who founded an orphanage in the west Serbian town of Bajina Bašta, established similar ties to Yugoslavia through their wartime experiences, but remained rare exceptions. Želimir Dj Mikić, *Ever Yours Sincerely: The Life and Work of Dr Katherine S. MacPhail*, trans. Muriel Heppell (Cambridge: Perfect Publishers, 2007), 128–9.
42 Francesca M. Wilson, *In the Margins of Chaos: Recollections of Relief Work in and between Three Wars* (London: John Murray, 1944), 11–12, 111.
43 Krippner, *Quality of Mercy*, 13.
44 Sandes, *Autobiography*, 63–85.
45 Gordon Gordon-Smith, *Through the Serbian Campaign* (London: Hutchinson & Co., 1916), 265–75.
46 McPhail recounted being called upon to perform an autopsy in 1917 – despite having no experience beyond assisting senior practitioners. Krippner, *Quality of Mercy*, 13–14; Mikić, *Ever Yours*, 59–60.
47 Wilson, *In the Margins of Chaos*, 31–2.
48 Davies, *A Farmer in Serbia*, 71.
49 Douglas Walshe, *With the Serbs in Macedonia* (London: The Bodley Head, 1920), 237–9.
50 Stobart, *Flaming Sword*, 124.
51 Krippner, *Quality of Mercy*, 53. Ehrlich's research grants this maternal analogy a degree of scientific validation, noting that interpersonal bonds between mothers and sons tended to be closer in Serbia, Montenegro, and 'highland' areas where attitudes regarding male heirs as 'future protectors and providers' retained stronger resonance. St. Ehrlich, *Family in Transition*, 96–9.
52 Sandes, *Autobiography*, 9, 12.
53 Hammond, *British Literature*, 86.
54 Wheelwright, *Amazons and Military Maids*, 145–8; Lee, 'A Nurse and a Soldier', 99–100.
55 A British advance guard had arrived in the Thessaloniki in late September.
56 Over the centuries, the city's cosmopolitanism had given rise to several variations on the Greek appellation of Thessaloniki: *Salonica/Salonika* (Ladino), *Sārunā* (Armenian), *Solun* (Old Church Slavonic) and *Selanik* (Turkish). Palmer, *The Gardeners of Salonika* (London: Andre Deutsch, 1965), 11.
57 Maintaining an Entente base in Thessaloniki was actually deemed vital to securing naval transit routes between the war's African, Middle Eastern and Western theatres. (Captain) A. J. Mann, *The Salonika Front* (London: A. & C. Black, 1920), vi–vii; D. J. Dutton, 'The Calais Conference of December 1915', *The Historical Journal* 21 (1978): 145–9.

58 See Craig Gibson, *Behind the Front: British and French Civilians, 1914-1918* (Cambridge: Cambridge University Press, 2014).
59 Keith Jeffery, *1916: A Global History* (London: Bloomsbury Publishing, 2015), 2-3. See also Robert Gerwarth and Erza Manela (eds), *Empires at War: 1911-1923* (Oxford: Oxford University Press, 2015).
60 Cyril Falls, *Military Operations, Macedonia (Volume 1): From the Outbreak of War to the Spring of 1917* (London: HMSO, 1933), 5-9.
61 A British division had also engaged the Bulgarians at Dojran as part of a French-led offensive in 1916 where it suffered equally heavy losses. Wakefield and Moody, *Under the Devil's Eye*, 82-3, 96-8, 217-19.
62 By October 1917, over 20 per cent of all BSF personnel were listed as hospitalized, yet only 18,187 of these were recorded as combat-related cases. T. J. Mitchell and G. M. Smith, *History of the Great War – Medical Services: Casualties and Medical Statistics of the Great War* (London: John Murray, 1931), 187.
63 Much of the archival material held at the IWM includes preserved plant specimens and sketches of local landscapes. Michail, *The British and the Balkans*, 65.
64 'Macedonian Medley 1917-1918, undated', *Private Papers of Dr. T. Stephanides*, IWM Documents: 13891, 41-2.
65 H. Collinson Owen, *Salonika and After: The Sideshow that Ended the War* (London: Hodder & Stoughton, 1919), v-vi.
66 'IWM Interview with Rumney, Mary Millicent (3 March 1976)', IWM Sound Archive, Catalogue no. 739.
67 'A Conducted Tour, with all Found, and a Shilling a Day to Spend, ca.1970', *Private Papers of C.R. Hennessey*, IWM Documents: 12705, 150-2; 'Untitled Memoir, undated', *Private Papers of R. Gwinnel*, IWM Documents: 11601, 24-7.
68 Palmer, *Gardeners of Salonika*, 145.
69 Owen, *Salonika and After*, 118.
70 'Reports (dated 28 April and 12 May 1917)', *Private Papers of H. Fitch*, IWM Documents: 76/191/1.
71 'Report (dated 5 October 1916)', Ibid., 'Diary (dated April 1916)', *Private Papers of T.G. Craddock*, IWM Documents: 16826, 36.
72 A form of classification based on anthropological and ethnographic theories of cultural, historical, racial and social hierarchy and used to rationalize the recruitment of 'warlike' ethnic or social groups, such as Scottish Highlanders, Punjabi Sikhs, Nepalese Gurkhas or men from specific Indian castes, by British imperial forces. See Heather Streets, *Martial Races: The Military, Race and Masculinity in British Imperial Culture, 1857-1914* (Manchester: Manchester University Press, 2010).
73 A Habsburg province encompassing most of the Monarchy's southern borderlands which served as a *cordon sanitaire* against the Ottoman Empire from 1553 to its dissolution in 1881. Although dominated by Croats and Serbs, its population also included Germans, Hungarians, Romanians and Slovaks.
74 Ford, 'Montenegro in the Eyes of the English Traveller', 361-74; Suonpää, *British Perceptions of the Balkan Slavs*, 90-2, 105-9.
75 The Balkan Wars left the Serbian army overstretched and lacking in food, transportation, weaponry, uniforms, or proper footwear. James Lyon notes that even in July and August 1914, lines of 'exhausted conscripts' marched to battle in civilian clothes. By contrast, the Austro-Hungarians boasted the latest model of rifle and fielded some of the war's most advanced artillery. Nevertheless, Serbia's victories at Cer and Kolubara exposed the Monarchy's lack of experience in contemporary

warfare; this was exacerbated by the inept leadership of the invasions' commander, Oskar Potiorek: the governor of Bosnia-Herzegovina who had been responsible for security arrangements during Franz Ferdinand's fateful visit to Sarajevo. By November 1914, a 'peasant mob' had 'destroyed the Dual Monarchy's Fifth and Sixth Armies, leaving the Empire's southern border almost completely undefended'. James Lyon, *Serbia and the Balkan Front, 1914: The Outbreak of the Great War* (London: Bloomsbury Academic, 2015), 3, 75–91; Charles J. Vopicka, *Secrets of the Balkans* (Chicago: Rand, McNally & Co., 1921), 34.
76 Goldsworthy, *Inventing Ruritania*, 30–1.
77 See George Robb, *British Culture and the First World War*, 2nd edn (Basingstoke: Palgrave Macmillan, 2015).
78 Ibid., 35; Alice and Claude Askew, *The Stricken Land: Serbia As We Saw It* (London: Eveleigh Nash Company, 1916), 45; Owen, *Salonika and After*, 119–20; Walshe, *With the Serbs*, 219–22.
79 Lake, *In Salonika*, 112; Mann, *The Salonika Front*, 65–70.
80 'Letter, undated', *Private Papers of W.G. Ostler*, IWM Documents: 12335; Mann, *The Salonika Front*, 22–3. While being 'the best comrades to have on the ground', a former German pilot recalled how Bulgarian peasant soldiers would intermittently open fire 'on anything that flew', claiming to have no memory of their actions afterwards. Georg Wilhelm Haupt-Heydemarck, 'War Flying in Macedonia', in W. E. Johns (ed.), *Wings: Flying Stories*, 1:3 (London: John Hamilton Limited, 1935), 59–60.
81 Aleksandar M. Stojićević, *Istorija naših ratova za oçlobodenje i ujedinjenje od 1912-1918 god* (Belgrade: Štamparija Gl. Saveza Srpskih Zemljorad Zadruga, 1932), 301.
82 'BBC Interview with Henry Fitch (2 April 1941)'. IWM Sound Archive Catalogue no. 29987.
83 Walshe, *With the Serbs*, 240.
84 Stebbing, *At the Serbian Front in Macedonia* (London: John Lane, 1917), 101.
85 'I Saw the Futile Massacre at Doiran', in (Sir) John Alexander Hammond (ed.), *The Great War – I Was There! Undying Memories of 1914-1918*, 3:46 (London: Amalgamated Press, 1939), 18. See also Richard C. Hall, *Balkan Breakthrough: The Battle of Dobro Pole 1918* (Bloomington: University of Indiana Press, 2010).
86 The only formal acknowledgement of the BSF's contribution to the war effort was a letter from the bishop of London, published in *The Times* on 8 November 1918. Arthur Winnington-Ingram, 'Our Army in Salonika: A Gallant Force: Testimony of The Bishop of London', *The Times* (8 November 1918), 5; Wakefield and Moody, *Under the Devil's Eye*, 233. As Mazower has argued, BSF personnel's experience of wartime engagement in Macedonia, particularly in Thessaloniki, represents a rich yet critically under-examined avenue of enquiry in both Balkan and First World War historiography. Mazower, 'Travellers and the Oriental City', 59, 108–9.
87 Leneman, *Service of Life*, 82–3.
88 Davies, *A Farmer in Serbia*, 39.
89 Jan Gordon, *A Balkan Freebooter: Being the True Exploits of the Serbian Outlaw and Comitaj Petko Moritch* (London: Smith, Elder & Co., 1916), 3–4.
90 'The Mad Escapades of a War Nurse', *Pinniger*. IWM Documents: 2320, 54; Krippner, 'The Work of British Medical Women', 77.
91 Berry et al., *Story of a Red Cross Unit*, 123.
92 Askew, *Stricken Land*, 94–5.
93 (Private) H. Sinclair, *Highland Memories in Macedonia: Reprinted from the Balkan News (1917-1918)* (Salonika: The BSF Library Vol. 3, 1919), 6–7.

94 Askew, *Stricken Land*, 361; Berry et al., *Story of a Red Cross Unit*, 119; Davies, *A Farmer in Serbia*, 141; Matthews, *Experiences of a Woman Doctor*, 43; Sandes, *English Woman-Sergeant*, 44–5; Monica M. Stanley, *My Diary in Serbia: April 1ˢᵗ – Nov 1st 1915* (London: Simpkin, Marshall, Hamilton, Kent & Co., 1916), 102; Walshe, *With the Serbs*, 14–15; Mann, *The Salonika Front*, 59.
95 Stanley, *My Diary in Serbia*, 68; Hammond, *Debated Lands*, 135–7.
96 Berry et al., *Story of a Red Cross Unit*, 137.
97 'The Mad Escapades of a War Nurse', Pinniger. IWM Documents: 2320, 52.
98 Berry et al., *Story of a Red Cross Unit*, 231–2; Davies, *A Farmer in Serbia*, 225–6.
99 Michail, *The British and the Balkans*, 60–2.
100 An early review praised *The Luck of Thirteen* for its humour and realism, drawing comparisons with Kinglake's *Eōthen*. 'The Luck of Thirteen by Mr. and Mrs. Jan Gordon', *Birmingham Daily Post* (19 April 1916), 2–3. See (Mr. and Mrs.) Jan Gordon, *The Luck of Thirteen: Wanderings and Flight through Montenegro and Serbia* (London: Smith, Elder, & Co., 1916); Idem, *Balkan Freebooter*.
101 '"A Living Snake with Heads for Scales": The Refugees on the Trail during the Great Serbian Retreat', *The Illustrated London News* (25 December 1915), 4–5.
102 Berry et al., *Story of a Red Cross Unit*, 129–30.
103 Owen, *Salonika and After*, 212–13.
104 Berry et al., *Story of a Red Cross Unit*, 130.
105 Everard Wyrall, *The Gloucestershire Regiment in the War 1914-1918* (London: Methuen & Co., 1931), 191.
106 Stebbing, *At the Serbian Front*, 72.
107 Owen, *Salonika and After*, 128.
108 Askew, *Stricken Land*, 154; H. I. W., *The Experiences of a Unit in the Great Retreat (Serbia 1915)* (Cambridge: Crompton & Sons, 1916), 23; Davies, *A Farmer in Serbia*, 134.
109 Gordon, *Balkan Freebooter*, 127; Norris, *In the Wake*, 32–3.
110 A traditional Serbian Orthodox celebration of a patron saint.
111 'Serbia: Reminders from Ostrovo (October 1917–May 1918)', *Private Papers of Dr. J. Rose*, IWM Documents: 6776.
112 Stobart, *Flaming Sword*, 131; 'The Mad Escapades of a War Nurse', 52.
113 A circular folk-dance common to most of the South Slavonic Balkans.
114 Hammond, *Debated Lands*, 131.
115 H. I. W., *The Experiences of a Unit*, 14.
116 Ibid., 226.
117 'Life of an Army Chaplain (Padre) 1917-1919, undated', *Private Papers of Reverend J. Sellors*, IWM Documents: 1277, 50.
118 Berry et al., *Story of a Red Cross Unit*, 124–5.
119 Askew, *Stricken Land*, 87–8; Berry et al., *Story of a Red Cross Unit*, 239.
120 Abraham, *Balkan Log*, 127.
121 Gordon, *Luck of Thirteen*, 43–4.
122 H. I. W., *The Experiences of a Unit*, 19.
123 'A Conducted Tour', 121–2.
124 See Wakefield and Moody, *Under the Devil's Eye*.
125 'A Living Snake with Heads for Scales', 4–5.
126 Quoted in Krippner, *Quality of Mercy*, 112.
127 Stobart, *Flaming Sword*, 164.

128 Askew, *Stricken Land*, 25–6; Gordon-Smith, *Through the Serbian Campaign*, 37–8; Matthews, *Experiences of a Woman Doctor*, 107–8.
129 Sandes, *English Woman-Sergeant*, 206.
130 Mikić, *Ever Yours*, 42.
131 Olive Lodge, *Peasant Life in Jugoslavia* (London: Seeley, Service & Co., 1942), 17.
132 Fortier Jones, *With Serbia into Exile* (New York: The Century Co., 1916), 296–7.
133 Ibid., 447.
134 Askew, *Stricken Land*, 362–3; Sandes, *English Woman-Sergeant*, 113–15; Stobart, *Flaming Sword*, 294–5.
135 Gallant, *Experiencing Dominion*, 55.
136 Hammond, *British Literature*, 254.
137 Indira Duraković, 'Serbia as a Health Threat to Europe: The Wartime Typhus Epidemic, 1914–1915', in Joachim Bürgschwentner, Matthias Egger and Gunda Barth-Scalmani (eds), *Other Fronts, Other Wars?: First World War Studies on the Eve of the Centennial* (Leiden and Boston: Brill, 2014), 274–6.
138 Dearmer, *Letters*, 134.
139 Rotha Lintorn-Orman, who, in 1923, founded the 'British Fascisti', Britain's first avowedly fascist political movement, had been a volunteer for the SWH in Thessaloniki. Vron Ware, *Beyond the Pale: White Women, Racism and History* (London: Verso, 2015 [1992]), 149–50; Martin Durham, 'Britain', in Kevin Passmore (ed.), *Women, Gender and Fascism in Europe 1919–45* (Manchester: Manchester University Press, 2003), 215–16.
140 Todorova, *Imagining*, 119–20.
141 Matthews, *Experiences of a Woman Doctor*, 23–4.
142 Dearmer, *Letters*, 135.
143 Ibid., 182.
144 William George Willoughby and Louis Cassidy (RAMC), *Anti-Malarial Work in Macedonia among British Troops* (London: H.K. Louis, 1918), 31–7; Mitchell and Smith, *History of the Great War*, 187.
145 Duraković, 'Serbia as a Health Threat to Europe', 271–2.
146 Berry et al., *Story of a Red Cross Unit*, 142–3.
147 The Serbian military surgeon V. Soubbotitch claimed that the disease was spread to Serbia externally, tracing the outbreak to infected Habsburg soldiers abandoned in the Western city of Valjevo in August 1914. V. Soubbotitch, 'A Pandemic of Typhus in Serbia in 1914 and 1915', *Proceedings of the Royal Society of Medicine: Section of Epidemiology and State Medicine* 11 (1918): 31–2.
148 Richard P. Strong, *Typhus Fever with Particular Reference to the Serbian Epidemic* (Cambridge, MA: Harvard University Press, 1920), 14–29.
149 Ibid., 16–19.
150 Leneman, *Service of Life*, 17–18.
151 Colonel Vladimir Stanojević, the director of the Niš military hospital, calculated that of the country's 534 trained doctors, 132 were already dead when the epidemic peaked in March 1915. Cited in Zoran Vesić, Branislav Popović, Mirjana Korica and Zorica Stošić, *Srpski vojni sanitet* (Belgrade: Ministarstvo Odbrane, 2009), 48.
152 Abraham, *Surgeon's Journey*, 135.
153 Gordon, *Luck of Thirteen*, 4.
154 Similar complaints were levied against French soldiers on the Western Front. Balfour, *Elsie Inglis*, 164.
155 Quoted in Krippner, *Quality of Mercy*, 55.

156 Strong, *Typhus Fever*, 25–8.
157 Edward Stuart, 'Sanitation in Serbia', *The American Journal of Public Health* 10, no. 2 (1920): 124.
158 Smith, *British Women of the Eastern Front*, 155–6.
159 Balfour, *Elsie Inglis*, 211; Matthews, *Experiences of a Woman Doctor*, 72; McLaren, *The History of the Scottish Women's Hospitals*, 366.
160 Sandes, *English Woman-Sergeant*, 63; eadem, *Autobiography*, 14; Lee, 'A Nurse and a Soldier', 95.
161 Owen, *Salonika and After*, 131–46.
162 N.D.M., 'To a Military Policeman', in *Salvos from Salonika* (Carlisle: Charles Thurman & Sons, 1919), 16.
163 'Life of an Army Chaplin (Padre) 1917-1919', 28.
164 Berry et al., *Story of a Red Cross Unit*, 118.
165 The British Red Cross had also refused to accept female volunteers at the beginning of the war prompting many to register with its Belgian, French or even Serbian counterparts.
166 Hammond, *British Literature*, 82.
167 'Diary (30-31March 1917)', *Private Papers of Miss L. Creighton*, IWM Documents: 1898.
168 'Diary (7 January 1916)', *Private Papers of Dame K. Courtney*, IWM Documents: 9785.
169 Lee, 'A Nurse and a Soldier', 95.
170 Sandes, *Autobiography*, 14.
171 'Letter (dated 21 July 1915)', *Private Papers of Miss M. Ingram,* IWM Documents: 2786; 'Journal, undated', *Private Papers of Miss G. Holland*, IWM Documents: 1042, 160–8.
172 Walshe, *With the Serbs*, 50–1.
173 Quoted in C. E. J. Fryer, *The Destruction of Serbia in 1915* (Boulder: Colombia University Press, 1997), 150–3.
174 Lake, *In Salonika*, 188; Owen, *Salonika and After*, 27.
175 Askew, *Stricken Land*, 109; Matthews, *Experiences of a Woman Doctor*, 79; Stobart, *Flaming Sword*, 163.
176 Elsie Corbett, *Red Cross in Serbia, 1915-1919: A Personal Diary of Experiences* (Banbury: Cheney & Sons, 1964), 67.
177 'IWM Interview with Ernest Victor John Jones (undated)', IWM Sound Archive, Catalogue no. 12678.
178 Davies, *A Farmer in Serbia*, 46.
179 'Letter to Lewis Einstein (US *charge d'affairs*, Sofia) (24 May 1916)', *Paget Papers (3rd Series) Vol.XX 1914-1945*, BL Western Manuscripts: Add MS 51261.
180 Goff and Fawcett, *Plea for the Primitive*, ix–x, 37–8.
181 Ibid., 35.
182 Lake, *In Salonica*, 287.

Chapter 6

1 Scully, *British Images of Germany*, 129. See also, Pennell, *A Kingdom United*; Toby Thacker, *British Culture and the First World War: Experience, Representation and Memory* (London: Bloomsbury Academic, 2014).

2. Perkins, 'Peasants and Politics', 55–6.
3. Norris, *In the Wake*, 33; Hammond, *Debated Lands*, 125.
4. Evans, *Great Britain and the Creation*, 5; Drapac, *Constructing Yugoslavia*, 64.
5. See Ramsay Muir, *The Expansion of Europe: The Culmination of Modern History*, 2nd edn (London: Constable & Co., 1917); R. W. Seton-Watson, *The Rise of Nationality in the Balkans* (London: Constable & Co., 1917).
6. See Michael Sanders and Philip M. Taylor, *British Propaganda during the First World War, 1914-18* (Basingstoke: Macmillan, 1982).
7. See Garth S. Jowett and Victoria O'Donnell, *Propaganda and Persuasion*, 7th edn (Los Angeles: Sage Publications, 2018).
8. Sluga, 'Narrating Difference', 192.
9. Winter, 'British National Identity', 276–7.
10. Đorđe Stanković, *Srbija i stvaranje Jugoslavije* (Belgrade: Službeni glasnik, 2009), 65–6.
11. Seton-Watson, *Making of a New Europe*, 108–9.
12. Connie Robinson, 'Yugoslavism in the Early Twentieth Century: The Politics of the Yugoslav Committee', in Dejan Djokić and James Ker-Lindsay (eds), *New Perspectives on Yugoslavia: Key Issues and Controversies* (Abingdon: Routledge, 2011), 14–16.
13. The only wartime engagements to take place on British territory were between the Royal and Imperial German navies in the North Sea, and the aerial dogfights that later ensued during German bombing raids.
14. These included Evans; the former Viceroy for India and Conservative peer, George Curzon; and the Archbishop of Canterbury, Randall Davidson, with Mary of Teck, the wife of King George V, serving as the SRF's patron throughout the war. Krippner, 'The Work of British Medical Women', 72–3.
15. In 2018, these totals can be estimated as £117,000 and £200,000 when adjusted for inflation. Sandes, *The Autobiography*, 15; Leah Leneman, *Elsie Inglis: Founder of Battlefield Hospitals Run Entirely by Women* (Edinburgh: NMSE Publishing, 1998), 6.
16. Approximately £60,000,000 when adjusted for inflation in 2018. R. W. Seton-Watson, *Masaryk in England* (Cambridge: Cambridge University Press, 1943), 36.
17. Snežana Toševa, *Srbija i Britanija: kulturni dodiri početkom xx veka* (Belgrade: SANU, 2007), 24, 37.
18. Mikić, *Ever Yours*, 81.
19. *Serbia's Cup of Sorrow* (London: Serbian Relief Fund, 1915), 2–4.
20. Bailey was very likely referring to Croatia-Slavonia's large Serb population. W. F. Bailey, *The Slavs of the War Zone* (London: Chapman & Hall, 1916), 158.
21. Ibid., 158–9.
22. While other groups adopted a similar tone, the campaign's core message was monopolized by the SRF. See *Serbia's Cup of Sorrow*; (Lady) L. Paget, *With Our Allies the Serbs* (London: Serbian Relief Fund, 1915); *An Appeal for Serbian Prisoners of War* (London: Serbian Relief Fund, 1917); *The Serbian Colonies in Corsica* (Corsica: Serbian Relief Fund, 1917).
23. May Wynne [Mabel Winifred Knowles], *An English Girl in Serbia: The Story of a Great Adventure* (London & Glasgow: Collins Clear Type Press, 1916), 27, 115–17.
24. See Archibald Reiss, *How Austria-Hungary Waged War in Serbia: Personal Investigations of a Neutral* (Paris: A. Colin, 1915); Idem, *The Kingdom of Serbia. Infringements of the Rules and Laws of War Committed by the Austro-Bulgaro-Germans: Letters of a Criminologist on the Serbian Macedonian Front* (London: G. Allen & Unwin, 1919).

25 Ibid., 612.
26 'Life of an Army Chaplin', 36–8; Milovan Pisarri, 'Bulgarian Crimes against Civilians in Occupied Serbia during the First World War', *Balcanica* 44 (2013): 373.
27 'Letter to Einstein (22 April 1916)', *Paget Papers*.
28 Bastian Matteo Scianna, 'Reporting Atrocities: Archibald Reiss in Serbia, 1914-1918', *The Journal of Slavic Military Studies* 25, no. 4 (2012): 613–14.
29 'Reporting Atrocities', 617; Pisarri, 'Bulgarian Crimes against Civilians in Occupied Serbia', 389–90.
30 Norka Machiedo Mladinić, 'Prilog proučavanju djelovanja Ivana Meštrovića u Jugoslavenskom odboru', *Revue d'histoire contemporaine* 39, no. 1 (2007): 134–5.
31 See Evans, *Great Britain and the Creation*.
32 R. W. Seton-Watson, 'The Archduke Francis Ferdinand', *Contemporary Review* 800 (1914): 288–303.
33 'Letter to May Seton-Watson (6 August 1914)', SEW/3/3/3.
34 *The New Europe*'s co-founders also included the archaeologist Ronald Burrows (who was instrumental in helping London and Paris steer Greece into the Entente camp) and the Liberal MP Frederick Whyte, with Masaryk as its key political consultant. Seton-Watson, *Making of a New Europe*, 112. On the Entente's wider international efforts at anti-Habsburg propaganda, see Mark Cornwall, *The Undermining of Austria-Hungary: The Battle for Hearts and Minds* (Basingstoke: Palgrave Macmillan, 2000).
35 See I. W. Roberts, *History of the School of Slavonic and East European Studies, 1915-1990* (London: SSEES, 1991).
36 In exchange for entering the war, the Entente had promised Italy various territorial acquisitions at the Monarchy's expense including the Austrian Littoral; nearly a third of Carniola; northern Dalmatia, and most of its adjacent islands; and a protectorate over Albania. Incidentally, Montenegro and Serbia were also promised territory despite neither having been aware of the agreement. Dragovan Šepić, 'The Question of Yugoslav Union in 1918', *The Journal of Contemporary History* 3, no. 4 (1968): 35–6.
37 Bogumil Vošnjak, *A Bulwark Against Germany: The Fight of the Slovenes, the Western Branch of the Jugoslavs, for National Existence*, trans. Fanny Copeland (London: George Allen & Unwin, 1917), 3–5; R. G. D. Laffan, *The Guardians of the Gate: Historical Lectures on the Serbs* (Oxford: The Clarendon Press, 1918), 89. See also Crawfurd Price, *Serbia's Part in The War, Vol I, Being the Political and Military Story of the Austro-Serbian Campaigns: The Rampart against Pan-Germanism* (London: Simpkin, Marshall, Hamilton, Kent & Co., 1917).
38 (JO), *The Southern Slav Library I: The Southern Slav Programme* (London: Nisbet & Co., 1915), 12.
39 Ibid., 13.
40 Srdjan Tucić, *The Slav Nations*, trans. Fanny S. Copeland (London: Hodder & Stoughton, 1915), 144.
41 'Manifesto', 6–9.
42 Tucić, *Slav Nations*, 177.
43 Robinson, 'Yugoslavism in the Early Twentieth Century', 19.
44 Laffan, *The Guardians of the Gate*, 167–82.
45 Jovan Byford, *Denial and Repression of Antisemitism: Post-Communist Remembrance of the Serbian Bishop Nikolaj Velimirović* (Budapest: Central European University Press, 2008), 24–8.
46 Nicholas Velimirović, *The Soul of Serbia* (London: The Faith Press at the Faith House, 1916), 18–20, 78–81.

47 Mijo Radešević and Franjo Markić, *Memorandum: Addressed by the Jugoslav Socialists to the International Socialist Peace Conference in Stockholm* (London: Jugoslav Workman's Association, 1917), 3–11.
48 H. M. Hyndman, 'British Policy and the Rights of the People', *The New Europe* 1, no. 2 (1916): 329–34.
49 Its closest equivalent was the *Near East* that ostensibly dealt with Middle Eastern affairs but would also frequently cover the Balkans. Hanak, *Great Britain and Austria-Hungary*, 188.
50 'J.B.' [James Bone], 'The Temple of Kosovo', *The Spectator* (10 July 1915), 9–10; Perkins, 'Peasants and Politics', 56.
51 Elizabeth Clegg, 'Meštrović, England and the Great War', *The Burlington Magazine* 144, no. 1197 (2002): 745.
52 Ibid., 745–6. See also Andrew Wachtel, *Making a Nation, Breaking a Nation: Literature and Cultural Politics in Yugoslavia* (Stanford: Stanford University Press, 2002).
53 'Letter to Milenko Vesnić (17 July 1916)', SEW 3/3/3.
54 A religious holiday commemorating the Serbian at the battle of Kosovo. While the event itself was believed to have taken place on 15 June 1389, based on the calendar system in use at the time, it is now popularly associated with the 28th.
55 Hanak, *Great Britain and Austria-Hungary*, 76–7.
56 Robinson, 'Yugoslavism in the Early Twentieth Century', 19.
57 Bogumil Vošnjak, *Jugoslav Nationalism: Three Lectures* (London: Polsue Limited, 1916), 13.
58 Ibid., 23.
59 Bogumil Vošnjak, a leading Slovene representative in the JO, cited the medieval principality of Carantania – the inhabitants of which were viewed as the ancestors of the modern Slovenes – as the progenitor of these democratic peasant traditions. Hereditary monarchy, a concept reviled as 'foreign and unnatural' to Carantania's 'honest peasant soul', had been shunned in favour of directly electing the ruling dukes, in ceremonies reminiscent of medieval Scotland. (JO), *The Southern Slav Library I*, 5–6; Bogumil Vošnjak, *A Chapter of the Old Slovenian Democracy* (London: J. Murray, 1917), 8–9.
60 (JO), *The Southern Slav Library VI: Political and Social Conditions in Slovene Lands: Carniola, Carinthia, Illyria and Styria* (London: The Near East, 1916), 16–18.
61 As further details of the Treaty of London were leaked to the press, the JO even sought to reassure Italy that 'her justified supremacy in the Adriatic' would be safeguarded by a large anti-German state on its eastern shore. *South Slav Bulletin* 12 (1916): 1.
62 'Adriatic Imperialism', *The New Europe* 1, no. 2 (1916): 49.
63 An economic ideology derived from Catholic social teachings that existed in opposition to both capitalism and socialism. Distributionist theory classifies property ownership as a fundamental human right while arguing that the means of production should be spread as broadly as possible across the social spectrum, allowing individuals and families to work for themselves rather than others.
64 G. K. Chesterton, 'This Thing Called a Nation: The Spiritual Issue of the War' (reprinted from the *Daily News*), in *The Lay of Kosovo: History and Poetry on Serbia's Past and Present* (London: The Kosovo Day Committee, 1917), 18, 32–5.
65 R. W. Seton-Watson, *Serbia: Yesterday, Today and Tomorrow. A School Address* (London: Vacher & Sons, 1916), 13–16.
66 Ibid., 22–3.

67 Vošnjak, *Jugoslav Nationalism*, 7.
68 Askew, *Stricken Land*, 353.
69 Lampe, *Yugoslavia as History*, 105–6.
70 Seton-Watson, *Making of a New Europe*, 140.
71 Gale Stokes, 'The Role of the Yugoslav Committee in the Formation of Yugoslavia', in Dimitrije Djordjević (ed.), *The Creation of Yugoslavia 1914-1918* (Santa Barbara: Clio Books, 1980), 55; Mladinić, 'Prilog proučavanju djelovanja Ivana Meštrovića u Jugoslavenskom odboru', 146–9.
72 Seton-Watson, *Making of a New Europe*, 140–1.
73 'Abridged Report by Mr. Alex Devine, 2–3; 8–9', *Viscount Gladstone Papers Vol.XXX 1916-1926*, BL Western Manuscripts: Add MS 46014.
74 'Letter to Herbert Gladstone (2 June 1917)', Ibid.
75 'Letter to F.C.J. Hearnshaw (28 March 1917)', SEW/3/2/7; Seton-Watson, *Making of a New Europe*, 197–8.
76 Anticipating little or no public interest, the 1918 commemorations were used instead to commemorate Inglis, who had died in from cancer in November 1917. Hanak, *Great Britain and Austria-Hungary*, 77–8.
77 Noel and Charles Roden Buxton, *The War and the Balkans*, 2nd edn (London: George Allen & Unwin, 1915), 9; Grogan, *The Life of J.D. Bourchier*, 163–6; Hanak, *Great Britain and Austria*-Hungary, 197.
78 Evans, *Great Britain and the Creation*, 116–18.
79 Cornwall, *The Undermining*, 174.
80 Ibid., 238–40, 443–4.
81 Robinson, 'Yugoslavism in the Early Twentieth Century', 23–4.
82 Evans, *Great Britain and the Creation*, 4.
83 Čedomir Antić, *Neizabrana Sabezinca: Srbija i Velika Britanija u prvom svetskom ratu* (Belgrade: Zavod za udžbenike, 2012), 495.

Chapter 7

1 Despite being established before the Paris Peace Conference, a final settlement on the Kingdom of Serbs, Croats and Slovenes' border with Italy wasn't ratified until 1928. See Dejan Djokić, *Pašić & Trumbić: The Kingdom of Serbs, Croats and Slovenes* (London: Haus Publishing, 2010); Leonard V. Smith, *Sovereignty at the Paris Peace Conference of 1919* (Oxford: Oxford University Press, 2018).
2 Michail, *The British and the Balkans*, 19–20; Dragan Bakić, *Britain and Interwar Danubian Europe: Foreign Policy and Security Challenges, 1919-1936* (London: Bloomsbury Academic, 2017), 5.
3 The 2010s witnessed a significant shift towards a more historicized focus on culture, economics, religion and society. See Djokić and Ker-Lindsay (eds), *New Perspectives on Yugoslavia* (2010); Christian Axboe Nielsen, *Making Yugoslavs: Identity in King Aleksandar's Yugoslavia* (Toronto: University of Toronto Press, 2014); John Paul Newman, *Yugoslavia in the Shadow of War: Veterans and the Limits of State Building 1903-1945* (Cambridge: Cambridge University Press, 2015); Pieter Troch, *Nationalism and Yugoslavia: Education, Yugoslavism and the Balkans before World War II* (London: I.B. Tauris, 2015); Nada Boskovska, *Yugoslavia and Macedonia before Tito: Between Repression and Integration* (London: Bloomsbury, 2017); Richard

Mills, *The Politics of Football in Yugoslavia: Sport, Nationalism and the State* (London: I.B. Tauris, 2018).
4   Brad Beaven, *Leisure, Citizenship and Working-Class Men in Britain, 1850-1945* (Manchester: Manchester University Press, 2005), 180–1.
5   Goldsworthy, *Inventing Ruritania*, 101–2.
6   Michail, *The British and the Balkans*, 103.
7   Political and Economic Planning, *Report on the British Press* (1938). Cited in ibid., 104.
8   Goldsworthy, *Inventing Ruritania*, 104–11; Kostova, *Tales*, 197.
9   Ross McKibbin, 'Great Britain', in Robert Gerwarth (ed.), *Twisted Paths: Europe 1914-1945* (Oxford: Oxford University Press, 2007), 40–1.
10 Timothy D. Hoyt, 'The Easter Rising and the Changing Character of Irregular Warfare', in Enrico Dal Lago, Róisín Healy and Gearóid Barry (eds), *1916 in Global Context: An Anti-Imperial Moment* (London: Routledge, 2018), 19–26.
11 W. J. Lowe, 'The War against the R.I.C, 1919-1921', *Éire-Ireland* 38, nos. 3–4 (2002): 79–82; D. M. Leeson, *The Black and Tans: British Police Auxiliaries in the Irish War of Independence, 1920-1921* (Oxford: Oxford University Press, 2010), 128.
12 Pavlović, *Balkan Anschluss*, 111; Boskovska, *Yugoslavia and Macedonia before Tito*, 23–4. See also Robert Gerwarth and John Horne (eds), *War in Peace: Paramilitary Violence in Europe after the Great War* (Oxford: Oxford University Press, 2012).
13 Christopher Harvie, *No Gods and Precious Few Heroes: Scotland since 1914* (Edinburgh: Edinburgh University Press, 1993), 17.
14 See John Stevenson and Chris Cook, *The Slump: Britain in the Great Depression* (London: Routledge, 2009).
15 Alun Howkins, 'Death and Rebirth? English Rural Society, 1920-1940', in Paul Brassley, Jeremy Burchardt and Lynne Thompson (eds), *The English Countryside Between the Wars: Regeneration of Decline?* (Woodbridge: The Boydell Press, 2006), 21–4; Christopher Bailey, 'Rural Industries and the Image of the Countryside', in ibid, 135–43.
16 Paul Brassley, Jeremy Burchardt and Lynne Thompson, 'Conclusion', in ibid, 239.
17 Winter, 'British National Identity', 273–5.
18 Alex King, *Memorials of the Great War in Britain: The Symbolism and Politics of Remembrance* (Oxford: Berg, 1998), 12.
19 Beaven, *Visions*, 153, 163–74.
20 Seton-Watson, *Making of a New Europe*, 315–21.
21 David N. Dilks, 'Public Opinion and Foreign Policy: Great Britain', *Collection de l'École française de Rome* 54, no. 2 (1981): 57, 68–9; Finney, 'Raising Frankenstein', 321; Miklós Lojkó *Meddling in Middle Europe: Britain and the 'Lands Between', 1919-1925* (Budapest: Central European University Press, 2006), 1–3; Michail, *The British and the Balkans*, 20; Bakić, *Britain and Interwar Danubian Europe*, 30.
22 F. S. Copeland, 'Who are the Yugoslavs', *The Balkan Review* 1, no. 1 (1919): 32–3; M. R. Vesnitch, 'The Aspirations of Serbia', *The Balkan Review* 1, no. 2 (1919): 265–8.
23 M. A. St. Clair Stobart, 'Peace Celebrations and Serbia', *The Times* (23 August 1919), 6.
24 'Letter to Wickham Steed (8 October 1920)', SEW/17/26/6; R. W. Seton-Watson, 'A Farewell Survey', *The New Europe* 17, no. 2 (1920): 52.
25 Roberts, *History of the School of Slavonic and East European Studies*, 20–3.
26 Conversely, Seton-Watson's lobbying activities did little to impede his post-war academic career. In 1921 he was a founding member of the University of London's

Institute of Historical Research and co-founder of *The Slavonic Review* in 1922. Seton-Watson, *Making of a New Europe*, 332, 418.

27 'Balfour to Curzon (27 June 1919)', FO 371/3578; 'Letter to Herbert Gladstone (dated April 1924)', *Viscount Gladstone Papers*.
28 Drapac, *Constructing Yugoslavia*, 127–34; Michail, *The British and the Balkans*, 95–6.
29 Seton-Watson, *Making of a New Europe*, 430–1.
30 Michail, *The British and the Balkans*, 50–1.
31 F. M. L. Thompson, 'Epilogue: The Strange Death of the English Land Question', in Cragoe and Readman (eds), *The Land Question*, 259–67.
32 See Ivo Banac, *The National Question in Yugoslavia: Origins, History, Politics* (Ithaca: Cornell University Press, 1988).
33 Dragan Bakić, '"Must Will Peace": The British Brokering of "Central European" and "Balkan Locarno", 1925-9', *Journal of Contemporary History* 48, no. 1 (2013): 26.
34 Idem, *Britain and Interwar Danubian Europe*, 177–81.
35 Inderjeet Parmar, *Think Tanks and Power in Foreign Policy: A Comparative Study of the Role and Influence of the Council on Foreign Relations and the Royal Institute of International Affairs, 1939-1945* (Basingstoke: Palgrave Macmillan, 2004), 167–8.
36 Ibid., 169; 'The Royal Institute of Foreign Affairs, HC Deb (21 November 1939)', *Hansard*, Vol. 353, cc1037-40W.
37 W. N. Medlicott, *Britain and Germany: The Search for Agreement, 1930-1937* (London: The Athlone Press, 1969), 4.
38 Finney, 'Raising Frankenstein', 319; Lojkó, *Meddling in Middle Europe*, 44–5.
39 Diplomatic correspondence from the end of 1939 noted that most of the club's 520-strong membership were junior military offices, more interested in 'having a good time' at the various dances and social gatherings than 'Anglo-Saxon' culture and history. Ioannis Stefanidis, *Substitute for Power: Wartime British Propaganda in the Balkans, 1939-1944* (Farnham: Ashgate, 2012), 245.
40 Although Belgrade was reported to have a '[L]arge English-speaking colony', its Anglophone residents were mostly North Americans. 'What Struck me Most About Belgrade', *South Slav Herald* (June 1933), 2.
41 'Reich's Overwhelming Role in Yugoslav Economy', *South Slav Herald* (January–February 1939), 8; Antić, *Neizabrana Sabezinca*, 496.
42 Kuklick, *Savage Within*, 68–70.
43 James Hinton, *The Mass Observers: A History* (Oxford: Oxford University, 2013), 7–8.
44 Quoted in David Hall, *Worktown: The Astonishing Story of the Project that launched Mass Observation* (London: Weidenfeld & Nicolson, 2015), 25; Christopher Hilliard, 'Popular Reading and Social Investigation in Britain, 1850-1940', *The Historical Journal* 57, no. 1 (2014): 265.
45 Joseph Preston Baratta, *Politics of World Federation: From World Federalism to Global Governance* (Santa Barbara: Greenwood Publishing Group, 2004), 74.
46 Richard Baxell, *British Volunteers in the Spanish Civil War: The British Battalion in the International Brigades, 1936-1939* (London: Routledge, 2004), 18–19, 66–9.
47 Horatiu Burcea, '"Times of Unbelief": Staging the Rise and Fall of British Travel Writing During the Interwar Period', *Études britanniques contemporaines* 56 (2019), https://journals.openedition.org/ebc/6366.
48 See Frank Trentmann, 'Beyond Consumerism: New Historical Perspectives on Consumption', *Journal of Contemporary History* 39, no. 4 (2004): 373–401; Peter J. Gurney, 'Co-operation and the "New Consumerism" in Interwar England', *Business History* 54, no. 6 (2012): 905–24; Matthew Hilton, *Consumerism in Twentieth-*

Century Britain: The Search for a Historical Movement (Cambridge: Cambridge University Press, 2012).
49 Neither the Communist Party of Great Britain (established in 1920) nor Oswald Mosley's British Union of Fascists (founded in 1932) attracted a mass following. While the latter (capitalizing on the support of the *Daily Mail*) achieved a peak membership of 50,000 in mid-1934, its embrace of antisemitism, and rising violence at public demonstrations, saw most of this fall away in 1935. The former enjoyed even less success before 1942, with the number of registered members having plateaued at 15,000 to 20,000 by the outbreak of the Second World War. G. C. Webber, 'Patterns of Membership and Support for the British Union of Fascists', *Journal of Contemporary History* 19, no. 4 (1984): 595–9; Andrew Thorpe, 'The Membership of the Communist Party of Great Britain', *The Historical Journal* 43, no. 3 (2000): 781.
50 Stevenson and Cook, *The Slump*, 18.
51 McKibbin, 'Great Britain', 48; Stevenson and Cook, *The Slump*, 19.
52 John Stevenson, *British Society 1914-45* (Harmondsworth: Penguin, 1984), 398.
53 'Book Reading in Wartime. Report on Material obtained from Publisher, Book Clubs, Libraries and Book Sellers', File Report 1937-49, Tom Harrisson Mass-Observation Archive. Quoted in Beaven, *Leisure, Citizenship and Working-Class Men*, 186.
54 Hilliard, 'Popular Reading and Social Investigation', 264.
55 George Orwell, *The Road to Wigan Pier* (London: V. Gollancz, 1937), 72, 80.
56 McKibbin, 'Great Britain', 52.
57 Ibid., 53; Mills, *The Politics of Football*, 20.
58 Yugoslavia went on to win 2-1 before a crowd comprising Albanians, Bulgarians, Greeks and Hungarians whose interest in attending was suspected of being as much about politics as it was a love of the game. '"Fans" Excited at Coming Match, Yugoslavia v England at Football in May', *South Slav Herald* (January–February 1939), 11; 'Belgrade Sensational Football Victory over England', *South Slav Herald* (June 1939), 1.
59 Tom Buchanan, '"A Far Away Country of Which we Know Nothing"? Perceptions of Spain and its Civil War in Britain, 1931-1939', *Twentieth Century British History* 4, no. 3 (1993): 4; John. K. Walton, 'The Origins of the Modern Package Tour?: British Motor-Coach Tours in Europe, 1930-70', *The Journal of Transport History* 32, no. 2 (2011): 148.
60 Charles Graves. *And the Greeks* (London: G. Bles 1930), 20–2.
61 Djokić, *Pašić & Trumbić*, 124–6.
62 John K. Walton, 'Preface: Some Context for Yugoslav Tourism History', in Hannes Grandits and Karin Taylor (eds), *Yugoslavia's Sunny Side: A History of Tourism in Socialism (1950s–1980s)* (Budapest: Central European University Press, 2010), xiv.
63 Ann Bridge [Mary Dolling], *Facts and Fictions: Some Literary Recollections* (London: McGraw-Hill, 1968), 45–6. *Illyrian Spring* proved to be a bestseller in Britain and Australia, earning Dolling critical distinction as a Book Society 'Choice' in 1935. Nicola Wilson, 'British Publishers and Colonial Editions', in eadem (ed.), *The Book World: Selling and Distributing British Literature, 1900-1940* (Leiden: Brill, 2016), 23.
64 Ann Bridge [Mary Dolling], *Illyrian Spring* (London: Daunt Books, 2012 [1935]), 56. See also Ethel Lina White, *The Wheel Spins* (Harmondsworth: Penguin Books, 1955 [1936]).
65 See Oona H. Ball, *Dalmatia* (London: Faber & Faber, 1932). See also Grace Mary Ellison, *Yugoslavia: A New Country and Its People* (London: John Lane, 1933).
66 'Delightful Dalmatia', *Great Britain and the East* (11 March 1937), 12.

67 John B. Allcock, 'The Historical Development of Tourism in Yugoslavia to 1945', in John B. Allcock and Joan Counihan (eds), *Two Studies in the History of Tourism in Yugoslavia* (Bradford: University of Bradford, 1989), 13–19.
68 A. Vidakovič, 'Jugoslavia', in Eugene Fodor (ed.), *1938 in Europe: Aldor's Entertaining Travel Annual* (London: W. Aldor, 1938), 1293–4; 'Where Shopping is Easy on the Purse', *South Slav Herald* (January–February 1939), 5.
69 Muriel Innes Currey, *Yugoslavia: A Guide Book approved by the Official Tourist Department for Yugoslavia* (London: Chatto & Windus, 1939), 5–6, 11–14, 146–9.
70 Vidakovič, 'Jugoslavia', 1293–338; Thomas Cook (& Son), *Summer Holidays Abroad on the Continent and Overseas 1939* (London: Thomas Cook & Son, 1939), 331–3, Michail, *The British and the Balkans*, 52. Dolling's *Illyrian Spring* might have played a role in perpetuating these cultural anxieties by depicting her characters' discomfort and isolation during an expedition to Dalmatia's hinterland. [Dolling], *Illyrian Spring*, 211–16.
71 Jan and Cora Gordon, *Two Vagabonds in the Balkans* (London: The Bodley Head, 1925), 86, 128.
72 Ball, *Dalmatia*, 184; Currey, *Yugoslavia*, 211.
73 Gordon, *Two Vagabonds*, 27–8.
74 Stephen Graham, *The Moving Tent: Adventures with a Tent and Fishing-rod in Southern Jugoslavia* (London: Cassel and Company, 1939), 148.
75 Ibid., 332–3; Walton, 'Preface', xvi.
76 'Anglo-Saxon will form the Majority Part of Yugoslavia's Tourists in 1932', *South Slav Herald* (23 February 1932), 5; Geoffrey Gibson, 'Market Day in Trebinje: A Hercegovina Vignette', *South Slav Herald* (September 1933), 3.
77 [Frank Green], *A Journey through Bosnia, Herzegovina, and Dalmatia* (London: privately printed at the Chiswick Press, 1928), 4–5.
78 Howkins, 'Death and Rebirth?', 16.
79 Paul Brassley, Jeremy Burchardt and Lynne Thompson, 'Conclusion', in idem, *The English Countryside Between the Wars*, 239.
80 Ibid., 239–40.
81 Todorova, *Imagining*, 63.
82 See for example, Ellen Chivers Davies, *Tales of Serbian Life* (London: G. Harrap, 1919).
83 Richard M. Dorson, 'Folklore Studies in England', *Journal of American Folklore* 74, no. 294 (1961): 302–10. See also, Iorwerth C. Peate, 'Folklore Studies in Wales', *Folklore* 68, no. 4 (1957): 471–3.
84 Richard Clarke and Marija Anteric, '(British) Anthropological Tourism in Slovenia 1932-2007', *Anthropological Notebooks – Društvo antropologov Slovenije* 15, no. 1 (2009): 3.
85 Ball, *Dalmatia*, 209; Currey, *Yugoslavia*, 10–12.
86 Jan and Cora Gordon, 'Two Vagabonds in the Balkans', *The Geographical Journal Reviews* 66, no. 1 (1925): 59.
87 Gordon, *Two Vagabonds*, 50.
88 'What Struck me most about Ljubljana' *South Slav Herald* (May 1933), 3. Richard Clarke and Maria Anteric, 'Fanny Copeland and the Geographical Imagination', *Scottish Geographical Journal* 127, no. 3 (2011): 180.
89 'Yugoslav Art Show in Liverpool and Glasgow', *South Slav Herald* (June 1939), 10.
90 West, *Black Lamb*, [Vol. 1], 55.

91 H. Gregarious Brown, 'A Leeds Man's Tour in Serbia: Crossing the Country on Foot', *The Yorkshire Evening Post* (30 September 1919), 8; 'On Foot through Serbia', *The Mercury Press* (14 May 1929), 5; F. S. Copeland, 'Where a Snail is Chained Up!', *South Slav Herald* (January–February, 1939), 10–11; 'How Croat & Serb Peasant can Cooperate: Prof Herceg's Plan', *South Slav Herald* (February 1940), 6.
92 *Kingdom of Yugoslavia 1919-1929* (Belgrade: Central Press Bureau, 1930), 3; Rudolf Andrejka, Stevan Ivanitch and Miloslav Stojadinovitch (eds), *European Conference on Rural Life, National Monographs Drawn up by Governments: Yugoslavia* (Geneva: League of Nations, 1939), 40–1.
93 Ernest H. R. Collings, 'The Exhibition of Serbo-Croat Art', *Balkan Review* 2, no. 2 (1919): 349–50; 'Peasant Painters', *South Slav Herald* (January–February 1939), 12.
94 Allcock, *Explaining Yugoslavia*, 54–6.
95 'Krekov tabor v Komendi', *Slovenec* (29 February 1920). Quoted in Banac, *The National Question in Yugoslavia*, 343.
96 Joel. M Halpern and E. A. Hammel, 'Observations on the Intellectual History of Ethnology and other Social Sciences in Yugoslavia', *Comparative Studies in Society and History: An International Quarterly* 11, no. 1 (1969): 20–1.
97 Edith Durham, 'A Bird Tradition in the West of the Balkan Peninsula', *Man* 23 (1923): 55–7.
98 'Notes on Peasant Traditions, undated', *Lodge Collection (1919-1956)*, SSEES, LOD/1; Durham, *Twenty Years*, 48.
99 Fanny S. Copeland, 'Three Go South: Through Montenegro to the South Land', *South Slav Herald* (December 1933), 3.
100 Dudley Heathcote, *My Wanderings in the Balkans* (London: Hutchinson & Co, 1925), 83–4.
101 Larry Wolff, 'This Time, Let's Listen', *The New York Times Book Review* (10 February 1991), 28.
102 *The Croats under Yugo-Slavian Rule. The Result of an Enquiry by Rhys J. Davies and Ben Riley* (dated 26 October–8 November). LP/WG/YUG/1-4.
103 R. H. Bruce Lockheart, 'A Peasant State. The Crisis in Yugoslavia', *The Times* (26 April 1927), 15.
104 Lovett Fielding Edwards, *A Wayfarer in Yugoslavia* (New York: Robert M. McBride & Company, 1939), 211–12.
105 Itinerant bards famous for their recitals of epic poetry while playing the iconic single-stringed *gusle*. Fanny S. Copeland, *Beautiful Mountains in the Jugoslav Alps* (Chelmsford: The Mercury Press, 1931), 24–5; eadem, *Poems*, unpublished, dated 1954, 3.
106 Clarke and Anteric, 'Fanny Copeland and the Geographical Imagination', 182.
107 'Letter to Charles Saroléa (4 February 1922)', cited in ibid., 184.
108 William Miller, *The Balkans: Roumania, Bulgaria, Servia, and Montenegro*, 3rd edn (London: T. Fisher and Unwin, 1923), 514.
109 Ibid., 510–14.
110 Copeland, 'Three Go South', 3.
111 Cvijić, *Péninsule Balkanique*, 322–3; A. Davies, 'Slovenia', in Laurence Dudley Stamp (ed.), *Slovene Studies: Being Studies Carried Out By Members of the Le Play Society in the Alpine Valleys of Slovenia (Yugoslavia)* (London: The Le Play Society, 1933), 14; Kaser, 'Balkanization of the Balkans', 92–3.
112 Davies, 'Ethnography', in Stamp (ed.), *Slovene Studies*, 23–4.

113 Nora Lavrin, *Jugoslav Scenes; Dry Points by Nora Lavrin* (London: Stanley Nott, 1935), 11.
114 Horatio F. Brown, *Dalmatia* (London: A & C Black, 1925), 33. From 1929, Belgrade also boasted Europe's only Buddhist temple outside of Russia (constructed for the city's émigré community of Kalmyk's who had fled the Russian Civil War). 'Painter-Mystics's Gift', *South Slav Herald* (September 1932), 1.
115 Quoted in Ilana R. Bet-El, 'Unimagined Communities: The Power of Memory and the Conflict in the Former Yugoslavia', in Jan-Werner Müller (ed.), *Memory and Power in Post-War Europe: Studies in the Presence of the Past* (Cambridge: Cambridge University Press, 2002), 220.
116 L. S. Amery (Rt. Hon), 'Salute to Jugoslavia!', *Illustrated London News* (12 April 1941), 1–11.

Chapter 8

1 W. D. Rubinstein, *Capitalism, Culture, & Decline in Britain, 1750-1990* (London: Routledge, 2001 [1994]), 11–12; Richard Overy, *The Morbid Age: Britain between the Wars* (London: Allen Lane, 2009), 29, 51–67, 297–309.
2 Ibid., 241.
3 West, *Black Lamb [Vol. 1]*, 54; Allcock, 'Constructing the Balkans', 237–8; Marina MacKay, *Modernism and World War II* (Cambridge: Cambridge University Press, 2010), 35.
4 Andrew Hammond, 'The Escape from Decadence: British Travel Literature on the Balkans 1900-45', in Michael St. John (ed.), *Romancing Decay: Ideas of Decadence in European Culture* (Farnham: Ashgate, 1999), 142–3.
5 West, *Black Lamb [Vol. 1]*, 482.
6 Hammond, 'Escape from Decadence', 146–8; Idem, *British Literature*, 141.
7 Gordon, *Two Vagabonds*, 186–7.
8 Hammond, 'Escape from Decadence', 147.
9 Ibid., 149.
10 MacKay, *Modernism*, 44–7.
11 See Daniele Conversi, 'Moral Relativism and Equidistance in British Attitudes to the War in the Former Yugoslavia', in Thomas Cushman and Stjepan G. Meštrovič (eds), *This Time We Knew: Western Reponses to Genocide in Bosnia* (New York: New York University Press, 1996), 244–81; Branimir Anzulovic, *Heavenly Serbia: From Myth to Genocide* (London: Hurst & Co., 1999); Brendan Simms, *Unfinest Hour: Britain and the Destruction of Bosnia* (London: Penguin, 2002).
12 West, *Black Lamb [Vol. 1]*, 288; Hammond, *British Literature*, 159–60.
13 West, *Black Lamb [Vol. 1]*, 1, [*Vol.2*], 426, 543–4; Goldsworthy, *Inventing Ruritania*, 196; Lene Hansen, *Security as Practice: Discourse Analysis and the Bosnian War* (Abingdon: Routledge, 2006), 163–4; MacKay, *Modernism*, 35–7; Overy, *Morbid Age*, 219–20.
14 Graham, *Moving Tent*, v.
15 Ibid., 15–18.
16 While the novel's setting is left unnamed, it's famous 1938 film adaptation, *The Lady Vanishes*, takes place in the fictional East European country of 'Bandrika', a cultural pastiche of Switzerland, Czechoslovakia and Alpine Yugoslavia.

17 White, *The Wheel Spins*, 16.
18 West, *Black Lamb [Vol. 1]*, 53.
19 'Admiralty to Foreign Office (15 January 1919)', FO 371/3507.
20 Noel Buxton and T. P. Evans Conwil, *Oppressed Peoples and the League of Nations* (London: J.M.Dent & Sons, 1922), 88–9; *The Croats under Yugo-Slavian Rule*, LP/WG/YUG/1-4; R. W. Seton-Watson, 'The Jugoslav Dictatorship', *The Contemporary Review* 793 (1932): 23–31; idem, 'King Alexander's Assassination', *International Affairs* 14, no. 1 (1935): 41–7; Robert Gower (Sir.), *The Hungarian Minorities in the Successor States* (London: G. Richards, 1937), 85–9.
21 [*Pathé News*] 'ASSASSINATION OF KING ALEXANDER – Vivid Pictures from the Scene of the Tragedy at Marseilles (October 1934)' (London: Associated British-Pathe). Available online: www.britishpathe.com/video/assassination-of-king-alexander/ (accessed 17 September 2019).
22 Michail, *The British and the Balkans*, 131.
23 West, *Black Lamb [Vol. 1]*, 457.
24 Nielsen, *Making Yugoslavs*, 86–7.
25 'Italy and Jugoslavia, Kennard to FO (14 April 1928)', *Political Central: Yugoslavia*, FO 371/12978.
26 Gordon, *Two Vagabonds*, 55, 149–50.
27 Stephen Graham, *Alexander of Jugoslavia: Strong Man of the Balkans* (London: Cassel and Company, 1938), 122.
28 R. G. D. Laffan, *Jugoslavia since 1918* (London: The Yugoslav Society of Great Britain, 1929), 8–9.
29 M. E. Durham, 'King Nikola of Montenegro', *The Contemporary Review* 664 (1921): 473–5.
30 King Aleksandar's ancestor and the leader of the First Serbian Uprising in 1804, Karađorđe Petrović, claimed decent from one of Montenegro's historic tribes.
31 M. E. Durham, 'Croatia and Great Serbia', *The Contemporary Review* 695 (1923): 503–6.
32 See Alexander Devine, *Off the Map: The Suppression of Montenegro, the Tragedy of a Small Nation* (London: Chapham and Hall, 1921).
33 'Report of the British Mission to Montenegro 1919-1920', *Gladstone Papers*, BL: MS 46014.
34 [Herbert Vivian], *Myself not Least, Being the Personal Reminiscences of 'X'* (New York: Henry Holt and Company, 1923), 223.
35 Even before the King's suspension of parliament, Seton-Watson's rising concerns saw him attempting to dissuade the City of London from issuing a loan to the Yugoslavian government in 1928. 'Strictly confidential: Some Considerations on the Situation in Yugoslavia, c.1931-1932', SEW 9/2/1.
36 Following the assassination, the *Herald* dedicated more of its column space to foreign affairs, including stories focusing on other countries.
37 Evelyn Wrench, 'Journal of a Balkan Tour . . .; 14 Aug.-10 Oct. 1935'. *Wrench Papers Vol. XXXVIII*, BL Western Manuscripts: Add MS 59578, 84.
38 Hammond, *British Literature*, 28.
39 West, *Black Lamb*, 123.
40 [Anon], *The Jugoslav Minority in Italy* (Geneva: International Union of Associations for the League of Nations, 1927), 34–42; F. S. Copeland, 'The S. E. Face of the Mojstrovka', *The Alpine Journal* 40, no. 2 (1928): 46; Fran Barbalić, 'National

Minorities in Europe – V: The Jugoslavs of Italy', *The Slavonic and East European Review* 15, no. 43 (1936): 179–84.
41 Clarke and Anteric, 'Fanny Copeland and the Geographical Imagination', 186.
42 West, *Black Lamb [Vol. 1]*, 124.
43 Edith Durham, 'Croatia and Greater Serbia', *The Contemporary Review* 129 (1923): 504.
44 Riley had lost his seat in the 1931 general election but regained it in 1935. LP/WG/YUG/ 1-4.
45 See Mark Mazower, *Dark Continent: Europe's Twentieth Century* (London: Allen Lane the Penguin Press, 1998).
46 I. Monte Radlovic, *Tito's Republic* (London: Coldharbour Press, 1948), 48.
47 Burr was expelled by the Yugoslavian government in the summer of 1940 following accusations of sabotage against stretches of railway administered by Germany. Sebastian Ritchie, *Our Man in Yugoslavia: The Story of a Secret Service Operative* (London: Routledge, 2004), 35–6; Stefanidis, *Substitute for* Power, 247.
48 'How the Yugoslav Nation Found its Soul', *The War Illustrated* 4, no. 85 (April 1941): 386. Probable oversight on the part of the articles' author puts the date of the coup, and Churchill's subsequent pronouncement, as 28 March.
49 'R. W. Seton-Watson, Radio Message (27 March 1941)' (Yugoslavia, RWSW's radio broadcasts, 1940-1945), SEW/15/3/1.
50 'Letter from Paget to Ivan Subbotić (Jugoslavian ambassador to Great Britain), (30 March 1941)'; 'N. Henderson, Radio Message Transcript (April 1941)', *Paget Papers*.
51 'Yugoslavia Revolts', *Western Daily Press and Bristol Mirror* (Friday, 28 March 1941), 3; 'What We Think, Yugoslavia Finds her Soul!', *Sunderland Daily Echo and Shipping Gazette* (Thursday, 27 March 1941), 2.
52 'Recent Travel Publications', *Outlook and Independent*, 156 (New York: The Outlook Company, 1930), 368.
53 M. F. Melville, *Balkan Racket: The Inside Story of the Political Gangster Plot which Destroyed Yugoslavia and Drove Britain out of the Balkans* (London: Jarrolds, 1941), 94–9.
54 Mandler, 'Against "Englishness"', 171–2.
55 Much of rural England and Wales remained fairly traditional and underpopulated prior to the Second World War. The growth of 'White Collar' suburban communities was largely concentrated in the south those counties directly adjacent to financial and light-industrial centres such as Surrey, Middlesex and Cheshire. Alun Howkins, *The Death of Rural England: A Social History of the Countryside since 1900* (London: Routledge, 2003), 98.
56 Richard Clarke and Marija Anteric, '(British) Anthropological Tourism in Slovenia 1937-2007', *Anthropological Notebooks - Društvo antropologov Slovenije* 15, no. 1 (2009): 8–9; Kuklick, *Savage Within*, 68–71.
57 Brown, *Dalmatia*, 33; Olive Lodge, *Peasant Life in Yugoslavia* (London: Seeley, Service & Co, 1941), 18–19.
58 Lampe and Jackson, *Balkan Economic History*, 334–5; Ehrlich, *Family in Transition*, 48.
59 Ibid., vi, 49, 243.
60 Hasma Humo, 'Rare Moslem Festivals in Yugoslavia', *South Slav Herald* (1–16 September 1937), 4.
61 '"Mass Observation" by a "Herald" Reader', *South Slav Herald* (August 1939), 4.
62 'Journal of a Balkan Tour', *Wrench Papers Vol. XXXVIII*, 14.

63 F. S. Copeland. 'Three Go South: Through Montenegro to the South Land', *South Slav Herald* (November 1933), 7; Lodge, *Peasant Life*, 75.
64 'Journal of a Balkan Tour', *Wrench Papers Vol. XXXVIII*, 81.
65 Lodge, *Peasant Life*, 292.
66 Jovana Babović, *Metropolitan Belgrade: Culture and Class in Interwar Yugoslavia* (Pittsburgh: University of Pittsburgh Press, 2018), 107–8.
67 Wrench, 'Journal of a Balkan Tour', 25–7.
68 West, *Black Lamb [Vol. 1]*, 337; *[Vol. 2]*, 2.
69 Anna Kay, 'Louise Rayner: An English Women's Experiences in Wartime Yugoslavia', in Allcock and Young (eds), *Black Lambs*, 164.
70 Louisa Rayner, *Woman in a Village: An Englishwoman's Experiences of Life in Yugoslavia under German Occupation* (London: William Heinemann, 1957), 12–13, 78–82.
71 Rudolf Bićanić, *Kako živi narod: život u pasivnim krajevima* (Zagreb: Tisak 'Tipografija' 1936), 3.
72 F. S. Copeland, 'Lost World in Carniola', *The Alpine Journal* 52, no. 260 (1940): 96.
73 Ibid.
74 Evans, *Through Bosnia and Herzegovina*, 89.
75 Michail, *The British and the Balkans*, 27.
76 Overy, *Morbid Age*, 29.
77 Tito's status as a founder of the Non-Aligned Movement in 1961 further enhanced his internationalist reputation. Ibid., 112–14. See also B. Vivekanandan, 'Britain and Non-Alignment', *International Studies* 20, nos. 1–2 (1981): 477–87.
78 These cultural re-enactments still provoked controversy over how Yugoslavia's pre-socialist past should be presented in relation to Marxist historical theory. Patrick Hyder Patterson, 'Yugoslavia as It Once Was: What Tourism and Leisure Meant for the History of the Socialist Federation', in Grandits and Taylor (eds), *Yugoslavia's Sunny Side*, 384, 392.

Conclusion

1 Searle, *A New England?*, 365.
2 Readman, 'The Edwardian Land Question', 182–3.
3 Thompson, *British Political Culture*, 140–1, 224–32.
4 Evans, *Great Britain and the Creation*, 9–10, 91; Drapac, *Constructing Yugoslavia*, 80–3.
5 Scianna, 'Reporting Atrocities', 617.

Bibliography

Unpublished archival documents

Great Britain

London, British Library
   Paget Papers (3rd Series) Vol. XX 1914-1945, BL Western Manuscripts: Add MS 51261.
   Viscount Gladstone Papers Vol. XXX 1916-1926, BL Western Manuscripts: Add MS46014.
   'Diaries of John Evelyn Wrench, Vol I. The Tour in 1901, 31 Aug.-2 Oct. 1901'. Wrench Papers Vol. XVI. BL Western Manuscripts: Add MS 59556.
   'Journal of a Balkan tour; 14 Aug.-10 Oct. 1935'. Wrench Papers Vol. XXXVIII, BL Western Manuscripts: Add MS 59578.

London, Imperial War Museum Archive and Sound Archives, London
   'BBC Interview with Henry Fitch, 2nd April 1941', IWM Sound Archive Catalogue no. 29987.
   'IWM Interview with Ernest Victor John Jones, undated'. IWM Sound Archive Catalogue no.12678.
   'IWM Interview with Mary Millicent Rummney, 3rd March 1976'. IWM Sound Archive, Catalogue no. 739.
   Private Papers of Dame K. Courtney, IWM Documents.9785.
   Private Papers of TG Craddock, IWM Documents.16826.
   Private Papers of Miss L Creighton, IWM Documents.1898.
   Private Papers of H. Fitch, IWM Documents. IWM Documents.76/191/1.
   Private Papers of R. Gwinnel, IWM Documents.11601.
   Private Papers of C.R. Hennessey, IWM Documents.12705.
   Private Papers of Miss K Hodges, IWM Documents.1974.
   Private Papers of Miss G Holland, IWM Documents.1042.
   Private Papers of Miss M Ingram, IWM Documents. 2786.
   Private Papers of Dr K S Macphail, IWM Documents 6767.
   Private Papers of W. G. Ostler, IWM Documents.12335.
   Private Papers of Miss A.J. Pinniger, IWM Documents.2320.
   Private Papers of Dr Jean K Rose, IWM Documents.6776.
   Private Papers of Reverend J Sellors, IWM Documents.1277.
   Private Papers of Dr T Stephanides, IWM Documents.13891.
   London, The National Archives
   Foreign Office Class 195.
   Foreign Office Class 294.
   Foreign Office Class 371.
   Foreign Office Class 800.

London, Royal Anthropological Institute of Great Britain and Ireland
   My Balkan Notebook Vol. II: Montenegro [1940], Durham, Mary Edith 'Collection', RAI: MS 41.

Durham, Mary Edith *'Collection'*, RAI: MS 42.
Durham, Mary Edith *'Collection'*, RAI: MS 43.
Durham, Mary Edith *'Collection'*, RAI: MS 45.

London, UCL School of Slavonic and East European Studies
Lodge Collection (1919-1956), LOD/1.
Seton-Watson (Professor Robert William) Collection, SEW/1.
Seton-Watson (Professor Robert William) Collection, SEW/3.
Seton-Watson (Professor Robert William) Collection, SEW/15.
Seton-Watson (Professor Robert William) Collection, SEW/17.
Manchester, Labour History Archive and Study Centre (People's History Museum)
The Croats under Yugo-Slavian Rule. The Result of an Enquiry by Rhys J. Davies and Ben Riley (Dated 26th October-8th November). LP/WG/YUG/1-4.

Serbia

Belgrade, Arhiv Srbije [Archive of Serbia]
Ministarstvo inostranich dela, Političko odeljenje, 1904, Fascikla – III, Docije – IV, I/9 Pov.b r. 2191, Jovičić-Pašiću, 2/15. XI 1904.

Belgrade, Arhiv Srpske akademije nauka i umetnosti (ASANU) [Archive of the Serbian Academy of Sciences and Arts], Belgrade.
Stead, A. *Memorandum o odnosima između Engleske i Srbije*, ASANU. No.12880/3.

Published Documents, Correspondence and Broadcast Media

[Anon] (1914), *Report of the International Commission to Inquire into the Causes and Conduct of the Balkan War*, Washington, DC: The Endowment.
[Anon] (1915), *Census of England and Wales*, 1911, London: H.M.S.O.
[Anon] (1915), *The Serbian Blue Book*, New York: American Association for International Conciliation.
[Pathé News] (1934), 'ASSASSINATION OF KING ALEXANDER - Vivid Pictures from the Scene of the Tragedy at Marseilles', London: Associated British-Pathe, www.britishpathe.com/video/assassination-of-king-alexander/.
Howe, A. and S. Morgan eds, (2015), *The Letters of Richard Cobden: Volume IV*, Oxford: Oxford University Press.
Layard, H. (Sir), W. N. Bruce and A. Otway eds, (1903), *Autobiography and Letters from his Childhood until His Appointment as H.M. Ambassador at Madrid*, London: John Murray.

Newspapers and Periodicals

Belfast News Letter
Birmingham Daily Post
Edinburgh Evening News
Great Britain and the East
Hansard

Hull Daily Mail
New Review
Review of Reviews
Sheffield Evening Telegraph
South Slav Herald (Britain/USA/Yugoslavia)
St James's Gazette
Sunderland Daily Echo and Shipping Gazette
The Balkan Review
The Contemporary Review
The Economist
The Fortnightly Review
The Humanitarian
The Illustrated London News
The Irish Times
The Manchester Guardian
The Mercury Press
The Monthly Review
The National Review
The Nation
The New York Times Book Review
The Spectator
The Southern Slav Bulletin
The Times
The War Illustrated
The Western Times
The Wide World Magazine
The Yorkshire Evening Post
Western Daily Press and Bristol Mirror

Diaries, Memoirs, Pamphlets and Contemporary Literature

[Anon] (1904), *Report of the Inter-departmental Committee on Physical Deterioration: Vol. 1 Report and Appendix*, London: Printed for H.M. Stationery Off., by Darling & Son.
[Anon] (1912), 'First International Eugenics Congress', *The British Medical Journal*, 2: 253–5.
[Anon] (1913), *The British Red Cross in the Balkans*, London: Cassell and Company.
[Anon] (1915), *Serbia's Cup of Sorrow*, London: SRF.
[Anon] (1917), *The Lay of Kosovo: History and Poetry on Serbia's Past and Present*, London: The Kosovo Day Committee.
[Anon] (1925), 'Two Vagabonds in the Balkans', *The Geographical Journal Reviews*, 66 (1): 59.
[Anon] (1927), *The Jugoslav Minority in Italy*, Geneva: International Union of Associations for the League of Nations.
[Anon] (1929), *Dr Elsi Inglis memorijal-bolnica za žene i decu*, Belgrade: Štamparija 'Jovanović'.
[Anon] (1930), *Kingdom of Yugoslavia 1919–1929*, Belgrade: Central Press Bureau.

[Anon] (1939), 'I Saw the Futile Massacre at Doiran', in John Alexander Hammond (Sir) (ed.), *The Great War- I was there! Undying Memories of 1914–1918*, Vol. 3, 1–22, London: Amalgamated Press.
Abbott, G. F. (1903), *The Tale of a Tour in Macedonia*, London: Edward Arnold.
Abraham, J. J. (1922), *My Balkan Log*, New York: E. Dutton & Company.
Adam, R. (1764), *Ruins of the Palace of Emperor Diocletian at Spalatro in Dalmatia*, London: Printed for the Author.
Andrejka, R., S. Ivanitch and M. Stojadinovitch eds, (1939), *European Conference on Rural Life, National Monographs Drawn up by Governments: Yugoslavia*, Geneva: League of Nations.
Angell, N. (1912), *Peace Theories and the Balkan War*, London: Horace Marshall & Son.
Arbuthnot, G. (Lieut) (1862), *Herzegovina; Or, Omer Pacha and the Christian Rebels*, London: Longman, Roberts, & Green.
Askew, A. and C. Askew (1916), *The Stricken Land: Serbia as We Saw It*, London: Eveleigh Nash Company.
Bailey, W. F. (1916), *The Slavs of the War Zone*, London: Chapman and Hall.
Balfour, F. (Lady) (1918), *Dr Elsie Inglis*, London: Hodder and Stoughton.
Barbalić, F. (1936), 'National Minorities in Europe –V: The Jugoslavs of Italy', *The Slavonic and East European Review*, 15 (43): 177–90.
Barrington, R. (Mrs Isabel Emilie) (1912), *Through Greece and Dalmatia*, London: Adam and Charles Black.
Barry, J. P. (Lieut-Col) (1906), *At the Gates of the East: A Book of Travel among Historic Wonderlands*, London: Longmans, Green, and Co.
Berry, J., F. M. Dickinson Berry, and W. Blease Lyon [and Other Members of the Unit] (1916), *The Story of a Red Cross Unit in Serbia*, London: J & A Churchill.
Bićanić, R. (1936), *Kako živi narod: život u pasivnim krajevima*, Zagreb: Tisak 'Tipografija'.
Block, A. (Sir) (1913), *Come over to Macedonia and Help us*, Constantinople: Le Comité de Publication D.A.C.B.
Booth, John C. L. (1905), *Trouble in the Balkans*, London: Hurst and Blackett.
Booth, W. (General) (1890), *In Darkest England and the Way Out*, London: Funk and Wagnells.
Brailsford, H. N. *Macedonia: Its Races and their Future*, London: Methuen, 1906.
de Bunsen, V. and N. Buxton (1907), *Macedonian Massacres: Photos from Macedonia*, London: The Balkan Committee.
Buxton, N. (1907), *Europe and the Turks*, London: John Murray.
Buxton, N. and C. R. Buxton (1915), *The War and the Balkans*, 2nd edn, London: George Allen & Unwin.
Buxton, N. and T. P. Conwell-Evans (1922), *Oppressed Peoples and the League of Nations*, London: J. M. Dent & Sons.
Chirol, V. (Sir) (1914), *Serbia and the Serbs*, Oxford: Oxford Pamphlets.
Comyn-Platt, T. (1904), *The Turk in the Balkans*, London: Alston Rivers.
Conway, A. E. (1917), *A Ride through the Balkans, On Classic Ground with a Camera*, London: Robert Scott.
Copeland, F. S. (1928), 'The S.E. Face of the Mojstrovka', *The Alpine Journal*, 40 (2): 331–8.
Copeland, F. S. (1940), 'Lost World in Carniola: A Record of Mountain Adventure and Scientific Observation by Members of the Alpine Club', *The Alpine Journal*, 52 (260): 89–96.
Crawfurd Price, W. H. (1913), *The Balkan Cockpit: The Political and Military Story of the Balkan Wars in Macedonia*, London: T. Werner Laurie.

Creagh, J. (1876), *Over the Borders of Christendom and Eslamiah*, Vol. II, London: Samuel Tinsley.
Cvijić, J. (1906), *Nekolika promatranja o etnografiji makedonskih Slovena*, Belgrade: Štamparija 'Dositije Obradović'.
Cvijić, J. (1918), *La Péninsule Balkanique: Geographie Humaine*, Paris: Librairie Armand Colin.
Dangerfield, G. (1936), *The Strange Death of Liberal England*, London: Constable & Co.
Davies, E. C. (1916), *A Farmer in Serbia*, London: Methuen & Co.
Dearmer, M. (1915), *Letters from a Field Hospital*, London: Macmillan & Co.
Denton, W. (Rev) (1877), *Montenegro: Its People and their History*, London: Daldy, Isbister & Co.
Diouritch, G. (1919), 'A Survey of the Development of the Serbian (Southern Slav) Nation: An Economic and Statistical Study', *Journal of the Royal Statistical Society*, 82 (3): 293–342.
Drage, G. (1909), *Austria-Hungary*, London: John Murray.
Durham, M. E. (1904), *Through the Lands of the Serb*, London: Edward Arnold.
Durham, M. E. (1905), *The Burden of the Balkans*, London: Edward Arnold.
Durham, M. E. (1909), *High Albania*, London: Edward Arnold.
Durham, M. E. (1914), *The Struggle for Scutari (Turk, Slav and Albanian)*, London: Edward Arnold.
Durham, M. E. (1917), 'Albania Past and Present', *Journal of the Central Asian Society*, 4 (1): 3–16.
Durham, M. E. (1920), *Twenty Years of Balkan Tangle*, London: George Allen & Unwin.
Durham, M. E. (1925), *The Serajevo Crime*, London: G. Allen & Unwin.
[Eliot, C.] 'Odysseus'. (1900), *Turkey in Europe*, London: Edward Arnold.
Evans, A. J. (1876), *Through Bosnia and Herzegovina on Foot during the Insurrection*, London: Longmans, Green and Co.
Evans, A. J. (1878), *Illyrian Letter: A Revised Selection of Correspondence from the Illyrian Provinces*, London: Longmans, Green and Co.
Falls, C. (1933), *Military Operations, Macedonia (Volume 1): From the Outbreak of War to the Spring of 1917*, London: HMSO.
Fennimore, J. (1913), *A Boy Scout in the Balkans*, London: W & R. Chambers.
Fraser, J. F. (1906), *Pictures from the Balkans*, London: Cassell and Company.
Gibbs, P. and B. Grant (1913), *The Balkan War: Adventures of War with Cross and Crescent*, Boston: Small, Maynard and Company.
Gladstone, W. E. (MP) (1876), *Bulgarian Horrors and the Question of the East*, London: John Murray.
Goff, A. and H. A. Fawcett (1921), *Macedonia: A Plea for the Primitive*, London: John Lane, The Bodley Head.
Gordon, J. and C. Gordon (1915), *The Luck of Thirteen: Wanderings and Flight through Montenegro and Serbia*, London: Smith, Elder and Co.
Gordon, J. and C. Gordon (1916), *A Balkan Freebooter: Being the True Exploits of the Serbian Outlaw and Comitaj Petko Moritch*, London: Smith, Elder & Co.
Gordon, J. and C. Gordon (1925), *Two Vagabonds in the Balkans*, London: John Lane.
Gordon-Smith, G. (1916), *Through the Serbian Campaign: The Great Retreat of the Serbian Army*, London: Hutchinson & Co.
Gower, R. (Sir.) (1937), *The Hungarian Minorities in the Successor States*, London: G. Richards.
Graham, S. (1939), *The Moving Tent: Adventures with a Tent and a Fishing Rod in Southern Jugoslavia*, London: Cassel and Company.

Graves, C. (1930), *And the Greeks*, London: G. Bles.
[Green, F]. (1928), *A Journey through Bosnia, Herzegovina, and Dalmatia*, London: Privately printed at the Chiswick Press.
Grogan, E. (Lady) (1926), *The Life of J.D Bourchier*, London: Hurst & Blackett.
Hadži-Vasiljević, J. (1902), *Prilep i njegova okolina: istorijsko-geografska izlaganja*, Belgrade: Štam Jockovića.
Henderson, P. E. (1909), *A British Officer in the Balkans*, London: Seeley and Co.
H. I. W. (1916), *The Experiences of a Unit in the Great Retreat (Serbia 1915)*, Cambridge: Crompton & Sons.
Hichens, R. (1913), *The Near East: Dalmatia, Greece and Constantinople*, London: Hodder & Stoughton.
Holbach, M. M. (1908), *Dalmatia: The Land where East Meets West*, London: John Lane, The Bodley Head.
Holbach, M. M. (1910 [1909]), *Bosnia and Herzegovina: Some Wayside Wanderings*, London: John Lane, The Bodley Head.
Hulme-Beaman, A. G. (1898), *Twenty Years in the Near East*, London: Methuen & Co.
Jackson, H. F. (1908), *The Shores of the Adriatic, The Austrian Side*, London: John Murray.
James, L. (Colonel) (1929), *Times of Stress*, London: John Murray.
Johns, W. E. (Captain, ed) (1935), *Wings: Flying Stories*, 1 (3), London: John Hamilton Limited.
[JO] (1915), *The Southern Slav Library-I: The Southern Slav Programme*, London: Nisbet & Co.
[JO] (1916), *The Southern Slav Library- VI: Political and Social Conditions in Slovene Lands: Carniola, Carinthia, Illyrian and Styria*, London: The Near East.
Jovanović, V. M. (1909), *An English Bibliography on the Near Eastern Question, 1481–1906*, Belgrade: The Government Press.
Kinglake, A. W. (1844), *Eōthen, or, Traces of Travel, Brought Home from the East*, London: John Oliver.
Laffan, R. G. D. (1918), *The Guardians of the Gate: Historical Lectures on the Serbs*, Oxford: The Clarendon Press.
Laffan, R. G. D. (1929), *Jugoslavia since 1918*, London: The Yugoslav Society of Great Britain.
Lake, H. (1917), *In Salonika with our Army*, London: A. Melrose.
Lavrin, N. (1935), *Jugoslav Scenes; Dry Points by Nora Lavrin*, London: Stanley Nott.
[Le Queux, W] (1907), *An Observer in the Near East*, London: T. Fisher and Unwin.
Lodge, O. (1942), *Peasant Life in Jugoslavia*, London: Seely, Service & Co.
Mackenzie, G. M. and A. Irby. (1877 [1867]), *Travels in the Slavonic Provinces of Turkey-in- Europe*, Vol. 1, 2nd edn, London: Daldy, Isbister & Co.
Mann, A. J. (Captain) (1920), *The Salonika Front*, London: A & C Black.
Mason, D. M. (1903), *Macedonia and Great Britain's Responsibility*, London: T. Fisher Unwin.
Matthews, C. (Dr.) (1916), *Experiences of a Woman Doctor in Serbia*, London: Mills and Boon.
McLaren, Eva Shaw (ed.) (1919), *A History of the Scottish Women's Hospitals*, London: Hodder and Stoughton.
Melville, M. F. (1941), *Balkan Racket: The Inside Story of the Political Gangster Plot which Destroyed Yugoslavia and Drove Britain out of the Balkans*, London: Jarrolds.
Mijatovich, C. (1908), *Servia of the Servians*, London: Sir Isaac Pitman & Sons.
Miller, W. (1898), *Travel and Politics in the Near East*, London: T. Fisher Unwin.
Miller, W. (1923), *The Balkans: Roumania, Bulgaria, Servia, and Montenegro*, 3rd edn, London: T. Fisher and Unwin.

Misirkov, K. (1903), *Za makedonckite raboti*, Sofia: Pečatnica na 'Liberalnij Klub'.
Mitchell, T. J. and G. M. Smith (1931), *History of the Great War- Medical Services: Casualties and Medical Statistics of the Great War*, London: John Murray.
Mitton, G. E. (1914), *Austria-Hungary*, London: Adam and Charles Black.
Munro, R. (1900 [1895]), *Rambles and Studies in Bosnia-Herzegovina and Dalmatia*, 2nd edn, Edinburgh: William Blackwood & Sons.
Namier, L. B. (1917), *The Case for Bohemia*, London: The Czech National Alliance in Great Britain.
N. D. M. (1919), *Salvos from Salonika*, Carlisle: Chas. Thurman & Sons.
Orwell, G. (1937), *The Road to Wigan Pier*, London: V. Gollancz.
Owen, H. C. (1919), *Salonica and After: The Sideshow that Ended the War*, London: Hodder and Stoughton.
Paton, A. A. (Esq.) (1845), *Servia, Youngest Member of the European Family*, London: Longman, Brown, Green and Longmans.
Radešević, M. and F. Markić (1917), *Memorandum: Addressed by the Jugoslav Socialists to the International Socialist Peace Conference in Stockholm*, London: Jugoslav Workman's Association.
Rowntree, B. S. (1911), *Land and Labour: Lessons from Belgium*, London: Macmillan and Co.
Sandes, F. (1916), *An English Woman-Sergeant in the Serbian Army*, London: Hoddar and Stoughton.
Sandes, F. (1927), *The Autobiography of a Women Solider: A Brief Record of Adventure in the Serbian Army, 1916–1919*, New York: Frederick A. Stokes Company.
Scott-James, R. A. (1908), *Modernism and Romance*, London: John Lane, The Bodley Head.
Scott-James, R. A. (1910), *An Englishman in Ireland: Impressions of a Journey in a Canoe by River, Lough and Canal*, London: J. M. Dent & Sons.
Seton-Watson, R. W. (1911), *The Southern Slav Question and the Habsburg Monarchy*, London: Constable and Co.
Seton-Watson, R. W. (1915), *The Spirit of the Serb*, London: Nisbet.
Seton-Watson, R. W. (1916), *Serbia: Yesterday, To-day and Tomorrow: A School Address*, London: Vacher & Sons.
Seton-Watson, R. W. (1935), 'King Alexander's Assassination: Its Background and Effects', *Royal Institute of International Affairs*, 14 (1): 20–47.
Sinclair, H. (Private) (1919), *Highland Memories in Macedonia*, Salonika: The B.S.F Library 3.
Soubbotitch, V. (1918), 'A Pandemic of Typhus in Serbia in 1914 and 1915', *Proceedings of the Royal Society of Medicine: Section of Epidemiology and State Medicine*, 11: 31–9.
Stamp, L. Dudley (ed.) (1933), *Slovene Studies*, London: Le Play Society.
Stanley, M. M. (1916), *My Diary in Serbia: April 1st – Nov 1st 1915*, London: Simpkin, Marshall, Hamilton, Kent & Co.
St.Clair Stobart, M. A. (1913), *War and Women: From Experience in the Balkans and Elsewhere*, London: G. Bell & Sons.
St.Clair Stobart, M. A. (1916), *The Flaming Sword in Serbia and Elsewhere*, London: Hodder and Stoughton.
St.Clair Stobart, M. A. (1935), *Miracles and Adventures: An Autobiography*, London: Rider & Co.
Stebbing, E. (1917), *At the Serbian Front in Macedonia*, London: John Lane, The Bodley Head.
Stojićević, A. M. (1932), *Istorija naših ratova za oçlobođenje i ujedinjenje od 1912–1918 god*, Belgrade: Saveza Srpskih Zemljorad Zadruga.

Stuart, E. (1920), 'Sanitation in Serbia', *The American Journal of Public Health*, 10 (2): 124–31.
Strong, R. (1920), *Typhus Fever with a Particular Reference to the Serbian Epidemic*, Cambridge, MA: Harvard University Press.
Trevor, R. (1911), *My Balkan Tour: An Account of some Journeyings and Adventures in the Near East*, London: John Lane, The Bodley Head.
Trevor, R. (1913), *Montenegro: A Land of Warriors*, London: Adam and Charles Black.
Truhelka, Ć. (1907), *Hrvatska Bosna (Mi i 'oni tamo')*, Sarajevo: Tiskara Vogler.
Velimirović, N. (1916), *The Soul of Serbia*, London: The Faith Press at the Faith House.
Vidaković, A. (1938), 'Jugoslavia', in Eugene Fodor (ed.), *1938 in Europe: Aldor's Entertaining Travel Annual*, 1293–338, London: W. Aldor.
Vivian, H. (1897), *Servia; The Poor Man's Paradise*, London: Longmans, Green and Co.
Vivian, H. (1904), *The Servian Tragedy, with some Impressions of Macedonia*, London: G. Richards.
Vopika, C. J. (1921), *Secrets of the Balkans*, Chicago: Rand, McNally & Co.
Vošnjak, B. (1916), *Jugoslav Nationalism: Three Lectures*, London: Polsue Limited.
Vošnjak, B. (1917), *A Bulwark against Germany: The Fight of the Slovenes, the Western Branch of the Jugoslavs, for National Existence*, trans. Fanny Copeland, London: George Allen & Unwin.
Vošnjak, B. (1917), *A Chapter of the Old Slovenian Democracy*, London: John Murray.
Walpole, H. and T. Park (1806), *A Catalogue of the Royal and Noble Authors of England, Scotland, and Ireland*, Vol. 5, London: John Scott.
Walshe, D. (1920), *With the Serbs in Macedonia*, London: The Bodley Head.
West, R. (1941), *Black lamb and Grey Falcon: The Record of a Journey through Yugoslavia in 1937*, Vols 1 and 2, London: MacMillan.
Whitwell, E. R. (Mrs) (1909), *Through Bosnia and Herzegovina with a Paintbrush*, Darlington: William Dresser & Sons.
Willoughby, W. G. and L. Cassidy (1918), *Anti-Malarial Work in Macedonia among British Troops*, London: H. K. Louis.
Wills, L. M. (1906), *A Captive of the Bulgarian Brigands: Englishman's Terrible Experiences in Macedonia*, London: Ede, Allom & Townsend.
Wilson, H. W. and J. A. Hammerton eds, (1914), *The Great War: The Standard History of the all-Europe Conflict*, Vol. 1, London: The Amalgamated Press.
de Windt, H. (1907), *Through Savage Europe*, London: T. Fisher Unwin.
Wynne, M. [Knowles M. W.] (1916), *An English Girl in Serbia: The Story of a Great Adventure*, London: Collins' Clear-Type Press.
Wyon, R. and G. Prance (1903), *The Land of the Black Mountain: The Adventures of Two Englishmen in Montenegro*, London: Methuen & Co.
Wyon, R. (1904), *The Balkans from Within*, London: James Finch & Co.
Wyrall, E. (1931), *The Gloucestershire Regiment in the War 1914–1918*, London: Methuen & Co.

Secondary Literature

Abraham, J. J. (1957), *Surgeon's Journey*, London: Heinemann.
Alan, L. (1976), *The Origins of the Popular Press in England, 1855–1914*, London: Rowman & Littlefield.

Allcock, J. B. (2000), *Explaining Yugoslavia*, New York: Columbia University Press.
Anderson, B. (2016), *Imagined Communities: Reflections on the Origins and Spread of Nationalism*, rev edn, London: Verso.
Antić, Č. (2012), *Neizabrana Sabezinca: Srbija i Velika Britanija u prvom svetskom ratu*, Belgrade: Zavod za udžbenike.
Ayerst, D. (1985), *Garvin of the Observer*, London: Croom Helm.
Babović, J. (2018), *Metropolitan Belgrade: Culture and Class in Interwar Yugoslavia*, Pittsburgh: University of Pittsburgh Press.
Barnard, F. M. (2003), *Herder on Nationality, Humanity, and History*, Montreal and Kingston: McGill-Queen's University Press.
Baratta, J. (2004), *Politics of World Federation: From World Federalism to Global Governance*, Santa Barbara, CA: Greenwood Publishing Group.
Bartulin, N. (2014), *The Racial Idea in the Independent State of Croatia*, Leiden & Boston: Brill.
Baxell, R. (2004), *British Volunteers in the Spanish Civil War: The British Battalion in the International Brigades, 1936–1939*, London: Routledge.
Beaven, B. (2005), *Leisure, Citizenship and Working-Class Men in Britain, 1850–1945*, Manchester: Manchester University Press.
Beaven, B. (2012), *Visions of Empire; Patriotism, Popular Culture and the City, 1870–1939*, Manchester: Manchester University Press.
Berber, N. (2010), *Unveiling Bosnia-Herzegovina in British Travel Literature (1844–1912)*, Pisa: Pisa University Press.
Bridge, A. [Dolling, M.] (2012 [1935]), *Illyrian Spring*, London: Daunt Books.
Butler, D. and G. Butler (2011), *British Political Facts*, 10th edn, London: MacMillan.
Byford, J. (2008), *Denial and Repression of Antisemitism: Post-communist Remembrance of the Serbian Bishop Nikolaj Velimirović*, Budapest: Central European University Press.
Carmichael, C. D. (1991), 'Two Gentleman Travellers in the Slovene Lands in 1737', *Slovene Studies*, 13 (1): 19–26.
Cary, J. (2000), *Memoir of the Bobotes*, London: Weidenfeld & Nicolson.
Colley, L. (1992), *Britons: Forging the Nation, 1707–1837*, New Haven, CN: Yale University Press.
Corbett, E. (1964), *Red Cross in Serbia, 1915–1919: A Personal Diary of Experiences*, Banbury: Cheney and Sons.
Cornwall, M. (2000), *The Undermining of Austria-Hungary: The Battle for Hearts and Minds*, Basingstoke: Macmillan.
Demirci, S. (2006), *British Public Opinion towards the Ottoman Empire during the Two Crises: Bosnia-Herzegovina (1908–1909) and the Balkan Wars (1912–1913)*, Istanbul: Isis.
Despot, I. (2012), *The Balkan Wars in the Eyes of the Warring Parties: Perceptions and Interpretations*, Bloomington, IN: iUniverse.
Djokić, D. (2010), *Pašić & Trumbić: The Kingdom of Serbs, Croats and Slovenes*, London: Haus Publishing.
Drapac, V. (2010), *Constructing Yugoslavia: A Transnational History*, Basingstoke: Palgrave Macmillan.
Durham, M. (2003), 'Britain', in K. Passmore (ed.), *Women, Gender and Fascism in Europe 1919–45*, 214–34, Manchester: Manchester University Press.
St. Erlich, V. (1966), *Family in Transition: A Study of 300 Yugoslav Villages*, Princeton, NJ: Princeton University Press.

Evans, J. (2008), *Great Britain and the Creation of Yugoslavia: Negotiating Balkan Nationality and Identity*, London: Tauris Academic Studies.
Fryer, C. E. J. (1997), *The Destruction of Serbia in 1915*, New York: Colombia University Press.
Gallant, T. W. (2002), *Experiencing Dominion: Culture, Identity, and Power in the British Mediterranean*, Notre Dame, IN: University of Notre Dame Press.
Gere, C. (2009), *Knossos and the Prophets of Modernism*, Chicago, IL: University of Chicago Press.
Goldsworthy, V. (1998), *Inventing Ruritania: The Imperialism of the Imagination*, New Haven, CT: Yale University Press.
Hadžiselimović, O. (2001), *At the Gates of the East: British Travel Writers on Bosnia and Herzegovina from the 16th to the 20th Centuries*, New York: Columbia University Press.
Hall, D. (2015), *Worktown: The Astonishing Story of the Project that launched Mass Observation*, London: Weidenfeld & Nicolson.
Hall, R. C. (2000), *The Balkan Wars 1912-1913: Prelude to the First World War*, London: Routledge.
Hammond, A. (2007), *The Debated Lands: British and American Representations of the Balkans*, Cardiff: University of Cardiff Press.
Hammond, A. (2010), *British Literature and the Balkans: Themes and Contexts*, Amsterdam: Rodopi Press.
Hanak, H. (1962), *Great Britain and Austria-Hungary during the First World War*, London: Oxford University Press.
Hanssen, L. (2006), *Security as Practice: Discourse Analysis and the Bosnian War*, Abingdon: Routledge.
Harvie, C. (1993), *No Gods and Precious Few Heroes: Scotland since 1914*, Edinburgh: Edinburgh University Press.
Hauser, G. A. (1999), *Vernacular Voices: The Rhetoric of Publics and Public Spheres*, Columbia, SC: The University of South Carolina Press.
Herzfeld, M. (1987), *Anthropology through the Looking-Glass: Critical Ethnology in the Margins of Europe*, Cambridge: Cambridge University Press.
Hinton, J. (2013), *The Mass Observers: A History, 1937-1949*, Oxford: Oxford University Press.
Hoade, E. (1970 [1952]), *Western Pilgrims (1322-1392)*, Jerusalem: Fransciscan Printing Press.
Howkins, A. (2003), *The Death of Rural England: A Social History of the Countryside since 1900*, London: Routledge.
Hughes, M. (1997), *Inside the Enigma: British Officials in Russia, 1900-1939*, London: Hambledon Press.
Hyman, A. (1972), *The Rise and Fall of Horatio Bottomley: The Biography of a Swindler*, London: Cassell.
Jeffery, K. (2015), *1916: A Global History*, London: Bloomsbury.
Jezernik, B. (2004), *Wild Europe: The Balkans in the Gaze of Western Travellers*, London: Saqi.
Julian, P. (1974), *The Triumph of Art Nouveau: Paris Exhibition, 1900*, London: Phaidon Press.
Karadžić, V. S. and G. Dobrašinović eds, (1975 [1837]), *Crna Gora i Crnogorci*, Cetinje: Obod.
Keisinger, F. (2008), *Unzivilisierte Kriege im zivilisierten Europa? Die Balkankriege und die öffentliche Meinung in Deutschland, England und Irland 1876-1913*, Paderborn: Ferdinand Schöningh.

Kelly, G. (1992), *Revolutionary Feminism: The Mind and Career of Mary Wollstonecraft*, Basingstoke: MacMillan.
Kidd, C. (1993), *Subverting Scotland's Past; Scottish Whig Historians and the Creation of Anglo-British Identity, 1689-c.1830*, Cambridge: Cambridge University Press.
King, A. (1998), *Memorials of the Great War in Britain: The Symbolism and Politics of Remembrance*, Oxford: Berg.
Kostova, L. (1997), *Tales of the Periphery: The Balkans in Nineteenth-Century British Writing*, Veliko Tŭrnovo: Universitetsko izd-vo Sv. sv. Kiril i Metodii.
Krippner, M. (1980), *The Quality of Mercy: Women at War in Serbia 1915-18*, London: David and Charles.
Kucklick, H. (1991), *The Savage Within: The Social History of British Anthropology, 1885-1945*, Cambridge: Cambridge University Press.
Lampe, J. R. and M. R. Jackson (1982), *Balkan Economic History, 1550-1950: From Imperial Borderlands to Developing Nations*, Bloomington, IN: Indiana University Press.
Lampe, J. R. (2000), *Yugoslavia as History: Twice there was a Country*, Cambridge: Cambridge University Press.
Laycock, J. (2009), *Imagining Armenia: Orientalism, Ambiguity and Intervention*, Manchester: Manchester University Press.
Leeson, D. M. (2010), *The Black and Tans: British Police Auxiliaries in the Irish War of Independence, 1920-1921*, Oxford: Oxford University Press.
Leneman, L. (1994), *In the Service of Life: The Story of Elsie Inglis and the Scottish Women's Hospital*, Edinburgh: Mercant Press.
Leneman, L. (1998), *Elsie Inglis: Founder of Battlefield Hospitals run Entirely by Women*, Edinburgh: NMS Publishing.
Lojkó, M. (2006), *Meddling in Middle Europe: Britain and the 'Lands Between', 1919-1925*, Budapest: Central European University Press.
MacKay, M. (2010), *Modernism and World War II*, Cambridge: Cambridge University Press.
Magill, Allen. (1987), 'The Reception of Foucault by Historians', *Journal of the History of Ideas*, 48 (1): 117-41.
Markovich, S. G. (2000), *British Perceptions of Serbia and the Balkans, 1903-1906*, Paris: Dialogue.
Marx, K. and F. Engels (2010), *Collected Works, Vol. 8 1848-9*, London: Lawrence and Wishart.
Mathias, P. (1969), *The First Industrial Nation: An Economic History of Britain, 1700-1914*, London: Methuen.
McCourt, J. (2000), *The Years of Bloom: James Joyce in Trieste 1904-1920*, Madison: University of Wisconsin Press.
Medlicott, W. N. (1969), *Britain and Germany: The Search for Agreement, 1930-1937*, London: Athlone Press.
Meštrović, S. G. (1991), *The Coming Fin de Siècle: An Application of Durkheim's Sociology to Modernity and Postmodernism*, London: Routledge.
Michail, E. (2011), *The British and the Balkans: Forming Images of Foreign Lands, 1900-1950*, London: Continuum.
Mikić, Ž. (Dj.) (2007), *Ever Yours Sincerely: The Life and Work of Dr Katherine S. MacPhail*, trans. Muriel Heppell, Cambridge: Perfect Publishers.
Mills, R. (2018), *The Politics of Football in Yugoslavia: Sport, Nationalism and the State*, London: I.B. Tauris.

Mills, S. (1991), *Discourse of Difference: An Analysis of Women's Travel Writing and Colonialism*, London: Routledge.
Morrison, K. (2008), *Montenegro: A Modern History*, London: I.B. Tauris.
Morris, A. J. A. (1984), *The Scaremongers: The Advocacy of War and Rearmament 1896–1914*, London: Routledge & Kegan Paul.
Mulley, C. (2009), *The Woman Who Saved the Children: A Biography of Eglantyne Jebb Founder of Save the Children*, Oxford: Oneworld Publications.
de Nie, M. (2004), *The Eternal Paddy: Irish Identity and the British Press, 1789–1882*, Madison: The University of Wisconsin Press.
Norris, D. A. (1999), *In the Wake of the Balkan Myth: Questions of Identity and Modernity*, Basingstoke: Macmillan.
Overy, R. (2009), *The Morbid Age: Britain between the Wars*, London: Allen Lane.
Palairet, M. (1997), *The Balkan Economies c.1800–1914: Evolution without Development*, Cambridge: Cambridge University Press.
Palmer, A. (1965), *The Gardeners of Salonika*, London: Andre Deutsch.
Parmar, I. (2004), *Think Tanks and Power in Foreign Policy: A Comparative Study of the Role and Influence of the Council on Foreign Relations and the Royal Institute of International Affairs, 1939–1945*, Basingstoke: Palgrave Macmillan.
Parry, J. (2006), *The Politics of Patriotism: English Liberalism, National Identity and Europe, 1830–1886*, Cambridge: Cambridge University Press.
Pavlović, S. (2008), *Balkan Anschluss: The Annexation of Montenegro and the Creation of the Common South Slavic State*, West Lafayette, IN: Purdue University Press.
Pavlowitch, S. K. (1961), *Anglo-Russian Rivalry in Serbia, 1837–1839: The Mission of Colonel Hodges*, Paris: Mouton & Co.
Pennell, C. (2012), *A Kingdom United: Popular Responses to the Outbreak of the First World in Britain and Ireland*, Oxford: Oxford University Press.
Pick, D. (1989), *Faces of Degeneration: A European Disorder, c.1848–c.1918*, Cambridge: Cambridge University Press.
Powell, D. (1996), *The Edwardian Crisis: Britain, 1901–1914*, Basingstoke: Palgrave.
Priestley, J. B. (1970), *The Edwardians*, London: Heinemann.
Prior, C. (2013), *Edwardian England and the Idea of Racial Decline: An Empire's Future*, Basingstoke: Palgrave MacMillan.
Radlovic, I. M. (1948), *Tito's Republic*, London: Coldharbour Press.
Rayner, L. (1957), *Woman in a Village: An Englishwoman's Experiences of Life in Yugoslavia under German Occupation*, London: William Heinemann.
Readman, P. (2008), *Land and Nation in England: Patriotism, National Identity, and the Politics of Land, 1880–1914*, Woodbridge: The Boydell Press.
Ritchie, S. (2004), *Our Man in Yugoslavia: The Story of a Secret Service Operative*, London: Routledge.
Rodogno, D. (2012), *Against Massacre: Humanitarian Interventions in the Ottoman Empire, 1815–1914*, Princeton, NJ: Princeton University Press.
Rubinstein, W. D. (2001 [1994]), *Capitalism, Culture, & Decline in Britain, 1750–1990*, London: Routledge.
Said, E. W. (2003 [1978]), *Orientalism*, London: Penguin Books.
Scully, R. (2012), *British Images of Germany: Admiration, Antagonism & Ambivalence 1860–1914*, Basingstoke: Palgrave Macmillan.
Seaman, L. C. B. (1973), *Victorian England: Aspects of English and Imperial History, 1837–1901*, London: Methuen.
Searle, G. R. (2004), *A New England? Peace and War 1886–1918*, Oxford: Clarendon Press.

Seton-Watson, H. and C. Seton-Watson (1981), *The Making of a New Europe: R. W. Seton-Watson and the Last Years of Austria-Hungary*, London: Methuen.
Soloway, R. A. (1990), *Demography and Degeneration: Eugenics and the Declining Birthrate in Twentieth-Century Britain*, Chapel Hill: University of North Carolina Press.
Smith, A. K. (2016), *British Women on the Eastern Front: War Writing and Experience in Serbia and Russia, 1914–20*, Manchester: Manchester University Press.
Sparks, M. (2014), *The Development of Austro-Hungarian Sarajevo, 1878–1918, An Urban History*, London: Bloomsbury Academic.
Stanković, Đ. (2009), *Srbija i stvaranje Jugoslavije*, Belgrade: Službeni glasnik.
Stavrianos, L. S. (2000), *The Balkans since 1453*, London: Hurst.
Steiner, Z. S. (1969), *The Foreign Office and Foreign Policy, 1898–1914*, Cambridge: Cambridge: University Press.
Steiner, Z. S. and Neilson, K. (2003), *Britain and the Origins of the First World War*, 2nd edn, Basingstoke: Palgrave MacMillan.
Stevenson, J. (1984), *British Society 1914-45*, Harmondsworth: Penguin.
Sugar, P. F. (1963), *The Industrialization of Bosnia-Hercegovina, 1878–1918*, Seattle, WA: University of Washington Press.
Suonpää, M. P. (2008), *British Perceptions of the Balkan Slavs: Professional and Popular Categorizations before 1914*, PhD Thesis, University of Hull.
Symons, J. (1955), *Horatio Bottomley: A Biography*, London: The Cresset Press.
Stefanidis, I. (2012), *Substitute for Power: Wartime British Propaganda in the Balkans, 1939–1944*, Farnham: Ashgate.
Thompson, J. B. (2007 [1990]), *Ideology and Modern Culture*, Cambridge: Polity Press.
Thompson, J. (2013), *British Political Culture and the Idea of 'Public Opinion', 1867–1914*, Cambridge: Cambridge University Press.
Todorova, M. (1997), *Imagining the Balkans*, Oxford: Oxford University Press.
Toševa, S. (2007), *Srbija i Britanija: kulturni dordiri početkom xx veka*, Belgrade: SANU.
Vesić, Z., Popović, B., Korica, M. and Stošić, Z. (2009), *Srpski vojni sanitet*, Belgrade: Ministarstvo Odbrane.
Wakefield, A. and Moody, S. (2004), *Under the Devil's Eye: Britain's Forgotten Army at Salonika, 1915–1918*, Stroud: Sutton Publishing.
Wallace, W. (1977), *The Foreign Policy Process in Britain*, London: George Allen & Unwin.
Ward, P. (2004), *Britishness since 1870*, London: Routledge.
Ware, V. (2015 [1992]), *Beyond the Pale: White Women, Racism, and History*, London: Verso.
Weller, T. (2009), *The Victorians and Information: A Social and Cultural History*, Saarbrücken: Verlag Dr. Mülle.
Wheelwright, J. (1989), *Amazons and Military Maids: Women who dressed as Men in Pursuit of Life, Liberty and Happiness*, London: Pandora.
White, E. L. (1955 [1936]), *The Wheel Spins*, Harmondsworth: Penguin Book.
Wild-Bićanić, S. (2006), *British Travellers in Dalmatia 1757–1935*, Zagreb: Zaprešić Fraktura.
Wilson, F. M. (1944), *In the Margins of Chaos: Recollections of Relief Work in and Between Three Wars*, London: John Murray.
Wolff, L. (1994), *Inventing Eastern Europe: The Map of Civilization on the Mind of Enlightenment*, Stanford, CA: Stanford University Press.
Wolff, L. (2001), *Venice and the Slavs: The Discovery of Dalmatia in the Age of Enlightenment*, Stanford, CA: Stanford University Press.
Yosmaoğlu, İ. (2014), *Blood Ties: Religion, Violence and the Politics of Nationhood in Ottoman Macedonia, 1878–1908*, Ithaca, NY: Cornell University Press.

Journal Articles and Book Chapters

Allcock, J. B. (1989), 'The Historical Development of Tourism in Yugoslavia to 1945', in J. B. Allcock and Joan Couniham (eds), *Two Studies in the History of Tourism in Yugoslavia*, 1–25, Bradford: University of Bradford.

Allcock, J. B. (2000 [1991]), 'Constructing the Balkans', in J. B. Allcock and A. Young (eds), *Black Lambs and Grey Falcons: Women Travellers in the Balkans*, 217–40, New York: Berghahn Books.

Bailey, C. (2006), 'Rural Industries and the Image of the Countryside', in P. Brassley, J. Burchardt and L. Thompson (eds), *The English Countryside Between the Wars: Regeneration or Decline?*, 132–49, Woodbridge: The Boydell Press.

Bakić, D. (2013), "Must Will Peace": The British Brokering of "Central European" and "Balkan Locarno", 1925–9', *Journal of Contemporary History*, 48 (1): 24–56.

Bet-El, I. R. (2002), 'Unimagined Communities: The Power of Memory and the Conflict in the Former Yugoslavia', in J. -W. Müller (ed.), *Memory and Power in Post-War Europe: Studies in the Presence of the Past*, 206–22, Cambridge: Cambridge University Press.

Béliard, Y. (2014), 'Introduction: Revisiting the Great Labour Unrest, 1911–1914', *Labour History Review*, 79 (1): 1–17.

Biondich, M. (2016), 'The Balkan Wars: Violence and Nation-Building in the Balkans', *Journal of Genocide Research*, 18 (4): 389–404.

Bracewell, W. (1988), 'Opinion-Makers: The Balkans in Popular Literature', in Petar Kačavenda (ed.), *Jugoslovensko-britanski odnosi/ British Yugoslav Relations, 1856–1876*, 91–117, Belgrade: Institut za savremenu istoriju.

Bracewell, W. (2009), 'New Men, Old Europe: Being a Man in Balkan Travel Writing', in W. Bracewell and A. Drace-Francis (eds), *Balkan Departures: Travel Writing from Southeastern Europe*, 137–60, New York: Berghahn Books.

Brassley, P., J. Burchardt and L. Thompson (2006), 'Conclusion', in P. Brassley, J. Burchardt and L. Thompson (eds), *The English Countryside Between the Wars: Regeneration or Decline?*, 235–9, Woodbridge: The Boydell Press.

Bridge, R. F. (2002), 'The British Foreign Office and National Questions in the Dual Monarchy', in R. Evans, D. Kováč and E. Ivaničková (eds), *Great Britain and Central Europe 1867-1914*, 45–60, Bratislava: VEDA.

Broks, P. (1993), 'Science, Media and Culture: British Magazines, 1890–1914', *Public Understanding of Science*, 2 (2): 123–39.

Buchanan, T. (1993), 'A Far Away Country of Which we Know Nothing'? Perceptions of Spain and Its Civil War in Britain, 1931–1939', *Twentieth Century British History*, 4 (3): 1–24.

Burcea, H. (2019), '"Times of Unbelief": Staging the Rise and Fall of British Travel Writing during the Interwar Period', *Études britanniques contemporaines* 56, https://journals.openedition.org/ebc/6366

Carmichael, C. (2002), 'A People Exists and that People has Its Language', in S. Barbour and C. Carmichael (eds), *Language and Nationalism in Europe*, 221–39, Oxford: Oxford University Press.

Chew, W. L. (III.) (2006), 'What's in a National Stereotype? An Introduction to Imagology at the Threshold of the 21st Century', *Language and Intercultural Communication*, 6 (3–4): 179–87.

Church, R. (1987), 'Edwardian Labour Unrest and Coalfield Militancy', *The Historical Journal*, 30 (4): 841–57.

Clarke, R. and M. Anteric (2009), '(British) Anthropological Tourism in Slovenia 1937–2007', *Anthropological Notebooks - Društvo antropologov Slovenije*, 15 (1): 5–25.

Clarke, R. and M. Anteric (2011), 'Fanny Copeland and the Geographical Imagination', *Scottish Geographical Journal*, 127 (3): 163–92.

Clegg, E. (2002), 'Meštrović, England and the Great War', *The Burlington Magazine*, 144 (1197): 740–51.

Dilks, D. N. (1981), 'Public Opinion and Foreign Policy: Great Britain', *Actes du Colloque de Rome*, 54 (2): 57–79.

Dorson, R. M. (1961), 'Folklore Studies in England', *Journal of American Folklore*, 74 (294): 302–12.

Douglas, R. (1976), 'Britain and the Armenian Question, 1894–7', *The Historical Journal*, 19 (1): 113–33.

Dubisch, J. (1998), 'Europe through the Back Door: Doing Anthropology in Greece', in S. Parman (ed.), *Europe in the Anthropological Imagination*, 34–45, Upper Saddle River, NJ: Pearson Education.

Duraković, I. (2014), 'Serbia as a Health Threat to Europe: The Wartime Typhus Epidemic, 1914–1915', in J. Bürgschwentner, M. Egger and G. Barth-Scalmani (eds), *Other Fronts, Other Wars?: First World War Studies on the Eve of the Centennial*, Leiden and Boston: Brill.

Duijizings, G. (2003), 'Changes in the Social Roles of Western Anthropologists and Indigenous Ethnologists', *Xenopoliana (Iași)*, 11 (1–2): 9–13.

Dutton, D. J. (1978), 'The Calais Conference of December 1915', *The Historical Journal*, 21: 143–56.

Emmet, B. Ford (Jr.) (1959), 'Montenegro in the Eyes of the English Traveller, 1840–1914', *Südost-Forschungen: Internationale Zeitschrift für Geschichte, Kultur und Landeskunde Südosteuropas*, 18: 350–80.

Finney, P. (2003), 'Raising Frankenstein: Great Britain, "Balkanism" and the Search for a Balkanlocarno in the 1920s', *European History Quarterly*, 33 (3): 317–42.

Fleming, K. E. (2000), 'Orientalism, the Balkans, and Balkan Historiography', *The American Historical Review*, 105 (4): 1232–3.

Foley, M. (2007), 'James David Bourchier: An Irish Journalist in the Balkans', *Irish Communication Review*, 10: 57–63.

Foster, S. (2013), 'British Medical Volunteers and the Balkan Front, 1914–1918: The Case of Dr Katherine Stuart MacPhail', *University of Sussex Journal of Contemporary History*, 14 (1): 4–16.

Foster, S. (2017), 'The Balkan Wars and "the Macedonian Question" through the Eyes of British Nationals', in N. Garrett (ed.), *Macedonia 2013: 100 Years after the Treaty of Bucharest*, 95–108, Ottawa: Legas.

Foster, S. (2018), 'Reviving the Völkerabfälle: The South Slavonic Left, Balkan Federalism and the Creation of the First Yugoslavia', *Socialist History*, 25 (1): 47–68.

Gamble, A. (2016), 'The Conservatives and the Union: The "New English Toryism" and the Origins of Anglo-Britishness', *Political Studies Review*, 14 (3): 359–67.

Gould, J. (1987), 'Women's Military Service in First World War Britain', in M. R. Higonnet (ed.), *Behind the Lines: Gender and the Two World Wars*, 114–25, New Haven, CT: Yale University Press.

Gounaris, B. C. (2005), 'Preachers of God and Martyrs of the Nation: The Politics of murder in Ottoman Macedonia in the early 20th Century', *Balkanologie*, 9 (1–2): 31–43.

Halpern, J. M. and E. A. Hammel (1969), 'Observations on the Intellectual History of Ethnology and other Social Sciences in Yugoslavia', *Comparative Studies in Society and History*, 11 (1): 17-26.

Hammond, A. (1999), 'The Escape from Decadence: British Travel Literature on the Balkans 1900-45', in Michael St. John (ed.), *Romancing Decay: Ideas of Decadence in European Culture*, 141-53, Farnham: Ashgate.

Hilliard, C. (2014), 'Popular Reading and Social Investigation in Britain, 1850-1940', *The Historical Journal*, 57 (1): 247-71.

Hodgson, J. (2000 [1991]), 'Edith Durham: Traveller and Publicist', in J. B. Allcock and A. Young (eds), *Black Lambs and Grey Falcons: Women Travellers in the Balkans*, 9-31, New York: Berghahn Books.

Howkins, A. (2006), 'Death and Rebirth? English Rural Society, 1920-1940', in P. Brassley, J. Burchardt and L. Thompson (eds), in *The English Countryside Between the Wars: Regeneration or Decline?*, 10-25, Woodbridge: The Boydell Press.

Howkins, A. (2014), 'The Discovery of Rural England', in R. Colls and P. Dodd (eds), *Englishness: Culture and Politics, 1880-1920*, 2nd edn, 85-112, London: Bloomsbury.

Hoyt, T. D. (2018), 'The Easter Rising and the Changing Character of Irregular Warfare', in E. D. Lago, R. Healy and G. Barry (eds), *1916 in Global Context: An Anti-Imperial Moment*, 18-28, London: Routledge.

Jelavich, B. (1955), 'The Abuses of Ottoman Administration in the Slavonic Provinces', *The Slavonic and East European Review*, 33 (81): 396-413.

Johnson, P. W. and J. O. Baylen (1994), 'Dillon, Dr. Emile Joseph, 1854-1933', in J. L. Wieczynski and G. V. Rhyne (eds), *The Modern Encyclopaedia of Russian and Soviet History*, Vol. 9, 106, Gulf Breeze, FL: Academic International Press.

Kardjilov, P. (2012), '"Cinematograms" of a Balkan Conflict: Charles Rider Noble in Bulgaria, 1903-1904', *Film History*, 24 (3): 302-23.

Kaser, K. (1998), 'Anthropology and the Balkanization of the Balkans: Jovan Cvijić and Dinko Tomašić', *Ethnologia Balkanica*, 2 (1): 89-99.

Kay, A. (2000 [1991]), 'Louise Rayner: An English Women's Experiences in Wartime Yugoslavia', in J. B. Allcock and A. Young (eds), *Black Lambs and Grey Falcons*, 155-65, New York: Berghahn Books.

Knezhevich, S. (1992), 'Pochasni konzul Srbiye Arnold Myuir Vilson', *Istoriyski chasopis*, 39: 165-80.

Krippner, M. (2000 [1991]), 'The Work of British Medical Women in Serbia during and after the First World', in J. B. Allcock and A. Young (eds), *Black Lambs and Grey Falcons: Women Travellers in the Balkans*, 71-89, New York: Berghahn Books.

Láslo, P. (2002), 'The European Balance of Power and R.W. Seton-Watson's Changing Views on the National Question of the Habsburg Monarchy', in R. Evans, D. Kováč and E. Ivaničková (eds), *Great Britain and Central Europe 1867-1914*, 87-101, Bratislava: VEDA.

Leerssen, J. (2007), 'Imagology: History and Method', in Manfeld Beller and J. Leerssen (eds), *Imagology: The Cultural Construction and Literary Representation of National Characters, A Critical Survey*, 17-32, Amsterdam: Rodopi Press.

Liebich A. (2012), 'The Antisemitism of Henry Wickham Steed', *Patterns of Prejudice*, 46 (2): 180-208.

Mandler, P. (1997), 'Against "Englishness": English Culture and the Limits to Rural Nostalgia, 1850-1940', *Transactions of the Royal Historical Society*, 7: 155-75.

Mazower, M. (2002), 'Travellers and the Oriental City, c.1840-1920', *Transactions of the Royal Historical Society*, 12: 59-111.

McCormick, R. B. (2004), 'Noel Buxton, The Balkan Committee and Reform in Macedonia, 1903-1914', in N. C. Pappas (ed.), *Antiquity and Modernity: A Celebration of European History and Heritage in the Olympic Year 2004*, 151-66, Athens: Institute for Education and Research.

McKibbin, R. (2007), 'Great Britain', in R. Gerwarth (ed.), *Twisted Paths: Europe 1914-1945*, 33-59, Oxford: Oxford University Press.

Mencej, M. (2005), 'Witchcraft in Eastern Slovenia and Western Macedonia – A Comparative Analysis', in Zmago Šmitek and Aneta Svetieva (eds), *Post-Yugoslav Lifeworlds: Between Tradition and Modernity*, 37-67, Ljubljana: Univerza v Ljubljani.

Michail, E. (2012), 'Western Attitudes to War in the Balkans and the Shifting Meaning of Violence 1912-91', *The Journal of Contemporary History*, 47 (2): 219-39.

Mladinić, N. M. (2007), 'Prilog proučavanju djelovanja Ivana Meštrovića u Jugoslavenskom odboru', *Revue d'histoire contemporaine*, 39: 133-56.

Mollan, S. and R. Michie. (2012), 'The City of London as an International Commercial and Financial Center since 1900', *Enterprise and Society*, 13 (3): 538-87.

Moynahan, J. (1972), 'Pastoralism as Culture and Counter-Culture in English Fiction, 1800-1928: From a View to a Death', *Novel: A Forum on Fiction*, 6 (1): 20-35.

Okey, R. (2002), 'British Impressions of the Serb-Croat Speaking Lands of the Habsburg Monarchy – Reports to the Foreign Office 1867-1908', in R. Evans, D. Kováč and E. Ivaničková (eds), *Great Britain and Central Europe 1867-1914*, 61-76, Brastislava: VEDA.

Patterson, P. H. (2010), 'Yugoslavia as It Once Was: What Tourism and Leisure Meant for the History of the Socialist Federation', in H. Grandits and K. Taylor (eds), *Yugoslavia's Sunny Side*, 367-402, Budapest: Central European University.

Pavlowitch, K. S. (2003), 'The First World War and the Unification of Yugoslavia', in Dejan Djokić (ed.), *Yugoslavism: Histories of a Failed Idea 1918-1992*, 27-41, Madison: University of Wisconsin Press.

Pejitć, R. (2013), 'Herbert Vivian: A Late Nineteenth-Century British Traveller in Serbia', *Balcanica*, 44: 255-84.

Perkins, J. (2015), 'The Congo of Europe: The Balkans and Empire in Early Twentieth-Century British Political Culture', *The Historical Journal*, 58 (2): 565-87.

Perkins, J. (2017), 'Peasants and Politics: Re-thinking the British Imaginative Geography of the Balkans at the Time of the First World War', *European History Quarterly*, 47 (1): 55-77.

Petkov, K. (1997), 'England and the Balkan Slavs 1354-1583: An Outline of a Late Medieval and Renaissance Image', *The Slavonic and East European Review*, 76 (1): 86-117.

Pisarri, M. (2013), 'Bulgarian Crimes against Civilians in Occupied Serbia during the First World War', *Balcanica*, 44: 357-90.

Potkonjak, S. (2013), 'In Women's Arms: Croatian Ethnography between 1945 and 1990', in Aleksandar Bošković and Chris Hann (eds), *The Anthropological Field on the Margins of Europe, 1945-1991*, 237-58, Zürich: Lit Verlag.

Readman P. (2010), 'The Edwardian Land Question', in Matthew Cragoe and P. Readman (eds), *The Land Question in Britain, 1750-1950*, 181-200, Basingstoke: Palgrave Macmillan.

Robinson, C. (2011), 'Yugoslavism in the Early Twentieth Century: The Politics of the Yugoslav Committee', in Dejan Djokić and James Ker-Lindsay (eds), *New Perspectives on Yugoslavia: Key Issues and Controversies*, 10-26, Abingdon: Routledge.

Rusinow, D. (2003), 'The Yugoslav Idea before Yugoslavia', in D. Djokić (eds), *Yugoslavism: Histories of a Failed Idea 1918-1992*, 11-26, Madison: University of Wisconsin Press.

Scianna, B. M. (2012), 'Reporting Atrocities: Archibald Reiss in Serbia, 1914–1918', *The Journal of Slavic Military Studies*, 25 (4): 596–617.
Sekeruš, P. (2007), 'Serbs', in Manfeld Beller and Joep Leerssen (eds), *Imagology: The Cultural Construction and Literary Representation of National Characters, A Critical Survey*, 234–7, Amsterdam: Rodopi Press.
Sezgin, P. J. D. (2013), 'Between Cross and Crescent: British Public Opinion towards the Ottoman Empire in Resolving the Balkan Wars, 1912–1913', in M. H. Yavuz and I. Blumi (eds), *War and Nationalism: The Balkan Wars, 1912–1913, and their Sociopolitical Implications*, 423–73, Salt Lake City: The University of Utah Press.
Skinner, S. (2013), 'Religion', in David Craig and James Thompson (eds), *Languages of Politics in Nineteenth-Century Britain*, 93–117, Basingstoke: Palgrave Macmillan.
Sluga, G. (2002), 'Narrating Difference and Defining the Nation in Late Nineteenth and Early Twentieth Century "Western" Europe', *European Review of History: Revue européenne d'histoire*, 9 (2): 183–97.
Soloway, R. (1982), 'Counting the Degenerates: The Statistics of Race Deterioration in Edwardian England', *Journal of Contemporary History*, 17 (1): 137–64.
Steele, D. (2014), 'Three British Prime Ministers and the Survival of the Ottoman Empire, 1855–1902', *Middle Eastern Studies*, 50 (1): 43–60.
Steward, J. (2008), '"The Balkans in London": Political Culture and the Cultural Politics of Exhibitions at Earl's Court, 1906–1908', *Balkan Studies (Études Balkaniques)*, 44 (4): 64–89.
Stokes, G. (1980), 'The Role of the Yugoslav Committee in the Formation of Yugoslavia', in D. Djordjević (eds), *The Creation of Yugoslavia 1914–1918*, 51–71, Santa Barbara, CA: Clio Books.
Šepić, D. (1968), 'The Question of Yugoslav Union in 1918', *The Journal of Contemporary History*, 3 (4): 29–43.
Thompson, F. M. L. (2010), 'The Strange Death of the English Land Question', in M. Cragoe and P. Readman (eds), *The Land Question in Britain, 1750–1950*, 257–70, Basingstoke: Palgrave Macmillan.
Thorpe, A. (2000), 'The Membership of the Communist Party of Great Britain', *The Historical Journal*, 43 (3): 777–800.
Vogel, R. (1990), 'Noel Buxton: The "Trouble-Maker" and His Papers', *Fontanus*, 3: 131–50.
Vittorelli, N. (2002), 'An "Other" of One's Own': Pre-WW1 South Slavic Academic Discourses on the *Zadruga*', *Spaces of Identity*, 2 (3): 27–43.
Walton, J. K. (2010), 'Preface: Some Contexts for Yugoslav Tourism History', in H. Grandits and K. Taylor (eds), *Yugoslavia's Sunny Side: A History of Tourism in Socialism (1950s–1980s)*, ix–xxii, Budapest: Central European University Press.
Walton, J. K. (2011), 'The Origins of the Modern Package Tour?: British Motor-Coach Tours in Europe, 1930–70', *The Journal of Transport History*, 32 (2): 145–63.
Watt, D. C. (1971), 'The British Reactions to the Assassination at Sarajevo', *European Studies Review*, 1 (3): 233–47.
Webber, G. C. (1984), 'Patterns of Membership and Support for the British Union of Fascists', *Journal of Contemporary History*, 19 (4): 575–606.
Wheelright, J. (2000 [1991]), 'Captain Flora Sandes: A Case Study in the Social Construction of Gender in a Serbian Context', in J. B. Allcock and A. Young (eds), *Black Lambs and Grey Falcons: Women Travellers in the Balkans*, 90–8, New York: Berghahn Books.
Wilson, N. (2016), 'British Publishers and Colonial Editions', in N. Wilson (ed.), *The Book World: Selling and Distributing British Literature, 1900–1940*, 15–30, Leiden: Brill.

Winter, J. M. (1996), 'British National Identity and the First World War', in S. J. D. Green and R. C. Whiting (eds), *The Boundaries of the State in Modern Britain*, 261–77, Cambridge: Cambridge University Press.

Wolff, L. (2014), 'The Western Representation of Eastern Europe on the Eve of World War I: Mediated Encounters and Intellectual Expertise in Dalmatia, Albania and Macedonia', *The Journal of Modern History*, 86 (2): 381–407.

Živančević-Sekeruš, I. (2007), 'Balkans', in Manfeld Beller and Joep Leerssen (eds), *Imagology: The Cultural Construction and Literary Representation of National Characters, A Critical Survey*, 103–8, Amsterdam: Rodopi Press.

Index

Abraham, John   80, 97
Adam, Robert   15, 16
Adriatic, *see also* Dalmatia
   tourism   14, 38, 115, 129
agriculture, *see also* rural depopulation
   and identity   14
   in Britain   23, 32, 35
Albania   49, 69, 72, 77, 148
Aleksandar I, King of Serbia   41
Aleksandar I, King of Yugoslavia
   Crown Prince of Serbia   91, 113
   Royal Dictatorship   142, 143
Anderson, Benedict   2, 3, 6
Anglo-American-Yugoslav Club   124
Anglo-Britishness
   and foreign cultures   17, 27
   'Anglo-British paradigm'   120–5, 155
   political concept   115
anthropology
   and colonialism   51
   and race   30
   professionalization   27
atrocities   13, 17, 49, 50, 60, 68, 69, 104–6, 144, 178 n.30
Atherton, Terence   145, 148, *see also South Slav Herald*
Austria-Hungary, *see also* Henry Wickham Steed; Robert William Seton-Watson
   in propaganda   56, 102
   invasion of Serbia   106
Axis Powers   1

Balkan Committee (BC)   48, 50, 53, 55, 60, 70, 124
Balkanism   3, 4, 119, 155
   'Balkanist thesis'   4, 5, 154
Balkan League   67–9, 73
Balkan Relief Fund (BRF)
Balkan Wars (1912–1913)   1, 8, 29, 49, 61, 63, 67–72
Belgrade   33, 37, 39, 47, 54, 62, 68, 74, 76, 82, 86, 99, 123, 134–7, 142, 145, 149
   growth of   36

Belgium
   First World War   103
   tourism   128
Berry, Mary Dickinson   62
Berry, John   62
Bićanić, Rudolf   149, 150
Blount, Henry   15
Bosnia-Herzegovina
   Annexation Crisis (1908)   55, 73
   occupation by Austria-Hungary (1878)   21, 144
   Ottoman culture   17, 18
Bottomley, Horatio William   74, 75, *see also John Bull*
Bourchier, James David   21, 42, 46, 48, 49, 114, 123, 172 n.39
Brailsford, Henry Noel   43, 46, 48, 49, 51, 53, 58, 59, 69, 73, 100, 114, 123, 171 n.15
British identity   1, 2, 6, 67, 154, 155
British public sphere   1, 8, 37, 47, 119
   'rhetorical public sphere'   7
British Salonika Force, (BSF)   84–7, 89, 92, 93, 96, 98–100, 131, 185 n.86
Browne, Edward   161 n.24
Bulgaria
   Balkan Wars   1, 8, 29, 49, 53, 61, 63, 67–73, 76–9, 84, 86, 89, 97, 102, 144
   First World War   79, 102, 154
   Great Eastern Crisis   17, 67
   public perceptions   81, 86
Bugojno   53
Burr, Malcolm   145
Buxton, Noel   40, 48–50, 53, 54, 114, 123, 124

Carnegie Endowment for International Peace   69
   report on the Balkan Wars (1914)   73
Central Powers   75, 77, 78, 93, 103, 107, 111, 146
'Celtic Fringe'   6

Cetinje 39, 44, 47, 53, 58, 161 n.33, 177 n.141
Chatham House 124
Chesterton, Gilbert Keith 112
Chirol, Ignatius Valentine 50, 75
Christianity
    Anglicanism 22, 23, 61, 108
    Catholicism 36, 42, 44, 112, 120, 133, 138
    Eastern Orthodoxy 22, 41
    Nonconformism 23, 48
    rural folk traditions 34, 109, 133
Christmas Uprising (1919) 141
Churchill, Winston 28, 146, 151
class, *see also* British identity
    aristocracy/upper class 7, 16, 26, 31, 50, 56, 71, 96, 99, 128
    middle class 6, 9, 13, 17, 20, 21, 24, 25, 29, 31, 32, 41, 42, 47, 48, 128, 129, 136, 138, 149
    working class 8, 18, 23, 27, 28, 31, 34, 35, 77, 121, 124, 127
Conservative-Liberal Unionist coalition 28
consumerism 9, 126, 127, 152, 155
Copeland, Fanny Susan
    Italianization 145
    Slovenia 134, 135, 148
Croatia
    Culture 30
    in Yugoslavia 130
Cvijić, Jovan 2, 30, 31, 133, 135

Dalmatia 15, 16, 19, 29, 33, 38, 41, 44, 47, 56, 57, 107, 128, 129, 131, 136, 142, 148
    tourism 33, 40, 128
Davies, Rhys John 145
Dearmer, Jessie Mabel Pritchard 74, 96, 180 n.56
Devine, Alexander 113, 114, 123, 144
Dillon, Emile Joseph 46, 48, 55, 68, 69, 170 n.4
Dolling, Mary Ann (Ann Bridge)
Dorson, Richard Mercer 131
Dubrovnik 17, 55, 130, 171 n.8
    tourism 40
Durham, Mary Edith 7, 35, 37, 39, 40, 42, 43, 45–50, 57–9, 61, 62, 70–3, 114, 123, 125, 132, 133, 141, 143, 145, 155
    Balkan Wars 71

Edward VIII, King of the United Kingdom 125, 128
Ehrlich, Vera Stein 2, 148, 183 n.51
Enemy Propaganda Department (Crewe House) 114
Engels, Friedrich 13
England, *see also* Anglo-Britishness; British identity; 'Celtic fringe'
    cities 21, 36
    culture 26, 33, 36, 126
    romanticism 33, 35, 149
    Scottish identity 78
Entente Powers 105
eugenics 27, 29
Evans, Arthur
    Balkan correspondence (1875–1877) 5
    Balkan Wars 102
    excavations at Knossos 27

Fascism, *see* Germany, Italy
folklore, *see also* anthropology; tourism
    in Britain 15
    in the South Slavic Balkans 135
Filipović, Milenko, 149
First World War, *see also* Anglo-Britishness; British identity
    humanitarianism
    Balkan Front 79
    British Home Front 106
    female volunteers 79
    propaganda 104
    Western Front 72
Foreign Office (FO)
    and experts 47, 50
    and the press 46
    and public opinion 114
Fortis, Abbe Alberto 16
France
    and civilization 84
    foreign policy 123
    Little Entente 123–4
Franz Ferdinand, Archduke of Austria-Este 63, 73, 76, 106, 109
Franz Joseph I, Emperor of Austria 106
French Revolution 16
    and the Balkans 17

Gaster, Moses 15
Germany 29, 69, 74, 75, 77, 83, 102, 104, 107, 112, 126
  pan-Germanism 55, 75, 106–8
Gladstone, Herbert 123
Gladstone, William 7, 18, 19, 21–4, 35, 43
Gordon, Cora 90, 91, 93, 132, 138, 139, 142
Gordon, Jan 90, 91, 93, 97, 129, 131
Graves, Charles Patrick 128
Great Eastern Crisis (1875–1878) 17
Greece 5, 13, 17, 20, 21, 67, 69, 84, 101, 146, *see also* Philhellenism
  war of independence (1821–1832) 13, 16
Grey, Edward 55, 73

Harmsworth, Alfred (Viscount Northcliffe) 109, *see also* Enemy Propaganda Department (Crewe House)
Herder, Johann Gottfried 16, 44
Hitler, Adolf 146
Hodges, Katherine 80
Hope (Hawkins), Anthony 20, 180 n.56
Hoppé, Emil Otto 139
Hrebeljanović, Lazar (Prince) 109
Hulme-Beaman, Ardern George 14, 23, 59

Ilinden–Preobrazhenie Uprising 31
Imagology 2, *see also* Balkanism
India 23, 30, 54, 70, 109, 136
Industrialization 8, 26, 27, 33, 37, 52, 150, *see also* rural depopulation; urbanization
  'Great Unrest' (1911–1914) 28, 68, 120
Inglis, Elsie Maud 79–81, 98, 100, 110, 146, 182 n.27
Internal Macedonian Revolutionary Organization (VMRO) 20, 29, 31, 50, 60–2, 105, 121, 142, 165 n.40
internationalism
  before 1914, 67
  interwar period 126, 138, 148, 150, 152
Irby, Adeline Paulina 17, 18, 48, 71

Ireland, *see also* Anglo-Britishness; British identity
  Home Rule 5, 28, 56
  Irish identity 9
  'Land War' (1879–1909) 22
  war of Independence (1919–1921) 120
Islam 15, 30, 42, 43, 108, 134, *see also* Christianity; Ottoman empire
Istanbul (Constantinople) 87
Italy 20, 107, 112, 114, 115, 129, 132, 134, 142, 144, 145, 190 n.36, 191 n.61

Jebb, Eglantyne 72, 80, 179 n.42
Jews
  antisemitism 30
John Bull 74, 75
Jones, Foriter 94
Joyce, James 36, 71
Julian Alps 148

Kennard, Howard William 142
Kinglake, Alexander William 17, 138
Kosovo 35, 45, 49, 69, 70, 72, 109, 111, 113, 139, 145
Kossovo Day Committee 110
Kragujevac 82, 93, 96

Labour Party 28
Laffan, Robin 108, 124, 143
Lake, Harold 79, 99, 100
land reform
  in Bosnia-Herzegovina 19
  in Britain 23, 35
Lavino, William 21, 49
Le Play Society 131, 147
liberal
  party 28
  opinion 71
Lipton, Thomas Johnstone 78, 181 n.10
Liverpool general transport strike (1911) 68
Ljubljana 61, 131
Lloyd George, David 73, 75, 120, 122
Lodge, Olive 94, 131, 133, 147, 148
Long Depression (1873–1896) 7, 23
Lord Byron 13

MacDonald, Ramsay 123
Macedonia 8, 14, 19–21, 29–31, 36–8, 42, 43, 45, 49, 53, 54, 59, 61, 62, 69,

70, 72, 77, 80, 84, 85, 87, 98–100, 105, 133, 134, 145, 148, 153, 154
Mackenzie, Georgina Muir   17, 18, 48
MacPhail, Katherine Stuart   80–2, 94, 100, 104, 182 n.27
medicine
   and hygiene   95, 97
   First World War   72, 95
Mass-Observation (M-O)   7, 125, 127, 148
'May Coup' (1903)   41
Meštrović, Ivan   109–11, 133
Miller, William   19, 52, 135
Montenegro
   attitudes to women   57
   Balkan Wars   1
   First World War   77

national efficiency   7, 8, 23, 27, 28, 31, 32, 45, 153
   'national efficiency paradigm'   26–32
New Europe   107, 109, 114, 122
Nietzsche, Friedrich   24, 108
Nikola I, Prince of Montenegro   44, 50, 57, 72, 144, 174 n.69
Nostalgia   6, 25, 26, 34, 37, 121, 148

Ohrid   43, 45, 53, 61, 108, 130
Orientalism   2
Owen, Harry   85, 90, 91, 98, 99

Pacifism   137, 138, 141, *see also* internationalism
Paris Peace Conference (1919–1920)   122, 124, 132
Pašić, Nikola   103, 113, 143, 179 n.53
Paton, Andrew Archibald   17, 23, 32
Petar I, King of Serbia   54
Philhellenism   13, 17, *see also* Greece, Lord Byron
Podgorica   71
Prilep   38, 39
Prisap   53
Priština   94
Punch   21, 22, 74, 111, 113

race   21, 29, 30, 33, 36, 38, 51, 53, 83, 106, 108, *see also* eugenics; national efficiency
   decline   31

Radić, Stjepan   142, 143
railways   15, 38, 40, 52, 60, 140
Rayner, Louisa   149
Red Cross   70–2, 78, 80, 88–90, 104, 122
   Serbian   99
Reiss, Rudolphe Archibald   105, 106
relief aid
   Ilinden–Preobrazhenie Uprising (1903)   31
   Balkan Wars   78
   First World War   78
   wartime atrocities against Serbs   69
Rijeka   144
Riley, Ben   145
Romania   21, 139, 146, 171 n.10
Royal Anthropological Institute of Great Britain and Ireland (RAI)   125, 131, *see also* Mary Edith Durham
rural depopulation   23, 38
rural poverty   138, 149
Rušanj   149

Said, Edward   1–4, *see also* Orientalism
Sandes, Flora   81, 83, 94, 98–100, 104, 146, 182 n.36
Sandžak of Novi Pazar   19
Sarajevo   30, 36, 40, 44, 55, 67, 73–6, 129, 135, 138, 149
   development of   37
School of Slavonic and East European Studies (SSEES)   173 n.63, 190 n.35, 197 n.98
Scotland, *see also* Anglo-Britishness; British identity; 'Celtic fringe'
   Culture   45
   romanticism   33
Scottish Women's Hospitals for Foreign Services (SWH)   78–82, 87, 92, 93, 97, 104, 182 n.27, 183 n.41, 187 n.139
Scott-James, Rolfe Arnold   28, 36, 45, 110
Second Boer War   7, 25
Second World War   1, 9, 123, 127, 132, 135, 145, 146, 200 n.55
Serbian Relief Fund, (SRF)   78, 83, 89, 96, 99, 104, 113, 181 n.10
Serbian retreat (1915)   94

Serbia
    Balkan Wars   55, 86, 97
    Culture   31, 54, 76, 87
    First World War   105
Seton-Watson, Robert William
    organized opinion   40, 50
    political activism   48, 55, 106
Skala (Slovenian Mountaineering
    Club)   145
Skopje   38, 80, 97, 149, 175 n.115
Slovenia   131, 133–5, 145, 148
socialism   35, 141, 191 n.63
    fear of   28
South Slav Herald   124
Soviet Union   124
Spain
    tourism   128
Split   15, 16, 34, 103, 144
sport , 50, 127
Special Operation's Executive   145
Soltau, Eleanor   82, 83
Steed, Henry Wickham   49, 74, 107, 109, 113, 114, 122
Stobart, Mabel Annie St Clair, *see also* humanitarianism; Women's suffrage
    Balkan Wars   72
    First World War   79
    political activism   72, 79, 110
suburbanization   9, 147, 150
Sušak   144

Thessaloniki (Salonica)   38, 84–6, 98, 99, 167 n.82, 175 n.115, 183 n.57, 185 n.86
The Times   21, 40, 46, 49, 50, 53, 74, 109, 130
Tito, Josip Broz   1, 145, 151
Todorova, Maria   3, 4, 14, 17, 25, 42, 59, 67, 158 n.16
Toynbee, Arnold   110
transport   28, 68, 83, 93
travel literature   3, 7, 15, 46, 86, 128, 134, 138, 147
travel   3, 5, 13–15, 17, 26, 33, 35, 39, 48, 49, 57, 60, 62, 81, 126, 128, 130, 137, 146

Treaty of Berlin (1878)   19, 60
Trebinje   130
Trieste   36
Trogir   38, 40
Trumbić, Ante   103, 106, 113
Tsarist Russia   30

Upper Savinja   131, 135
United States of America   3, 148
urbanization   23, 31, 33, 45, 73, 142, 153
urban poverty   8, 26, 33, 51, 79, 153

Veles   38
Velika Planina   150
Velimirović, Nikolaj   108, 110, 112
Vidovdan (St. Vitus Day)   110, 112, 114
Victoria, Queen of the United Kingdom   6
Vienna   21, 23, 38–40, 43, 49, 54, 55, 74
violence   3, 8, 20, 22, 45, 50, 57, 59–63, 68–71, 73, 76, 78, 91, 105, 106, 119–21, 141, 154
Vivian, Herbert   23, 32, 33, 43, 54, 62, 63, 70, 76, 139, 144
Vošnjak, Bogumil   111–13, 191 n.59

Wales   35, 36, 120, 130, *see also* Anglo-Britishness; British identity; 'Celtic fringe'
West, Rebecca   1
White, Ethel Lina   140
Wrench, Evelyn   29, 52, 144, 148, 149

Yugoslav Committee, (JO)   103
Yugoslavia, *see also* First World War
    and modernity   150
    culture   135, 137, 150
    politics   141
    propaganda   102, 107, 113
Yugoslavism   109, 133

Zadar   38, 135
Zagreb   36, 38, 47, 123, 129, 130, 133, 134, 142, 149
Zeune, Johann August   16

www.ingramcontent.com/pod-product-compliance
Lightning Source LLC
Chambersburg PA
CBHW062215300426
44115CB00012BA/2064